Joint Production and Responsibility
in Ecological Economics

ADVANCES IN ECOLOGICAL ECONOMICS

Series Editor: Jeroen C.J.M. van den Bergh, *Professor of Environmental Economics, Free University, Amsterdam, The Netherlands*

Founding Editor: Robert Costanza, *Director, University of Maryland Institute for Ecological Economics and Professor, Center for Environmental and Estuarine Studies and Zoology Department, USA*

This important series makes a significant contribution to the development of the principles and practices of ecological economics, a field which has expanded dramatically in recent years. The series provides an invaluable forum for the publication of high quality work and shows how ecological economic analysis can make a contribution to understanding and resolving important problems.

The main emphasis of the series is on the development and application of new original ideas in ecological economics. International in its approach, it includes some of the best theoretical and empirical work in the field with contributions to fundamental principles, rigorous evaluations of existing concepts, historical surveys and future visions. It seeks to address some of the most important theoretical questions and gives policy solutions for the ecological problems confronting the global village as we move into the twenty-first century.

Titles in the series include:

Sustainability in Action
Sectoral and Regional Case Studies
Edited by Jörg Köhn, John Gowdy and Jan van der Straaten

Sustaining Agriculture and the Rural Environment
Governance, Policy and Multifunctionality
Edited by Floor Brouwer

The Economics of Technology Diffusion and Energy Efficiency
Peter Mulder

Time Strategies, Innovation and Environmental Policy
Edited by Christian Sartorius and Stefan Zundel

America's Changing Coasts
Private Rights and Public Trust
Edited by Diana M. Whitelaw and Gerald R. Visgilio

Economic Growth, Material Flows and the Environment
New Applications of Structural Decomposition Analysis and Physical Input-Output Tables
Rutger Hoekstra

Joint Production and Responsibility in Ecological Economics
On the Foundations of Environmental Policy
Stefan Baumgärtner, Malte Faber and Johannes Schiller

Joint Production and Responsibility in Ecological Economics

On the Foundations of Environmental Policy

Stefan Baumgärtner, Malte Faber

University of Heidelberg, Germany

Johannes Schiller

UFZ Centre for Environmental Research Leipzig-Halle, Germany

ADVANCES IN ECOLOGICAL ECONOMICS

Edward Elgar
Cheltenham, UK • Northampton, MA, USA

Published by
Edward Elgar Publishing Limited
Glensanda House
Montpellier Parade
Cheltenham
Glos GL50 1UA
UK

Edward Elgar Publishing, Inc.
136 West Street
Suite 202
Northampton
Massachusetts 01060
USA

A catalogue record for this book
is available from the British Library

ISBN-13: 978 1 84064 872 0
ISBN-10: 1 84064 872 4

Printed and bound in Great Britain by MPG Books Ltd, Bodmin, Cornwall

Contents

Authors and Co-Authors

This book has a number of authors and co-authors who have contributed to the overall product in different ways and roles.

Three **main authors** have composed and principally written the book:

Stefan Baumgärtner – Background in physics (MSc) and economics (PhD), Assistant Professor of Ecological Economics, Alfred-Weber-Institute of Economics, University of Heidelberg, Germany (baumgaertner @uni-hd.de).

Malte Faber – Background in mathematics and economics (MA, PhD), Professor Emeritus of Economics, Alfred-Weber-Institute of Economics, University of Heidelberg, Germany (faber@uni-hd.de).

Johannes Schiller – Background in physics (MSc) and economics (PhD), Senior Researcher, Department of Economics, UFZ Centre for Environmental Research, Leipzig-Halle, Germany (johannes.schiller@ufz.de).

Cooperating authors have made significant contributions that have essentially shaped the overall argument and the character of the book. Their role is acknowledged in the respective chapters of the book:

Thomas Petersen – Background in philosophy (MA, PhD), Assistant Professor of Philosophy, Institute of Philosophy, University of Heidelberg, Germany (thomas.petersen@urz.uni-heidelberg.de).

John Proops – Background in mathematics and physics (BA), engineering physics (MSc) and economics (PhD), Professor of Ecological Economics, School of Politics, International Relations and the Environment, Keele University, Keele, UK (j.l.r.proops@keele.ac.uk).

Ralph Winkler – Background in physics (MSc) and economics (MA, PhD), Marie-Curie Fellow, School of Politics, International Relations and the Environment, Keele University, Keele, UK (r.t.winkler@pol.keele. ac.uk).

Contributing authors have made important contributions to individual chapters of the book. Their role is acknowledged in the respective chapters:

Jakob de Swaan Arons – Background in chemical engineering (MSc, PhD), Professor Emeritus of Chemical Engineering, Delft University of Technology, Delft, The Netherlands, and Chair of Industrial Ecology, Tsinghua University, Beijing, China (jakobdeswaanarons@yahoo.com).

Harald Dyckhoff – Background in mathematics, physics, business administration (MA) and economics (PhD), Professor of Industrial Economics and Environmental Economics, Institute of Business Administration, Technical University of Aachen, Germany (dyckhoff@lut.rwth-aachen.de).

Frank Jöst – Background in economics (MA, PhD), Assistant Professor of Economics, Alfred-Weber-Institute of Economics, University of Heidelberg, Germany (frank.joest@uni-hd.de).

Eva Kiesele – Background in physics and economics (MSc), Research Assistant, Alfred-Weber-Institute of Economics, University of Heidelberg, Germany (kiesele@eco.uni-heidelberg.de).

Georg Müller-Fürstenberger – Background in chemistry (BSc) and economics (MA, PhD), Assistant Professor of Economics, Institute of Applied Microeconomics, University of Berne, Switzerland (georg.mueller @vwi.unibe.ch).

Preface

This book lies at the interface of the natural sciences, economics and philosophy. It builds on the results of a major research programme that has evolved over the last fifteen years in various strands, with the aim of providing conceptual foundations for ecological economics and for environmental policy.

As in any jointly authored book, each chapter has a different weight of contribution by the three authors. However, our collaboration in research and in writing this book was so extremely close that even when the original version of a chapter was drafted by only one or two of us, a significant influence of all three of us is present in every chapter. Furthermore, in writing various chapters of this book we have been very fortunate to enjoy the collaboration of a number of colleagues with backgrounds in business administration, chemistry, economics, engineering, mathematics, philosophy, physics. Each of them has made a unique and very different contribution, as acknowledged on pages vii–viii. As a result, this book is fundamentally interdisciplinary.

The University of Heidelberg's Interdisciplinary Institute for Environmental Economics provided an ideal platform for conducting this research. We are grateful for the opportunity to benefit from its environment of intellectual openness and scientific excellence. Indeed, all three authors, and most of the cooperating and contributing authors, have been associated with this institution in one way or another. We are also grateful for the comments and ideas that emerged from discussion with students when one of us (S.B.) taught courses on this material in Heidelberg in 2002/03 and 2004/05. In particular, we thank Christoph Heinzel, Eva Kiesele, Philipp Krohn, Karoline Rogge, Christian Traeger and Torsten Stein.

Over the years, we have received comments on the ideas and material presented here from a large number of colleagues. We are grateful for critical and constructive comments, as well as for stimulating discussions, to Frank Ackerman, Shmuel Amir, Peter Bernholz, Guido Bünstorf, Mick Common, John Coulter, Harald Dyckhoff, Bernhard Eckwert, John Ehrenfeld, Stefan Felder, Karin Frank, Manuel Frondel, Jörg Hüfner, Frank Jöst, Bernd Klauer, Andreas Lange, Reiner Kümmel,

Thomas Kuhn, Heinz D. Kurz, Markus Lehmann, Günter Liesegang, Reiner Manstetten, Georg Müller-Fürstenberger, Ulf Moslener, Jürg Niehans, Richard B. Norgaard, Charles Perrings, Rüdiger Pethig, Dan Phaneuf, John Proops, Clemens Puppe, Martin Quaas, Till Requate, Mario Schmidt, Armin Schmutzler, Jeroen van den Bergh, Ralph Winkler, Ulrich Witt, as well as anonymous reviewers of the journals *Ecological Economics, Economic Theory, Environmental and Resource Economics, Environmental Values, Journal of Environmental Economics and Management, Journal of Industrial Ecology, Resources, Conservation and Recycling, Resource and Energy Economics, Structural Change and Economic Dynamics* and *Zeitschrift für Politikwissenschaft*.

When preparing the final draft of the manuscript we very much appreciated the high-quality editorial support from Edward Elgar Publishing. Also, Dale Adams, Maximilian Mihm and Paul Ronning have helped improve language and style. Simone Bauer has helped editing the references.

We thank the following publishers for permission to use material from previously published articles, as indicated in the respective chapters. Elsevier Science for the use of material from

> S. Baumgärtner (2004), 'Price ambivalence of secondary resources: Joint production, limits to substitution, and costly disposal', *Resources, Conservation and Recycling*, **43**(1), 95–117.

> S. Baumgärtner, H. Dyckhoff, M. Faber, J.L.R. Proops and J. Schiller (2001), 'The concept of joint production and ecological economics', *Ecological Economics*, **36**, 365-372.

> S. Baumgärtner, M. Faber and J. Proops (2002), 'How environmental concern influences the investment decision. An application of capital theory' in *Ecological Economics*, **40**(1), 1–12.

> S. Baumgärtner and R. Winkler (2003), 'Markets, technology and environmental regulation: price ambivalence of waste paper in Germany', *Ecological Economics*, **47**(2–3), 183–195.

> M. Faber, K. Frank, B. Klauer, R. Manstetten, J. Schiller and C. Wissel (2005), 'On the foundation of a general theory of stocks', *Ecological Economics*, **55**, 155–172.

> R. Winkler (2005), 'Structural change with joint production of consumption and environmental pollution: a neo-Austrian approach', *Structural Change and Economic Dynamics*, **16**(1), 111–135.

MIT Press for the use of material from

> S. Baumgärtner and J. de Swaan Arons (2003), 'Necessity and inefficiency in the generation of waste. A thermodynamic analysis', *Journal of Industrial Ecology* **7**(2), 113–123.

Springer-Verlag for the use of material from

> S. Baumgärtner and F. Jöst (2000), 'Joint production, externalities, and the regulation of production networks', *Environmental and Resource Economics*, **16**(2), 229–251.

Last, not least, we are grateful for financial support from the German Research Foundation (Deutsche Forschungsgemeinschaft DFG) and from the Volkswagen Foundation for several research projects over the past fifteen years.

Heidelberg and Leipzig, June 2006
Stefan Baumgärtner, Malte Faber, Johannes Schiller

1. Introduction: Joint Production and Ecological Economics[*]

with Harald Dyckhoff and John Proops

1.1 INTRODUCTION

Human existence is unthinkable without its relationship to nature. This relationship is twofold. On the one hand, humans depend in a variety of ways on nature and the services it provides. Examples include resources such as water, food and fuels; functions such as the regulation of climate, floods and diseases; cultural services such as recreation as well as aesthetic and spiritual fulfilment; and the space for unfolding all kinds of human activity. On the other hand, human activity impacts the natural environment: humans intentionally shape their natural environment to form their space of living; they take resource materials from, and release substances into, natural ecosystems; and in so doing they alter natural processes and functions.

The imperative of sustainability requires sustaining nature's functioning and services for humans over the long run. So, the relationship between humans and nature must be of a certain quality. This poses a challenge for how humans should act towards nature. The challenge has many facets which have to be addressed when studying the relationship between humans and nature, and when developing recommendations for sustainable policy:

- There is an inextricable interaction of processes from the natural sphere, traditionally analysed by the natural sciences; the social and economic sphere, traditionally analysed by the social sciences; and categories of human thinking, which is the domain of philosophy. This requires an interdisciplinary approach.

---

[*]Sections 1.2–1.6 are based on Baumgärtner, Dyckhoff, Faber, Proops and Schiller (2001).

1

- Natural, social and economic processes are dynamic and characterised by the modification of stocks on a multitude of different time scales. In addition, they may be irreversible.

- The imperative of sustainability requires consideration of long time horizons.

- Since natural, social and economic processes are inextricably intertwined, one faces complex systems. This complexity is aggravated when considering the long run.

- Knowledge about the relevant processes and systems is generally restricted by a high degree of uncertainty and fundamental ignorance. Again, this restriction is aggravated when considering the long run.

- Human action is multifarious and cannot analytically be grasped by one single paradigm. The concept of *homo economicus*, which highlights self-centred optimising behaviour and dominates the current social sciences, needs to be complemented by other concepts of the human that feature, for example creativity, free will, communal sense and responsibility.

In the face of such a major challenge, some people may just resign and decide that sustainability is a myth and of hardly any practical relevance; others may revert to isolated ad-hoc action which falls short of addressing the challenge of sustainability in a proper way. But what is actually needed is an all-encompassing, consistent and systematic perspective on the problem and corresponding guidance for action.

In this book, we argue that the concept of *joint production* can be an essential element of such a perspective, and a fruitful tool to develop guidance for sustainable policy. The notion of joint production denotes the phenomenon that several outputs *necessarily* emerge together from economic activity. These joint outputs may all be desired and positively valued goods. But in the vast majority of instances, some of them are undesired and may even be harmful to the natural environment. An example is the refining of crude oil, in which gasoline, kerosene, light heating oil and other mineral oil products are produced; but harmful sulphurous wastes and carbon dioxide emissions are also necessarily generated.

The concept of joint production captures the particular characteristic of human activity – namely that it always has unintended side effects – which is the structural cause of many environmental problems. With this, it is a natural starting point for analysing how environmental problems emerge and how they can be solved in a sustainable manner. Also, the concept of joint production is suitable for the systematic and unified consideration of all the aspects mentioned above.

With this book, we aim at a comprehensive analysis of economy-environment interaction which takes the aspects mentioned above seriously. We develop concepts that are interdisciplinary and allow a general, consistent and systematic analysis. In so doing, we contribute to the conceptual foundation of environmental policy. With this, our book should be of central interest to the field of *ecological economics*, which is commonly understood as 'the science and management of sustainability' (Costanza 1991) and, thus, has the same research aim. Besides making a significant contribution to ecological economics, this book is also relevant to other research fields, such as environmental and resource economics, environmental policy and regulation, environmental valuation, as well as environmental ethics and responsibility.

In this introductory chapter, we outline the argument of the book. The remainder of the book then elaborates this argument in detail. In Section 1.2, we make reference to the laws of thermodynamics in order to show how joint production is implied by the First and Second Laws. There is a review of the analysis of joint production in economics in Section 1.3, pointing out its extensive history and range of applications. Section 1.4 relates joint production to philosophy, showing how its consideration gives rise to ethical and epistemological concerns. The comprehensibility of joint production is stressed in Section 1.5, while Section 1.6 shows how the concept of joint production is constitutive and supportive of such notions as holistic policy analysis, the precautionary principle, time horizons and external effects. Section 1.7 explains the approach and plan of the book.

1.2   Joint Production and Thermodynamics

Why is joint production such a ubiquitous phenomenon and useful notion in ecological economics? We believe that this is because joint production is intimately related to the laws of thermodynamics. The application of thermodynamics is widely recognised as an essential element in much current ecological-economic thought, since it gives rich insights into the nature of economy-environment interactions. The usefulness of thermodynamics derives from its applicability to *all* real production processes, which are the basis of economic activity. Thus, thermodynamics relates ecological economics to the natural sciences, such as chemistry, biology and ecology, which also facilitates interdisciplinary research.

The laws of thermodynamics lead us to recognise that the human economy is an open subsystem embedded in the larger, but finite, system of the natural environment (Boulding 1966, Georgescu-Roegen 1971, Daly 1977, Ayres 1978, Faber et al. 1995[1983], and many more). The strength of the concept of joint production is that it allows us to incorporate this insight about economy-environment interactions into ecological economics. This can be seen in the following argument.

From a thermodynamic point of view, energy and matter are the fundamental factors of production. Every process of production is, at root, a transformation of these factors. Hence, in this view production processes are subject to the laws of thermodynamics, which in an abbreviated form can be stated as follows:

First Law: Energy and matter can be neither created nor destroyed, that is, in an isolated system matter and energy are conserved.

Second Law: In every real process of transformation a positive amount of entropy is generated.

One can describe the process of production as a transformation of a certain number of inputs into a certain number of outputs, each of which is characterised by its mass and its entropy. From the laws of thermodynamics it then follows that every process of production is joint production; that is, it results necessarily in more than one output (Faber et al. 1998, Baumgärtner 2000: Chapter 4). In particular, industrial production processes which generate low entropy desired goods *necessarily and unavoidably* jointly produce high entropy waste by-products. We can represent this thermodynamic constraint on real production processes as in Figure 1.1. For example, in the production of iron one starts from

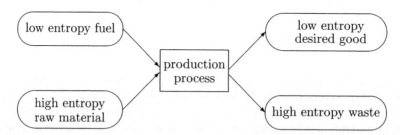

Figure 1.1   Production processes generating low entropy desired goods necessarily and unavoidably jointly produce high entropy waste materials.

iron ore. In order to produce the desired product iron, which has lower specific entropy than iron ore, one has to reduce the raw material's entropy. This is achieved by employing a low entropy fuel, for example coal, which provides the energy necessary for this process. From a thermodynamic point of view, one may therefore consider production as a shifting of high entropy from the raw material to the waste product. At the same time, it becomes apparent that the inputs are also joint in the sense that high entropy iron ore and low entropy fuel are complementary (cf. Christensen 1989: 28–29). Hence, the fundamental idea of joint production applies on both the input and the output side.

In that sense, the concept of joint production can capture the essential thermodynamic constraints on production processes as expressed by the First and Second Laws, through an easy-to-use and easy-to-understand economic concept.

This holds for production in both economic systems and ecosystems. Joint production, therefore, is also a fundamental notion in ecology, even though it is not often expressed as such in that discipline. Organisms and ecosystems, as open, self-organising systems, necessarily take in several inputs and generate several outputs, just as does an economy. Indeed, such natural systems are the earliest examples of joint production.

The power and generality of the joint production concept can be demonstrated through the way it embraces four central issues in ecological economics: irreversibility; limits to substitution; the ubiquity of waste; and the limits to growth.

Irreversibility is explicitly included within the above thermodynamic formalisation of joint production, as it is necessarily the case that the production process generates entropy and is therefore irreversible. *Limits to substitution* are also included, as the requirement that high entropy materials inputs must be converted into lower entropy desired goods requires that the material inputs be accompanied by an irreducible minimum of low entropy fuels. The *ubiquity of waste* can be easily derived from the thermodynamically founded joint production approach. It follows from the necessity of jointly producing high entropy, which very often is embodied in undesired material, and hence constitutes waste (for example CO_2, slag, etc.). The combination of the above three issues leads to the notion of *limits to growth*, further emphasising the power and generality of the joint production concept for ecological economics.

1.3   JOINT PRODUCTION AND ECONOMICS

The analysis of joint production actually has a long tradition in economics. Many economists – for example Adam Smith, John Stuart Mill, Karl Marx, Johann Heinrich von Thünen, William Stanley Jevons, Alfred Marshall, Arthur Cecil Pigou, Heinrich von Stackelberg, John von Neumann, Piero Sraffa – devoted considerable effort to the study of joint production. As a matter of history, the analysis of joint production contributed to the abandonment of the classical theory of value and the establishment of the neoclassical theory of value (Kurz 1986, Baumgärtner 2000: Chapters 5–8). For ecological economists it is interesting to note that several of these authors, in particular von Thünen, Marx and Jevons, emphasised that environmental pollutants come into existence as joint products of desired goods.

There is a substantial body of both theory and applications of joint production in the economics and business administration literature. In general, within this literature two cases are distinguished:

1. all joint products are desired goods, and

2. at least one output is undesired while at least one other is desired.

While the former is the case which has received most treatment in the literature, the thermodynamic discussion suggests that it is the second case that is of particular interest in ecological economics.

The theory of joint production has been extensively developed in business administration (for example Dyckhoff 1996a). For example, joint production is necessarily the case in chemical transformation processes, and in processes of splitting and separation (Riebel 1955, Oenning 1997). A range of computer-based models and methods has been developed to solve the resulting problems concerning the planning and cost allocation of joint production (Oenning 1997). Further, the quantitative relations between inputs and outputs in joint production can be described with input/output graphs, and one can use linear or non-linear algebraic systems generalising Koopmans' (1951) activity analysis. There are also relevant dynamic and stochastic graph-theoretic models in computer science (for example Petri nets) as well as models in process engineering and chemistry, which are particularly important for balancing and managing the flows of material and energy (Spengler 1999). Even the problem of allocating ecological effects to joint products is being addressed (Schmidt and Häuslein 1997).

Important theoretical results about the economics of joint production include the following. Joint production of private and public goods may reduce the usual problem of under-provision of public goods in a decentralised economy (Cornes and Sandler 1984). Under joint production of goods and polluting residuals, and making the realistic assumption that the assimilative capacity of the natural environment for these pollutants is limited, a steady state growth path does not exist (Perrings 1994, O'Connor 1993).

The modern literature on general equilibrium theory does – with a few exceptions (for example Sraffa 1960, Pasinetti 1980, Salvadori and Steedman 1990, Kurz and Salvadori 1995) – not explicitly investigate the properties of economies characterised by joint production. Instead, it is focussed on identifying the most general assumptions under which certain results hold, for example existence and efficiency of general equilibrium. Yet, by doing so it implicitly supplies insights into the economics of joint production. Arrow and Debreu (1954) and Debreu (1959) have shown that even in cases of joint production – be they goods or bads – under standard assumptions there exists a general equilibrium in a competitive economy if (i) the individual production sets are all convex and (ii) the possibility of free disposal is given, that is unwanted and harmful joint outputs can be disposed of at no costs. McKenzie (1959) showed the same result using a weaker assumption about disposal (disposal is possible but not necessarily free and the economy is 'irreducible'), yet only for a technology characterised by constant returns to scale. Furthermore, any general competitive equilibrium, in particular under joint production, is Pareto efficient in the absence of negative externalities (Arrow 1951a, Debreu 1951). Pigou (1920) and Lindahl (1919) have conceived mechanisms to internalise such externalities, thereby re-establishing optimality of the equilibrium. In the case of negative externalities exhibiting the character of public bads, however, this mechanism can only be established under very restrictive and unrealistic assumptions. In particular, every individual is assumed to reveal a personalised willingness to pay for the absence of the public bad and not to act as a free rider.

In summary, while modern economic theory has produced many interesting results concerning the existence and efficiency of equilibrium under joint production, in the case which is most relevant from the ecological-economic point of view – joint production of bads causing public negative externalities – we are essentially left with a negative result.

1.4   JOINT PRODUCTION AND PHILOSOPHY

The concept of joint production, with its foundation in thermodynamics and economics, stresses that economic activity generally produces two kinds of output: the intended principal product and unintended by-products. We would expect, and indeed observe, that producers will focus their attention and energies on the former, while the latter will be largely ignored, at least to the extent permitted by legal constraints and social mores. This inattention to the undesired products raises two issues of a philosophical nature, one relating to responsibility, that is ethical, and one relating to knowledge, that is epistemological.

Turning first to ethics, the thermodynamically necessary by-products bring with them new issues of moral responsibility. This becomes obvious if we consider the hypothetical case of single production where *no* by-products are generated. In such an idealised world, assuming the existence of perfect markets and a fair social and legal order, the ethical problem for producers of a desired product is narrowly limited as long as they trade their products on the market and obey the legal order. In contrast, joint production implies that economic activity, in addition to the intended products, also results in *unintended* outputs, which often go unnoticed. This lack of knowledge and attention often results in a social and legal order that typically neglects joint products. However, these joint products may be harmful, for example to other producers, consumers, or to the natural environment. As a consequence, both the producer, and the wider society demanding the desired principal product, now face complex ethical problems. Inattention to joint production may therefore easily result in ethical negligence. An example is the inattention to waste in the nuclear industry. From the inception of nuclear power it was recognised that very dangerous and long-lived waste materials would be produced as by-products. Nevertheless, for the first thirty years of commercial power generation, unconscionably little attention was paid to the disposal of this waste (Proops 2001).

Concerning the second issue, epistemology, the area to which we draw attention is that of surprise and ignorance (Faber et al. 1992). Even if one were to suppose that it were possible to produce only principal products, this could still give rise to unanticipated and unwanted environmental effects (for example CFCs are a principal product, not a by-product). However, we believe that unwanted waste by-products are likely to be a greater source of unpleasant environmental surprises because, as mentioned above, they are not the focus of attention for their producers. The story of waste chlorine in the nineteenth century is one of ignorance of, and inattention to, the effects of emitting this waste product, with damaging and unforeseen consequences for air and water quality (Faber et al. 1996b; see also Chapter 16).

What lessons can we learn from this discussion? Considering the concept of joint production naturally leads one to address issues of ethics and epistemology, requiring one to discuss economic questions in a philosophical context. In particular, the concept creates an awareness of both (i) the ethical dimension of economic action due to unintended joint outputs, and (ii) our potential ignorance, primarily of the effects of unwanted by-products.

1.5 JOINT PRODUCTION AS A COMPREHENSIBLE PRINCIPLE

It is clearly desirable that fundamental concepts of ecological economics should be easily comprehensible. It has often been noted in the literature (for example by Norton 1992) that the scientific approach is sufficient neither for the recognition of environmental problems, nor for their solution. Concerning recognition, as a matter of history, the awareness of environmental degradation was, to a large extent, brought about not by the scientific community, but by laypeople. Often, it was individuals or small groups who first publicly noted that the natural environment was being changed. For, in everyday life, attentive human beings can recognise many dimensions of the natural environment, while science, by its nature, has to reduce the wholeness of an event to only those aspects to which its methods are suited.

The second important reason why central concepts of ecological economics should be easily comprehensible for 'the person in the street' concerns the solution of environmental problems. In democratic societies, decisions about what kind of environmental policy is to be enacted are made (effectively) by ballot. Hence, voters have to understand environmental issues and their proposed solutions.

We have often noted in discussions with scientists who had no background in economics, but also with laypeople, that they were able to comprehend the nature of an environmental problem and to appreciate a proposed solution much more easily when such issues were explained in terms of joint production, rather than in other economic terms, for example production functions, damage functions, externalities, Pigouvian taxes, etc.

1.6 THE CONCEPT OF JOINT PRODUCTION AND ENVIRONMENTAL POLICY

We have outlined the relationship of joint production to thermodynamics, economics and philosophy, and argued that joint production is also an eminently comprehensible notion. Furthermore, the notion of joint production is particularly useful for the discussion of some environmental policy issues. The concept of joint production naturally leads to these issues, which are currently being discussed in ecological economics, as part of a single framework of analysis. This further demonstrates, we believe, the power of the joint production approach.

Universality of the concept

The concept of joint production may be employed at several different levels of aggregation. It can be used for the analysis of an individual production process, of a firm, of an economic sector, or of a whole economy. It is also suited to examine environment-economy interactions in which economic activities and resulting environmental effects are separated by long time intervals, as in the example of CO_2 emissions. In both cases today's effects on the natural system are caused by stocks of these substances, which were accumulated mainly from emissions up to several decades ago.

Holistic approach to policy

Taking a joint production approach to economy-environment interactions stresses the necessary relationships between various sorts of inputs into production processes, and the corresponding sorts of outputs. As illustrated in Figure 1.1, much, even most, production requires inputs of low entropy fuels and high entropy raw materials, and generates low entropy desired goods and high entropy wastes. Thus, this thermodynamically based joint production representation shows us that the two issues, of natural resource use and of pollution from waste, are necessarily and intimately related: the resource is the mother of the waste. So it is conceptually incomplete to consider natural resources and pollution as separate issues. Seeking to understand either on its own leaves out this relationship, with potentially profound implications for policy analysis. In summary, the theory of joint production tells us that sound environmental policy can come only from an integrated and holistic conceptualisation of the production and consumption processes.

Time scales and time horizons

Joint production leads one to the recognition of different time scales and time horizons. Desired principal products are generally produced and consumed over relatively short time scales, leading to relatively short time horizons of decision makers with regard to such outputs. However, jointly produced waste outputs are often emitted into the environment, where they can accumulate over significantly longer time scales. Such accumulation may, and often does, lead to the unanticipated and unpleasant surprises discussed earlier. Clearly, the social management of such problems demands much longer time horizons than those typically applied to the principal products.

Precautionary principle

The discussion in Section 1.4, concerning how awareness of potential ignorance and responsibility follows from the perspective of joint production, gives additional support to applying the precautionary principle. Indeed, a frequently perceived weakness of this principle is its lack of apparent conceptual foundation. We consider it supportive of both the concept of joint production and the precautionary principle that an analysis of the former so directly gives rise to the latter.

External effects

Within the environmental economics literature, with its roots in welfare economics, the usual analytical method for understanding environmental damage is through the notion of external effects. There is postulated a relationship between economic actors, which is asymmetrical and not mediated by a market; for example if one smokes in a lift, it causes uncompensated offence to one's fellow passengers. In the usual externality approach this relationship is conceptualised as an issue of welfare/utility loss of the person affected by the external effect. That is, the description is based on the effect. One could, however, recast this relationship starting from the cause of the effect. Very often one would observe that the starting point is an unintended joint product. In the example of smoking in the lift the desired product of nicotine in the bloodstream has an unwanted joint product of smoke in the lift. Therefore, we observe that there exists a duality between an explanation based on the effect, that is the externality approach, and an explanation starting from the cause of the effect, that is the joint production approach.

We also note that welfare effects will only be taken account of once they have been experienced; that is, external effects are matters of the ex post. On the other hand, the concept of joint production can alert one to the potential of environmental harm; that is, considering joint production ex ante creates a motive for actively exploring as yet unknown potential welfare effects (Baumgärtner and Schiller 2001: Section 6, Baumgärtner 2000: 293–294). We therefore argue that the concepts of joint production and externality are complementary.

1.7   APPROACH AND PLAN OF THE BOOK

The discussion in Sections 1.2–1.6 has suggested that the concept of joint production can unify the different perspectives of the natural sciences, economics and philosophy, and thus serve as a fruitful tool to develop guidance for environmental policy. In the different parts of the book, we investigate joint production from these different perspectives. In this sense, the book is heterogeneous. Different specific methods are employed, for example mass, entropy and exergy balances (Chapter 3), constrained optimisation (Chapters 8 and 10), and philosophical reasoning (Chapters 11–14). While this heterogeneity may pose a potential problem, it also allows the reader to take alternative entries to the subject of joint production and this book. Also, the diversity of perspectives is unified by the common subject of joint production, a common conceptual framework, and a common way of presenting arguments so that they can easily be related to each other.

Part I lays the conceptual foundations of joint production. As a starting point, we take the observation that joint production is a ubiquitous phenomenon. Employing a natural science perspective, in particular from thermodynamics, we show that this is not accidental, but a necessary characteristic of all productive activity. Accordingly, we define joint production in such a way that the inevitability of joint outputs is captured, and the temporal dimension is taken into account. On a conceptual level, we go on to explore implications of joint production for the dynamics of ecological-economic systems – such as multiple stock dynamics and complexity – and investigate the role of joint production for the emergence and solution of environmental problems.

Part II approaches joint production from a welfare economic perspective. To start with, we survey how joint production was analysed in the history of economic thought. Thereby, we identify remaining gaps in the current economic understanding of the issue. One of these gaps is related to the valuation of joint products, which is crucial for dealing with joint production. We study the particular aspect of ambivalence, that is, a joint product may potentially be both positively and negatively valued. We also study how joint production of harmful pollutants affects intertemporal economic decision-making and the dynamics of capital and pollutant stocks. One important conclusion from this part will be that taking joint production and stock dynamics seriously increases the complexity of economic valuation up to a point where the economic approach of 'rational' and 'efficient' policy-making ceases to be a helpful tool in meeting the challenge associated with sustainability (see Section 1.1).

In response to this, in Part III we adopt an ethical perspective on joint production as a complement. It is centred around the concept of responsibility. We define this concept and explore the limits of responsibility, and we relate it to joint production, complexity, and uncertainty. This forms a conceptual basis for the precautionary principle. Distinguishing between individual and collective responsibility, we discuss the role of both the individual as economic agent and politics at large. From this perspective, we sketch an approach to sustainable policy which complements the economic approach where it falls short of meeting the challenge of sustainability (cf. Section 1.1). We find that politics has to assume responsibility to a much greater extent than currently acknowledged.

While the analysis in Parts I through III is mainly theoretical, Part IV presents empirical case studies from the paper, chlorine, cement and sulphur industries. These serve to illustrate the general results from the previous parts, and offer an empirical approach to the phenomenon of joint production. Indeed, these (and other) real-world cases of joint production in some ways inspire our conceptual and theoretical analysis of the phenomenon. Ultimately, they demonstrate that the perspective of joint production developed in this book is fruitful in that it allows one to see real-world problems in a new way and to identify the policy-relevant structure of the respective problems.

After studying joint production from different perspectives in the four parts of the book, the concluding Chapter 19 summarises the key insights and draws conclusions concerning the foundations of environmental policy.

PART I

Conceptual Foundations

INTRODUCTION

The first part of the book analyses the phenomenon of joint production and its consequences for economy-environment interactions on a general and abstract level. Phenomena of the real world – the occurrence and consequences of joint production – are translated into the language of science. For that sake, we employ different disciplinary perspectives from the social and natural sciences, in particular from economics, system theory and thermodynamics. The chapters in this part thereby lay the conceptual foundations for the further analysis in the subsequent parts of the book.

Chapter 2 introduces the general notion of joint production by reviewing different definitions from the economic literature. On this basis, we develop our own definition which is suitable for the purpose of an encompassing analysis of long-term economy-environment interactions. We also link the concept of joint production to a traditional analytical tool from economics, the concept of externality. This chapter develops the language in which we will discuss joint production and its consequences throughout the book. Using arguments from the natural sciences, in particular from thermodynamics, Chapter 3 justifies why joint production is ubiquitous, and, thus, why the concept of joint production is universally suited to the analysis of economy-environment interactions. Introducing a time-dimension into the analysis, Chapter 4 points to long-term evolutionary consequences of the phenomenon. The logic of the argument developed there is then applied to the dynamics of environmental problems in Chapter 5.

2. Conceptualising Joint Production*

2.1 INTRODUCTION

Joint production has many faces. The account of the analysis of joint production in the history of economic thought in Chapter 6 and the case studies in Part IV illustrate various aspects of the phenomenon which are relevant when analysing economy-environment interactions. Also the economic literature displays a large variety of different notions of joint production. In this chapter, we develop a concept of joint production that is concise and consistent, yet general enough to capture this variety of relevant aspects in one concept. Such a concept is necessary for an encompassing scientific analysis of ecological-economic systems. The chapter is organised as follows. In Section 2.2, we survey different notions of joint production that have been developed in the economic and business literature. Before introducing our own definition of joint production in Section 2.4, we discuss our science-theoretic approach to the analysis of production systems in Section 2.3. Section 2.5 concludes.

2.2 THE ECONOMIC CONCEPT OF JOINT PRODUCTION

The phenomenon of joint production has long been studied by economists (cf. Chapter 6). In the literature there is a huge number of classifications and terms referring to different types of multi-output production. Most of them are not compatible with each other, and one and the same term is used by different classification schemes to denote very different production patterns (Riebel 1981: 298).

2.2.1 Joint Production in the Economic Literature

The traditional notion of joint production[1]

The notion of joint production prevalent among classical economists is that of a single process of production in which two different outputs are

---

*This chapter draws on Baumgärtner (2000: Sections 9.1–9.3), Baumgärtner and Schiller (2001) and Schiller (2002: Sections 2.1–2.3, 7.1–7.2, 7.5–7.6).

necessarily produced together at one point in time and in fixed proportion to each other. Adam Smith (1976[1776]: 178) illustrates this notion by the example of hunting, where meat and skins of some animal are necessarily produced together at the same time and in fixed proportion. Similarly, John Stuart Mill (1965[1848]: 570) refers to the production of coke and coal-gas. The idea that the various joint outputs are produced in *fixed proportion* dominates the notion of joint production among classical economists until William Stanley Jevons (1911[1879]).

The classical notion of joint production with fixed output proportion is generalised by Johann Heinrich von Thünen, Karl Marx and Alfred Marshall. They all stress that the various outputs, which are jointly produced at one point in time from one process of production, do not need to come in fixed proportion. For instance, the proportion of the output quantities produced can be *flexible* within certain limits depending on technical parameters of the production process, such as temperature or input mix (for example von Thünen 1921[1826]: 196, Marx 1959[1894]: 103, Marshall 1925[1890]: 389).

The assumption of flexibility in the output proportion is sometimes stretched to the extreme. Some authors go so far as to include the limit case, in which nothing at all of one of the outputs is produced, as one example of flexible joint production. Karl Marx and Heinrich von Stackelberg, who both study joint production not on the level of an individual production process but on the level of a firm, employ such a very broad notion of joint production (for example von Stackelberg 1948: 31–32, 1952: 29). As compared to the classical notion of joint production this very wide notion gives up not only the assumption of fixed proportion, but also the aspect that the various outputs are *necessarily* produced together.

The temporal structure of joint production processes, that is the possibility that the various joint outputs are not necessarily produced *at the same point in time*, is also discussed by some authors. For instance, Johann Heinrich von Thünen and Piero Sraffa stress that some factors of production, such as land or fixed capital, after having been used, leave the production process as outputs and may be used as inputs in the production of different commodities again at some later time (see for example von Thünen 1921[1826]: §§14, 21–23, Sraffa 1960: Chapter X). In this sense, outputs which are produced at different points in time are joint by land or capital.

Systems of production

The idea that various joint outputs are not necessarily produced in fixed proportion, but may be produced in flexible proportion, turned out to be fruitful for further development of the theory of joint production. However, empirical examples suggest that in most cases of joint production within one process of production, the outputs come in fixed proportion or the flexibility of output proportion is confined within very narrow limits.[2]

In this context the notion of joint production is further generalised in the 1930s by Frederik Zeuthen and John von Neumann. They both study systems of joint production which comprise several processes of production. Under the assumption that there is more than one process in which the same outputs are jointly produced in fixed, yet different proportions, it is possible to vary the output proportion in which the joint outputs are produced at the level of the entire system by varying the activity levels of the different production processes. This means that the joint outputs are produced in fixed proportion at the level of an individual production process, but in flexible proportion at the level of the entire system (Zeuthen 1933: 15, von Neumann 1937, 1945/46).

Within the vast and still growing literature that goes back to Sraffa (1960) economic problems of joint production are exclusively analysed by studying systems of production comprising several processes of production with fixed output proportions.[3]

Multi-product firms and industrial organisation

Joint production became an issue in the field of industrial organisation in the 1970s. At the origin is the question of what influence multi-product firms exert on the market structure within one industry and what policy advice can be inferred from this (Baumol 1977, Panzar and Willig 1977a, 1977b, 1981 and Willig 1979).[4] Within this literature, a multi-output firm that produces n different outputs in quantities y_1, ..., y_n is typically described by a cost function $C(y_1, \ldots, y_n)$. The special case in which the cost function is not completely separable in functions which only depend on one output variable, that is $C(y_1, \ldots, y_n) \not\equiv C_1(y_1) + \ldots + C_n(y_n)$ ('non-separable cost function'), corresponds to an interdependence in the production of outputs, as, for instance, established by joint production.[5, 6]

This conceptualisation poses the following problem as far as the description of a technical phenomenon such as joint production is concerned. The cost function is the dual (value-based) description of the firm's production possibilities, with the production function being the associated primal (real) concept. Under certain (sufficient) conditions, the primal and the dual concept are equivalent in the sense that both the production function and the cost function contain the same information regarding the production technology. These conditions are (Chambers 1988: 82–92, Varian 1992: 83):

1. the firm is minimising its costs,

2. the firm is a price taker on all factor markets, and

3. the firm's technology is characterised by an input requirement set which is regular, convex and monotonic.[7]

If one of these conditions is violated, duality does not need to hold and the cost function cannot necessarily be taken as a valid source of information on the technical production possibilities of the firm. Hence, the primal concept in the description of production seems to be better suited to an analysis which focuses on the technical phenomenon of joint production – a phenomenon which genuinely stems from the primal side and is defined there in the first place.

Modern production theory

There are several attempts to explicitly capture joint production by the primal concepts of modern neoclassical production theory, such as the production function, production correspondences, distance functions or the production possibility set. While some contributions are motivated by an interest in analysing multi-output production of several desired goods, other important contributions take their motivation and starting point from the analysis of joint production of desired goods and environmentally harmful bads (Kohn 1975, Mäler 1974, Pethig 1979 or Whitcomb 1972).

Pioneering contributions are those of Färe (1988), Färe et al. (1994), Färe and Primont (1995), Frisch (1965), Krelle (1969) and Shephard (1970), who all base their description of production on certain *functions*, for example production functions (or correspondences) as well as input or output distance functions. In principle, such a conceptualisation can be applied to both joint production of several desired goods and joint production of desired goods and unwanted bads. But in any case, this procedure presupposes some prior knowledge about the character of outputs, that is whether they are desired goods or undesired bads. Hence, it cannot be applied to the most general case where the character of some output is not a priori clear but has yet to be determined in the analysis. We will study this aspect of 'ambivalent' joint production in Chapter 8 below.

Conceptualisations that are based on the production possibility *set* do not encounter this problem. Since they do not presuppose any value judgement about the outputs, they offer, in principle, the most general description of production. For example, Pethig (1979: 7–8, our translation) employs the following definition of joint production:

> A production possibility set $Y \subseteq \mathbb{R}^n$ is characterised by joint production if there is some feasible production vector $y = (y_1, \ldots, y_n) \in Y$ with $y_j, y_k > 0$ for some $j, k = 1, \ldots, n$ ($j \neq k$) and there is no other feasible production vector $y' \in Y$ with $y'_j \geq y_j$, $y'_k < y_k$ and sign y'_h = sign y_h for all $h = 1, \ldots, n$.

This definition may be interpreted as follows. Output k is a joint product of output j if it is not possible to reduce the amount produced of good k while at the same time not reducing output j and keeping constant the roles of all other goods as inputs or outputs.

Joint production and the concept of externality

Within the context of an economic analysis of environmental problems (Baumol and Oates 1988, Hanley et al. 1997, Kolstad 2000, Siebert 2004, Tietenberg 2003) joint production is typically modelled in an implicit way – using the economic concept of externality (for example by Malinvaud 1985: 232). A standard definition of an externality is given, for instance, by Mas-Colell et al. (1995: 352):

> An *externality* is present whenever the well-being of a consumer or the production possibilities of a firm are directly affected by the actions of another agent in the economy. [...] When we say 'directly', we mean to exclude any effects that are mediated by prices.

Hence, externalities express the following kind of interactions between economic agents: The economic activity of agent A influences the well-being or possibilities of economic action of agent B without A and B having a business relationship concerning that matter. The modelling of such influences is normally done by modelling the effect upon B.

Let us think of A and B as two firms. Firm A's activity brings forward a polluting joint product which negatively influences the activity of firm B. This interaction can be modelled using the following production functions

$$y_A = f^A(x_1),$$

$$y_B = f^B(x_2, y_A) \quad \text{with} \quad \frac{\partial f^B}{\partial y_A} < 0,$$

in which x_1 and x_2 are any inputs of the two firms, and y_A and y_B are the outputs of A and B respectively. The emergence of the joint output of firm A is, however, modelled implicitly via its effect on firm B.[8]

Hence, without affected economic agents and their valuation of the effect, an externality does not exist. As some effects of current joint production will show up and can be evaluated only in the future, the concept of externality is not universally suited to capturing the physical phenomenon of joint production.

2.2.2   Joint Production in the Business Literature

The business literature approaches the issue of joint production from an applied and empirical point of view.[9] At the centre of attention is the individual production and business unit.

Riebel's notion of joint production

Riebel (1981: 296; similarly 1996: 993), one of the important authors dealing with joint production from the business point of view, gives the following definition (our translation):

> Out of a single common process of production emerge, either for natural or for technical reasons, necessarily two or more different products (of which often only one is desired).

While this definition appears to be clear and plausible at first sight, it raises a number of questions (Dyckhoff 1996a: 175) and turns out to be too narrow to deal with joint production from an ecological-economic point of view:

1. What is a 'product'? Does this term denote everything that emerges from the production process, or is it more restrictive?

2. What is the time frame of consideration of the process? Are two outputs that emerge from the process one after the other, and necessarily so, joint products?

3. The definition is coined for 'process[es] of production'. Is this the appropriate level of analysis for the purpose of an ecological-economic study? One could as well think of analysing joint production on the level of a firm, an industry, a sector, or the entire economy.

Dyckhoff's notion of joint production

Dyckhoff (1996a), by defining the concept in a relative way, has a much more encompassing notion of joint production than Riebel:

> Joint production [...] holds with respect to a system of production, if in pursuing the system's purpose at least one output under consideration, which is of a different kind than the one related to the system's purpose, is necessarily produced together with the latter. Every output of an input/output-system which corresponds to the system's purpose is called main [...] product; every other output under consideration is called by-product. A main product or a by-product is a joint product of the system, if it unavoidably emerges when pursuing the system's purpose and if it does not, by its kind, correspond to the system's purpose. (Dyckhoff 1996a: 176; similarly Dyckhoff et al. 1997: 1149–1150; our translation)

Dyckhoff's definition is relative with respect to the system under consideration in a threefold manner. (i) The system, according to Dyckhoff (1996a: 176), is described by its 'accounting boundary', which is defined as the 'spatial, temporal and functional' boundary of the system. (ii) The definition refers to 'outputs under consideration'. (iii) Another characteristic feature of the system is the 'system's purpose'. Thus, whether some system of production is characterised by joint production or not may depend on what one takes to be the system's purpose.

Dyckhoff's definition generalises Riebel's definition in an essential and constructive way:

1. The definition can be applied not just to *processes* of production, but to *systems* of production at all levels.

2. Explicitly introducing the 'system's purpose' as a genuine element in the definition allows for describing systems whose purpose is not standard, say the production of goods, but whose purpose consists, for example, in the reduction of pollutants (Dyckhoff 1996b).

3. Referring to 'outputs under consideration' acknowledges and addresses the obvious problem that many flows of outputs may be neglected when describing a production activity.

2.3 SYSTEMS AND REPRESENTATIONS OF SYSTEMS

As the previous section has shown, there exists a wide variety of different notions of joint production in the literature, each tailored to capture one particular aspect of joint production. In this section and the next one, we shall develop a general and encompassing definition of joint production, which is inspired by Dyckhoff's (1996a: 176) definition and resembles Pethig's (1979: 7) definition in its formal structure. Capturing the variety of relevant aspects discussed above as particular expressions of one general idea, it is suitable for an ecological-economic analysis. One of its characteristic features is that it explicitly takes into account the time structure of production.

Since we are mainly interested in studying economy-environment interactions when considering inputs or outputs of production, we focus on flows of energy and matter, as it is almost exclusively by such flows that economy-environment interactions take place. Our notion of joint production is not restricted to one particular class of systems, such as production processes or manufacturing plants. Rather, the notion is suitable for describing systems at any level, for instance, individual production processes, firms, sectors of the economy, or a geographical region. In this section, we first specify the system under study and an observer's representation of this system. We then formally define joint production in Section 2.4.

2.3.1   The System under Study

To start with, and as a reference point for subsequent discussion, we specify the system under study, which may or may not display joint production.

Definition 2.1.   A *system* is a part of reality, which

(i) is separated from its surroundings by a spatial boundary for all times $t \in [t_0, t_0 + T]$, where t_0 is the initial time of description of the system and T is the system's remaining lifetime, and

(ii) contains $n \geq 1$ endogenous elements, which potentially interact with each other and are potentially influenced by exogenous elements in the system's surroundings.

The essence of a system, thus, is its boundary, which separates the system (endogenous elements) from its surroundings (exogenous elements). In Definition 2.1, this boundary is spatial and temporal. From an applied point of view, a system's boundary is often specified in functional terms (for example by Dyckhoff 1996a: 176). For systems whose interaction with their surroundings can be fully specified in terms of energy and material flows, such a functional boundary can always be reduced to a spatial-temporal boundary, which may, however, be very complicated.[10] With the system specified, the system's properties and behaviour are determined by two classes of interactions: *endogenous* and *exogenous* interactions.

Definition 2.2.

(a) An *endogenous interaction* is an interaction among endogenous elements of a system.

(b) An *exogenous interaction* is an influence from an exogenous element on an endogenous element of a system.

Endogenous interactions denote the interactions which take part within the system, whereas exogenous interactions denote the influence of the system's surroundings on the system. The interplay between these two classes of interactions determines a system's behaviour and evolution over time (Figure 2.1).

The distinction between endogenous and exogenous elements as well as interactions is analytical, that is, it is introduced by the observer of a system. Only the observer's choice of a particular system under study, and the separation between system and surroundings associated with this choice, separate endogenous from exogenous elements. As the choice of a particular system under study may be motivated by subjective reasons, for example the observer's interest of study, this raises the question whether, or to what extent, an objective description of reality is possible at all.

2.3.2   Objectivity of a Model: The System Representation

One might think of two different subjective elements which could possibly have an influence on the description of reality (Figure 2.2). One of them is the observer's interest when observing, describing and analysing the system; it depends on the context of his scientific investigation. For the sake of conceptual clarity, we assume that the observer is not part of the system to be described, but that he is observing the system from the outside. The context of the investigation and the observer's cognitive interests influence his choice of a particular representation of the system to be described. This is subject to a detailed discussion in Section 2.3.3. The second subjective element stems from the valuation of states of the system by the individuals in the system. For example, if the system is an economy with production and consumption, one source of subjectivity are the preferences of the individual economic agents in this economy. They value all outputs of production according to their subjective preferences. This includes not only desired goods and products, but also wastes, pollutants and their respective environmental impact. This valuation introduces a subjective element into the analysis and is subject to a detailed discussion in Section 2.3.5.

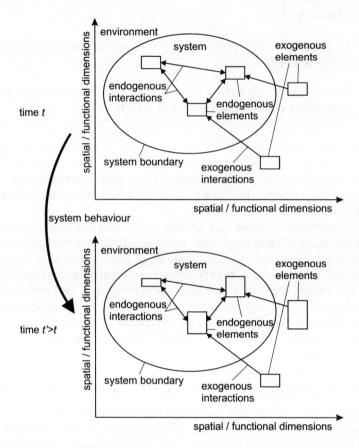

Figure 2.1   Endogenous and exogenous interactions determine the system's evolution from time t to time t′ > t. (Figure adapted from Schiller 2002: 41.)

   The assumption that the observer describes the economy from the outside is a simplification. In reality, any observer of the system is at the same time an economic agent who has certain preferences for the different outputs of production. The observer's individual preferences as well as other individuals' preferences will influence the observer's cognitive interest when describing the system. For example, the generally increased appreciation of the natural environment led to a boost for environmental sciences in the 1980s. As a result, the description of some economic processes changed such as to include the environmental impact of these processes.

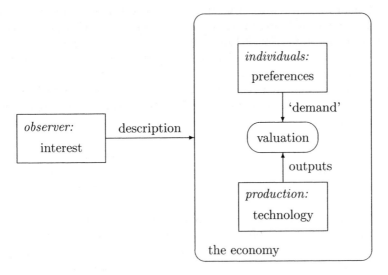

Figure 2.2   The influence of the subjective elements, (i) observer's cognitive interest and (ii) individuals' preferences, on the description of the production process. (Figure taken from Baumgärtner 2000: 171.)

2.3.3   The Choice of a System Representation

The description of a system by an observer is motivated by his interests.[11] Depending on these interests – and the context of the investigation – he will (i) choose the system boundary so as to confine the object under study accordingly, and (ii) make further simplifications when specifying the endogenous and exogenous elements of the system. Thus, the observer does not describe a *system proper*, but he chooses a particular *representation of the system*.[12]

Definition 2.3.   A *representation of a system* (or: *system representation*) is the description of a system by the observer which specifies

- which endogenous elements and interactions of the system and

- which exogenous interactions from the surroundings on the system

are being considered.

A representation of a system is an abstract description of the system – one could also say: a *model* of the real system – which is in general simplified compared with a complete description of the system.[13]   In particular, a system representation may comprise less than all endogenous and exogenous elements as well as interactions. The choice of a particular system representation by an observer depends on several factors. Among them are, in particular, the observer's scientific and other interests, his state of knowledge and ignorance with respect to the various interactions, as well as technical conditions (such as measurability of elements and interactions).

For every system there exists a wide variety of representations. One particular kind of representation is given by thermodynamic representations.

Definition 2.4.   A *thermodynamic representation of a system* is a system representation in which all exogenous interactions are being considered that can be described by energy and material flows.

Thermodynamic representations play a special role for systems which can be completely described in terms of energy and material flows. For such systems, a thermodynamic representation amounts to a *complete* description of the system. For the analysis of economy-environment interactions, thermodynamic representations are important as a reference point for modelling because they do not only include desired material flows, but also all undesired and harmful pollutants. In Chapter 3, we will see that in a thermodynamic representation every process of industrial production is necessarily joint production (Section 3.3).

A complete, thermodynamic description of real systems can only be achieved in a very few cases. Moreover, it is very possible that the observer's cognitive interests are such that he explicitly does not even *want* to consider all inputs and outputs, since this would considerably complicate the description of the system without contributing any relevant insights.

As an illustrative example, consider the production system of a power plant. The system under study consists of an (idealised) transformation technology and the associated flows of inputs and outputs (Figure 2.3). The numbers refer to the brown-coal-fired power plant Niederaußem in North-Rhine-Westphalia, Germany (RWE 1986). Figure 2.3a-c shows the system in three stylised representations:

- *Thermodynamic representation* (Figure 2.3a, cf. Definition 2.4): A complete description of the material and energetic inflows and outflows.

- *Accounting representation* (Figure 2.3c): Only flows associated with real or accounting payments in money units are taken into consideration. Free goods that are used as inputs are not considered. Similarly, outputs that are not marketable and do not

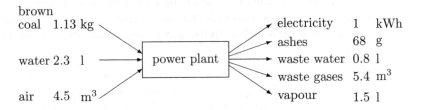

(a) thermodynamic representation

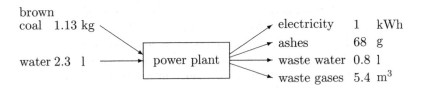

(b) environmental-economic representation

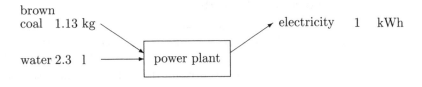

(c) accounting representation

Figure 2.3   Idealised description of the system 'brown-coal-fired power plant' in three different representations: (a) thermodynamic representation; (b) one possible environmental-economic representation; (c) accounting representation (no environmental regulation). (Data from RWE 1986; figure adapted from Baumgärtner 2000: 174.)

lead to any payments (for example disposal or emission fees), are not considered either.[14]

- *Environmental-economic representation* (Figure 2.3b): In addition to the accounting representation, an environmental-economic representation would also include inputs and outputs that are either relevant as natural resources or have the potential to be environmentally harmful. In general, for every system there is a large number of representations that could be classified as environmental-economic ones. The reason is that one might consider a different selection of inputs and outputs, according to the problem under study.

Obviously, the choice of a particular representation has an influence on how the observer will describe the production structure and whether or not he will detect the environmental impact of production. In particular, the choice of a representation will influence the answer to the question of whether or not the system under study is characterised by joint production. In the accounting representation (Figure 2.3c) electricity is produced in single production. In contrast, in the environmental-economic representation (Figure 2.3b) and in the thermodynamic representation (Figure 2.3a) the system is characterised by joint production.

In choosing a particular system representation, an observer simplifies not only the representation of exogenous interactions of a system with its surroundings, that is the flows of inputs and outputs. In general, a particular system representation may also be a simplification as far as the representations of endogenous elements and interactions are concerned.

2.3.4   The Choice of a Time Horizon

In addition to choosing a particular system representation, the observer chooses a time horizon of observation. The *time horizon* τ is the time span over which the system's activity is considered.[15] Like the system representation, the observer's time horizon τ depends on his interests and the scientific context of the study. One normally chooses a time horizon τ according to the problem to be studied (Faber and Proops 1996). For example, if one wants to study the return on investment of a new production facility in the chemical industry, then one typically employs a time horizon of a few years. If, however, one wants to study the ecological impact of this production facility, then the time horizon chosen has to be considerably longer, since for this purpose the slow accumulation of pollutant stocks has to be taken into account (see Section 5.2).

So far, we have argued that the chosen degree of completeness in the description of some system, as well as the time horizon τ, depends on the observer's cognitive interest. Furthermore, the completeness of description and the time horizon are influenced by the observer's *knowledge* and *ignorance*. This might be illustrated by the following example. If waste incineration is carried out at low temperatures, dioxins are produced in small amounts as joint outputs of this activity. As long as one did not know about the emergence and toxicity of these substances, dioxins were not considered as joint outputs of waste incineration, that is, they were not part of the system representation. If, however, the toxicity is known and their emergence falls within the observer's interests, he will be likely to include the dioxins in the description of the process of waste incineration.

2.3.5 The 'Purpose' of a System

We have seen in the previous sections that the observer's cognitive interest is crucial for the choice of a system representation and a time horizon. This necessarily introduces a subjective element into the description of production. In this section, we argue that the second potential subjective element in the description of production – valuation of outputs based on individuals' subjective preferences (cf. Figure 2.2) – should not matter for this choice.

Statements about the value of outputs go beyond a purely material and energetic description of the production process. The value of some output, and its character as a good or a bad, is not an intrinsic property of the output but depends on many factors (Debreu 1959: 33). Among them are people's preferences, lifestyles and cultural backgrounds; society's initial endowment with resources; conditions of production and available technologies; environmental impact of emissions, as well as their perception and valuation etc. Since the purpose of a production system is, at least in part, based on the value of its inputs and outputs, only a total analysis of the entire economy can reveal the system's purpose, and, thus, which outputs can be considered as the main products and the by-products. Chapter 8 provides a theoretical analysis of this aspect of valuation, and Chapters 15 and 18 case studies.

As long as the definition of joint production refers to the system's purpose (for example Dyckhoff 1996a: 176), economic agents' preferences do have an influence on the description of production.[16] In contrast, we consider joint production to be a natural and technical phenomenon, which should be defined as a property of some system. Once the observer has chosen a particular system representation, it is determined whether the system (in this representation) is characterised by joint production or not. The subjective preferences of economic agents, which may also be part of the system under study, should not make any difference for such a classification. Hence, the description of production and the treatment of subjective valuation of outputs should be conceptually separated in the first place.

Summing up, we advocate the following procedure in the analysis of ecological-economic systems. First, the representation of the system under study and a time horizon are chosen. This choice depends on the observer's cognitive interest as well as his knowledge and ignorance (cf. Section 2.3.3). With the representation and time horizon chosen, one may then give a description of production which is solely based on physical quantities and the technical relationships between them. Our definition of joint production (cf. Section 2.4 below) reflects this procedure, as it is free of any value judgements. Based on such a material description of production, questions of valuation may then be addressed.

2.3.6   Criteria for System Boundaries, System Representation and Time Scale

So far, we have discussed the system and, in particular, the system representation as the object of a scientific investigation. We have seen that both are chosen by the observer according to his scientific interest. Nothing has been said so far, however, about criteria for the choice of a *suitable* system, system representation, and time horizon. The fact that this choice is influenced by subjective factors does not, by any means, indicate that it is arbitrary. During scientific research, the context of a scientific investigation is determined intersubjectively to meet the requirements of the scientific community. Generally speaking, the quality of a scientific investigation partly depends on its context being suitably chosen. This means, for example, that it should reflect any prior scientific experience of the problem at hand. Also societal judgements with respect to a suitable time scale of observation and suitable time horizons should be taken up.

Hence, a suitable choice of system boundaries, system representation and time scale of observation has to meet certain criteria. When establishing the system boundaries and representation, the *interaction* between endogenous and exogenous elements is approximated by a one-way influence of exogenous on endogenous elements (see Section 2.3.1). In mathematical terms: the exogenous elements become the boundary conditions of the evolving system. In this section, we propose criteria for discussing the question of how 'good' this approximation of reality is.[17]

The 'quality' of the approximation introduced by the artificial division between the system and its environment is determined by

- the relationship between the time scale of change of the boundary conditions, the time scale of observation of the system behaviour, and the observer's time horizon, and

- the relative strength of the neglected interaction between exogenous and endogenous elements.

After introducing the time scale of observation T_{obs} we shall elaborate on these two aspects. A third aspect – the practicability of a certain choice of system boundaries and a system representation – will be discussed afterwards.

The time scale of observation

Each investigation of the temporal development of a system (or system element) is based on a time scale of observation T_{obs}, which is the typical duration on which modifications of the state of the system are to be monitored or modelled. Depending on this time scale of observation, one given temporal development of a system can be characterised very differently: For example, the motion of the system 'automobile' can be investigated on the scale of 10^{-15} to 10^{-11} s to see the thermal motion of the molecules leading to heat radiation, on the scale of 10^{-4} to 10^{-1} s to see the mechanical oscillation of components leading to noise radiation, and on the scale of 1 to 10^4 s to see the macroscopic motion of the automobile on the road.

Setting a time scale of observation T_{obs} means determining the 'time units' used for the investigation; it sets the temporal resolution – the 'rhythm' – at which a temporal development is gauged. (For an illustrative application see Figure 4.1 on page 73.) The exact length of the time units involved need not be precisely defined; instead it suffices to set the time scale of observation by specifying a temporal order of magnitude – for example seconds, minutes, hours, or days – for which the dynamics of the system observed are to be described. In the same way as the time horizon τ, the time scale of observation T_{obs} is not objectively given; instead they both result from the observer's cognitive interest.[18]

The relationship of time scales

Besides T_{obs}, two other time scales are important for analysing the quality of choice of system boundaries and representation: the time scale of the development of the exogenous elements, that is, the time scale of the variations of the boundary conditions, T_{bc}, and the time horizon of the observer, τ. For reasons of consistency we only consider situations with

$$T_{\mathrm{obs}} \leq \tau, \tag{2.1}$$

in which the observer's time horizon is long enough in order to monitor the movement he is interested in. If Condition (2.1) is not met, the observer has a static perspective – a situation which we do not want to discuss further as we are interested in investigating system behaviour over time.

If, in addition to Condition (2.1), we also have

$$\tau \ll T_{\mathrm{bc}}, \tag{2.2}$$

then the boundary conditions are quasi static on the time scale of observation and relative to the time horizon. Hence, neglecting the repercussions from the system on exogenous elements (which is implied by the choice of system boundaries) can be considered as a valid approximation, because the repercussions are too slow to be of interest to the observer. In the opposite case of $T_{bc} \leq \tau$, the approximation has to be considered as a bad approximation with respect to time scales.

To summarise: Apart from the aspect of the strength of the interaction between the system and its environment (which is to be developed in the next section), a choice of system boundaries can be regarded as a good approximation of reality if the time scale of the change of boundary conditions and the time scale of observation are sufficiently distinct, that is $T_{obs} \ll T_{bc}$,[19] and the time horizon of the observer is not too long. Both can be summarised in the following condition:

$$T_{obs} \leq \tau \ll T_{bc}, \tag{2.3}$$

which is sufficient for a good choice of system boundaries concerning time scales.

The relative strength of the interaction

The above comparison of time scales is not the only criterion for estimating the quality of a choice of system boundaries and representation. Even if Conditions (2.2) and (2.3) are not met, that is, the boundary conditions are not static over the time horizon of the observer, it may still be sensible to neglect the repercussions from the system on its environment. This is the case if the relative influence of the system onto the exogenous elements is small compared to the influence of other exogenous determinants. In that situation, boundary conditions are explicitly time dependent on the time scale of observation and compared to the time horizon. However, they can be taken to be independent of the evolution of the system with good approximation.

Practical considerations

In a real situation of choosing system boundaries and representation other criteria also play a significant role. Models incorporating all significant elements according to the above quality criteria are often too complex. In those cases, even for the purpose of prediction, the respective model has to be further simplified by, for example, choosing simplified system representations.[20] Criteria for such further simplifications are closely dependent on the observer's cognitive interest. For instance, to understand a certain interrelation it is a classical scientific strategy to separate the corresponding interactions and to neglect all other influences. This approach is very common in the natural sciences but also in some social sciences such as economics. So, in practical situations, trade-offs between the different kinds of criteria may exist and the observer has to judge according to his scientific interests and the context of the investigation.

2.4 DEFINITION OF JOINT PRODUCTION

Having discussed the system under study, the choice of system boundaries, system representation, time horizon, and the quality of this choice, we can now formally define joint production. We will first present the definition, and then discuss its properties. In order to define joint production, we focus our analysis on exogenous interactions from the system's surroundings on the system which take place in the form of flows of energy and matter.

Definition 2.5. Let t_0 be the initial time of description of a system and T its remaining lifetime. A *flow of input*, $x_i(t)$ with $t \in [t_0, t_0 + T]$, is the flow of a specified kind i of matter or energy that enters the system at some point in time t. A *flow of output*, $y_j(t)$ with $t \in [t_0, t_0 + T]$, is the flow of a specified kind j of matter or energy that leaves the system at some point in time t. Inputs are *transformed* into outputs by endogenous elements in the system.

The quantities $x_i(t)$ and $y_j(t)$ are flow quantities of the dimension amount of energy or matter per time. They can be specified for one given point in time t, and they are measured over some finite time interval dt around t.[21] The indices i and j serve to distinguish between different kinds of energy and matter. Examples of inputs into a system 'steel furnace' are coke, ore, air and labour force; examples of outputs are steel, ashes, waste heat and vapour.

The notion of joint production can now be defined with respect to a system representation. There are two aspects to be distinguished:

- An *output* may be characterised as a joint product of some other output.

- A *system* may be characterised by the property of joint production.

It will become obvious that the second aspect is a non-trivial extension of the first.

Definition 2.6. For a given system representation with n outputs and time horizon τ, output B is called a *joint product* (or: *joint output*) of output A at time t_0, if and only if the aggregated amount of output B over the time span $[t_0, t_0 + \tau]$ cannot be reduced to zero without the aggregated amount of output A over the same time span necessarily also being reduced to zero. Formally:

$$Y_B = 0 \quad \Rightarrow \quad Y_A = 0 \quad \text{with} \quad A,B \in \{1,\ldots,n\} \text{ and } A \neq B, \quad (2.4)$$

where

$$Y_j \equiv \int_{t_0}^{t_0+\tau} y_j(t)dt \quad \text{for} \quad j = 1,\ldots,n. \quad (2.5)$$

Definition 2.7.   For a given system representation with n outputs and time horizon τ, the system is characterised by *joint production* at time t_0, if and only if there is at least one output, output A, with the following property: a strictly positive aggregated amount of output A over the time span $[t_0, t_0 + \tau]$ necessarily entails a strictly positive aggregated amount of some other output over the same time span. Formally:

$$\exists_{A \in \{1,\ldots,n\}} \quad Y_A > 0 \quad \Rightarrow \quad \sum_{\substack{j=1 \\ j \neq A}}^{n} Y_j > 0, \quad (2.6)$$

where Y_j is defined by Equation (2.5).

The crucial aspect of both definitions is the *necessity* by which the production of one output entails the emergence of some other output. This necessity is the core idea behind the notion of joint production. The properties of Definitions 2.6 and 2.7 are now discussed in detail.

What are the systems under study?

Definitions 2.6 and 2.7 focus on systems which can be described in terms of flows of energy and matter between the system and its surroundings. This includes production systems, but also 'reduction' systems, for example waste incineration plants. While the description of systems solely by their energy/matter inputs and outputs may not be sufficient for a complete economic description of production, it nevertheless gives insight into the essential aspect of production as far as environmental impact is concerned.

The system can be at any level of economic organisation. As for a production system, it may be a particular technical device, a process, a plant, an entire sector of the economy or a geographically defined area, for example a country. Thus, Definitions 2.6 and 2.7 can be applied in both microeconomic and macroeconomic analysis.

A particular feature of Definitions 2.6 and 2.7 is that joint production is defined with respect to a system representation and not with reference to the system proper. This takes into account that a complete and objective description of real systems is neither possible nor sensible. The system proper is of importance for the argument only insofar as it constitutes the reference point for all representations related to that system.

Independence of the 'system's purpose'

In contrast to Dyckhoff's definition of joint production (see Section 2.2.2), Definitions 2.6 and 2.7 do not refer to the 'system's purpose'. As dicussed in Section 2.3.5, our aim is to describe production in a first step solely based on flows of energy and matter as well as on technical relationships. Value statements, such as the classification of outputs into goods, free goods or bads (Dyckhoff 1994: 67), are not necessary at this stage. In particular, value statements at this stage should not make any difference in answering the question of whether certain outputs are produced in joint production.[22]

Asymmetric joint production

In Definition 2.6, the two outputs, A and B, are not treated symmetrically. Output B is a joint product of output A, as the production of output A necessarily entails output B. But the converse does not need to hold, that is output A is not necessarily a joint product of output B.[23] In such a case one may speak of *asymmetric joint production* with respect to the output pair (A, B).

Definition 2.6, which is based on the characterisation of pairwise relationships between different outputs, allows us to state for each individual output of a multi-product firm, an industry, or a national economy, whether it is produced in single production or jointly with some other output.

Joint products and joint production

Clearly, if a system comprises at least one joint product it is also characterised by joint production. However, one might imagine systems which are characterised by joint production in the sense of Definition 2.7 where no single output is a joint product in the sense of Definition 2.6. This is the case for systems where the production of an output A entails the generation of some by-product. This by-product can be avoided, but only at the expense of generating some other by-product, and vice versa. Hence, none of these by-products is a joint product as defined above, but the production of A necessarily entails some by-product, which means it is characterised by joint production.

Such cases of 'joint production without joint products' are exceptional. They describe a situation where the 'substitution' of one by-product by another is possible without modification of the system. Usually, however, such a substitution requires modification of the system. Then, we actually talk about two different systems – one with and one without the modification – each of which is characterised by joint production (Definition 2.7) *and* comprises at least one joint product (Definition 2.6).[24]

Having separate definitions for joint products and joint production is nevertheless useful, because the two definitions capture different aspects of jointness which are important for analysing economy-environment interactions. Joint products as identified by Definition 2.6 are typically a concern of environmental policy because of their specific properties; they might be toxic or have severe ecological impact etc. Hence, what matters is the control of that particular substance and its origin as a joint output. End-of-pipe abatement strategies in many cases focus on specific joint products. Joint production as a property of a system (Definition 2.7) puts the emphasis on the consequences of producing some output A which may be, for instance, a desired consumption good. Joint production means that it is impossible to produce this output without by-products, even if every single one of these by-products can be avoided. This aspect of jointness has implications for the structure of ecological-economic systems and their dynamics (cf. Chapters 4 and 5), and for taking responsibility, as we will discuss in detail in Part III of this book.

Time of observation t_0 and time horizon τ

The characterisation of a system representation by joint production depends on the time of observation, t_0. The reference to the time of observation allows us to capture changes in the system's behaviour over time in terms of joint production. It is possible to explicitly state that a system representation is characterised by joint production at one point in time, but not at a later point in time (see, for example, Figure 2.4). Such a situation is possible if by, for example, technical progress a harmful joint output, which is unavoidable in the short run, can be avoided in the long run. For a detailed discussion of such processes, see Section 5.2.

The characterisation of a system representation by joint production at the time of observation t_0, according to Definition 2.7, also depends on the observer's time horizon τ. The time horizon τ determines the time span over which the different outputs are aggregated. Thereby, our notion of joint production is very encompassing. The choice of different time horizons τ reduces this general notion of joint production to more specialised concepts:

- For infinitesimally short time horizons $\tau = dt$, where dt is the time interval over which input and output flows are measured and, therefore, the elementary time unit of observation, the notion of joint production of Definition 2.7 reduces to a notion of joint production in which different outputs leave the production system *simultaneously* in t_0.

- For very long time horizons, $\tau \gg dt$, Definition 2.7 covers the case that outputs which are necessarily produced together leave the system *at different points in time*. In the extreme case, $\tau = T$, where T is the system's remaining lifetime, all outputs that ever leave the system are being considered. This includes, for example, the 'leftover' of a shut-down production plant.

The notion of joint production introduced by Definitions 2.6 and 2.7, hence, allows a unified treatment and, at the same time, a distinction between two aspects of joint production – namely the simultaneous generation of several output flows on the one hand, and the time-lagged, but also necessarily coupled, generation of several output flows on the other hand. In addition to the treatment of the first aspect, which has mainly been discussed in the literature so far, it is thus possible to deal with the necessarily linked emergence of several outputs that do not leave the system at the same time but at different times.[25]

The second aspect is particularly important when studying long-term economy-environment interactions. A dynamic analysis of these interactions has to take into account threshold effects and the accumulation of stocks in both the economic and the ecological systems. For this, an explicit description of the temporal structure of production is necessary, that is an explicit description of when inputs enter and outputs leave the various systems. Definitions 2.6 and 2.7 are particularly suited to such a temporally explicit description of economic systems. In such a dynamic framework, they allow one to identify a phenomenon as joint production – in the sense of an inevitable link between different outputs – which so far has scarcely been described as joint production, namely the *inevitable intertemporal* link between outputs.

In order to illustrate the role of the time of observation t_0 and the time horizon τ for the property of joint production, consider the following example (Figure 2.4). A (stylised) production plant continuously produces a desired output and, as a waste joint output, a broken component at discrete times $t = (3, 6, 14)$. Assume that until $t = 6$ the component lasts for three time periods (for example years) before it breaks and needs to be replaced. After $t = 6$, because of technical progress the component lasts for eight time periods. The answer to the question, whether the

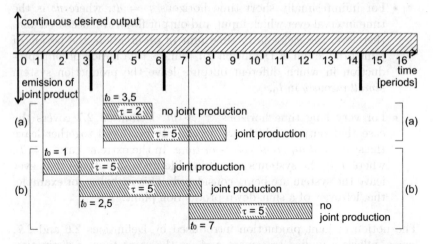

Figure 2.4   Joint production depends on the time horizon τ and the time of observation t_0. A (stylised) production plant continuously produces a desired output and a broken component at discrete times $t = (3, 6, 14)$. For fixed time of observation $t_0 = 3.5$, there exists joint production depending on the time horizon τ (a). For a fixed time horizon τ = 5, there exists joint production for observation at $t_0 = 1$ and $t_0 = 2, 5$, but not for observation at $t_0 = 7$ (b). (Figure adapted from Schiller 2002: 213.)

production plant is characterised by joint production, now depends on both the chosen time horizon τ and the time of observation t_0. For example, for a fixed time of observation $t_0 = 3.5$ the system is characterised by joint production if a time horizon τ ≥ 2.5 is chosen, but not for τ < 2.5 (Figure 2.4a). And for a fixed time horizon, for example τ = 5, there exists joint production for times of observation $t_0 ≤ 6$ (Figure 2.4b shows $t_0 = 1$ and $t_0 = 2, 5$), but not for later times of observation $t_0 > 6$ (Figure 2.4b shows $t_0 = 7$).

2.5   CONCLUSION

Joint production is treated here as an objective, real-world phenomenon which is independent of individual or collective valuation. This is reflected in our conceptualisation of the phenomenon: Definitions 2.6 and 2.7 build on technical and natural relationships regarding the flows of energy/matter which are a property of the system under study. They do not make recourse to value terms. Of course, there is a subjective element in the description of systems which is inherent in any scientific endeavour, namely the observer's cognitive interest. This is embraced in our conceptualisation by referring to a system representation and a time horizon which are chosen by the observer, rather than to the system proper.

With this perspective on the phenomenon, some methods of modelling joint production are better suited than others. In particular, models of joint production should not contain any a priori value judgements, but should start from a physical description of the system. Therefore, concepts like activity analysis (Koopmans 1951), production vectors and production sets are better suited than cost and production functions or externalities (cf. Section 2.2.1). In particular, the concept of externality, which is widely used in environmental economics to capture side effects of production, crucially depends on the valuation of those side effects by economic agents.

In Section 2.4, we have identified two aspects of jointness in production: specific joint products, which occur as by-products of desired goods, and general joint production in a system, which captures a jointness in production irrespective of the occurrence of specific by-products. We will study important implications of the first aspect particularly in Part II by performing an economic analysis. Ethical implications of the second aspect will be discussed in Part III in terms of responsibility.

In the remainder of Part I, we will further elaborate on joint production and its consequences on a conceptual level. In Chapter 3, joint production is conceptualised as a natural and ubiquitous phenomenon. We shall show that the laws of nature imply that every process of (industrial) production is joint production. The consequences of joint production for the dynamics of ecological-economic systems are discussed in Chapters 4 and 5.

Notes

1.   Chapter 6 gives a more detailed account of how economists have analysed joint production in the history of economic thought.

2.   For instance, Müller-Fürstenberger (1995: 289–295) gives an empirical analysis of production processes in the chemical industry which are characterised by the fact that the various outputs are produced in fixed proportion. Another example is the joint production of electricity and steam for space-heating in cogeneration power plants: when using a back-pressure turbine the two outputs are produced in fixed proportion; in contrast, when using an extraction-condensing turbine the two outputs are produced in flexible proportion, but the flexibility of output proportion is confined within narrow limits (Funk 1990: 93, 105).

3.   See, for instance, the contributions collected in Pasinetti (1980), Salvadori and Steedman (1990: Vol. II) and Steedman (1988). The most accessible, yet thorough,

presentation of the problem of joint production within a modern classical approach is that of Kurz and Salvadori (1995: Chapter 8).

4.　Bailey and Friedlaender (1982) give a survey of the literature. The theoretical side has been most fully expounded by Baumol et al. (1988).

5.　If a complete separation is possible, that is $C(y_1, \ldots, y_n) = C_1(y_1) + \ldots + C_n(y_n)$, a multi-product firm is characterised by multiple, yet independent production. See Nehring and Puppe (2004) for a more general discussion of the implications of joint production for the structure of the cost function.

6.　The idea of defining joint production in terms of a firm's costs of production goes back to Alfred Marshall (1925[1890]: 388), who defines:

> When two or more things are produced by one and the same process; so that the expenses of producing them all together are not greater than the expenses of producing one of them alone would be; then these things are called *joint products*.

7.　The input requirement set $V(y)$ is the set of all input vectors x that allow the production of at least the output vector $y = (y_1, \ldots, y_n)$. $V(y)$ is called *regular* if it is a closed, non-empty set for all $y \geq 0$; it is called *convex* if $x, x' \in V(y)$ implies that $tx + (1-t)x' \in V(y)$ for all $0 \leq t \leq 1$; it is called *monotonic* if $x \in V(y)$ and $x' \geq x$ imply that $x' \in V(y)$ (Varian 1992: 6–9). While regularity is a technical assumption, convexity and monotonicity have a substantial meaning. Convexity states that average input combinations yield an output at least as high as the one attainable for extreme input combinations. Convexity holds, for example, if there are different processes that can produce the same outputs and if these processes can be scaled up and down and combined with each other. If, however, processes cannot be, say, scaled down, for example because of indivisibilities, then convexity does not need to hold. Monotonicity states that 'free disposal' of inputs is possible. But often, this is not the case, in particular when input substances are environmentally harmful and, thus, are subject to regulation.

8.　In a more explicit presentation, firm A's activity leads to emissions $e_A = e_A(y_A)$, which is an argument of B's production function, $y_B = g^B(x_2, e_A(y_A)) \equiv f^B(x_2, y_A)$.

9.　See, for instance, Dyckhoff (1994), Fandel (1994), Oenning (1997), Riebel (1955, 1981, 1996) and Strebel (1981).

10.　Specifying a system boundary solely in spatial-temporal terms may pose problems, in particular, for social systems which interact with their surroundings by information flows.

11.　Implicit in this argument is the idea that *any* observation and increase in knowledge is guided and structured by interests. While it is, of course, possible that there are observations and learning processes which are not guided by interests, the latter are not considered here.

12.　Dyckhoff (1996a) is well aware of this when speaking of 'outputs under consideration'.

13.　Mäki (2002: 11) defines a *model* as 'a simple system used as a representation of [...] a more complex system'. In this book, we avoid the term 'model' and employ the term 'system representation' instead, because the former is generally used in many different specific, and partially contradictory, meanings.

14.　The implicit assumption behind Figure 2.3 is that there are no disposal costs for solid and liquid wastes or fees on emissions.

15.　In order to avoid the problems that stem from a finite lifetime T of the system, in the following we always assume that at the time of observation, t_0, the time horizon τ does not exceed the remaining lifetime of the system: $\tau \leq T$.

16.　Consider the example of a production system that uses wooden boards of 7 m length as raw material input to produce wooden boards of 2 m length and of 1 m length (Oenning 1997: 20 gives a very similar example). If there is a persistent demand for

1 m boards and no demand for 2 m boards, the former must be considered as the main product, the production of which defines the system's purpose. With reverse demand relations, however, the system's purpose would consist in the production of 2 m boards. They would then be the main product and 1 m boards would be an unavoidable joint product. According to Dyckhoff's definition (cf. Section 2.2.2), in the first scenario the production process is not characterised by joint production; and in the second scenario, the process would be one of joint production, although the technical conditions of production have not changed at all.

17.   In establishing criteria for the 'quality' of an approximation, we consider mainly predictional purposes of modelling. For other modelling purposes, different criteria are equally relevant.

18.   The choice of the time scale of observation T_{obs} in relation to the time horizon τ (cf. Definition 2.3) is essentially only limited by the trivial relation $T_{obs} < \tau$, and for a truly dynamic investigation by the condition $T_{obs} \ll \tau$. For reasons of practicability, however, there often exists also a lower bound for a suitable choice of T_{obs}.

19.   This condition is necessary so that Conditions (2.1) and (2.2) can hold simultaneously.

20.   This is even more relevant for other modelling purposes such as studying specific causal relations in 'toy' models or 'paradigm' models.

21.   The choice of this measuring time interval dt is not arbitrary and may give rise to problems. A sensible time scale dt for measuring flow quantities depends on the dynamical properties of the system (representation). On the one hand, dt is bounded from above by the slowest temporal variation of an in- or output of the system that still falls under the scope of description. On the other hand, it is not sensible to choose a measuring time scale dt which is smaller than the fastest variation of an in- or output that still falls under the scope of description. For example, consider a system in which the output is turned out once per year and the quantity of output produced cyclically varies with a period of 20 years. If one wants to properly take account of the cyclical variation with its period of 20 years, one has to choose the measuring time scale such that dt is much smaller than 20 years. In principle, descriptions are the more detailed the shorter the measurement intervals. However, in this example it is not sensible to choose dt shorter than one year.

22.   Consider again the example of 2 m boards and 1 m boards which are produced from 7 m boards (cf. note 16). According to Definition 2.6, 1 m boards always appear as the joint product of 2 m boards, irrespective of the system's purpose and the factors determining the system's purpose, such as market demand for the two outputs.

23.   Consider again the example of 2 m boards and 1 m boards which are produced from 7 m boards (cf. note 16). It is obvious that the 2 m boards cannot be produced in single production, that is as the sole output of the production process. For 1 m boards are necessarily produced as joint products with the 2 m boards. However, the converse does not hold. 1 m boards can well be produced in single production. This means that 1 m boards are joint products of 2 m boards, but 2 m boards are not joint products of 1 m boards.

24.   An example is the installation of a catalytic converter into a car's exhaust pipe which reduces NO_x-emissions from combustion but increases CO_2-emissions. In this example, the car with and the car without a catalytic converter actually constitute two different systems each of which is characterised by joint production and comprises joint products.

25.   This second aspect, for example, allows one to treat capital goods as joint products. It goes back to von Neumann's (1937, 1945/46) and Sraffa's (1960: Chapter X) view of fixed capital as a joint product.

3. Thermodynamics of Joint Production[*]

with John Proops and Jakob de Swaan Arons

3.1 INTRODUCTION

As the joint products of some desired good are often undesired and harmful to the natural environment, why don't we just avoid their occurrence?
One possible answer to this question that most economists will give is
that the occurrence of waste by-products and their disposal in many
instances constitute an *inefficiency* due to an externality, that is, the
consequences of producing and disposing of waste are not internalised in
market prices. In this economic view the occurrence of waste is due to
a market failure, which could, in principle, be cured by imposing suitable policy measures, such as, for example, Pigouvian taxes or tradable
permits on waste.

While the problem indeed is to some extent due to a market (and
policy) failure, taking a thermodynamic point of view reveals a different
relevant aspect. For, from a thermodynamic point of view, the occurrence of joint outputs appears as an *unavoidable necessity* of industrial
production. This view is presented in detail in this chapter.

It has been argued, based on the thermodynamic laws of mass conservation and entropy generation, that in industrial production processes
the occurrence of joint outputs is as necessary as the use of material
resources (Ayres and Kneese 1969, Faber et al. 1998, Georgescu-Roegen
1971). On the other hand, it seems to be quite obvious that the sheer
amount of waste currently generated in modern industrial economies[1]
is to some extent due to various inefficiencies and might, in principle,
be reduced. In this chapter, we analyse the question to what extent
the occurrence of joint outputs is actually an unavoidable necessity of
industrial production, and to what extent it is an inefficiency that may,
in principle, be reduced.

---

[*]This chapter draws on Faber, Proops and Baumgärtner (1998), Baumgärtner
(2000: Chapter 4), Baumgärtner and de Swaan Arons (2003), and Baumgärtner
(2004b).

For that sake, we employ the laws of thermodynamics as an analytical framework within which results about current 'industrial metabolism' (Ayres and Simonis 1994) may be rigorously deduced in energetic and material terms.[2] As we will show in this chapter, the concept of joint production captures essential physical aspects of production. So, by describing production in terms of joint production, essential physical effects of production are automatically embraced. In contrast to the complex notions and laws of thermodynamics, the concept of joint production is very concrete and comparatively easy to understand, as well as to apply. Thus, the concept of joint production can serve as a pedagogical tool to teach the lessons of thermodynamics about economy-environment interactions to economists who are, after all, far more familiar with the concept of joint production than with the laws of thermodynamics.

In Section 3.2, we develop the rationale for analysing economy-environment interactions from a thermodynamic point of view. In Section 3.3, we then use the concepts and laws of thermodynamics to demonstrate that industrial production is necessarily and unavoidably joint production. This means that the occurrence of joint products is unavoidable in the industrial production of desired goods. In Section 3.4, we analyse the degree of thermodynamic (in)efficiency of industrial production processes, and the associated amounts of waste by-products due to these inefficiencies. In Section 3.5, we discuss the thermodynamic properties of joint outputs, and how these relate to the occurrence of environmental problems. Section 3.6 concludes.

3.2 THE THERMODYNAMIC PERSPECTIVE ON ECONOMY-ENVIRONMENT INTERACTIONS

3.2.1 Duality Between the Real and Monetary Descriptions

When economists started to analyse the flow of resources, goods, services and money in an economy, the picture was pretty simple: there are two groups of economic agents, consumers and producers; producers deliver goods and services to consumers, and consumers provide the resources with which they are endowed, labour in particular, to producers. Thus, there is a circular flow of commodities in an economy. There is an equivalent circular flow of money counter to that primary flow, as consumers pay money to producers for the goods they consume, and producers remunerate the labour force they receive from the consumers/labourers.[3]

Since the two corresponding flows, the primal flow of real commodities and the dual flow of monetary compensation, are exactly equivalent, it seems superfluous to always study both of them when analysing economic transactions and allocations. Hence, the convention was established in economics to focus on the monetary flow. The current system of national economic accounts, which is meant to be a full representation of economic activity in an economy over one time period, therefore captures all transactions in monetary units, for example the provision of labour and capital, the trading of intermediate goods and services between different sectors of the economy, and final demand for consumer goods.

Of course, this picture is too simple. It neglects the use of natural resources and the emission of pollutants and wastes. Both activities are unavoidable aspects of economic action. In the early twentieth century, the subdiscipline of environmental and resource economics emerged to deal with the question of how to account, in an economic sense, for the use of natural resources on the one hand and the emission of pollutants and wastes on the other (Gray 1913, 1914, Hotelling 1931, Pigou 1912, 1920). The picture now appeared as follows: there is a circular flow – actually: two equivalent circular flows – between consumers and producers which form the core of economic activity. In addition, there is an inflow of natural resources and an outflow of emissions and wastes. Thus, a linear throughflow of energy and matter drives the circular flow of economic exchange.

Environmental and resource economics faced one conceptual problem from the very beginning. Economic analysis, including environmental and resource economics, is based on the idea of duality (that is equivalence) between the flow of real commodities and services (measured in physical units) and an equivalent value flow (measured in monetary units), and consequently focuses on the value dimension. But the inflow of natural resources, as well as the outflow of emissions and wastes, do not have an apparent value dimension. Markets do not indicate these values, as markets often do not exist in this domain. And where they exist, the resulting values are distorted due to ubiquitous externalities and public goods.

As a result, the valuation of environmental goods, services and damages has to be set up explicitly as a non-market process, and elaborate theories and techniques have been proposed for this purpose.[4] All these techniques require, to a greater or lesser extent, an adequate, prior description – in real terms – of the particular commodity or service to be valued. In other words, before individuals or society can value something, they have to have an adequate idea of what exactly that something is. This holds, in particular, for the energy and material resources used in production as well as for the emissions and wastes generated as by-products of desired goods.

And here lies the relevance of thermodynamics. Being the branch of physics that deals with transformations of energy and matter, thermodynamics is an appropriate foundation in the natural sciences to provide a description in real terms of what goes on when humans interact with the non-human environment. In particular, thermodynamics captures the energy/matter dimension of economy-environment interactions. Thus, it is a necessary complement and prerequisite for economic valuation.

3.2.2   The Fundamental Factors of Production

In line with the duality argument presented above, the economic literature has long abstracted from the physical basis of production. However, a description of economic systems based on monetary measures necessarily neglects real transactions that are not coupled to the exchange of (positive or negative) value. In particular, such transactions are excluded from an economic analysis. For that reason, analysing interrelations within the economy, or relationships between the economy and environment, based on a thermodynamic description which does not yet presuppose any value judgements, is a necessary ingredient for building ecological economics (Ayres 1978: vi).

While we consider energy (actually: exergy; see Section 3.4.1 below) and matter as the fundamental factors of production, the classical or neoclassical view on the input side of production is different. In the traditional (neo-)classical view, 'labour' and 'capital' are considered as homogeneous factors of production. This description abstracts from real production processes, which are always transformations of energy and matter.[5] Even the use of a third factor of production, 'land', once made by the classical economists as a reminder that all production relies on a natural basis, has practically been abandoned by neoclassical economists for a long time.

The reason for this abstraction from the physical reality of production is twofold. First, the choice of labour and capital as the fundamental factors of production reflects the strong interest of classical economists in the conflict over the distribution of the national income among those social groups involved in its production, namely capital owners and labourers.[6] Second, neoclassical economics is mainly preoccupied with the question of allocative efficiency. The neoclassical world is a 'model of pure exchange' (Pasinetti 1977: 24–26). With this emphasis, technical details of production did not get the attention they deserve from an ecological-economic point of view. As a consequence, production is often modelled in the most simple conceivable way, namely by writing down a production function with capital and labour as arguments.[7]

In contrast to the neoclassical concern, we are interested in describing economy-environment interactions. For that reason we focus on the material basis of all economic action. When we speak of 'production' we always have in mind transformations of energy and matter.[8] Such a material view of the process of production reveals the severe repercussions that production has on the natural environment. As discussed in Chapter 5, it is exactly the unwanted, yet unavoidable, joint products, such as CO_2, which cause some of the major current environmental problems. The traditional approach of environmental economics to describing these problems is based on the theory of public goods and externalities. Joint products which come as unwanted pollutants are considered as special cases, to be treated and eliminated by appropriate regulation or taxation:

> [T]here has been a tendency in the economics literature to view externalities as exceptional cases. [...] We believe that at least one class of externalities – those associated with the disposal of residuals resulting from the consumption and production process – must be viewed quite differently. They are a normal, indeed, inevitable part of these processes. (Ayres and Kneese 1969: 282)

Similarly, Georgescu-Roegen (1975: 357) claims that

> [g]iven the entropic nature of the economic process, waste is an output just as unavoidable as the input of natural resources.

In the next section, we are going to show that this claim is indeed true. Single production will turn out to be a mere idealisation, not existent in the real world; and environmental pollution as a consequence of the process of production appears as an inherent effect of production, rather than an exceptional external effect.

3.3 JOINT PRODUCTS ARE UNAVOIDABLE IN INDUSTRIAL PRODUCTION

Production can in the most general way be conceived of as the transformation of a number of inputs into a number of outputs. In thermodynamic terms, energy (actually: exergy) and matter are the fundamental factors of production (Ayres 1998, Baumgärtner 2000, Faber et al. 1998, Ruth 1993). From a thermodynamic view, two quantifiable characteristics of an input or an output are its mass, m, and its entropy, S. Alternatively, one could use its exergy instead of its entropy; this will be done in the next section. Because both mass and entropy are extensive quantities, it is useful to introduce the ratio of the two, $\sigma = S/m$, for $m > 0$ as an intensive quantity. σ is called *specific entropy* and measures the entropy per unit mass of a bulk of matter irrespective of that bulk's size.[9]

Let us now narrow down the analysis to the particular type of production which is found in most developed countries and which is most relevant as far as economy-environment interactions are concerned. This is what one may call *industrial production*. For that sake, consider the following reference model of industrial production (Baumgärtner 2000: Chapter 4). A raw material is transformed into a final product. The exergy necessary to carry out that transformation is typically provided by a material fuel. As the analysis of the reference model will reveal, it is then unavoidable that a by-product is jointly produced with the desired product. The analysis will also show that the joint product is characterised by high specific entropy, which suggests that this joint product may often be considered an unwanted waste. The industrial production process can, thus, be depicted as in Figure 3.1. An example of such an industrial production process is the production of pure iron as a desired product from iron ore as raw material (Ruth 1995a). The fuel in that example is coke, and there are slag, carbon dioxide and heat as waste joint products.

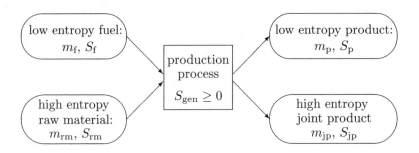

Figure 3.1 The thermodynamic structure of industrial production in terms of mass and (specific) entropy. (Figure modified from Baumgärtner 2000: 74.)

The focus on industrial production processes justifies building the reference model on the assumption of two kinds of inputs, raw material and fuel, and not more than two kinds of outputs, desired product and joint product.[10] In the notation introduced above, m_j and S_j are the mass and the entropy of the inputs and outputs involved and σ_j is their respective specific entropy (where $j =$ rm, f, p, jp stands for raw material, fuel, product, joint product). One may then formally define the notion of industrial production in thermodynamic terms.

Definition 3.1.   Within the formal framework of the reference model, a process of production is called *industrial production* if and only if it exhibits the following three properties:

$$m_{\text{rm}}, m_{\text{p}} \ > \ 0, \tag{3.1}$$

$$\sigma_{\text{rm}} \ > \ \sigma_{\text{p}}, \tag{3.2}$$

$$m_{\text{f}} \ > \ 0. \tag{3.3}$$

Property (3.1) means that the production process essentially consists of a material transformation, that is, a raw material is transformed into a material desired product. Property (3.2) states that the direction of this material transformation is such as to transform a raw material of relatively high specific entropy into a desired product of lower specific entropy. In our example, iron oxide (Fe_2O_3) and pure iron (Fe) have a specific entropy of 87.4 J/mole K and 27.3 J/mole K respectively (see Table 3.1; Kondepudi and Prigogine 1998: Appendix). The underlying idea is that most raw materials are still impure and, therefore, can be thought of as mixtures from which the desired product is to be obtained by de-mixing of the different components of the raw material. More generally, desired products are thought of as matter in a more orderly state than the raw material. From basic thermodynamics we know that such a transformation process requires the use of exergy. Property (3.3) states that the exergy input also has mass, that is, the exergy necessary to carry out the desired transformation is provided by a material fuel, such as oil, coal or gas.

The constraints imposed on production processes by the laws of thermodynamics can be formalised as follows:

$$m_{\text{rm}} + m_{\text{f}} \ = \ m_{\text{p}} + m_{\text{jp}}, \tag{3.4}$$

$$S_{\text{rm}} + S_{\text{f}} + S_{\text{gen}} \ = \ S_{\text{p}} + S_{\text{jp}} \ \text{ with } S_{\text{gen}} \geq 0. \tag{3.5}$$

The thermodynamic Law of Mass Conservation (Equation 3.4) states that the total ingoing mass has to equal the total outgoing mass because mass is conserved in the production process. The Second Law of Thermodynamics (Equation 3.5), the so-called Entropy Law, states that in the production process a non-negative amount of entropy is generated, S_{gen}, which is added to the total entropy of all inputs to yield the total entropy of all outputs.

For the system representation specified by the reference model, the two laws of thermodynamics, Equations (3.4) and (3.5), together with the assumption of industrial production, Properties (3.1)–(3.3), imply that the second output necessarily exists (Baumgärtner 2000: 77).

Proposition 3.1.   For any process of industrial production of a desired product (Properties 3.1–3.3), the laws of thermodynamics (Equations 3.4 and 3.5) imply the existence of at least one joint product.

This result is formally proven in Appendix 3A. It means, the occurrence of a joint product is necessary and unavoidable in every process of industrial production. One may actually speak of a *joint product* and of *joint production* in the sense of Definitions 2.6 and 2.7, since the desired product and the joint product are necessarily produced together.

The intuition behind this result is the following. One obvious reason for the existence of joint outputs besides the desired product is simply conservation of mass. If, for instance, pure iron is produced from iron ore with a carbon fuel, the desired product, which is pure iron, does not contain any carbon. Yet, the carbon material from the fuel has to go somewhere. Hence, there has to be a joint product containing the carbon. But there is a second reason for the existence of joint products besides and beyond conservation of mass, and that is the generation of entropy according to the Second Law of Thermodynamics. Think of a production process where all of the raw material and the material fuel end up as part of the desired product, for example, the production of cement (cf. Chapter 17). In that case, mass conservation alone would not require any joint product. But because the desired product has lower specific entropy than the raw material, and there is some non-negative amount of entropy generated by the process, there is a need for a joint output taking up the excess entropy. In many cases, as in the example of cement production, this happens in the form of low-temperature heat, which may be contained in the product, a by-product or transferred to the environment.

In most cases of industrial production, both of these reasons – the one based on mass conservation and the one based on entropy generation – hold at the same time. Therefore, the joint product is typically a high entropy material. Due to its high entropy it will most often be considered useless and, therefore, an undesired waste. However, one should be careful to note that the classification of an output as 'waste' carries a certain value judgement, which cannot be inferred from thermodynamics alone.[11] We will come back to the question of whether the joint product is a desired good or an undesired waste in Chapter 8.

3.4   THERMODYNAMIC (IN)EFFICIENCY OF INDUSTRIAL PRODUCTION

The thermodynamic analysis in the previous section has demonstrated that the existence of a high entropy joint product is necessary and unavoidable in every process of industrial production. In reality, however, much of the waste currently generated is obviously avoidable. Yet this observation is not in contradiction to the result derived above. While the reference model was based on the assumption of thermodynamic efficiency, current technology and production practices are to a large extent thermodynamically inefficient. As a consequence, while a certain amount of joint production is necessary and unavoidable for thermodynamic reasons, the actual amount of waste produced with current technologies is an expression of inefficiency. Thermodynamic considerations which originated in the applied field of engineering thermodynamics, in particular the exergy concept, can tell us exactly what amount of waste is due to inefficiency and may, in principle, be reduced (Ayres 1999, Bejan et al. 1996, Brodyansky et al. 1994, Cleveland and Ruth 1997, Creyts 2000, de Swaan Arons and van der Kooi 2001, de Swaan Arons et al. 2004, Dewulf et al. 2000, Ruth 1995b, 1995c).

3.4.1   Engineering Thermodynamics: The Exergy Concept

Exergy is defined to be the maximum amount of work obtainable from a system as it approaches thermodynamic equilibrium with its environment in a reversible way (Szargut et al. 1988: 7, Ayres 1998: 192). Exergy is also commonly called 'available energy' or 'available work' and corresponds to the useful part of energy, thus combining the insights from both the First and Second Laws of Thermodynamics. Hence, exergy is what most people mean when they use the term 'energy', for example, when saying that 'energy is used' to carry out a certain process. As the system might consist simply of a bulk of matter, exergy is also a measure of the potential work embodied in a material, whether it is a fuel, food or other substance (Ayres et al. 1998). The exergy content of different materials can be calculated for standard values specifying the natural environment, by considering how that material eventually reaches thermodynamic equilibrium with its environment with respect to temperature, pressure, chemical potential and all other intensive variables.

The relationship between the concepts of entropy and exergy is simple, as $B_{\text{lost}} = T_0 S_{\text{gen}}$ (Law of Gouy and Stodola), where B_{lost} denotes the potential work or exergy lost by the system in a transformation process, T_0 denotes the temperature of the system's environment, and S_{gen} denotes the entropy generated in the transformation. This means, as the system's entropy increases as a consequence of irreversible transformations according to the Second Law, the system loses exergy or some of its potential to perform work. Exergy, unlike energy, is thus not a conserved quantity. While the entropy concept stresses that with every transformation of the system something useless is created, the exergy concept stresses that something useful is diminished. These developments are two aspects of the same irreversible character of transformations of energy and matter. The character of industrial production, as sketched in Figure 3.1 above, therefore has a corresponding description in terms of exergy (Figure 3.2).

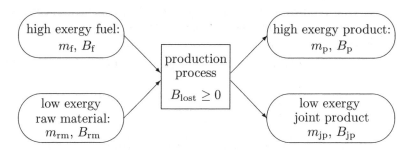

Figure 3.2 The thermodynamic structure of industrial production in terms of mass and exergy. (Figure from Baumgärtner and de Swaan Arons 2003: 118.)

With the strict correspondence, established by the Law of Gouy and Stodola, between the entropy generated in an irreversible transformation and exergy lost in this process, our entire analysis could, in principle, be based either on the entropy concept or on the exergy concept. Physicists usually prefer the entropy route, as entropy is the concept traditionally established in physics. On the other hand, exergy seems to be more popular with engineers and people interested in applied work. Instead of preferring one route to the other, or going all the way along both routes in parallel, we illustrate the fruitfulness of both approaches by employing them at different stages of the argument. While we have demonstrated above the result (Proposition 3.1) that industrial production necessarily yields waste joint products based on the entropy concept, we now switch to the exergy concept to analyse the efficiency of industrial production.

3.4.2 (In)Efficiency in Thermodynamic Equilibrium

In this section, industrial production is quantitatively analysed in exergy terms with regard to thermodynamic (in)efficiency. For that sake, we turn in detail to one particular step in the production process introduced above as an illustrative example. In the production of pure iron from iron ore, the first step is to extract the ore from the deposit. In the next step, the ore is separated by physical means into iron oxide and silicates. The third step, which we shall analyse in detail in this section, then consists of chemically reducing the iron oxide to pure iron. This reduction requires exergy. It is typically provided by burning coke, which, for the purpose of this analysis, can be taken to be pure carbon. So, in the terminology outlined earlier, the desired product of this transformation is pure iron (Fe), the raw material is iron oxide (Fe_2O_3) and the fuel is carbon (C). As a waste joint product in this reaction, carbon dioxide (CO_2) is generated. The chemical reaction in this production process may be written down as follows:

$$2\,Fe_2O_3 + 3\,C \rightarrow 4\,Fe + 3\,CO_2 \,. \qquad (3.6)$$

The molecular weight, specific entropy and exergy of the chemicals involved in the reaction are given in Table 3.1.

chemical	molecular weight [g/mole]	specific entropy [J/mole K]	exergy [kJ/mole]
Fe	56	27.3	376.4
Fe_2O_3	160	87.4	16.5
C	12	5.7	410.3
CO_2	44	213.8	19.9
O_2	32	161.1	4.0

Table 3.1 Molecular weight, specific entropy and exergy of the different chemicals involved in the reduction of iron oxide to pure iron. One mole is, by definition, the amount of some material that contains as many atoms as 12 g of carbon isotope ^{12}C. For every material, one mole contains 6.022×10^{23} particles. The molecular weight of a material is its mass per mole. Source: Kondepudi and Prigogine (1998: Appendix), Szargut et al. (1988: Appendix, Table I).

As one sees, the desired product Fe has a much higher exergy (that is lower specific entropy) than the raw material Fe_2O_3. It is the relatively high exergy content (that is low specific entropy) of the fuel C that provides the exergy for this transformation to happen. The waste CO_2 is then characterised by low exergy content (that is high specific entropy).

Mass balance

The chemical reaction equation (3.6) is correct in terms of the mass balance: all atoms of an element that go into the reaction come out of the reaction as well. Conservation of mass is the reason for the existence of the joint product CO_2. Producing four moles of Fe, thus, entails three moles of CO_2 as waste. That makes 0.75 moles of waste CO_2 emissions per mole of Fe produced (corresponding to 0.59 kg CO_2 per kg of Fe) for mass balance reasons alone.

Thermodynamically efficient energy balance

Checking the reaction equation (3.6) with the exergy values given in Table 3.1 reveals that while the reaction equation is written down correctly in terms of the mass balance, it is not yet correct in energetic terms. For, in order to produce four moles of Fe with an exergy content of 1,505.6 kJ, one needs the input of at least 1505.6 kJ as well. (Recall that exergy cannot be created, but always diminishes in the course of a transformation due to irreversibility.) But three moles of C only contain 1,230.9 kJ. Therefore, one actually needs more than three moles of C to deliver enough exergy for four moles of Fe to be produced from Fe_2O_3. We compensate for this shortage of exergy on the input side by introducing 0.76 additional units of the exergy source C. The reaction equation should, thus, be written down as follows to obey both laws of thermodynamics:

$$2\,Fe_2O_3 + 3.76\,C + 0.76\,O_2 \rightarrow 4\,Fe + 3.76\,CO_2 .$$
$$(33.0) \quad (1,542.7) \quad (3.0) \quad (1,505.6) \quad (74.8)$$
$$(3.7)$$

The numbers in brackets below each input and output give the exergy content in kJ of the respective amounts of inputs and outputs. On the input side 0.76 moles of oxygen (O_2) have been added to fulfil the mass balance with the additional 0.76 moles of C involved. This oxygen comes from the air and enters the transformation process when carbon is burned.

From reaction equation (3.7) we see that the exergy supplied to the reaction by its inputs (1,580 kJ) now suffices to yield the exergy of the outputs (1,580 kJ). As no exergy is lost in the reaction, that is, the exergy of the inputs exactly equals the exergy of the outputs, this corresponds to a thermodynamically 100 % efficient and reversible transformation, in which no entropy is generated and no exergy is lost. In mass terms, reaction equation (3.7) tells us that even in thermodynamically ideal transformations of Fe_2O_3 into Fe, 3.76 moles of CO_2 are generated as material waste when producing four moles of Fe. That makes

0.94 moles of waste CO_2 emissions per mole of Fe produced (corresponding to 0.74 kg CO_2 per kg of Fe). This amount is the minimum waste joint product generation required by the two laws of thermodynamics, as shown in Section 3.3 above to necessarily exist (Proposition 3.1).

Thermodynamic inefficiency

In real production processes the exergy content of carbon of 410.3 kJ/mole is never put to work with an efficiency of 100 %. Detailed data on pig iron production in real blast furnaces in Poland (Szargut et al. 1988: Table 7.3), where coke is burned together with atmospheric oxygen, imply that the efficiency of exergy conversion is only about 33 %.[12] This means that out of one mole of C one obtains only 135.4 kJ instead of the ideal value of 410.3 kJ. As a consequence, in order to deliver the exergy necessary to carry out the chemical reaction one needs to employ at least 12.42 moles of C. The reaction equation for a transformation that is only 33 % efficient in energy conversion would thus read:

$$2\,Fe_2O_3 \quad + \quad 12.42\,C \quad + \quad 9.42\,O_2$$
$$(33.0) \qquad\quad (5,095.9) \qquad (37.7)$$

$$\rightarrow \quad 4\,Fe \quad + \quad 12.42\,CO_2 \quad + \quad heat\,. \quad (3.8)$$
$$(1,505.6) \qquad\quad (247.2)$$

Out of the 5,095.9 kJ of exergy supplied by 12.42 moles of C only 33 %, or 1,681.6 kJ, are put to work in the reaction due to the inefficiency in energy conversion. The amount of exergy supplied by the inputs but not contained in the outputs of the reaction corresponds to exergy lost in the process, $B_{lost} = 3,413.8$ kJ, which is emitted from the reaction as waste heat.

From Equation (3.8) we see that due to the inefficiency in energy conversion the amount of material fuel that is necessary to drive the transformation has more than tripled. In order to produce four moles of Fe with a 33 % efficiency one needs 12.42 moles of C (Equation 3.8) instead of just 3.76 moles in the efficient case (Equation 3.7). As a consequence, the reaction generates 12.42 moles of CO_2 (Equation 3.8) instead of just 3.76 moles in the efficient case (Equation 3.8). That makes 3.11 moles of waste CO_2 emissions per mole of Fe produced (corresponding to 2.45 kg CO_2 per kg of Fe), with only 30 % (0.94 moles) due to thermodynamic necessity (cf. the discussion of Equation 3.7 above) and 70 % (2.17 moles) due to thermodynamic inefficiency.

From this analysis one might conclude that roughly two thirds of the waste currently generated in iron production is due to thermodynamic inefficiency, while one third is actually necessary for thermodynamic reasons. Therefore, even increasing thermodynamic process efficiency to the ideal value of 100 % will not reduce the amount of waste to zero, but only to one third of the amount currently generated.

3.4.3   Finite-Time/Finite-Size Thermodynamics

Pointing to the thermodynamic inefficiency of a real production process, and how it implies the occurrence of large amounts of waste, seems to suggest that the amount of waste can easily be reduced by increasing the thermodynamic efficiency at which the process is carried out. However, there are good economic reasons why this form of thermodynamic inefficiency may actually be desired.

The analysis so far was entirely based on concepts and methods from ideal equilibrium thermodynamics, which means that a level of 100 % efficiency in this framework is reached by operating processes in a completely reversible way between one equilibrium state and another equilibrium state, resulting in zero entropy generation (or: exergy loss) during the process. Recent research in the applied field of engineering thermodynamics has addressed the circumstance that chemical and physical processes in industry never happen in a completely reversible way between one equilibrium state and another equilibrium state. Rather, these processes are enforced by the operator of the process and they are constrained in space and time. This has led to an extension of ideal equilibrium thermodynamics, known under the name of *finite-time/finite-size thermodynamics* (Andresen et al. 1984, Bejan 1996, 1997, Bejan et al. 1996).

From the point of view of finite-time/finite-size thermodynamics it becomes obvious that the minimum exergy requirement and minimum waste production in chemical or physical processes is considerably higher than that suggested by the ideal equilibrium thermodynamics analysis carried out so far. The reason for the increased exergy requirement (which entails an increased amount of waste joint products at the end of the process) lies in the fact that chemical and physical transformations are forced to happen over a finite period of time by the operator of the production plant, which necessarily causes some dissipation of energy. In the language of the reference model described earlier, this shows in a strictly positive amount S_{gen} of entropy generated in the process.

The finite-time/finite-size consideration is a very relevant consideration for many production processes, in particular in the chemical industry. Finite-time/finite-size thermodynamics allows one to exactly identify, track down and quantify exergetic inefficiencies at the individual steps of a production process (Bejan 1996, 1997, Bejan et al. 1996, Brodyansky et al. 1994, Creyts 2000, Szargut et al. 1988), along the entire chain of a production process (Ayres et al. 1998, Cornelissen and

Hirs 1999, Cornelissen et al. 2000), and for whole industries (Dewulf et al. 2000, Hinderink et al. 1999). Thus, it yields valuable insights into the origins of exergy losses and forms a tool for designing industrial production systems in an efficient and sustainable manner (Connelly and Koshland 2001, de Swaan Arons and van der Kooi 2001, de Swaan Arons et al. 2004).

An example which demonstrates how large S_{gen} can actually be is the enrichment of uranium (Balian 1991: 347–348, 383–385). In the production of enriched uranium the actual exergy input is larger than the theoretical minimum calculated from ideal equilibrium thermodynamics by a factor of 70 million! At the Eurodif factory, the French enriching plant from which the data are taken, the process of enriching by isotope separation is realised by gas diffusion through a semipermeable membrane. An ideal process realisation would require letting the gas diffuse in thermodynamic equilibrium, which would take an infinite time span. In order to carry out the process in finite time, diffusion is enhanced by building up an enormous pressure difference between the two sides of the membrane, which requires an equally enormous amount of energy. Then, the process of diffusion is no longer an equilibrium process. Instead, it is irreversible and $S_{\text{gen}} > 0$. A comparison of the ideal separation process and the real process realisation shows that the huge irreversible loss of energy in the actual separation process is entirely due to the dissipation of energy in the many compressions and decompressions which are necessary to run the separation process under a pressure difference and, thus, in finite time. This dissipated energy leaves the process as waste heat.[13]

3.5   THERMODYNAMIC PROPERTIES OF JOINT OUTPUTS

In Section 3.3 we have seen that the occurrence of joint products is necessary and unavoidable in industrial production processes. Yet the quantitative amount in which they occur may vary according to the degree of thermodynamic (in)efficiency with which the process is carried out (Section 3.4). The explanation of the sheer amount of waste by-products (measured in mass terms) may be the most obvious result from a thermodynamic analysis of production. But beyond that, the thermodynamic view also allows one to make statements about the properties of this waste. From the simple reference model of industrial production analysed in Section 3.3 above it is obvious that, in some sense, high entropy may be seen as the fundamental characterisation of waste (Faber 1985). This idea has been operationalised by Kümmel (1989), who defines an aggregated measure for pollution as the rate of increase in entropy per unit volume of the biosphere where this increase occurs.

On the other hand, it is important to distinguish between high entropy waste in the form of heat and in the form of waste materials.[14] The former may be considered a minor problem since it can, in principle, be radiated into space.[15] It is only the latter which accumulates in the biosphere, thus causing major environmental problems. Waste materials, however, might cause environmental problems not because of their high entropy, but – just the opposite – because their entropy is not yet maximal. In other words, it is the exergy still contained in waste materials, that is the potential to initiate chemical reactions and perform work, which makes these wastes potentially harmful to the natural environment (Ayres and Martinás 1995, Ayres et al. 1998, Perrings 1987).[16]

3.6 CONCLUSION

Although the two examples studied in Section 3.4 (reducing iron oxide to iron and the enrichment of uranium) are rather specific, the insights from the analysis of these examples are fairly general and hold for industrial production processes at large. Our basic result is twofold:

1. First, based on a thermodynamic analysis we have shown that high entropy joint outputs are unavoidable and necessary in the industrial production of desired goods. This is the type of production technology that is currently in use and dominates production in industrial economies.

2. Second, thermodynamic analysis has also allowed us to quantify the amount of waste joint products which – beyond the thermodynamic minimum required – is due to inefficiencies.

We have identified three major reasons for the occurrence of large amounts of excessive material waste from industrial production:

1. The first reason is simply *conservation of mass*. Starting with a raw material, which is a mixture of different chemical elements, to produce a desired product, which is made up of only one particular chemical element, necessarily leaves a material waste.

2. The second reason is the use of a *material fuel*, which is a characteristic property of many industrial production technologies currently in use. The fuel – carbon in our example – only serves to provide

the exergy for the chemical reaction. The carbon material itself is actually neither wanted nor needed in the reaction. Because mass is conserved, the fuel material has to go somewhere after its exergy content has been stripped off. And that makes the waste. An alternative, immaterial way of providing exergy to production processes would be the use of renewable energy sources, such as solar, wind, tidal or hydro-energy.[17]

3. The third reason is the *thermodynamically inefficient performance* of current technologies when it comes to the conversion of exergy, which is a necessary factor of production in all production processes. In particular, this is due to the operation of production processes under *non-equilibrium conditions*, in order to have them completed in finite time. The shorter the time span within which one wants the process to be completed, the more energy will irreversibly be dissipated. This inefficiency not only considerably increases the need for fuel beyond the minimum exergy requirement; it also increases the amount of material waste generated far beyond the thermodynamic necessity. This holds, in particular, for carbon dioxide emissions when carbon (for example coal or coke) or hydrocarbons (for example oil or natural gas) are used as a fuel.

Hence, notwithstanding the fundamental insight that joint production is a necessary characteristic of industrial production technologies as they are currently in use, a large potential exists for the reduction of waste. Thermodynamics has proven to be a very useful analytical tool for studying and exploiting this potential.

On a conceptual level, the rooting of joint production in thermodynamics is important for ecological economics for the following reason. The thermodynamic concepts of matter, energy and entropy are the natural science basis for all processes in the economy, the environment, and the interactions between these two. The framework of thermodynamics thus creates a unifying perspective on the biogeophysical environment and the economy. This unifying framework, combined with economic analysis (cf. Part II of this book), enables the posing of questions that would not have been posed from the perspective of one scientific discipline alone. This is an important step in the interdisciplinary development of ecological economics.

However, thermodynamics is difficult. In particular, the notion of entropy is so difficult that even natural scientists have, more often than not, problems in applying it correctly. This holds, of course, even more for social scientists.[18] It is therefore expedient to supplement the notions and concepts of thermodynamics with a notion which is more concretely applicable, and easier for others to come to understand and use. We consider the notion of joint production to be a fundamental one for this purpose. The notion of joint production captures the essential insights from thermodynamics about production: (i) conservation of mass and (ii) irreversibility. In that sense, the concept of joint production appears to be a 'translation' of essential thermodynamic statements into the language of economics.

APPENDIX 3A PROOF OF PROPOSITION 3.1

In order to prove the proposition (see Baumgärtner 2000: 72–77), one should distinguish between different chemical elements, such as, for example, oxygen (O), carbon (C) or iron (Fe). Each input and each output of a production process may, in general, be composed of various such elements. For example, a raw material input into production may be iron oxide (Fe_2O_3), which consists of the two chemical elements of iron (Fe) and oxygen (O). In any chemical reaction, the mass of each element is conserved separately,[19] so that the thermodynamic Law of Mass Conservation (Equation 3.4) should be formulated more precisely as

$$\forall_e \quad m_{rm}(e) + m_f(e) \;=\; m_p(e) + m_{jp}(e) \tag{3.9}$$
$$\text{with } e = \ldots, O, \ldots, C, \ldots, Fe, \ldots \,,$$

where $m(e)$ denotes the mass of chemical element e. For instance, in the reduction of iron oxide (Fe_2O_3) into pure iron (Fe) by means of coke (C), the mass of all chemical elements – oxygen, carbon, iron and others – is conserved separately; that is, the mass of iron in the inputs must equal the mass of iron in the outputs, and similarly for the mass of oxygen, carbon, etc.

In the proof, a mass balance will explicitly be considered for only one chemical element, the so-called 'element under consideration'. Beyond that, it is only important that there exists more than one chemical element. But these other elements' mass balance is of no explicit interest. In order to simplify the presentation, we therefore omit the argument e where it is clear that we refer to the first element. The detailed mass balance (3.9) then reduces to Equation (3.4), but nevertheless is meant to refer to the first element.

In this interpretation, Properties (3.1) and (3.3) may be relaxed to

$$m_{rm}, m_p \;\geq\; 0, \tag{3.1'}$$
$$m_f \;\geq\; 0, \tag{3.3'}$$

with each of these quantities, m_{rm}, m_p and m_f, being strictly positive for at least one element. That is to say, the raw material input (as well as the fuel and the desired output) does not need to contain positive amounts of *all* elements; it is only assumed to contain *at least one* element. For instance, the raw material iron oxide (Fe_2O_3) contains iron and oxygen, but no carbon. If the element under consideration in the analysis should be, say, iron, then $m_{rm} > 0$; but if the element under consideration should be carbon, then $m_{rm} = 0$.

The proof is now carried out by showing that either the mass m_{jp} or the entropy S_{jp} (or both) of the second output is strictly positive. Note that not necessarily both the mass *and* the entropy have to be strictly positive for an output to exist, since the mass of an output – in our formalisation – will be zero if it does not contain the element under consideration. For carrying out the proof, we distinguish between the two cases that (i) the statement of Proposition 3.1 follows already from mass conservation alone and (ii) the Second Law is essential for the existence of a second output.

Joint production as a consequence of mass conservation

In many instances, the aspect of entropy is not necessary to understand why there exists a second output besides the main product. So, to start with, let us focus on the mass aspect of inputs and outputs and neglect their entropic character. Consider first the extreme case that $m_p = 0$; the complementary case of $m_p > 0$ will be dealt with later on. Most obviously, if $m_{rm}, m_f \geq 0$ with at least one, m_{rm} or m_f, strictly positive (according to Properties 3.1' and 3.3' and with a suitable choice of the element under consideration) and $m_p = 0$, it follows from the mass balance (Equation 3.4) that $m_{jp} = m_f + m_{rm} > 0$. This means, a joint product cogently exists.[20]

In general, mass balance considerations make the existence of at least one joint output necessary as soon as either the raw material or the fuel (or both) contain an element which is not contained in the desired product. Note that if such an argument holds for any one material of the, in general, many materials involved in a production process, then this already suffices to establish the result.

Joint production as a consequence of the Second Law

It remains to be shown that a second output necessarily exists if $m_p > 0$. In this case, the Law of Mass Conservation alone may not suffice to prove the existence of a joint output. For instance, for $m_p = m_f + m_{rm}$ and $m_{jp} = 0$ the mass balance is fulfilled and the existence of a joint output is not immediately obvious. In this case, however, the Second Law becomes crucial in establishing the result.

In order to build the argument in this case, let us come back to the entropic character of inputs and outputs in the reference model of industrial production. As far as the mass aspect is concerned, we make the assumption that $m_f = 0$.[21] The mass balance (Equation 3.4) then becomes

$$m_{rm} = m_p + m_{jp} ,$$

(3.10)

from which it follows that[22]

$$m_{rm} \geq m_p .$$

(3.11)

Consider now the entropy balance (Equation 3.5). It can be rearranged into

$$S_{jp} = S_f + \Delta S + (S_{rm} - S_p) .$$

(3.12)

The sign of the term $S_{rm} - S_p$ can be determined from considering the fraction S_{rm}/S_p which is, according to the definition of specific entropy as $\sigma = S/m$, given by:

$$\frac{S_{rm}}{S_p} = \underbrace{\frac{m_{rm}}{m_p}}_{\geq 1} \cdot \underbrace{\frac{\sigma_{rm}}{\sigma_p}}_{>1} > 1 ,$$

(3.13)

since $m_{rm} \geq m_p$ (Equation 3.11) and $\sigma_{rm} > \sigma_p$ (Property 3.2). Hence,

$$S_{rm} - S_p > 0 .$$

(3.14)

From this and Equation (3.12) it follows that

$$S_{jp} = \underbrace{S_f}_{\geq 0} + \underbrace{\Delta S}_{\geq 0} + \underbrace{(S_{rm} - S_p)}_{>0} > 0 .$$

This means that the existence of a joint product with entropy S_{jp} is cogently required in order to fulfil the entropy balance. It serves to take up the excess high entropy, which cannot be contained in the desired low specific entropy product.

NOTES

1. For example, in 1990 the amount of waste in West Germany (measured in physical units, such as tonnes) exceeded the amount of useful economic output (also measured in physical units) by more than a factor of four: out of a total material output of 59,474.6 million tonnes generated by all sectors of the economy, only 3,602.6 million tonnes (6.1 %) were contained in the different components of GDP, while 7,577.2 million tonnes (12.7 %) were intermediate outputs for reuse within the economy (including recovered and recycled materials) and 48,294.8 million tonnes (81.2 %) were

final wastes (Statistisches Bundesamt 1997). This huge dimension of material waste generation is also confirmed for other industrialised countries, for example Denmark, Italy and the USA (Acosta 2001).

2.   For those readers not familiar with classical thermodynamics, we recommend Callen (1985), Kondepudi and Prigogine (1998) or Zemansky and Dittman (1997) as comprehensive, yet accessible introductions. Baumgärtner (2004b: Section 6.4) provides a short and basic introduction to classical thermodynamics in non-technical terms. Bejan (1997) gives a good introduction to engineering thermodynamics.

3.   Later, this system was extended to include savings and investment, as well as imports and exports.

4.   For an overview see, for example, Freeman (2003) or Hanley and Spash (1993).

5.   Note that both labour and capital, when reduced to their material and energetic basis, appear as 'extremely heterogeneous aggregates [which] have all the scientific validity of the medieval elements of earth, air, fire, and water' (Boulding 1981: 28).

6.   Historically, the concept of a production function has been introduced by Wicksell (1893) and Wicksteed (1992[1894]) to analyse the *distribution* of income among the factor owners, and not its *physical production* (Schumpeter 1954: 1028, Sandelin 1976). But later on, the concept has come to dominate economists' thinking about the physically feasible production possibilities.

7.   It is typically argued that it is the engineers' responsibility to specify the detailed properties of the production functions. But

> there seems to have been a misunderstanding somewhere because the technologists do not take responsibility for production functions either. They regard the production function as an economist's concept, and, as a matter of history, nearly all the production functions that have actually been derived are the work of economists rather than of engineers. (Dorfman et al. 1957: 131)

8.   The production of services (for example hair-cutting or consulting) nevertheless falls into the scope of our analysis insofar as the production of services always requires a material basis and thus has to obey the laws of thermodynamics (see the discussion in Section 4.4.3).

9.   Thermodynamic variables, such as volume and particle number, which are proportional to the size of the system, are called *extensive* variables. Variables, such as temperature or pressure, that specify a local property and are independent of the size of the system, are called *intensive* variables. If one doubled a bulk of matter, then the two extensive quantities m and S would double as well, while the ratio of the two, $\sigma = S/m$, would remain constant. Specific entropy, thus, is an intensive variable.

10.   This assumption may be relaxed. It may be assumed that there are a number of additional inputs and outputs besides the ones mentioned in the text. The joint production result is not altered by the assumption of additional inputs or outputs.

11.   The notion of 'waste' is a difficult one, as a proper definition should build on a descriptive materials balance on the one hand, and normative human attitudes and valuation on the other hand (Bisson and Proops 2002). A single parameter, such as specific entropy, is therefore not sufficient to classify a substance as 'waste'. For a review of various attempts to construct a so-called 'entropy theory of value', and a refutation of these endeavours see Baumgärtner et al. (1996).

12.   Typical exergy conversion efficiencies in the process industry range from values as low as 4%, 6% and 9% in the production of nitric acid, oxygen and copper respectively up to values of 58% and 63% in the production of hydrogen and methanol (Hinderink et al. 1999: Table 1).

13.   Note that the efficiency of uranium enrichment in a centrifuge plant is about two orders of magnitude higher than in a membrane plant. Despite the tremendous exergetic inefficiency, enrichment of uranium makes sense, as the exergy loss in en-

richment is small with respect to the exergy content of enriched uranium as a fuel for nuclear fission.

14. Kümmel and Schüssler (1991) have suggested using heat equivalents for characterising different material pollutants. These heat equivalents are defined as the amount of heat that is inevitably produced when cleaning the environment from the respective pollutant or avoiding the occurrence of the pollutant altogether. Waste heat may thus be considered to be the ultimate form of waste.

15. Of course, waste heat that is directly released into ecosystems may cause harm to these systems, for example when heating up surface waters. Also, the ability to radiate heat into space may be impaired by the greenhouse effect that is caused by certain greenhouse gases in the Earth's atmosphere and further aggravated by anthropogenic emission of these gases.

16. The view that the 'waste exergy' of joint products can be seen as a measure for potential harm done to natural ecosystems, to be sure, is limited. It does not take into account the (eco-)toxicity of some inert materials, nor does it take into account purely physical effects of inert materials, for example global warming due to the carbon dioxide emitted into the atmosphere.

17. Note that, because the primary goal of carrying out the transformation studied using reaction equations (3.6)–(3.8) is to split Fe_2O_3 into Fe and O_2, the minimal way of doing that would be: $2\ Fe_2O_3 + \text{direct exergy} \rightarrow 4\ Fe + 3\ O_2$. The exergy necessary to achieve the splitting of Fe_2O_3 into Fe and O_2 could, for instance, be delivered by solar energy directly. Without any material fuel the amount of material waste would be considerably reduced. With four moles of Fe there would be three moles of O_2 jointly produced. That makes 0.75 moles of waste O_2 emissions per mole of Fe produced (corresponding to 0.43 kg O_2 per kg of Fe). However, running the chemical process in this direct way, that is, powered by solar energy instead of material fuel input, would require technologies very different from the ones we are currently using.

18. For an overview of 'entropy, information and confusion in the social sciences' see Proops (1987). An analysis of the often misleading 'use of the entropy concept in ecological economics' is given in Baumgärtner et al. (1996).

19. In principle, chemical elements may be transformed into each other by nuclear reactions. However, this possibility is neglected here.

20. Again, the assumption of $m_p = 0$ should *not* be interpreted as production resulting in no desired product at all, or only in an immaterial one. Nor should the assumption of $m_{rm} = 0$ or $m_f = 0$ be interpreted as saying that these inputs are absent from the production process. Recall that the mass balance (Equation 3.4) refers to one particular element, say carbon, but that there are other elements as well, say iron. Then, $m_p = 0$ only means that there is nothing of the element under consideration contained in the desired output. However, this output may well contain other elements, for example iron. In the example of iron production mentioned above, let carbon (C) be the element for which the mass balance is considered. Equation (3.4) can then be read as the mass balance of carbon, that is the mass of carbon in the inputs has to equal the mass of carbon in the outputs. Of course, there are also mass balances for the other elements, such as, for example, iron or oxygen, but they are of no interest for the argument. Then, $m_f = m_f(C) > 0$ (the fuel, coke plus oxygen, contains carbon), $m_{rm} = m_{rm}(C) = 0$ (there is no carbon in the raw material, iron ore), $m_p = m_p(C) = 0$ (the desired main product, pure iron, does not contain any carbon), and, hence, $m_{jp} = m_{jp}(C) > 0$. In sum, the existence of the joint output, carbon dioxide, is necessary because the carbon atoms which are originally contained in the fuel are not contained in the desired product and cannot disappear either.

21. Again, this should not be seen as restricting the generality of the treatment, since the mass balance (Equation 3.4) refers to one particular element. So, setting

$m_f = 0$ simply amounts to a suitable choice of the element under consideration. As an illustration, consider again the example of iron making and take iron (Fe) to be the element under consideration. Then $m_f = m_f(\text{Fe}) = 0$ only means that the fuel does not contain any iron.

22.   Note that if m_{rm} should be strictly larger than m_p, the existence of a second output with $m_{jp} > 0$ would follow immediately from mass balance considerations. Therefore, the interesting case which genuinely requires an entropy balance argument is actually $m_{rm} = m_p$.

4. Joint Production, Stocks, and Dynamics*

4.1 INTRODUCTION: SYSTEM DYNAMICS AS STOCK DYNAMICS

This book is about the phenomenon of joint production and its role in the interaction between the economy, society and the natural environment. Taking on the perspective of sustainability, it is necessary (i) to take the dynamics of these interactions into focus and (ii), in so doing, to adopt a long time horizon. When dealing with long-term behaviour of such coupled systems, many fundamental difficulties occur. For instance, system behaviour is likely to be very complex, and a lot of boundary and initial conditions are generally unknown. So, one has to deal extensively with uncertainty and ignorance. Also, interdisciplinary and transdisciplinary approaches are necessary because the systems under study generally transcend the scope of individual scientific disciplines.

A traditional way of approaching ecological-economic systems' long-term dynamics, which is in particular adopted in the natural sciences, is the use and coupling of process-based numeric models. The results are complex model systems which, on the one hand, display similar problems of hyper-complexity as real ecological-economic systems themselves but, on the other hand, still neglect many aspects which may be important for 'true' long-term prediction. While these approaches are important and valuable, we want to follow a different and, in our view, complementary path: In this chapter, we introduce the interdisciplinary concept of *stocks* for the investigation of long-term dynamics of ecological-economic systems. It is an important and rather simple concept which can be applied to a broad range of subjects. It allows one to capture the deterministic dynamics of systems.[1] The dynamics of a system representation (cf. Section 2.3.3) can be regarded as the dynamics of interacting stocks; the dynamics of an individual stock has to be underpinned by special exper-

---

*Parts of this chapter are based on Faber, Frank, Klauer, Manstetten, Schiller and Wissel (2005: Sections 2–3) and Schiller (2002: Sections 4.3, 7.3, 7.6–7.7).

tise, for example by a (disciplinary) process-model, in order to grasp the relevant dynamic features of the respective stock and its causes. After having introduced the concept of stocks (Section 4.2), in Section 4.3 we shall briefly sketch various ways of modelling stocks in different disciplinary contexts.

Using the concept of stocks, we then go on to investigate the general role of joint production in the dynamics of ecological-economic systems (Section 4.4). We shall see that there is an intimate relationship between the two concepts, joint production and stocks: Joint production leads to the modification of multiple stocks, and stocks are a source of joint production spread out in time. Thus, joint production is an important structural element governing the long-term behaviour of ecological-economic systems. In Section 4.4.3, we argue accordingly that joint production is a much more general phenomenon and not restricted to industrial production systems and energy/matter flows. Finally, in Section 4.5 we will draw general conclusions regarding the macro characteristics of ecological-economic systems. We discuss the role of joint production in aggravating complexity and irreversibility.

4.2   DETERMINISTIC CHANGE: THE CONCEPT OF STOCKS

4.2.1   The Basic Idea of Stocks

Dynamics as we observe them in the real world are often characterised by change. Typically, change is not instant, but the observed variables exhibit a certain *inertia*. Due to this inertia, the present state of a system can be regarded as being influenced by its past states – the inertia effectively functions as a system's 'memory'. In order to analytically grasp the inertial moment of permanency in an easy to use way, Faber et al. (2005) developed a notion of stocks which is introduced in this section.[2]

Stocks are entities which are characterised by a temporal durability relative to the time scale of observation, that is they exist over time. During the time span of their existence, they influence other interrelated elements. For example, economic activity at every point in time is contingent upon preconditions of all kinds, for example stocks of resources, raw materials, and capital goods necessary for production, but also upon restrictions such as stocks of hazardous substances released into the environment etc. So, future options of economic (and other human) activities depend on stocks existing at that time. The build-up or the degradation of a stock in the present has repercussions for future states of the system, for example the economy's productive potential and the availability of ecosystem functions. So, deterministic dynamics can, to a certain extent, be grasped as an interaction of stocks over time.

The attribute of permanency, which is the central characteristic of a stock, can generally refer to both quantifiable entities and entities which cannot be described quantitatively; the latter we shall call *non-quantifiable*. Both may possess the attribute of permanency. In the following section, we shall restrict ourselves to quantifiable stocks and give a formal definition. The definition is formulated in a general manner, based on set theory. The notion of non-quantifiable stocks will be further developed in Section 4.2.4.

4.2.2 Quantifiable Stocks: Formal Definitions

We now conceptually express the phenomenon of *permanency*, using a concept of *stocks*. It is based on set theory and, thereby, generally applicable. In so doing, we have to limit the formal notion of stocks to quantifiable entities. We further have to assume that the time horizon τ (see Section 2.3.4) and the time scale of observation T_{obs} (see Section 2.3.6) have been chosen according to the cognitive interest of the observer.

Before stocks can be formally defined, the terms *set* and *attribute of appertainment* need to be explained.

Definition 4.1. A *set* is a group of elements that possess a common attribute. This common attribute, which distinguishes the set, is called the *attribute of appertainment*.

The attribute of appertainment of a set must, by definition, be met by each element of the set. It is thus an attribute which characterises the individual elements of the observed set and therefore constitutes a microscopic perspective. In addition, the attribute of appertainment characterises the set as a whole. So it can also be seen as a macroscopic attribute. By delimiting the set from its environment by means of an attribute of the individual elements, our notion of stocks is stressing the homogeneity of the set.[3] The attribute of appertainment has to consist of one or several objectifiable attributes of the elements. They have to be suitably chosen depending on the context of the investigation carried out by the observer.[4] Consider, for example, a number of machines in a factory building. If we intend to investigate how much electricity is consumed by production activities in the factory building, a suitable attribute of appertainment of the set of machines would consist of the following elements: (i) the machines are located inside the building and (ii) they consume electrical energy when being operated.

As the central characteristic of a stock is its permanency, a set can only be referred to as a stock if it exists for a certain time. This basic idea brings us to the following definition of permanency and of a stock:

Definition 4.2.   In the context of an investigation, a set is *permanent* at time t_0 if it is non-empty for a period of time beginning at t_0 which is much greater than the time scale of observation T_{obs}. A permanent set is called a *stock*.

The permanency of a stock can only be defined relative to the time scale of observation T_{obs}. That time scale represents a yardstick against which permanency is measured, and is chosen by the observer according to his cognitive interest. Hence, T_{obs} is not an objective characteristic of the stock observed but a subjective element as discussed in Section 2.3.6. When describing stocks, however, it is useful to establish a measure of how long this stock will exist in absolute terms:

Definition 4.3.   The *duration* of a stock denotes its entire period of existence. The *remaining duration* of a stock T at the time of observation t_0 is the duration of its existence remaining at time t_0.

In contrast to the time scale of observation, the duration of a stock is an objective characteristic of the stock. With the notion of the (remaining) duration of the stock it is possible to re-phrase Definition 4.2 as a comparison of different time intervals. Three expressions of time are important for our notion of stocks: (i) the time of observation t_0 for which it is stated whether a set is permanent or not, (ii) the time scale of observation T_{obs} on which permanency in the sense of continuity is defined, and (iii) the remaining duration of a stock T at the time of observation t_0. By comparing these three expressions of time, a stock can now be alternatively formulated and more precisely defined.

Definition 4.4.   (*Equivalent definition of a stock.*) At time t_0 a set is called a *stock* if the remaining duration of the set at time t_0, T, is much larger than the time scale of observation T_{obs}, that is

$$T \geq AT_{obs}, \text{ with } A \gg 1. \tag{4.1}$$

Since the time scale of observation T_{obs} forms the temporal 'resolution' with which the stock dynamics are gauged by the observer, the condition in Definition 4.4 means that the remaining duration of the stock T extends over a large number of unit lengths (see Figure 4.1).[5] This is a reflection of the permanency which is at the core of the definition of a

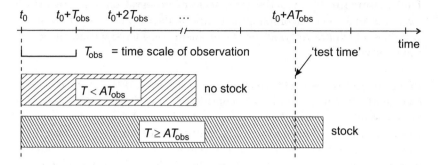

Figure 4.1 Illustration of Definition 4.4. The time scale of observation T_{obs} forms the temporal 'resolution' with which the system under investigation is gauged by the observer. If the remaining duration of the observed set T at time t_0 is much larger than the time scale of observation T_{obs}, that is $T \geq AT_{obs}$ with $A \gg 1$, the observed set is a stock.

stock. Hence, such a comparison of the periods can serve as a 'test' of whether or not a set represents a stock. Definition 4.4 can thus assist the empirical determination of permanency of a set.

Thus far, we have characterised stocks in two dimensions: (i) The attribute of appertainment characterises the stock and distinguishes it at the macroscopic level. (ii) The remaining duration of the stock T at every point in time characterises it in its temporal dimension. When investigating concrete problems using the notion of stocks, we are also interested (iii) in other attributes of the stock from a macroscopic perspective. If these attributes can be measured in a quantitative way,[6] we express them by stock variables:

Definition 4.5. A *stock variable* expresses a quantitative attribute of a stock, that is, an attribute of the stock which can be expressed on a cardinal scale at any time within time horizon τ.

Generally, it will be possible to view a variety of stock variables for any given stock. If, for example, a sand-heap is regarded as a stock, its temperature, mass, and weight on the earth's surface represent different stock variables. In a population of fish, the number of individuals and their entire biomass are different stock variables. When investigating a specific problem, it is therefore necessary to whittle down a large number of possible stock variables to those which are relevant for the problem at hand. Having defined a stock variable, we can finally get down to introducing the formal notion of stock dynamics.

Definition 4.6.   On the time scale of observation T_{obs}, the *stock dynamics* of a stock encompass the temporal developments of those stock variables which are relevant for the problem considered within the given time horizon τ.[7]

In this definition, we refer to stock dynamics even if the stock does not change at all during the period considered, that is the stock variables are constant over time. Furthermore, our notion of dynamics is relative to the time scale of observation T_{obs} and the time horizon τ. Both limit the investigation of the temporal development in the stock variables, which in general occurs on various time scales, to a certain 'window of analysis'. Temporal development which is more rapid than the time scale of observation is neglected because it cannot be tracked by the (slower) time resolution of the investigation (see Section 2.3.6). Similarly, temporal development which is so slow that it is not gauged within the time horizon will be neglected.

4.2.3   The Empirics of Stocks

Up to now we have introduced the notion of stocks as a purely theoretical concept. In this section, we shall briefly discuss different approaches to gaining factual information about stock dynamics.

Reasons for permanency: durability and reproduction

We defined a stock by its permanency, which is a macroscopic characteristic of the observable dynamics of a stock. But the observation of permanency does not say anything about how this permanency comes into being. In particular, merely identifying a set's character of being permanent is by no means enough to identify the determinants of its dynamics, and hence, the reasons for its permanency. In order to identify these causes, it is generally necessary to undertake an analysis at the level of the component elements of the corresponding stock. This may, for instance, include interactions with other endogenous and exogenous elements or internal dynamic processes within the elements, such as the radioactive decay of uranium and other substances.

Although the precise dynamics of every particular stock depends on its specific properties and its environment, two general processes can be identified at the microscopic level – that is at the level of individual elements – which underlie permanency at the macro-level. These are processes which characterise the internal dynamics of the stock: (i) the *durability* of individual elements of the corresponding set and (ii) the *reproduction* of elements of the set. Both processes reflect two fundamental mechanisms – permanency through survival and permanency through reproduction, that is through the generation of new elements with the same attributes.

Durability means that the individual elements exist, without interruption, on the time scale of observation and do not change with respect to the attribute of appertainment. The second process which may lead to permanency, and is essential particularly in stocks featuring living elements, is the reproduction of elements of a set. We talk of reproduction when one or more elements produce a new element of the same type. The reproduction of elements may result in the permanency of a stock without individual elements being durable on the time scale of observation.[8]

Stocks have a history

For empirically determining whether or not a concrete object of investigation is a stock, we are facing the following problem: According to Definition 4.2 and Definition 4.4, if the time of observation t_0 is interpreted as the present, the assessment of permanency of an observed set requires information about its future temporal development. Such information is, of course, always beset by a degree of uncertainty or even ignorance. In order to be able to provide meaningful information ex ante about the permanency of concrete objects of investigation, we need additional information about the stock dynamics.

In many concrete problems, one possible source of this additional information is past experience. Although knowledge of the history of a stock is not by itself enough to answer the question of current permanency, indications are normally provided by a stock's history.

When something is referred to today as a stock, this implies that, as a currently existing stock, it should necessarily continue to survive in the future and hence, exert influence on it. If the time of observation t_0 is shifted into the past, it follows that we will encounter stocks nowadays which originated in the past and which influence the present. By virtue of its permanency, a stock connects the past via the present to the future on the time scale of observation T_{obs}. Hence stocks act as bearers of influence from the past into the present – and thus as factors of history.

Further information about stocks' dynamics

The empirical permanency of a set in the past cannot by itself always provide information about a stock's continued survival in the future, that is about the current or future character of being permanent. As a rule, the dynamics of the set observed and its underlying mechanisms need to be analysed in order to obtain such information. Basically, this can take place at both a causal and a phenomenological level.

Consider for example a population of living organisms. The number of individuals in an ecosystem must not drop below a certain threshold if the constant reproducibility, and hence, the durable continuation of the population is to be secured. As a result, the mere knowledge of the existence of the population over a certain period in the past is not sufficient for statements about its current and future permanency. Other complementary information is needed to provide indications about future population dynamics – and hence indications concerning current and future permanency. Such information often has to be derived from specific theories regarding the dynamics of that particular stock.[9]

4.2.4   Non-quantifiable Stocks

The core of our concept of stocks is the temporal aspect of permanency. Given an attribute of appertainment, a stock's permanency does not depend on the character of its other attributes. In particular, for its permanency it does not matter which other attributes of the stock are quantifiable and can be described by stock variables, and which attributes are not quantifiable and are not amenable to a description by suitable quantitative measures. Indeed, stocks frequently do have attributes which cannot be adequately expressed using stock variables. This kind of attribute shall be called a *non-quantifiable attribute*.

For example, if the legal system of a country is regarded as a stock of laws, possible stock variables include the number of laws, the number of paragraphs, the number of printed pages, etc. However, even though the legal system's fairness is not a stock variable according to Definition 4.5, (i) it plays a crucial role with regard to the social structure and the stability of society, and (ii) the attribute 'fairness of the legal system' may persist over the lifetime of the stock itself. Hence, the existence of the fairness-attribute is connected to the temporal character of the stock 'legal system of the country'. Such non-quantifiable attributes may actually play an important or even dominant role in characterising a specific stock: The legal system's fairness, and the question of how long this fairness is persistent, may for certain problems be much more important than some stock variable like 'number of laws'.

Taking this argument further, many entities exist, in particular in socio-economic systems, which feature the attribute of permanency and are therefore important for dynamic investigations of such systems, but which can only be described very incompletely using quantitative measures such as stock variables. Their character is dominated by non-quantifiable attributes. We call such entities *non-quantifiable stocks*. Examples of non-quantifiable stocks include a society's rules, traditions, institutions in a broad sense, the agents' preferences, social identities, knowledge, know-how etc. Similar to quantifiable stocks, such entities may be permanent and, hence, bear influences from the present to future states of ecological-economic systems. The formal definitions of Section 4.2.2, however, are not applicable to them.

In many cases, it is the choice of the observer, however, to regard a specific object under investigation as a quantifiable or a non-quantifiable stock. The society's legal system is an example of an entity which can be framed in both ways. Depending on this choice, completely different aspects and characteristics of the entity are taken into focus in the investigation. Hence, this choice bears far-reaching repercussions for the investigation and has to be made carefully according to the observer's cognitive interest.

Investigating non-quantifiable stocks is a complex task which belongs to the genuine scope of social sciences like psychology, sociology, and politics. But there exist some fundamental difficulties:

- The delimitation of quantifiable stocks is based on distinguishable elements and a certain homogeneity of these elements (cf. Definitions 4.1 and 4.2). Neither feature can be used in a sensible way with regard to (purely) non-quantifiable objects. Let us, for example, consider stocks of knowledge. An existing stock of knowledge is never composed of *individual* elements sharing a certain common property. Gaining new knowledge, for example by carrying out research, can either be regarded as enlargement of an already existing stock of knowledge or as creation of an entirely new stock.[10]

- The notion of dynamics of non-quantifiable stocks has to be different from the notion of dynamics of quantifiable stocks. In particular, it cannot be described in a formal manner, since there are, for instance, no stock variables. As a consequence, theories of the formation, the modification, and also the durability of non-quantifiable stocks are likely to be non-mathematical theories. Therefore, empirical tests and ex ante predictions about non-quantifiable entities will also require a different basis.

One might therefore ask, what is the use of a characterisation of non-quantifiable entities using the concept of stocks? Even though the notion of non-quantifiable stocks is not yet fully developed with respect to an 'arithmetic' to capture their dynamics, they form important inertial elements in socio-economic systems. Hence, one has to include them when investigating the dynamic behaviour of ecological-economic systems. As will be discussed in the subsequent sections, like their quantifiable counterparts they are formed and modified by economic activity, in particular by joint production. Vice versa, they themselves exert significant influence on the system's temporal development.

4.3 MODELLING STOCKS

Before investigating the relationship between stocks and joint production in the following Section 4.4, we relate our general concept of stocks to well-established but more constricted concepts employed in various disciplines. We briefly sketch how permanent entities can be modelled in the physical environmental sciences (Section 4.3.1), in population ecology (Section 4.3.2) and in economics (Section 4.3.3).

4.3.1 Environmental Sciences: Pollutant Stocks

The dynamics of a pollutant stock can be modelled by specifying the material balance of the stock, and its inflows and outflows, over a time interval Δt. This reflects the thermodynamic Law of Mass Conservation (cf. Chapter 3):

$$S(t + \Delta t) = S(t) + f_{in}(t) \cdot \Delta t - f_{out}(t) \cdot \Delta t. \qquad (4.2)$$

In this equation, $S(t)$ denotes the stock at time t in mass units, for example tonnes; $f_{in}(t)$ and $f_{out}(t)$ denote the inflow and outflow, respectively, of matter at time t and are measured in units of mass per time, for example tonnes per day. The inflow and outflow describe elements that gain or lose, respectively, the attribute of appertainment of the stock. This may be due to, for example, matter flows across the spatial border of the stock, from the inside to the outside or vice versa. It may also be due to the transformation of elements, for example by radioactive decay.

The time interval Δt may be finite;[11] or it may be infinitesimally small. In the latter case, it follows from Equation (4.2) that

$$\lim_{\Delta t \to 0} \frac{S(t + \Delta t) - S(t)}{\Delta t} \equiv \frac{dS(t)}{dt} = f_{in}(t) - f_{out}(t). \qquad (4.3)$$

While Equation (4.2) is a difference equation that holds for discrete time models, Equation (4.3) is a differential equation that applies to models in continuous time.

When investigating the natural dynamics of environmental pollutants, we are particularly interested in the *lifetime* of the pollutant in the receiving natural compartment, that is, in the magnitude of its natural degradation rate. Generally, there is an inverse relationship between a pollutant's natural degradation rate, δ, and its lifetime. Formally, if a constant fraction δ (with $0 \leq \delta < 1$) of a stock S of pollution naturally degrades per time period, $dS/dt = -\delta S$,[12] then the stock will naturally degrade according to an exponential decay relationship: $S(t) = S_0 \exp(-\delta t)$.

As these pollutants are assumed to exhibit exponential decay, in one sense they last 'for ever'. However, the notion of a pollutant's 'lifetime' is often a useful descriptive device, and two obvious approaches can be established.

- First, the lifetime of a pollutant can be defined to be the time it takes for the amount of that pollutant to decay below the threshold of notice or damage. However, as such a threshold is contingent upon the state of detection technology as well as risk perception and valuing of society, this would give incommensurable lifetimes for different polluting materials and for different contexts.

- Therefore, another definition, which we shall adopt in the following, simply refers to the time the pollutant takes to decay to an arbitrary level.

Formally, we define the *lifetime* T of the stock pollutant to be the time span which it takes the original stock S_0 to decay to a fraction $1/e$ (Kuchling 1988: 544). Obviously then, $T = 1/\delta$ for pollutants decaying exponentially.[13] This means, the inverse of a pollutant's yearly degradation rate is just the lifetime of the pollutant in the environment, measured in years, and vice versa. If, for example, one tenth of the actual stock of some pollutant will be naturally degraded per year by biological, chemical or physical transformations, then this pollutant can be said to have a 'lifetime' in the natural environment of ten years.

There are some pollutants which are rather short-lived. For instance, sulphur dioxide (SO_2) and nitrogen oxides (NO_x), which are the main constituents of 'acid rain', stay in the atmosphere after emission for a few days up to several weeks, depending on current weather, until they are either deposited directly on the Earth's surface or washed out by rain (Klaassen 1996; cf. the detailed case study in Chapter 18). Over such short time spans no large stocks of these pollutants can accumulate in the atmosphere.

In contrast, most anthropogenic greenhouse gases have a much longer atmospheric lifetime, which is determined by complicated chemical and physical reactions in different layers of the atmosphere. For instance, carbon dioxide (CO_2) has an atmospheric lifetime of 50 to 200 years, methane (CH_4) of 12 years, nitrous oxide (N_2O) of 120 years (IPCC 1996: 15). These lifetimes correspond to natural degradation rates of 0.02 to 0.005 per year for CO_2, 0.083 per year for CH_4 and 0.0083 per year for N_2O. With such long lifetimes (that is, low degradation rates) the yearly emissions of these greenhouse gases contribute to an increase in the stock of the respective gases in the atmosphere. There are wastes with even smaller natural degradation rates than the greenhouse gases mentioned. For instance, plutonium (^{239}Pu), which is one particular constituent of nuclear waste, has a natural degradation rate of 0.000028 per year. This means plutonium has a lifetime of some 35,000 years, which, on typical human time scales, can be considered as infinite and, thus, causes severe problems for issues of nuclear waste disposal (Proops 2001).

Depending on the pollutant's lifetime and the time scale of observation, one can distinguish between flow pollution and stock pollution: Pollution due to pollutants that do not live longer than one time period is called *flow pollution*, since it is the flow of emissions that determines the extent of pollution. An example is noise pollution. In contrast, pollution by a long-lived pollutant is called *stock pollution*, since it is the accumulated stock of the pollutant that determines the extent of pollution. An example is the stock of anthropogenic greenhouse gases in the atmosphere, which causes global climate change.

4.3.2   Ecological Modelling: Populations

Main objects of interest in ecological modelling are populations of species and their dynamics. Just like the stocks of matter, we have dealt with in the last section, populations exhibit the characteristic of permanency and, hence, can be regarded as stocks under certain conditions (Faber et al. 2005).

Assuming that all attributes of individual members of a population can be depicted as effective attributes of a 'mean' individual – that is, assuming a certain homogeneity – the population can be described by the stock variable 'population size', $N(t)$. The dynamics of a closed population[14] can then be described by a growth equation of the form

$$\frac{dN(t)}{dt} = f(t, N(t)), \tag{4.4}$$

where the function $f(t, N(t))$ denotes the populations's total growth rate. Population dynamics depend, according to Equation (4.4), on the population's current size, and external factors like habitat, food supply etc., which might change over time – here represented by the explicit time dependence of f.

When investigating long-term dynamics of populations, the influence of such external factors can be neither neglected nor predicted in a deterministic way. Hence, stochastic concepts have to be used to describe population dynamics and, thus, stocks of populations. In ecological modelling, the concept of *persistence* (Grimm and Wissel 1997 and Frank 2005) can be used for that purpose. A population is persistent if its probability of survival $P_{surv}(t')$ at the point in time, t', until which the population's survival chance is to be assessed, is greater than or equal to 1 minus some residual risk of extinction, ε, which is considered by the observer. Thus a population is persistent if

$$P_{surv}(t') \geq 1 - \varepsilon. \tag{4.5}$$

If persistent stochastic populations are also regarded as permanent in the sense of Definition 4.4 (Equation 4.1), the formal condition for the persistence of a stochastic population from Equation 4.5 is to be rewritten as

$$P_{surv}(AT_{\text{obs}}) \geq 1 - \varepsilon, \tag{4.6}$$

where the time of observation has been set at $t_0 = 0$ for notational simplicity. Using a functional relationship from theoretical ecology between the population's probability of survival P_{surv} and its mean lifetime, T_{pop} (Grimm and Wissel 2004), it is possible to show that a stochastic population is a stock in the sense of Section 4.2 if the following necessary condition is fulfilled (Faber et al. 2005: 167–168):

$$T_{\text{pop}} \geq \left\{ -\frac{1}{\ln(1 - \varepsilon)} \right\} AT_{\text{obs}}, \text{ with } A \gg 1. \tag{4.7}$$

Comparing this expression to our alternative definition of a stock in Definition 4.4, it becomes obvious that both notions are consistent with each other, and identical in the case where the expression in brackets is equal to 1, that is $\varepsilon = 1 - e^{-1}$. Hence, for a given residual risk of $\varepsilon \approx 0.63$, persistence of a stochastic population is equivalent to this population being a stock in the sense of Definition 4.4.[15]

4.3.3 Economics: Stocks of Capital

Typical stocks in economics are stocks of capital goods or stocks of monetary capital (cf. Chapter 9). There exists a huge body of economic literature concerning the theory of capital stocks – *capital theory* (Barro and Sala-i-Martin 1995, Bliss 1975, Bliss et al. 2005, Burmeister 1980, Faber 1979, 1986b, Faber et al. 1999, Hicks 1946[1939], 1973, Malinvaud 1953, Solow 1963, Sraffa 1960, Stephan 1995, von Hayek 1941, von Weizsäcker 1971). While these treatments of capital employ different perspectives on the issue, the decisive characteristic of a capital good which is common to all these contributions is its temporal durability.

There has been a long controversy about the assumption of homogeneity of capital stocks. In one strand of the literature on capital theory, capital is modelled as a largely homogeneous stock (for an overview, see Barro and Sala-i-Marin 1995). Other strands of the literature explicitly take into account heterogeneous capital goods, for instance neo-Austrian capital theory (see Stephan 1995). However, in both schools capital is modelled by means of stock variables exhibiting certain dynamics.

Assuming discrete time periods, capital dynamics is typically modelled in the following form:

$$K_i(t+1) = K_i(t) + I_i(t) - \delta_i K_i(t),$$

$$\text{with } 0 \leq \delta_i \leq 1 \text{ and } i = 1, ..., k. \quad (4.8)$$

In Equation (4.8), $K_i(t)$ denotes the stock of (specific) capital of type i in period t, $I_i(t)$ denotes the (specific) investment into this stock, that is the amount of newly acquired capital goods of type i, and $\delta_i K_i(t)$ denotes capital depreciation, which is often assumed to be proportional to the respective capital stock. Depending on the size of δ_i, the capital stock denoted by K_i is long or short-lived. As a general rule, stocks of capital are assumed to be effective in production processes in each period t according to their current size in that period, $K_i(t)$.

4.4 STOCKS AND JOINT PRODUCTION

In the previous sections, we introduced the concept of stocks for analytically grasping the influence that a system's past exerts on its present, and we sketched the relationships of the concept to similar concepts which are well-established in various disciplines. In this section, we turn to the relationship between stocks and joint production. This relationship is twofold: (i) Joint production can be regarded as a source of change of a multiplicity of stocks, as will be argued in the following Section 4.4.1. (ii) On the other hand, stocks can be viewed as a source of the joint emergence of effects over time, which we shall discuss in Section 4.4.2. Putting both arguments together, in Section 4.4.3 we will argue that joint production is a more general phenomenon and not restricted to material production.

4.4.1 Joint Production as a Cause of the Change of Stocks

Let us, for a start, focus on production activity and its impact on *quantifiable* stocks of matter. Producing a material output necessarily involves the transformation of matter and energy – transformed material outputs emerge as the intended product or as unintended joint outputs from the production activity. The physical laws of the conservation of energy and matter (cf. Chapter 3) tell us that besides material or energetic outputs there must also be material or energetic inputs involved in such a transformation process. As a consequence, economic systems are characterised by production 'chains' of economic activities, linked by physical input-output relationships.

Such production chains occur in natural, in industrial economic, and in ecological-economic systems. In natural systems, many material input-output relationships have been established in a cyclical form during the long-term evolution of such systems, that is metabolic outputs of organisms are often re-used as inputs in matter/energy transformation by other organisms, and so on. Important examples for such cyclical structures are the natural carbon and water cycles.[16]

In modern economic and ecological-economic systems, however, production chains are non-circular. Hence, production activities necessarily entail the modification of some material or energetic stocks. These are either stocks from which production inputs are drawn, such as natural resources, or stocks in which production outputs are accumulated. This argument is even more relevant in a world of ubiquitous joint production. For, joint production (i) entails 'more' material outputs without direct economic use – leading to the accumulation of additional material stocks – and joint production (ii) entails material or energetic outputs also from those systems which are set up for producing services (see Section 4.4.3).

Consider now the effects of joint production on *non-quantifiable* stocks. Economic activity generally takes place within a social environment which implies that it is part of the agents' *lebenswelt*, that is it shapes their social environment and status, their habits, their preferences etc. The operation of a technology also forms the agents's and society's knowledge and know-how. In Section 4.2.4, we have conceptualised this as the modification of non-quantifiable stocks, which can be regarded as joint effects of economic activity. Hence, we can state that economic activity under joint production leads to the modification of a *multiplicity* of quantifiable and non-quantifiable stocks.

4.4.2   Stocks as a Source of Joint Production over Time

Having discussed the modification of stocks due to economic activity, we now want to turn to the *effects* of presently existing stocks in the future. Due to their permanency, current stocks will also be part of the system in the future. From a physical point of view, quantifiable stocks – being composed of matter or energy – take part in interactions with their environment. Given the multiplicity of their existence, this leads to complex interactions over (future) time.

From an economic perspective, human activity and economic choice at every point in time t_0 is contingent upon many prerequisites. Capital goods, infrastructure, resources, knowledge, know-how, institutions, preferences and many other (quantifiable and non-quantifiable) stocks which have been formed prior to t_0 determine, for example, production and consumption possibilities, income, economic wealth, and economic choice itself. Thus, currently existing stocks act as contingencies for future economic activity – they are at the origin of *future effects*.

If, however, (i) some effects of stocks are due to their mere existence, and if (ii) it is the nature of stocks to be permanent, then stocks can be regarded as a source of future effects over their lifetime. Hence, and according to the temporal aspect of Definition 2.7 (see also Figure 2.4 on page 42), stocks themselves can be identified as a source of *joint effects* which are spread out over time. In the following section, we shall further develop this argument and generalise our notion of joint production.

4.4.3   The 'General Principle' of Joint Production

Joint production is a ubiquitous characteristic of economic activity. In Chapter 3, we provided one explanation for this observation: given that most, if not all, economic activity involves the transformation of energy and matter, the laws of thermodynamics imply that joint production occurs in all these cases. The statement that 'all industrial production is joint production' may be referred to as the *principle of joint production*. While this principle, strictly speaking, only holds for thermodynamic system representations with respect to flows of energy and matter, we conjecture that this principle can be generalised to a *general principle of joint production*, which goes beyond considering energy/matter flows only. In this section, we briefly sketch four possible extensions: (i) joint production of private and public goods, (ii) joint production of services and material outputs, (iii) joint production of consumption and material outputs, and (iv) joint production of different effects of economic activity.

Private and public goods

Outputs from economic activity inherently possess a multitude of characteristics, some of which may be the reason for their production – these characteristics are valued positively by some economic agents. But once the outputs have come into existence, all of their other characteristics are potentially relevant for the same or other agents. For example, one branch of the economic literature going back to Olson (1965) and Cornes and Sandler (1984) investigates so-called impure public goods, that is economic goods which at the same time display the characteristics of a private and a public good. Producing such a good, hence, can be interpreted as joint production of private and public *characteristics*. For instance, commercially operating a truck at the same time provides transport service (characteristic of a private good) but also brings forward noise and pollution (characteristic of public goods – or, rather, bads).

Services and material joint outputs

The principle of joint production, which states that several outputs necessarily emerge together, is not restricted to purely material and energetic outputs. As discussed above, different characteristics of a material good may themselves be interpreted as different 'outputs' which – inevitably – emerge jointly. Developing this argument further, we can state that every service provided in an economy entails material joint products. For every service needs a material or energetic carrier. Performing a service means transforming the carrier medium which, in view of the thermodynamic argument developed in Chapter 3, entails joint products. As a prominent example, consider the transport of information via the Internet. The operation of 'the Internet' inevitably entails the use – that is the transformation – of significant amounts of electrical energy but also material products such as electronic equipment, cables, paper, ink cartridges etc.

Consumption and material joint outputs

The intimate connection between services and material or energetic joint products is not restricted to the production side of an economy but also includes the consumption side. Interpreting 'consumption' as the use of material goods, we find joint production of the consumption service – which is the reason for the consumption activity – and the material or energetic carrier emerging as a waste output from the consumption activity. The analogy to the sphere of production inspired Becker and Michael (1973) to draw a more sophisticated picture of consumption by developing the concept of 'household production'.

Joint production of different effects of economic activity

We have already seen that the principle of joint production is not restricted to material and energetic outputs but also holds for services or consumption. Generalising this observation one may argue that the principle of joint production holds for economic activity in general.

Economic activity changes the state of the world in a multifarious way (see Section 4.4.1): The use of material inputs, and the emergence of outputs, change the respective inventories in the ecological-economic systems, and performing the activity modifies the state of mind of the economic agents involved – that is, their knowledge, know-how, preferences, habits of consumption etc. Vice versa, these modified stocks themselves influence economic activity throughout their lifetime (see Section 4.4.2) – for example by determining individual and collective production and consumption possibilities, or by determining choice itself through modified preferences.

Extending the principle of joint production, we thus suggest a *general principle of joint production* which states that economic activity, in general, necessarily entails the joint emergence of different effects.[17] In addition to material outputs, this includes modifications of non-quantifiable stocks, such as the creation of knowledge, the formation of preferences of economic agents, the modification of institutions etc. In particular, the general principle of joint production implies that besides the intended effects of an economic activity, unintended effects jointly emerge, which can a priori be desired or undesired.

Taking the general principle of joint production seriously poses a challenge for the typical procedure of economics, which often limits its analysis to the *intended* result of economic activity. The general principle of joint production states that in addition to the intended outcome of one's action, a multitude of other effects will occur. In Part III of this book, we shall see that this has serious consequences for the possibility of economic and political agents to assume responsibility for their action.

4.5   CONCLUSION: JOINT PRODUCTION, COMPLEXITY, AND IRREVERSIBILITY

Joint production has been conceptualised in Chapter 2 as a characteristic of a system representation. It has been shown in a thermodynamic analysis (cf. Chapter 3) that joint production necessarily takes place on the level of an individual production process, that is on the micro-level. In the previous sections of this chapter, we have generalised this insight to a general principle of joint production, stating that economic activity entails effects in addition to those intended by the economic actor. From this general insight, we can draw some conclusions for the development of ecological-economic systems at the macro-level.

Complexity. The general principle of joint production implies that the results of any economic action are multi-dimensional. In particular, any action modifies various quantifiable and non-quantifiable stocks. Being permanent, these stocks interact and influence future states of the ecological-economic system. Hence, the multifarious effects of any economic action extend into the future. Also, ecological-economic systems, when regarded at a macro-level of observation, comprise many individual human actors and are, accordingly, influenced by a multitude of actions. As a result, joint production together with stock dynamics leads to a high complexity of ecological-economic systems and their dynamics, especially when analysed over the long run. Due to this complexity, it is impossible to foresee the development of such ecological-economic systems in detail. Joint production together with stock dynamics significantly aggravates our ignorance about the future development of ecological-economic systems.

Irreversibility. The ubiquity of joint production entails a high degree of interconnectedness between different economic, social, and natural processes. In addition to repercussions of this phenomenon upon the complexity of ecological-economic systems, the interconnectedness also entails consequences for the irreversibility of the temporal development of ecological-economic systems. If all individual processes were interrelated, irreversibility of just one process would lead to irreversibility of the aggregate development at the macro-scale. In the real world, many individual processes are irreversible at the temporal scale of human existence, for instance, loss of species, use of non-renewable resources, production of nuclear waste materials, spreading of artificial substances over natural compartments, desertification etc. If just one of the joint effects of a human action influences such an irreversible process, this action itself has to be considered as being irreversible with respect to its effects. The reason is that it is impossible to re-establish the state of the system prior to the action. Hence, joint production, in particular in its general principle, aggravates the irreversibility of human action.

NOTES

1. The dynamics of the real world can, idealistically, be dichotomised (Faber and Proops 1998: Section 1.3): The first category, deterministic dynamics, includes processes which are, *in principle*, predictable, that is they do not involve the emergence of novelty. Within the realm of this category, observed variables behave according to some 'laws of motion' which can be known in principle. However, complex interaction of different factors is possible, which *practically* limits the possibilities of prediction. The second category includes processes which do involve the emergence of novelty and are therefore, in principle, unpredictable.
2. The notion of stock dynamics developed here is phenomenological in that it refers to the observable change of variables in the first place. By itself it does not cover its causes.

3.   Regarding other attributes, the elements may be different. Hence, in this regard the set may be heterogeneous. Hence, the same set of elements could be regarded from a totally different perspective focussing on this heterogeneity.

4.   Our notion of stocks is essentially based on the time dimension. Very often, a stock also has a spatial dimension, which is self-evident for material, ecological, and most economic stocks. Formally speaking, any spatial dimension of stocks can be regarded as part of the attribute of appertainment and is a priori not distinguished from other attributes.

5.   The exact size of the constant A cannot be determined in general; it will usually depend on the problem observed.

6.   There are, in general, also attributes for which no suitable quantitative measure exists, for example, the 'beauty' of a landscape. We will discuss such 'non-quantifiable attributes' in Section 4.2.4.

7.   Similar to the abstraction from the internal structure of a stock by defining it by means of an attribute of appertainment, our notion of stock dynamics does not include the actual *causes* of the stock variables' temporal development at the micro-level. The notion is thus phenomenologically orientated and includes for example phenomenological regularities. The causes of such regularities can be observed (assuming corresponding cognitive interest and abilities) at a more detailed level of analysis in a complementary investigation.

8.   Examples of stocks in the context of typical economic questions are capital goods and reserves such as sets of buildings, machines, coffee, diamonds, ore, and oil etc., but also waste materials, CO_2 in the atmosphere, heavy metals in rivers etc. The attribute of permanency of most of these stocks is based on the durability of the individual elements. Examples of stocks in the ecological scope include lakes, rivers, forests, deserts, habitats and biotopes, and animal and plant populations. Concerning many of those kinds of stocks, permanency can be traced back to the processes of reproduction of individual elements, as is extensively discussed by Faber et al. (2005: Sections 4–5).

9.   Owing to the uncertainties existing ex ante, stochastic concepts are often helpful. The concept of stocks is extended also to encompass stochastic sets in Faber et al. (2005: Section 5); see also Section 4.3.2.

10.   For an extensive discussion on processes of gaining new knowledge see, for example, Schiller (2002: Chapter 6).

11.   In this case, Equation (4.2) is a linear approximation which is valid for small Δt.

12.   In general, the decay rate δ does not need to be a constant but can itself be a function of the stock S.

13.   By definition of the lifetime T, we have $S_0/e = S_0 \exp\{-\delta T\}$, which can be solved for $T = 1/\delta$.

14.   In a closed population, there is no exchange of individuals with other populations.

15.   For a more elaborate investigation of the relationship between persistence of stochastic populations and our notion of stocks, see Faber et al. (2005: Section 5).

16.   Even in 'purely natural' systems of energy and matter transformation as they existed before the rise of men, some stocks of 'waste' materials were accumulated, for example stocks of oxygen in the atmosphere and coal in the ground.

17.   This argument is not a formal proof of the proposed general principle of joint production – in contrast to the formal proof of the ubiquity of joint production of material and energetic outputs in industrial production systems in Chapter 3. Rather, the argument presented above is one of plausibility.

5. Joint Production and the Dynamics of Environmental Problems*

Up to now, we have developed some conceptual foundations for the concept of joint production. In this chapter, we shall change our perspective to investigate some structural implications of joint production for environmental problems. To begin with (Section 5.1), we adopt a static view, that is we focus on implications at a single point in time. In the subsequent Section 5.2, we shall take on a dynamic perspective, together with a long time horizon, and argue that the phenomenon of joint production together with the accumulation and degradation of stocks (cf. Chapter 4) leads to typical temporal patterns in the evolution of coupled ecological-economic systems over time.

5.1 THE STATIC VIEW ON JOINT PRODUCTION

5.1.1 Intended and Unintended Modifications of the Natural Environment

The traditional notion of an 'environmental problem' denotes a phenomenon at the interface of the spheres of 'the economy' and the surrounding natural ecosystems. Human economic action leads to deviations of the ecosphere's temporal development from its natural path because resource extraction, waste disposal, or other human influences change the affected ecosystems. From an economic perspective, such a deviation does not necessarily involve a value judgement. The deviation only becomes an 'environmental problem' once it is *valued* negatively by economic agents who are not compensated for this negative impact. In Part II of this book, we will discuss the problem of valuing joint production in detail.

The negative valuation of an environmental impact by some agents is necessarily part of an environmental problem. So, one might ask why environmental problems come into existence in the first place, why they cannot simply be avoided? The reason is to be found in the conflicting

---

*This chapter draws on Schiller (2002: Sections 7.3–7.4).

interests of different agents in the economy, who are linked by non-market interaction.[1] There are two possible manifestations of the problem:

1. It is exactly the *intended* result of an agent A's economic action itself which makes another economic agent B worse off. As an example, consider the clearing of a forest to construct a golf course. This landscape modification might be valued very differently by different people: whereas the owner of the course (agent A) – and potential customers – will most probably value this land-use change positively, other inhabitants of the region (agents B) might regret the disappearance of the woodland because of the loss of recreational area. In this case, to avoid the negative influence upon B the economic action 'construction of a golf course' has to be abandoned altogether. The reason is that it is precisely the intended (and desired) outcome of A's action which constitutes the negative impact on B.

2. In a second case, agent A may have some intention in pursuing his economic activity. In doing so, however, in addition to the desired outcome of his activity other side effects do jointly occur. If agent A's economic activity is a production activity, it will necessarily produce joint outputs in addition to the intended 'main' product (cf. Chapter 3).[2] The general principle of joint production (see Section 4.4.3) states that any economic activity will entail side effects, which, in general, do not correspond to the intention of the 'initiator' of the activity. In contrast to Case 1, in this case it is the impact of one of the side effects which may affect another agent B negatively. The environmental problem is caused by joint production. In a static view, the impact on B cannot be avoided due to the inevitability of the creation of the specific joint output for a given system at a given point in time.[3]

Adopting a static perspective, in both cases the only possibility of avoiding the negative impact on agent B would be to shut down the particular economic activity of agent A. In contrast to Case 1 however, in the second case the environmental problem constitutes mainly a 'technical' issue. As we shall discuss in Section 5.2, it can probably be avoided over time without shutting down agent A's economic activity if it is possible to modify this activity to avoid the emergence of the *specific* joint product.[4] Both of the mentioned causes of environmental problems are conceivable and relevant in modern society. In the following, we focus on the analysis of those environmental problems that are caused by joint production (Case 2 above).

5.1.2 Joint Production as a Cause of Environmental Degradation

Most of the currently known environmental problems can be traced back to the emergence of joint outputs, as has already been pointed out by Ayres and Kneese (1969: 282). So, joint production is extremely relevant for environmental degradation (Strebel 1981 and 1996), which in most cases can be regarded as a *public* bad. Rather than intentionally striving to deteriorate public goods, typically economic agents pursue a different economic interest. In doing so, they generally enhance economic welfare but at the same time unintentionally degrade environmental quality due to the joint outputs or side effects of their action.[5] This situation corresponds to Case 2 above. One prominent example is the emergence of CO_2 related to the use of fossil fuels; other examples are discussed in Part IV of this book.

There are three consecutive underlying reasons for the prominent role of joint products in causing environmental degradation: (i) the unavoidable emergence of joint outputs from economic action, (ii) the emission of the joint outputs into the natural environment by economic agents, and (iii) the resulting deviations of the natural ecosystems' temporal development from its natural path. Let us consider these points more closely.

(i) Without the unavoidability of joint products the emergence of each output of a given system could be controlled *individually*. In such a hypothetical situation, the operator of an economic system could freely choose the quantities of every output including a quantity of zero.[6] According to Definition 2.7, such a system would not display any joint production. Any output causing harm for the environment could just be avoided in case it is valued negatively by economic agents, and the corresponding environmental problem would not emerge or cease to exist. In a hypothetical world without any joint production a majority of environmental problems could be avoided, namely those which are caused by completely unwanted joint outputs (Case 2 above). Taking up the example of the emission of CO_2 into the atmosphere: Even when maintaining the current level of economic activity in the world, the problem of anthropogenic climate change could partly be avoided, if CO_2 did *not* emerge as an unavoidable joint output of fossil fuel use.

(ii) The second reason for the intimate connection between the emergence of joint outputs and the existence of environmental problems is the fact that emerging joint products are mainly emitted into the natural environment instead of being re-entered into the economic cycle. As material or energetic joint products emerge unintentionally from productive activity, they are not, in a natural way, inputs to another economic activity. Their disposal into the natural environment, however, is often easy and carries no private costs. Thus in many cases, economic agents release them into the surrounding ecosystems.

(iii) Finally, depending on the joint outputs' properties, their release into the natural ecosystems often entails a variety of effects on these ecosystems. If these substances accumulate to significant concentrations, they physically change ecosystems and may be toxic for species etc.

All three reasons suggest potential targets for environmental legislation in order to avoid environmental problems. Accordingly, it is often the aim of environmental regulation (i) to set incentives for avoiding the emergence of joint outputs in the first place (see also Section 5.2), (ii) to set incentives for avoiding the uncontrolled release of joint outputs into the environment, or (iii) to enhance the re-use of joint products within the economic cycle.[7] All three strategies, however, bear inherent problems: Strategy (i) cannot overcome the *general* occurrence of joint production, strategy (ii) often cannot guarantee secure long-term storage of hazardous joint products, and strategy (iii) faces the thermodynamic problem of downcycling and the fact that joint outputs, being unintentional outputs, often are not well suited to further economic use.

5.1.3   Joint Production and the Economic Concept of Abatement Costs

Within the framework of neoclassical environmental economics the problem of the emergence and avoidance of joint outputs is analysed using the concept of pollution abatement costs. The basic idea is that avoiding joint outputs is possible but costly, and that abatement costs rise with an increasing amount of avoided emissions.[8] Within this framework, it is the trade-off between (individual and social) abatement costs and benefits due to reduced environmental damage which governs the amount of emerging joint products in a production process.

The notion of joint production developed in this book does not contradict the concept of abatement costs. Rather it focusses on the underlying natural and technological structure which is the basis of the traditional neoclassical assumption of rising abatement costs. The phenomenon of joint production leads to positive and rising abatement costs, because avoiding joint outputs is only possible by modifying the respective production system. Such modifications take time and are costly, because they require the modification of capital and other stocks. In the following section, we investigate processes of this kind. We shall argue that the interplay of joint production and the time-consuming accumulation and degradation of the multiplicity of relevant stocks leads to typical dynamic structures in the interaction of economies and their natural environment.

5.2 THE DYNAMIC VIEW: PATTERNS OF DEVELOPMENT OF ENVIRONMENTAL PROBLEMS

According to the notion of joint production developed in Chapter 2 (Definition 2.7), a given representation of a system can – or cannot – be characterised by joint production at a certain point of time t_0 and taking into account a specific time horizon τ. Regarding one specific, for example a hazardous, joint output, it is therefore possible that the system representation exhibits joint production at one time of observation t_1, but does not exhibit joint production at a later time $t_2 > t_1$, even though at t_1 the emergence of the joint output was unavoidable. This contingency of our notion of joint production can be used to analyse typical temporal patterns in the development of environmental problems.

Economic systems with environmentally harmful joint products are not static but develop over time due to various influences from the outside world. Modifications of employed technologies can, for example, stop the emergence of a specific joint output. Hence, it is possible that the system stops being the cause of a corresponding environmental problem. In the following, we investigate a hypothetical, stylised scenario of the development of a production system[9] with the example of a combined system of several coal-fired power plants as in Figure 2.3 (page 31). For a start, let us choose a system representation that includes two output flows – the desired output A, electricity, and one harmful joint product B, for example sulphur dioxide (SO_2). We can then trace the following typical sequence (cf. Figure 5.1):

1. From a certain time t_1 on, a desired output A is produced in the system (electricity in our example). Along with the desired output the production activity brings forward a joint product B with no apparent economic use. Accordingly, it is released into the surrounding ecosystem (SO_2).[10] Due to the continuous operation of the production system, the released joint product B accumulates in the ecosphere, and the resulting stock increasingly causes modifications of the ecosystem and ecosystem functions.[11]

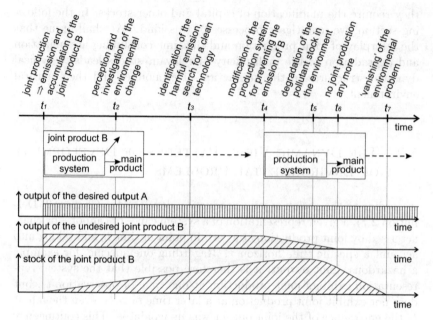

Figure 5.1   Stylised temporal pattern of an environmental problem and the production system at its origin: time series of the flows of the desired output A, the undesired joint output B, and the stock of the pollutant B in the environment. This particular representation of the system (main output A and joint output B) displays joint production for $t < t_6$ and single production for $t \geq t_6$.

2. At a later time $t_2 > t_1$, the modifications of the surrounding natural ecosystems become directly apparent to individuals and society as a whole. (Acid rain leads to acidification of lakes and damages to forests; see Chapter 18.) These modifications are valued negatively by economic agents and society as a whole. From t_2 on, general incentives exist to avoid or even reverse the modifications to nature. But to do so, the appropriate knowledge about the causal chain leading to the modifications has to be available. Usually, increased research effort has to be made in order to build up stocks of knowledge and to find the reasons for the problem.

3. At time $t_3 > t_2$, the emission of the joint product B is identified as the reason for the adverse effect on the environment (SO_2 in the atmosphere as a reason for acid rain). This forms a societal incentive to avoid the joint output B or its emission. However, as the desired output A (electricity) is highly desirable and necessary

for operating economic stocks, the short-term shut-down of the production activity is not a real option. But research activities are triggered in order to find possible ways of modifying the production system to avoid the undesired joint output, to convert it into a less harmful substance, or to re-enter it into the economic cycle.

4. At time $t_4 > t_3$, a modified or new production technology is available in the economy for producing the desired output A without the emission of the harmful joint product B (coal-fired power plants with flue gas desulphurisation). Society sets up incentives for individual agents (owners of the plants) or regulations leading to the implementation of the new technology. One by one the plants are modified; the rate of emission of B declines and reaches zero at time t_6.

5. At time $t_5 > t_4$, the (declining) rate of emission of the joint product is equal to the rate of deterioration of the pollutant stock in the environment, and the accumulated stock of the harmful joint product B in the natural compartments also starts to decline (SO_2 concentrations in the atmosphere are declining).

6. At time $t_6 > t_5$, the representation of the production system under study does not display joint production any more.

7. At time $t_7 > t_6$, the pollutant stock has almost vanished from the affected environmental compartments, that is the stock has ceased to be a stock, and with it the environmental problem.[12]

From the analysis of this hypothetical, but typical scenario, which is illustrated in Figure 5.1, we can draw a number of insights, which are discussed in detail in the following.

5.2.1   Joint Production as a Structural Cause of Environmental Degradation

At every point in time, the production system's feature of displaying joint production expresses the relevant structural characteristic which is the reason for the creation of the environmental problem. Assuming that the emerging joint product B is potentially harmful for the environment, the production system acts as a potential cause, as long as it displays joint production with respect to B and inevitably brings forward the joint product along with the production activity.[13] The concept of joint production is, hence, suitable for distinguishing time periods during which such a system is potentially environmentally harmful from other periods during which this is not the case.

Taking a more dynamic perspective, the concept of joint production as developed in Section 2.4 allows us to resolve the apparent contradiction between two possible but somehow naive interpretations of the scenario: (i) Regarding time $t = t_1$ in a static or short-term perspective one could state that the system displays joint production with respect to output B, that is production is inevitably connected to the emergence of B. (ii) In a more long-term and ex post perspective at times $t > t_6$ one could argue that output B did not emerge inevitably – it is obviously possible to avoid its production. The environmental problem, however, emerged nevertheless. This brings us to the second insight.

5.2.2   Joint Production and Stock Dynamics

The emergence of the environmental problem in the scenario is caused by the *temporal structure* in the interaction of the production system with its natural and social environment. The interaction is characterised by *time lags*, which can be described as time-consuming processes of accumulation and degradation of stocks. The perception of the environmental change is delayed by the necessary prior accumulation of the pollutant stock in the atmosphere. Prior to the modification of the production system it is necessary to build up (non-quantifiable) stocks of appropriate knowledge; the implementation process of the new technology itself is a process of the replacement of capital goods and, hence, time consuming. In our example, these time lags together with the temporary existence of joint production with respect to output B cause the environmental problem.

We would like to note that different kinds of stocks are involved in this dynamics: The accumulation of the pollutant stocks and the replacement of capital goods concern quantifiable stocks (cf. Section 4.2.2) whereas the building up of knowledge and of social pressure can be analytically grasped as the modification of non-quantifiable stocks (cf. Section 4.2.4).

5.2.3   'Substitution' between Joint Products

Up to now, we have been investigating a very limited system representation (comprising just one joint output B) which no longer displays any joint production for times $t > t_6$. From Chapter 3, however, we know that for thermodynamic representations this is impossible, because within thermodynamic representations *all industrial production is joint production*. Thus for the system investigated, there must exist at least one representation which, for $t > t_4$, displays joint production with respect to another joint output C. Avoiding the joint output B over time, hence, means 'substituting' it by another joint output C. (In the example that would be plaster from flue gas desulphurisation.) Figure 5.2 shows the

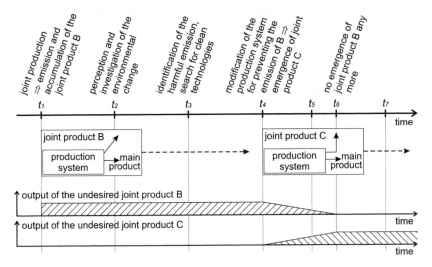

Figure 5.2 Stylised temporal pattern of the environmental problem and production system from Figure 5.1 in a more comprehensive system representation (desired output A, joint outputs B and C): time series of the flows of the joint outputs B and C. This representation displays joint production with respect to B for t < t$_4$, with respect to B and C for t$_4$ ≤ t < t$_6$, and with respect to C only for t ≥ t$_6$. The process of 'substitution' between joint outputs B and C takes place between t$_4$ and t$_6$.

system discussed above in another system representation comprising two joint products B and C besides the desired output A, and illustrates this gradual substitution process.

It depends on the characteristics of the novel joint product (C) whether or not a 'new' environmental problem is created due to its emergence. It is, however, typical of *end-of-pipe strategies* that in avoiding harmful joint outputs other environmental problems are introduced or intensified.[14] Generally, the properties of novel joint products when released into natural ecosystems are associated with a high degree of uncertainty, which implies low ex ante predictability with regard to the implications of their emergence and release.

In the event that the novel joint products cause new environmental problems, we may find long-term cyclical behaviour of environmental problems. Assuming reversible modifications to the affected ecosystems, the first negatively valued modification can be reversed over time, but is substituted by a different modification, which may also be negatively valued. Two cycles of this kind are illustrated in Figure 5.3. For reversible environmental modifications, the stocks of the polluting joint outputs B and C can be loosely interpreted as the 'strength' of the corresponding problem. So, one problem is 'substituted' by another problem with, typically, some overlap.[15]

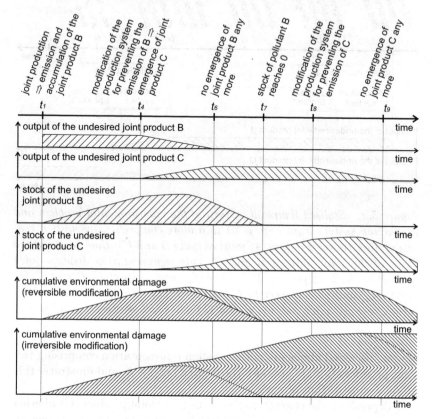

Figure 5.3   Stylised temporal pattern of the environmental problem and production system from Figures 5.1 and 5.2: time series of the flows of the joint outputs B and C, of the respective pollutant stocks in the natural environment, and of the resulting cumulative environmental damage in the cases of reversible and irreversible individual damages. At time t_8, the system starts to be modified to avoid the emergence of joint output C, at time t_9, joint output C is not emitted any more. In the case of reversible damage a cyclical cumulative damage occurs; in the irreversible case the cumulative damage is monotonously increasing.

If changes to the environment are irreversible, however, even *cumulative* environmental damage may be the result. In that case, every novel modification to the ecosystem may add some additional environmental

damage, whereas by avoiding a joint emission, one cannot reach a full recovery of the affected ecosystem. Examples of such worst case scenarios
include species and biodiversity loss. Figure 5.3 indicates the cumulative
environmental damage for the reversible and the irreversible case.[16]

5.3 SUMMARY AND CONCLUSIONS

The phenomenon of joint production or, more specifically, the emergence
of unintended joint products is the structural characteristic of produc-
tions systems that causes many environmental problems. Joint production, hence, is one of the key phenomena for understanding and modelling
environmental problems. Due to the ubiquitous nature of joint production, which stems from thermodynamic causes, it is not possible to avoid
harmful joint outputs altogether without compromising the emergence
of at least one other joint output. Often, by actively striving to avoid
a specific joint product other, novel joint products come into existence.
This phenomenon can be observed in the various case studies in Part IV
of this book. Ignorance and uncertainty concerning the environmental
impact of such novel joint outputs and time lags induced by the dynamics of various stocks lead to the possibility that 'substituting' joint
outputs can cause novel or enforce existing environmental problems.

The notion of joint production as developed in Chapter 2 conceptualises the very characteristics of economic systems which potentially lead
to the creation of environmental problems – namely the inevitable creation of joint outputs – in a useful way. It also facilitates the temporal
structuring of the phenomenon. So, the succession of anthropogenic
modifications to natural ecosystems and the emergence of cycles of environmental damage can be modelled and structurally explained by the
interplay of joint production and dynamics of quantifiable and non-
quantifiable stocks.

NOTES

1.   Within the economic approach to the analysis of environmental problems (see,
for example, Baumol and Oates 1988, Hanley et al. 1997, Kolstad 2000, Siebert 2004,
Tietenberg 2003) one central concept to model and analyse non-market interaction
of agents is the concept of 'externality'. Unregulated externalities lead to inefficiency
of the allocation of production factors in an economy. To avoid this inefficiency,
externalities have to be 'internalised'. That is, they have to be compensated in
an appropriate way. This can happen by means of, for example, suitable economic
instruments, assignment of private property rights etc. The modelling of an environmental problem using the concept of externality focusses on the impact on the

affected agent. In the widespread case of ignorance about the impact, this concept of modelling environmental problems is limited (for a discussion, see Schiller 2002: Section 7.5). Modelling approaches based on the concept of joint production can then serve as a complementary perspective; see Section 2.2.1.

2. This holds for a thermodynamic representation of the system under study (cf. Section 2.3.3, Definition 2.4), that is if one considers all outputs.

3. See Definition 2.7. The unavoidability of the creation of a joint output does not necessarily mean that it is created in the *same instant* of time; it can be created at a later time (within the time horizon τ).

4. This does not mean, however, that the occurrence of joint production can be avoided altogether (see the discussion in Section 2.4 on page 39).

5. The unintentionality of the side effects often results in them being neglected – economic agents often just fail to focus their attention on them, in particular, if joint products result in a public, but not in a private bad. In Chapters 12 and 13, we shall see that from an ethical perspective individual economic agents cannot be expected to assume responsibility for all unintended side effects of their action. However, the danger of neglect is also imminent at the societal level, in particular, if one solely uses the economic concept of 'externality' to analyse environmental problems (see Section 2.2.1).

6. At this point, we abstract from the potential costs for the operator of the system in doing so. In the real world, avoiding certain outputs may well be costly, an effect which is grasped in the economic concept of pollution abatement costs (see Section 5.1.3 below).

7. An example is the German *Recycling Management and Waste Act* ('Kreislauf-wirtschafts- und Abfallgesetz') which was enacted in 1994.

8. Neoclassical economists would claim that by assuming cost curves to rise to infinity for emissions reaching zero, one could also model the impossibility of avoiding a specific joint product.

9. We investigate this stylised scenario for didactic reasons: in order to highlight the basic temporal structure. In the example, many simplifying assumptions are made. Part IV of this book, however, contains several case studies investigating the development of real production systems in detail. In the case studies, we find very similar system behaviour (cf. Chapters 15, 16, and 18).

10. See Chapter 18 for a detailed description of how SO_2 emerges from productive activities and is released into ecosystems.

11. At this point, we assume (i) that the rate of release of the joint output into the ecosphere is higher than the rate at which it is deteriorated within the natural ecosystems and (ii) that the environmental modifications are dependent on the concentration of the substance in the respective environmental compartment, that is it is the *stock* of the pollutant which matters. Assumption (i) is typically true for newly developing environmental problems and assumption (ii) holds for many human interferences with ecosystems. For a detailed discussion of the environmental effects of SO_2 emissions, see Chapter 18.

12. Here, two heroic assumptions are made: (i) In real systems decay of substances often behaves exponentially. Hence, small amounts of the substance will remain for very long time periods – if not to infinity. In those cases, the pollutant stock retains its permanency even with an infinite time horizon. For a discussion of this problem, see Section 4.3.1. (ii) Modifications to environmental systems may often be irreversible, which means that the initial state cannot be reached again. We abstract from both facts in the example.

13. However, the mere emergence and release of a joint product is not sufficient for estimating its environmental impact because the effect of artificial substances in the natural environment is often uncertain.

14.   So-called *end-of-pipe* technologies typically transform the harmful output into another specification which then has to be disposed of. Furthermore, they often use fossil energy, which brings forward additional CO_2 emissions.

15.   A similar pattern is observed in the discussion concerning so-called 'environmental Kuznets curves' (EKC, Panayotou 1995). The concept of EKC postulates a specific relationship between aggregate income and the use of the environment as a sink for pollutants from economic activity. An existing EKC implies that with rising income the amount of pollution rises to a maximum and then declines again. There exists a broad discussion about empirical content and possible theoretical reasons for EKCs (summarised by Lieb 2001: Chapters 1 and 2). One of these reasons is the substitution between pollutants (Lieb 2001: Section 3.3).

16.   Figure 5.3 – like Figures 5.1 and 5.2 – is meant to provide a rough sketch of the structural pattern in principle, but not in any way to give a true qualitative, nor even quantitative, picture of the temporal development of the interaction between an economic system and the environment. For the sake of simplicity we therefore make heroic assumptions, for example (i) that both joint products B and C accumulate in the natural compartments in the same way, (ii) that both of them result in an environmental problem, (iii) that the environmental damage is proportional to the respective pollutant stock, and (iv) that both types of damage can be added to a cumulative environmental damage.

PART II

Economics

INTRODUCTION

As we have seen in Part I of this book, joint production has a number of systematic implications for ecological-economic systems. Traditionally, the economic consequences of joint production are analysed using the established methods and concepts from environmental and resource economics. These are based in welfare economics and are centred around the concept of externality. There is a large and well-understood body of literature in that strand; authoritative textbook treatments include Baumol and Oates (1988), Dasgupta and Heal (1979), Hanley et al. (1997), Hartewick and Olewiler (1998), Kolstad (2000), Siebert (2004) and Tietenberg (2003). However, this approach systematically leaves open a number of important questions. This part of the book employs the concept of joint production to address some of these issues.

Chapter 6 investigates how the analysis of joint production has influenced the history of economic theory and, vice versa, how in the history of economic theory the concept of joint production was shaped. We show that the concept of joint production is deeply rooted in economics and that there exists a vast body of knowledge on joint production which we can draw upon. We also identify remaining gaps in the current economic understanding of joint production. Chapter 7 then makes recourse to the philosophy of economics in order to explain why certain aspects of joint production are systematically neglected in modern economics.

The thermodynamic analysis of joint production in Chapter 3 has left open the question of the value of joint outputs, that is whether they are desired, undesired or neutral. But this is an important distinction because, traditionally, the character of joint outputs as desired or undesired entails a distinct way of modelling and theorising: desired joint outputs are subject to the theory of industrial organisation, while undesired joint products are subject to the theory of environmental economics. However, there are important examples of outputs which are ambivalent in the sense that they may potentially be desired or undesired. In Chapter 8, we study such ambivalence and draw conclusions for ecological-economic theory and policy.

Introducing the time dimension into the analysis, in Chapters 9 and 10 we employ capital theory to study the investment decision under joint production of consumption and environmental pollution, and the implications for structural change in ecological-economic systems.

6. Joint Production in the History of Economic Thought

6.1 INTRODUCTION

The analysis of joint production has long played an important role in the development of economic theory. Masterminds of economics – such as Adam Smith, John Stuart Mill, Karl Marx, Johann Heinrich von Thünen, William Stanley Jevons, Alfred Marshall, Irving Fisher, Francis Ysidro Edgeworth, Arthur Cecil Pigou, Heinrich von Stackelberg, John von Neumann, Piero Sraffa, and many more – devoted a considerable amount of effort to the analysis of joint production. As a result, there exists an extensive and well-understood body of knowledge about joint production in economics.

In this chapter, we outline how joint production has been analysed in the history of economic thought, starting from 1776 – the year in which Adam Smith's *Wealth of Nations* appeared, marking the beginning of modern economics – up until the 1970s, when the present general equilibrium theory of externalities as well as the present theory of multi-output firms and industries had taken shape.[1] This discussion serves several purposes, namely

- to highlight the various economic dimensions and implications of both the phenomenon and the concept of joint production;

- to outline the sources to which one might turn in order to use the extensive and powerful toolbox of economics for an analysis of joint production;

- to show how the analysis of joint production has shaped the analysis of general economics, and how this has led to our present understanding of both general economics and joint production in particular;

---

*This chapter is based on Baumgärtner (2000: Chapters 5–7).

- to argue that from the beginning, and long before the modern field of environmental and resource economics emerged, the economic analysis of joint production was motivated by the occurrence of environmental problems due to waste by-products and emissions;

- to identify remaining gaps in the current economic understanding of joint production and to point out that, although many aspects of joint production have been captured by various theories, up until today there is no general theory of joint production.

The chapter is organised as follows. Section 6.2 discusses the approach of classical value theory to joint production, and the fundamental problem that this approach encounters. Section 6.3 deals with one particular aspect of the value of joint products, namely that joint products may be unwanted and harmful to the environment. The analysis of this aspect has significantly contributed to the abandonment of classical value theory and the establishment of neoclassical value theory. Section 6.4 describes the neoclassical approach to explaining the value of joint products, which was put forward by Alfred Marshall and is based on partial equilibrium analysis. The challenge of moving from partial to general equilibrium analysis of joint production is discussed in Section 6.5. The current state of affairs, with many theories, but no general theory of joint production is presented in Section 6.6. Finally, Section 6.7 pulls together the multifaceted story: it summarises the historical developments and draws conclusions.

6.2   CLASSICAL VALUE THEORY

The classical era coincides with the beginning of industrialisation in the second half of the eighteenth century. Agriculture is still the predominant form of producing national income for most European countries. At the same time, and first in England, the industrial revolution takes place, making mining (for coal and ores) and industrial production an ever more important aspect of the economy. As joint production dominates the primary sector (agriculture and resource extraction) and is a characteristic feature of the industrial sector (cf. Chapter 3), it is not surprising that the analysis of joint production played an important role in economic thought at the time (Kurz 1986).

6.2.1   Adam Smith: Joint Production Requires Special Patterns of Explanation

Adam Smith (1723–1790) cites many examples of joint production in his *Inquiry into the Nature and Causes of the Wealth of Nations* (1976[1776]).

He is well aware of the fact that joint production is a ubiquitous phenomenon and, hence, deserves extensive treatment.

In classical value theory, the so-called 'natural price' of a product is given by the total costs of production, including wages, profits and rents (Smith 1976[1776]: 72). While in the short run the market price of a good may well deviate from its natural price due to market forces such as demand for that good, in the long run the market price will tend toward the natural price. The natural price can be described as acting as a 'centre of gravity' (Smith 1976[1776]: 75), attracting the market price in the long run. In the classical view it is, thus, the natural price of a good which corresponds to its true value.

Classical value theory was pervaded by the distinction between two kinds of goods (Niehans 1990: 241): goods with a fixed supply, such as land, and goods with a variable supply, such as cloth. In the first case, quantity is fixed and the price depends only on demand. In the second case, the price is determined solely by costs of production and demand only affects the quantity produced. For Adam Smith joint products, such as wool and mutton, did not fit into this scheme. He recognised the explanation of value of joint products as being special and, consequently, classified them as a 'third sort of produce' (Smith 1976[1776]: 234–235).

An important example of the existence of joint products is hunting or cattle-breeding (Smith 1976[1776]: 178). The production of meat from some animals goes hand in hand with the production of skins. One always gets both. Smith recognises the problem that arises from this fact: With joint production the proportion in which the joint outputs are produced need not coincide with that in which they are wanted. As a consequence, one or the other of the joint outputs is in excess supply:

> Land in its original rude state can afford the materials of cloathing and lodging to a much greater number of people than it can feed. In its improved state it can sometimes feed a greater number of people than it can supply with those materials; [...] In the one state, therefore, there is always a superabundance of those materials, which are frequently, upon that account, of little or no value. In the other there is often a scarcity, which necessarily augments their value. In the one state a great part of them is thrown away as useless [...]. In the other they are all made use of, and there is frequently demand for more than can be had. (Smith 1976[1776]: 178)

Obviously, Smith recognises – 'possibly for the first time in the history of economic thought' (Kurz 1986: 13) – what later became known as the 'rule of free goods': goods in excess supply have no value.

Smith analyses what determines which one of the joint products is in excess supply and finds that it is 'the extent of their respective market' (Smith 1976[1776]: 246), which in turn depends on the level of 'improvement' of the society (Smith 1976[1776]: 246) as well as on the foreign trade relationships with other countries at a different level of 'improvement' (Smith 1976[1776]: 178). As an example, Smith extensively discusses the domestic market for butcher's meat and foreign trade for the joint products of meat, wool, and raw hides. He demonstrates that in 'the progress of improvement' (Smith 1976[1776]: 246) of a country, the role of free good may be passed on from one of the joint products (meat) to the other (wool and raw hides).

While Smith clearly recognises that the market price of the individual joint products is influenced by a number of factors other than costs of production, he maintains that their value is ultimately given by their 'natural' price. Smith's notion of the 'natural' price of the joint products is the one developed in the case of single production, that is, total costs for producing all the joint products. However, this concept can only be applied to the sum of all joint products of some production process. As a consequence,

> [w]hatever part of this price, therefore, is not paid by the wool and the hide, must be paid by the carcase. The less there is paid for the one, the more must be paid for the other. In what manner this price is to be divided upon the different parts of the beast, is indifferent to the landlords and farmers, provided it is all paid to them. (Smith 1976[1776]: 251)

This observation, according to Smith, allows statements as to how the total natural price of all joint products is to be divided among the different joint products. Smith supports this conclusion with historical examples of how the price of wool and that of hides shifted relatively to the price of meat as a result of different trade regulations for wool imposed in England under the influence of mercantile ideas. Smith takes the empirical observations as support for his claim that the theory of natural prices is correct also in the presence of joint production and that, in particular, the total natural price of all joint products is independent of the manner in which it is divided between the different joint products.

Overall, Smith's analysis of joint production had a lasting impact on the development of economics in general and the economics of joint production in particular for two reasons:

1. Smith recognises joint products (a 'third sort of produce') as being distinct in the explanation of value. Joint products do not fit into the established scheme and explanations of classical value theory,

but they have to be treated differently to some extent. Thus, Adam Smith set the stage and suggested the direction for future study: the aim of the research after Smith was to find a framework for the explanation of value which is general enough to allow joint products to be treated just like any other kind of goods.

2. Although Smith recognises the explanation of value of joint products as being distinct, he nevertheless advocates the classical concept of natural prices also for this case. But it is obvious – also to Smith himself – that this approach is not sufficient to explain the prices of joint products. Smith is forced to introduce new elements of explanation into the classical theory: he refers in various ways to the demand side, for example when evoking the 'rule of free goods' or when talking about 'the market' for a product. But Smith's notion of demand is rather static. Throughout his analysis, Smith considers demand for a product as exogenously given, depending on the respective state of development of a country, and independent of the product's natural price.

6.2.2   John Stuart Mill: Demand and Supply

John Stuart Mill (1806–1873) developed in his *Principles of Political Economy* (1965[1848]) a theory of value and distribution which he intended to be a refined elaboration of the classical ideas. He was convinced that, in principle, the classical economists, in particular David Ricardo (1951[1817]), had already captured all the essential ideas.[2] But in fact, his analysis was an early critique of classical value theory and one step toward its abandonment.

Mill encounters fundamental problems in applying the classical theory of value and devotes a whole chapter to the discussion 'Of Some Peculiar Cases of Value' (Mill 1965[1848]: Chapter 16), which do not fit into the classical scheme of explanation. One of these 'peculiar cases' is joint production, which Mill (1965[1848]: 569–570) describes as follows:

> It sometimes happens that two different commodities have what may be termed a joint cost of production. They are both products of the same operation, or set of operations, and the outlay is incurred for the sake of both together, not part for one and part for the other. The same outlay would have to be incurred for either of the two, if the other were not wanted or used at all.

Although Mill does not consider examples of joint products to be important cases of the interchange of commodities, he nevertheless acknowledges that '[t]here are not a few instances of commodities thus associated in their production' (Mill 1965[1848]: 570). As examples, he mentions coke and coal-gas as well as examples from agriculture such as mutton/wool, beef/hides/tallow, calves/dairy products and chicken/eggs.

Mill (1965[1848]: 570) clearly recognises the classical approach's inability to give a complete answer to the question of how the value (in the sense of: natural price) of the individual joint outputs is determined:

> Cost of production can have nothing to do with deciding the value of the associated commodities relatively to each other. It only decides their joint value.

When answering this question himself, Mill goes far beyond the classical theory's focus on cost of production and supply, and gives considerations of demand an equally important role:[3]

> Since cost of production here fails us, we must revert to a law of value anterior to cost of production, and more fundamental, the law of demand and supply. The law is, that the demand for a commodity varies with its value, and that the value adjusts itself so that the demand shall be equal to supply. (Mill 1965[1848]: 570)

An implicit assumption in Mill's discussion is that the various joint outputs from some production process come in fixed proportions.[4] Consequently, in the case that supply does not equal demand for each joint product the possibility of an elastic adaptation of supply proportions is excluded by assumption. Instead, variations in the relative prices of the joint products and, thus, relative demand become important in explaining how an equilibrium between supply and demand for each joint product is attained. Mill's suggestion is that, while the total costs of production (including rent of land and profits) determine the joint natural value of all joint products, equilibrium between supply and demand for each product determines how the joint value is divided up between the individual joint products to give their individual value:

> When, therefore, two or more commodities have a joint cost of production, their natural values relatively to each other are those which will create a demand for each, in the ratio of the quantities in which they are sent forth by the productive process. (Mill 1965[1848]: 571)

So, Mill relies on the classical cost-of-production approach to justify the *joint value* of all outputs of some joint production process and uses the 'law of supply and demand' only to explain the *relative prices* of the joint outputs. This led Schumpeter (1954: 603) to the judgement that Mill built a 'halfway house'.

6.3   UNDESIRED JOINT OUTPUTS AND THE ABANDONMENT OF CLASSICAL VALUE THEORY

With John Stuart Mill's analysis, classical value theory had been clearly marked as unsatisfactory when it comes to explaining the value of joint products. Others have raised a similar critique, and also pointed to the important role of demand for explaining the value of joint products, in particular Johann Heinrich von Thünen, Karl Marx and William Stanley Jevons. Although these three authors are generally very different concerning method, focus and scope of their respective analyses, they all reach very similar conclusions as far as joint production and its consequences for the natural environment are concerned. For they emphasise that joint products may not only be wanted goods, but may be unwanted and even harmful. All three revert to early examples of environmental pollution when illustrating their claim.

6.3.1   Johann Heinrich von Thünen: Desired and Undesired Joint Products

The major concern of Johann Heinrich von Thünen (1783–1850) in his *Der isolierte Staat in Beziehung auf Landwirtschaft und Nationalökonomie* (1921[1826]) is with the optimal spatial allocation of different economic activities around a town that serves as a market centre, trading urban goods for the rural products of labour and land. Implicit in his argument is the assumption that goods are costly to transport, and that some goods, for example perishable food, cannot be transported at all over long distances.

Von Thünen draws on a rich set of practical examples of joint production, which dominates the primary sector of the economy. He realises that the various joint outputs of some processes of production do not necessarily occur in fixed proportion. Rather, the amounts in which they occur may depend on some parameter of the production process. For instance, von Thünen (1921[1826]: 196) points out that the proportion in which forestry yields timber and firewood depends on the age at which the trees are cut.

Von Thünen also notes that in the case of joint production one cannot speak a priori of a main product and its by-products. Which one of the joint outputs is considered to be the main product and which one, consequently, is considered as a by-product may well depend on the specific circumstances. Usually, in growing grain the grain is considered to be the main product whereas the straw is considered to be a by-product. However, von Thünen (1921[1826]: 14) points out that in the region close to the town, which should be specialised in the production of perishable goods such as vegetables or fresh milk, one needs hay and straw for cattle-breeding in order to produce milk from cows. Under these circumstances, hay and straw are the main purpose of growing grain, and grain is only a by-product.

Similarly, it cannot be ascertained a priori whether the various joint outputs are desired or not. This may also depend on the specific circumstances. In particular, an output may be desired if the process of production takes place in one place, while it may be undesired if the very same process of production is carried out in another place. As an example von Thünen points to the manure which is both a joint effect of human consumption and a joint product of cattle-breeding. For the inhabitants of the town the manure is an undesired side-effect of consumption, a 'bad' that has to be disposed of:

> The inhabitants of the town have to dispose of the dung, even if they do not receive anything in exchange for it but have to pay for its removal. (Thünen 1921[1826]: 209; our translation)

In contrast, for farmers the dung is a desired joint output of cattle-breeding since it is indispensable to the growing of crops.[5]

The fact that the by-products from a joint production process may or may not be desired, depending on the specific circumstances, has implications for the way in which a national economy should be spatially structured. In particular, different productive activities should be located such that the waste by-products of one process may serve as useful inputs for some other process.[6] Von Thünen proposes that the town be surrounded by several rings of different specialised economic activities and that, in general, more than one productive activity will be located in each ring. As an example, von Thünen (1921[1826]: 275) points out that distilling is best located in the sixth ring, since

> [t]he waste-products from distilling [...] can be most profitably used for stock feed; and as this ring of cattle-breeding depends on livestock anyway, and grain and firewood have their lowest possible value, everything combines in this ring which is in favour of distilling. (Translation by Kurz 1986: 20)

6.3.2 Karl Marx: Joint Products as Waste

Karl Marx (1818–1883), like Adam Smith, holds a classical theory of value and distribution. The world he describes and analyses, however, is radically different from Smith's, who lived almost exactly one hundred years earlier, or even from von Thünen's. In the meantime, the industrial revolution had taken place, and Karl Marx was very much interested in issues of technology and technical change, machinery and industry. In his works, especially in his excerpt books (Marx 1981, 1982), one finds many explicit descriptions of cases of joint production from all sectors of production: agriculture, animal-rearing, mining, forestry, paper manufacturing, the chemical industry, the textile industry, mechanical engineering etc. In his *Grundrisse der Kritik der politischen Ökonomie* he refers to joint products as 'accessory products' (Marx 1970[1857–1858]: 192). In the *Theories of Surplus Value* (Marx 1963[1905–1910], 1968) and *Capital* (Marx 1954[1867], 1956[1885], 1959[1894]), joint production is dealt with under the entries 'waste' and 'by-products', and joint products are also called 'excretions of production'.

Although Marx is well aware of the widespread existence of joint production, he nevertheless does not take this phenomenon into account in his theorising. His theory of the general rate of profit and prices of production (cf. Marx 1959[1894]: Part II) rests upon a model of single production. The reason for this can be found in Marx' implicit assumption that, in principle, the occurrence of waste by-products could be reduced to zero by running the production process efficiently (Kurz 1986: 16–17). According to Marx, although the existence of undesired joint products from industrial production is an empirical fact, it is not a necessary characteristic of production.[7]

Marx's ambiguous position of simultaneously stressing the empirical importance of the phenomenon of joint production and playing down its relevance for economic theory is best visible in Volume II of *Capital* (Marx 1959[1894]: Chapter 5, Section 4) where he discusses the issue under the heading 'Utilisation of the Excretions of Production'. Marx (1959[1894]: 101) introduces the subject with the empirical observation that '[t]he so-called waste plays an important role in almost every industry'. He recognises the intimate relationship between industrial production of desired goods and environmental pollution caused by unwanted joint outputs. This makes him think, at the same time, about how economic measures can result in a reduction of environmental pollution. Marx discusses in detail the possibility of recycling the waste by-products.[8] He notes that the recycling of waste is stimulated by the 'rising prices of raw materials' and identifies several conditions for the possibility of recycling (Marx 1959[1894]: 101):

1. The existence of large amounts of such waste, 'such as are available only in large-scale production'.

2. 'Improved machinery', such that even with inferior inputs production can be carried out.

3. 'Scientific progress, particularly of chemistry, which reveals the useful properties of such waste'.

Historical data from the flax, the cotton and the silk industries show, according to Marx (1959[1894]: 101–102, 109) that the first two conditions are fulfilled.[9] Concerning the third condition, Marx (1959[1894]: 102) observes that

> [t]he most striking example of utilising waste is furnished by the chemical industry. It utilises not only its own waste, for which it finds new uses, but also that of many other industries. For instance, it converts the formerly almost useless gas-tar into aniline dyes, alizarin, and more recently, even into drugs.[10]

According to Marx, recycling the waste by-products of production, turning them into useful products, and the prevention of their occurrence would act towards reducing the production of waste by-products, because competition spurs

> the capitalist's fanatical insistence on economy in means of production [... t]hat nothing is lost or wasted and the means of production are consumed only in the manner required by production itself. (Marx 1959[1894]: 83)

According to Marx, this strong force would ultimately lead to a reduction of waste by-products to zero, and the phenomenon of joint production would disappear. Hence, the observed widespread existence of joint production may be considered to be only a temporary phenomenon and would not last under the competitive pressure of employing capital efficiently.[11]

6.3.3   William Stanley Jevons: Marginal Utility Explains the Demand for Joint Outputs

William Stanley Jevons (1835–1882) was the first to give a complete refutation of the classical theory of value in his *Theory of Political Economy* (1911[1879]).[12] Just like Mill (cf. Section 6.2.2), he recognises the obvious problem that any labour theory of value, as well as any more general cost-of-production based theory of value, faces in the case of joint production of, say, two outputs X and Y:

> It is impossible to divide up the labour and say that so much is expended on producing X, and so much on Y. (Jevons 1911[1879]: 200)

This objection to the classical cost-of-production based theory of value is even more severe as

> these cases of joint production [...] form the general rule,
> to which it is difficult to point out any clear or important
> exceptions. (Jevons 1911[1879]: 198)

Hence, a cost-of-production based theory of value as put forward by the classical economists is severely deficient. Jevons argues that the conditions of production alone are not sufficient to explain the value of a good, but that demand is the other equally important ingredient in the explanation of value (Jevons 1911[1879]: 198–199). Whereas the insight that both supply and demand determine the value of a good is not new,[13] Jevons' genuine contribution to the theory of value is to give an explicit explanation of what determines demand.

According to Jevons, marginal utility – that is the utility gained from the consumption of one additional small unit of some good – is the key concept to explain demand. He also applies this concept to the explanation of the value of joint products (Jevons 1911[1879]: 199–202). Although his argument contains several flaws and stops short of really explaining prices or exchange ratios of the joint products (Baumgärtner 2000: 109–110), it appears to be aiming at what is now known as Gossen's Second Law (Kurz 1986: 28):[14] in equilibrium a household will choose among different goods in such a way that the marginal utility of that household is equal between any two goods. Thus, Jevons clearly recognises that marginal utility is needed as an element in the explanation of value in general, and in the explanation of the value of joint products in particular.[15]

Analysing joint production in terms of marginal utility leads Jevons to the insight that joint products may, in principle, be positively or negatively valued. The case in which a wanted good is jointly produced together with an output of low or even negative value is, according to Jevons, very common. Jevons (1911[1879]: 198–199) cites many empirical examples and concludes that in almost all cases of joint production the wanted good is accompanied by other outputs which are useless:

> [A]lmost every process of industry yields refuse results, of
> which the utility is zero or nearly so. (Jevons 1911[1879]: 202)

Formally, Jevons' conditions for the demand for joint products may even have negative solutions for the marginal utility (Jevons 1911[1879]: 202). Jevons realised that the interpretation of negative marginal utility is by no means obscure but rather straightforward: it means that one would be willing to sacrifice a certain amount of a wanted good to get rid of the unwanted substance characterised by negative marginal utility:

> [T]here cannot be the least doubt that people often labour,
> or pay money to other labourers, in order to get rid of things,
> and they would not do this unless such things were hurtful,
> that is, had the opposite quality to utility – disutility. [...]
> Reflection soon shows [...] that no inconsiderable part of the
> values with which we deal in practical economics must be
> *negative values*. (Jevons 1911[1879]: 127)

When giving examples of things of negative value, Jevons (1911[1879]:
129) reverts to cases of environmental pollution, for example 'the sewage
of great towns, the foul or poisoned water from mines, dye-works, etc.'
Also, Jevons identifies the importance of negatively valued joint outputs
in the first place as them being the origin of environmental pollution,[16,17]
which is very similar to Marx's view (cf. Section 6.3.2).[18] For instance,

> [t]he waste products of a chemical works [...] will sometimes
> have a low value; at other times it will be difficult to get rid of
> them without fouling the rivers and injuring the neighbouring
> estates; in this case they are discommodities and take the
> negative sign [of marginal utility]. (Jevons 1911[1879]: 202)

While Jevons emphasises and explicitly analyses the role of marginal
utility and demand for the determination of equilibrium prices and quantities for joint products, he takes a shortcut on the side of production
and supply conditions. His underlying model of production is that two
commodities are produced in fixed proportion in a single process with
labour as the only input (Jevons 1911[1879]: 199). The assumption of
fixed proportion is vindicated by the brief statement that 'in cases of
joint production there is no such freedom [of varying the quantities of
each output separately]' (Jevons 1911[1879]: 200). This simplifying assumption can be considered as a weakness in Jevons' approach (Stigler
1941: 18). In this respect, Jevons only half deserves to be called a 'marginalist': while he introduced the principle of substitution and marginal
quantities on the demand side, he failed to make this point on the supply
side. It fell to Alfred Marshall to evoke the principle of substitution and
marginal quantities in the supply of joint products (cf. Section 6.4.1).

6.4   NEOCLASSICAL VALUE THEORY

The classical approach to value and distribution was openly declared
to be insufficient around 1870 in the so-called 'marginalist revolution',
which is commonly associated with the works of William Stanley Jevons
(1911[1871]), Carl Menger (1871) and Léon Walras (1954[1874/77]). At

the end of this 'revolution' stood Alfred Marshall's *Principles of Economics* (1925[1890]) which established the so-called neoclassical explanation of value. Marginalism appeared to be a general principle for the determination of equilibrium and the explanation of value. Marshall (1925[1890]: 390) argued that this principle also holds for joint production, which seems to make the explanation of value of joint products a special case of a more general principle, and to put an end to its interpretation as a 'peculiar case'.

6.4.1 Alfred Marshall: Substitution in Demand and Supply

Alfred Marshall's (1842–1924) main interest was the analysis of individual and interrelated markets. Although he sketched a general equilibrium system in a short note,[19] Marshall focused on partial equilibrium analysis. The central idea in Marshall's analysis was that demand and supply are independent and equally important determinants of the price of some good. While the main insight of the 'marginalist revolution' was that demand largely depended on marginal utility, it was already obvious that marginal utility alone could not explain the price of a good (cf. Section 6.3.3, note 15). On the other hand, supply and the costs of production were not sufficient either to explain prices, as John Stuart Mill had already demonstrated (cf. Section 6.2.2). Marshall's ground breaking contribution to value theory was to put the two aspects of demand and supply together in one analytical framework, and to demonstrate that they jointly determine the price of a good. For Marshall, to dispute whether value is governed by utility or by costs of production, therefore, would be no more reasonable than to dispute whether it is the upper or the under blade of a pair of scissors that cuts a piece of paper (Marshall 1925[1890]: 675). This general scheme of explanation of price also holds, according to Marshall (1925[1890]: Book V, Chapter VI), for joint products.

Marshall (1925[1890]: 388) observes that joint products 'cannot *easily* be produced separately, but are joined in a common origin' (emphasis added).[20] Obviously, Marshall does not consider the jointness in the production of joint outputs to be an absolute one. This more general view on joint production extends the analytical scope beyond the more narrow view of many of Marshall's predecessors, such as John Stuart Mill (cf. Section 6.2.2) or William Stanley Jevons (cf. Section 6.3.3) who had always based their analysis on the assumption that joint outputs are produced in fixed proportion. In particular, it allows Marshall to generalise the principle of substitution that had been invoked by Jevons on the demand side to the production side.

To start with, Marshall analyses the case in which two goods (for example meat and hides) are produced in fixed proportion in a single process (for example the raising and slaughtering of a bullock) – the traditional paradigm of joint production. He uses a geometrical method for the simultaneous determination of the equilibrium prices and quantities of both joint products given the demand curves for both of them and the supply curve for the entity from which both joint products emanate:[21] from the demand curves for both joint products, that is demand for bullocks from meat users and demand for bullocks from hide users, Marshall derives a total demand curve for bullocks by vertical summation of these two. The intersection of this curve with the supply curve of bullocks (obtained by horizontal summation of all bullock-producing firms' supply curves) determines the equilibrium price and quantity of bullocks produced and sold. This equilibrium price is divided among the meat and the hide according to the demand curves for both joint products at the equilibrium quantity. Marshall (1925[1890]: 388) is well aware of the fact that this is only a partial equilibrium analysis:

> Other things must be assumed to be equal (that is, the supply schedule for the whole process of production must be assumed to remain in force and so must the demand schedule for each of the joint products except that to be isolated).

In the next step, Marshall generalises his analysis by abandoning the assumption that the two joint outputs are produced in fixed proportion, since

> [t]here are very few cases of joint products the cost of production of both of which together is exactly the same as that of one of them alone. (Marshall 1925[1890]: 389)

For instance, variations in the input proportions or variations in the parameters of the production process, such as temperature or pressure, may result in variations in the output proportion and, thus, may allow the producer to hold constant the amount of output of one product while varying the amount of the other. In this case it is possible to conceive the marginal costs of production separately for each of the joint outputs (Marshall 1925[1890]: 390). As a consequence, the principle of substitution also applies on the supply side. Whereas the notion of substitution in consumption had already been established by Jevons, for Marshall the notion of substitution is central to both consumption and production. Therefore

> the general principle can be applied, that the relative proportions of the joint products of a business should be so modified

that the marginal expenses of production of either product should be equal to its marginal demand price. (Marshall 1925[1890]: 395)

Marshall's conclusion from his partial equilibrium analysis is that joint production needs no longer to be considered as a peculiar case which deserves special methods for the explanation of value, as it has been claimed by classical economists such as Adam Smith or John Stuart Mill (cf. Section 6.2). Instead, the explanation of the value of joint products follows the same general explanatory principle that holds for all goods whatsoever. But while the classical economists had always performed a general equilibrium analysis, Marshall's analysis is limited by its focus on partial equilibrium. The question of how to determine the value of joint products in general equilibrium was not answered by Marshall.

6.4.2   Impact and Applications of Marshall's Principles

Marshall's authoritative *Principles of Economics* (1925[1890]), which had established the neoclassical explanation of value, soon became the predominant textbook on the issue and influenced two generations of economists, also as far as methods are concerned.[22] With partial equilibrium analysis being the underlying method of the *Principles*, the era between 1890 and the mid 1930s was also dominated by partial equilibrium analysis. It saw a number of contributions in the spirit of Marshall's conclusion that joint production is subject to the general explanatory principle according to which marginal utility and marginal costs of production determine the equilibrium price of a good, and thus can be treated by standard methods.

While Marshall (1925[1890]) had analysed the simultaneous determination of market prices and quantities of joint products, the focus of attention then shifted to the decision problem of a multi-output firm that faces given prices for its outputs (Marshall 1970[1911], Edgeworth 1925a[1911]: 84–91, Fisher 1892). One particular example receiving a lot of attention was railway transportation of passengers or freight (Pigou 1912: Part II, Chapter xiii, §3, 1913, 1920, Edgeworth 1925b[1915]: 485–491, Taussig 1891, 1913, 1933). Since in a given railroad system a trip from A to B necessarily implies a trip back from B to A, the two transportation services A-to-B and B-to-A are joint products that are produced in fixed proportion – albeit one after the other. Intertemporal joint production of these transportation services is directly analogous to the traditional case of simultaneous joint production of, say, meat and hides or grain and straw. Marshall's results on joint production are therefore directly applicable.[23]

Marshall himself moved beyond the static view on joint production underlying his *Principles of Economics* (1925[1890]), and introduced an explicitly dynamic perspective in his later work *Industry and Trade* (1970[1911]), where he discusses the innovation of new techniques or structural change in the economy due to the occurrence of new industries characterised by considerable jointness of production. According to Marshall, the general tendency in the structural development of an economy is to weaken the jointness in production and to render more flexible the proportion in which the outputs are produced. The reason is as follows: With an existing technique characterised by comparatively inflexible proportions of outputs there are strong incentives to invent and innovate a new technique characterised by comparatively more flexible proportions of outputs. This is particularly obvious in the case where some of the joint outputs are discommodities. With joint production techniques with more flexible output proportions available it is then possible to produce the desired good jointly together with less of the unwanted by-product. Marshall considers cases of free disposal of unwanted outputs as 'exceptional' and concludes that firms have a strong interest in abolishing 'wasteful' techniques of production and instead introducing less 'wasteful' techniques of production. Hence, joint production is one of the sources of induced technical change.[24]

Marshall also sees a different and to some extent opposing tendency at work. He argues that the existence of by-products, which are unwanted in the first place but need to be treated somehow, contributes to the tendency of business units to grow in size.[25] The reason is that one may solve the problem of valueless by-products by inventing new products, the production of which can make use of the formerly valueless substances, or by inventing new processes which can make use of these substances in order to produce already established goods. Also, one may find new uses for the well-known and hitherto undesired by-product:

> Something which was apparently almost valueless is suddenly made the foundation of an important product, either through a new technical discovery or through the rise of a new demand. (Marshall 1970[1911]: 238–239)

Among the empirical examples which Marshall mentions is the dye and pigment industry:

> Nothing is hastily dropped; every intermediate product and every by-product is tried in various combinations, with the hope of getting some new result of value in some industrial process, or of getting at an old result by a shorter or more economical method. (Marshall 1970[1911]: 240)

Apparently, Marshall is well aware of the dynamic forces which are stimulated by joint production. Technological and organisational change, as well as the innovation of new products, may spring from the existence of joint production.[26] In this respect, Marshall's view of the role of joint production for economic dynamics is very close to Marx's view (cf. Section 6.3.2). In contrast to Marx, Marshall identifies two opposing tendencies which are initiated by the intention to avoid unwanted by-products of some joint production process, so that the overall dynamic outcome is not clear: On the one hand, there is a tendency to innovate new techniques characterised by more flexible output proportions in order to reduce the occurrence of the unwanted by-product. On the other hand, unwanted by-products may be turned into wanted goods by product or process innovations. This results in a tendency to stick to the existing technique of production and to add other techniques to the former, thus resulting in large business units operating many processes at the centre of which is the old joint production process with comparatively inflexible output proportions.

6.5 FROM PARTIAL TO GENERAL EQUILIBRIUM ANALYSIS

Alfred Marshall's conclusion from his *Principles* in a sense was that the problem of analytically coming to grips with joint production was solved: the explanation of the value of joint products follows the same general explanatory principle that holds for all goods whatsoever. But Marshall's analysis was limited by its focus on partial equilibrium. The question of how to determine the value of joint products in general equilibrium was not answered by Marshall. In the early twentieth century, after decades of dominance by Marshallian partial equilibrium analysis, economists turned again to the question of general equilibrium in general, and joint production in particular.

Marco Fanno (1999[1914]), in his formal analysis of joint production, made a first attempt to go beyond the limited scope of Marshallian partial equilibrium analysis. He fully recognised the merits of general equilibrium theory and studied an approximated version of a general equilibrium system. Within this approximation, he was concerned with the supply at joint cost in the cases of perfect competition and monopoly, in both closed and open markets. But as his contribution was only available in Italian it did not have any significant impact on developments in economics.[27]

Most influential for the mainstream of economics was Gustav Cassel's (1866–1945) stripped down version of the Walrasian equilibrium system (Cassel 1967[1918]). It stimulated the research on general equilibrium especially among some German-speaking economists in Karl Menger's[28] seminar in Vienna in the 1930s.[29] John Hicks addressed the existence of a general equilibrium in *Value and Capital* (1946[1939]: 59), which introduced the English-reading theorists to the issue of general equilibrium, by simply counting unknowns and equations.[30] It soon became obvious that the problem of the existence of a general equilibrium was much more than just demonstrating the equality of the number of equations and the number of unknowns. For instance, the Cassel system might have negative values of prices or quantities as solutions. First results concerning the existence of a general equilibrium were derived, for example by Neisser (1932), von Stackelberg (1933), Zeuthen (1933), Schlesinger (1933/34).[31] It fell to Abraham Wald to give the first rigorous existence proof of a competitive general equilibrium in a series of alternative models (Wald 1933/34, 1934/35). But his papers were of 'forbidding mathematical depth, not only in the use of sophisticated tools, but also in the complexity of the argument' (Arrow and Hahn 1971: 11). Furthermore, he employed several very specialised assumptions, for example fixed proportions among the inputs and the single output of every process of production, thus ruling out joint production.

By the 1930s it had become obvious that general equilibrium analysis was a fairly complicated matter, requiring sophisticated mathematical tools, so that it was mostly based on simplified models of the economy, which most often ruled out joint production by assumption. Two contributions are of particular importance for how joint production was dealt with in the process of forming modern general equilibrium theory: Heinrich von Stackelberg's and John von Neumann's.

6.5.1   Heinrich von Stackelberg: Analogies to the Case of Single Production

Heinrich von Stackelberg (1905–1946) gives a careful and exhaustive treatment of the issue of joint production in his *Grundlagen einer reinen Kostentheorie* ('Foundations of a Pure Theory of Costs', von Stackelberg 1932), which has attracted wide attention both among German-speaking economists and within the international economic community immediately after it appeared (Eucken 1948: 133, Hicks 1935, Möller 1949, Niehans 1992: 194, Schneider 1933, Tinbergen 1933).[32] The aim of the book is to study the role that costs of (single or joint) production play in determining the optimal production programme of a profit-maximising firm in a partial equilibrium framework, that is given the firm's cost function and the inverse demand functions for all its products. Von Stackelberg's analysis of joint production in his *Kostentheorie* essentially recovers a number of results already obtained by Alfred Marshall in his *Principles* (1925[1890]). Yet, it improves on Marshall's arguments by employing innovative analytical instruments, and it is most relevant because of its conclusions on how to deal with joint production in a general equilibrium framework.

Von Stackelberg conceptualises joint production by introducing two new analytical tools:[33] the notions of 'length' and 'direction' of the production vector (von Stackelberg 1932: 54–55):[34] if one writes the various joint output quantities of one production activity as a vector ('production vector'), then its 'length' is given by its geometrical length in output space spanned by cartesian coordinate axes and its 'direction' is given by its orientation in output space as measured by the angles enclosed between the production vector and the coordinate axes. A production vector is uniquely determined by its length and its direction. Different vectors of equal length correspond to output combinations with different proportions of the joint products; different vectors of equal direction correspond to output combinations with the same proportions of the joint products, yet different total output.

To start with, von Stackelberg studies the case of fixed output proportion. In this case, the direction of all possible production vectors is the same and constant, and they differ only in their length. The bundle of outputs jointly produced in fixed proportion can then be treated as one fictitious product – a 'packet', as von Stackelberg (1932: 55) calls them. Obviously, as costs of production and sales, and thus the entire decision problem of the firm, depend only on the number of packets produced, the determination of the firm's profit-maximising production programme is formally by no means different from the case of single production. Von Stackelberg calls this result 'the fundamental proposition of joint production' and concludes that by this proposition the case of joint production with fixed output proportion is completely reduced to the case of single production (von Stackelberg 1932: 57).

Von Stackelberg then turns to the case of joint production with flexible output proportion, in which a firm can decide not only on the length but also on the direction of the production vector, that is on its relative composition. He uses a two-stage optimising procedure, which is based on isocost curves and isorevenue curves in output space, to analyse the optimal choice of the production vector as a choice over both the length and the direction of this vector.[35] In a first step, a firm would derive the so-called 'curve of the most favourable directions' (von Stackelberg 1932: 62–63) in output space, that is, it would narrow down the set of all potential output bundles to those output combinations which allow different levels of revenue to be achieved at lowest cost respectively. In a second step, the firm would then choose the profit-maximising output combination on this curve, that is, it would choose the optimal length of production given the curve of the most favourable directions. This problem has already been solved in the context of joint production with fixed output proportion. Von Stackelberg shows that under the two assumptions that (i) the isocost curves be strictly concave,[36] and (ii) the firm is a price taker on output markets, so that the isorevenue curves are linear, this two-stage procedure always yields a result. He concludes

> that by this construction the general case of joint production [that is joint production with flexible output proportion] is reduced to the special case of joint [that is fixed] output proportion, and from this case [...] to the case of single production of one good. (von Stackelberg 1932: 64–65)

Thus, the reduction of the analysis of the most general case of joint production to the case of single production seems to be complete. Very much in the spirit of Alfred Marshall, von Stackelberg has demonstrated that the general neoclassical principle of explaining value also holds for the special case of joint production, at least in a partial equilibrium framework.

The programmatic conclusion as to how to model production in economic theory which von Stackelberg (1932: 75) draws from his analysis, is that

> [t]he theory of joint production [...] allows us to use the image of single production for all sectors of an economy. All statements about the economy, which are based on the assumption of single production, are not altered by the fact, that joint production exists as well: [...] they only need to be supplemented. This enables us to greatly simplify our analysis: we only need to deal explicitly with the problem of joint production where the direction of production itself becomes subject of the theory.

Whereas von Stackelberg was extremely careful to distinguish the two cases of joint production with fixed and with flexible output proportion throughout his analysis, this crucial distinction is hardly noticeable in his conclusive formulation of the central result. To be more explicit and precise in terms of this distinction, one may reformulate von Stackelberg's findings about joint production in two general insights:

1. All statements about a firm's profit-maximising production programme derived under the assumption of single production remain

valid under joint production *with fixed output proportion* if one replaces 'amount of output' by 'length' of the production vector, that is the number of 'packets'.

2. For joint production *with flexible output proportion*, the theory of joint production goes beyond the theory of single production in that it also makes statements about the optimal output proportion, that is the 'direction' of the production vector.

The lasting impact of von Stackelberg's analysis of joint production on economic theory consists in the first part of his conclusion, while the second part of his conclusion was mostly ignored.[37] Von Stackelberg himself contributed to the (mis-)interpretation that the main result is the first part of his programmatic conclusion by consistently downplaying the second part of the conclusion in his textbooks (von Stackelberg 1943, 1948, 1952). For instance, the chapter on joint production in *The Theory of the Market Economy* (1952) is introduced by the statement:

> From the theory of costs in simple [that is: single] production we can derive a number of rules and build up in an abbreviated form the theory of joint production. (von Stackelberg 1952: 69)

The whole exposition of joint production in this textbook is guided by von Stackelberg's stressing the analogy between a theory of joint production and the theory of single production; and at no point does von Stackelberg explicitly distinguish between the cases of fixed and flexible output proportions or discuss the issue of 'direction' of production, that is the composition of product 'packets'. In the end, von Stackelberg (1952: 71) draws the conclusion:

> We observe therefore that the analogy between simple [that is: single] production and joint production is complete.

Von Stackelberg addresses the issue of general equilibrium in his *Marktform und Gleichgewicht* (1934), where he analyses equilibrium prices and quantities under different forms of competition.[38] However, vindicated by the (mis)interpretation of the results from the *Kostentheorie* described above, this general equilibrium analysis is entirely built upon the assumption of single production:

> In the following we shall predominantly be concerned with the case of single production and exclude joint production. This is [...] justified, because it can be shown, that the fundamental problems of this kind of production can be reduced to single production. (von Stackelberg 1934: 5; our translation)

But von Stackelberg's justification is untenable for two reasons. First, as pointed out above, the final conclusion of the *Kostentheorie* comprises two parts, to the first of which von Stackelberg refers in order to justify this simplification, and the second of which clearly states that the first part is not the whole story. Strictly speaking, it is not true 'that *the* fundamental problems of [... joint] production can be reduced to single production', as von Stackelberg (1934: 5; emphasis added) claims; it is only true that *some* problems of joint production can be reduced to single production.

Second, the results in the *Kostentheorie*, and the analogy between the theory of joint production and the theory of single production, are derived from a partial equilibrium analysis. Combining several joint outputs into a composite good may be appropriate in determining the optimal production programme for one individual firm and with all prices given. But it is inappropriate for the analysis of general equilibrium when quantities *and* prices for the joint products are to be determined simultaneously from the behaviour of many firms and consumers (Buchanan 1966: 405, Malinvaud 1985: 62, footnote). For different firms may produce the joint outputs in different proportions employing different technologies, or households may consume the joint products in different proportions. In any case, the 'product packet' interpretation breaks down with more than one firm and consumers entering the analysis.

In the end, von Stackelberg's legacy from his analysis of joint production is the programmatic misinterpretation that joint production does not make a difference and, therefore, does not need to be explicitly studied. He obviously overestimated the generality of his results, not realising that they were fundamentally limited by his partial equilibrium approach and, therefore, could not be carried over to general equilibrium analysis. It is hard to understand why von Stackelberg, who had clearly recognised that a general theory of joint production covering both fixed and flexible output proportions needed to go well beyond any theory of single production in requiring additional formal elements, always in his later works restricted himself to the case of single production. One reason might be that he had very well noticed that a general theory of joint production is rather complicated. Von Stackelberg's work on joint production, and his attitude toward the issue, cannot better be captured than by his own summary of the topic in his textbook *Grundzüge der theoretischen Volkswirtschaftslehre* (von Stackelberg 1943: 26; our translation):

> The theory of joint production is an important chapter of economics. However, it is rather messy. For that reason, in the following only single production is treated in detail.

6.5.2 John von Neumann: Duality of Process Intensities and Prices

Another line of research eventually helped to achieve a considerable simplification in the mathematics of general equilibrium analysis, namely John von Neumann's (1903–1957) theory of games (von Neumann 1928a, 1928b, von Neumann and Morgenstern 1944). It emanated from a fruitful interaction of John von Neumann and Oskar Morgenstern, with their roles clearly divided between them (Leonard 1995).[39] John von Neumann was primarily interested in mathematics, in particular in set theory. His intellectual background was the Hilbert school at Göttingen, which was characterised by an 'imperialistic drive to show how mathematical formalisation could constitute a widely applicable tool of explanation' (Leonard 1995: 732). With this background von Neumann's primary focus was the analysis of parlour games, not economics (Leonard 1995: 735), and his early papers on game theory were clearly written for a mathematical audience, not for economists. Von Neumann's powerful method was complemented by Oskar Morgenstern, an 'economist, in search of a method' (Leonard 1995: 739). The principal stimulation of game theory to economic equilibrium theory has been through the use of mathematical tools developed in game theory and used in economic equilibrium theory (Arrow and Hahn 1971: 10). This transfer of methods entailed significant consequences for the analysis of joint production, which will become obvious from a detailed discussion of von Neumann's contribution.

In his paper 'Über ein ökonomisches Gleichungssystem und eine Verallgemeinerung des Browerschen Fixpunktsatzes' ('On an economic system of equations and a generalisation of Brouwer's fixed-point theorem', 1937, 1945/46),[40] von Neumann considers an economy with many different goods, each of which has a price, and many different processes of production, which are all assumed to be linear. Production coefficients describe how much of some good is used as an input or produced as an output in each process, if this process is operated at the unit level. The activity level of each process can be scaled by a factor, the so-called 'process intensity'. Von Neumann's model thus fully allows for the possibility of intermediate products, the use of capital goods, and joint production. The model is one of pure production, that is, there is no final consumption: all inputs are producible and outputs serve only as inputs in future production.[41] The economy may grow at a constant rate, and there is an interest rate.

For this model, von Neumann (1937, 1945/46) proved the existence of a balanced growth equilibrium.[42] He also demonstrated that while the equilibrium growth rate and interest rate were uniquely determined, the prices and process intensities might not be unique. By this result von Neumann had solved the problem, initially posed by Cassel (1967[1918]), of demonstrating a general equilibrium in a uniformly expanding economy. His proof is based on the idea that the overall problem can be cast as two interrelated subproblems. In the primal problem the growth rate is maximised subject to the supply requirement as specified by the process intensities. In the dual problem the interest rate is minimised subject to the profitability requirement as specified by the prices. Thus, process intensities and prices are dual variables.[43] This is an essential conceptual property of the model, because it allows for duality arguments in the existence proof. Indeed, von Neumann's proof is a generalisation of his earlier theorem which showed the existence of an equilibrium in two-person zero-sum games based on duality arguments (von Neumann 1928a, 1928b).

John von Neumann's paper was ground breaking for the further development of general equilibrium theory because of the techniques which were employed in carrying out the proof (Koopmans 1964: 356): For the first time a fixed-point theorem had been employed in an economic proof, the paper stressed the duality of prices and production intensities as well as the convexity of the production and price sets induced by returns to scale and homogeneity, and it hinted at the fundamental relationship between the notions of equilibrium in game theory and in linear programming. It had demonstrated the fruitfulness, and for some problems even the necessity, of topology – a branch of mathematics – for economic analysis. A simplified version of von Neumann's saddle-point theorem was presented a few years later by the mathematician Shizuo Kakutani (1941), and Kakutani's theorem has been the basic tool in virtually all subsequent work on problems of existence of general equilibrium (Arrow and Hahn 1971: 10). Thus, von Neumann's work opened the door for modern neoclassical general equilibrium theory (cf. Section 6.6.1).

But von Neumann's breakthrough in terms of method actually amounted to a significant regression as far as the phenomenon of joint production is concerned. While his model is sufficiently general to allow for joint production in the first place, von Neumann nevertheless sacrifices one important aspect of joint production to mathematical convenience. His method of proof at hand rests on duality of prices and production intensities, and so, because production intensities cannot be negative, he simply assumes non-negativity of prices, too. But by making this assumption, von Neumann gives up the possibility of describing negatively valued bads, which may occur as joint products of desired goods. Although this procedure may be justified by von Neumann's interest in demonstrating the existence of a growth equilibrium for an economy comprising only wanted goods, the price to pay for the mathematical convenience of duality-based methods was the omission of undesired joint outputs from the analysis.

6.6 DIFFERENT STRANDS IN CURRENT THEORY

While John von Neumann's analysis had opened the door for modern general equilibrium theory as far as methods are concerned, it had also introduced a crucial distinction between positively and negatively valued (joint) outputs. This distinction structured the subsequent development of economic theory and persists until today. As a result, there are currently different strands in modern economic theory in general, and in dealing with joint production in particular. Neoclassical and neo-Ricardian general equilibrium theories (cf. Sections 6.6.1 and 6.6.2) perform a total analysis of the economy from the perspective of neoclassical and classical value theory respectively, focusing on desired outputs. Undesired and harmful joint outputs are dealt with, in partial and in general equilibrium, by the welfare theory of externalities (cf. Section 6.6.3). And the theory of industrial organisation deals with multi-output firms, which produce several marketable goods, and the resulting market structures (cf. Section 6.6.4).

6.6.1 Neoclassical General Equilibrium Theory

By 1950 set-theoretic concepts, such as convexity of the production set and fixed-point theorems, had found their way into economics. By the aid of these powerful methods it was now possible to address the issue of general competitive equilibrium in a far more general way than had been done by the Vienna school in the 1930s. Existence theorems of greater simplicity and generality than Wald's or von Neumann's were now accessible. The first such theorems were those of Lionel McKenzie (1954)[44] and Kenneth J. Arrow and Gérard Debreu (1954).

The use of the newly developed mathematical methods created a particular kind of problem when applied to real-world economic phenomena, as had already become obvious with von Neumann's proof (cf. Section 6.5.2): For the structure of assumptions, the terms in which they are formulated, and even to some extent their substantive content have to be such that they fit into the mathematical formalism. This created a special, sometimes limited focus on the phenomena. In order to illustrate this problem and its consequences for how joint production is incorporated in modern neoclassical general equilibrium theory, we shall discuss here the assumptions about production that are employed in the existence proof of Debreu (1959), which generalises the existence proof of Arrow and Debreu (1954) and has been credited with 'the most complete systematic account of the existence conditions' (Arrow and Hahn 1971: 11).[45] We will see that even though Debreu's formalisation seems to be general enough to fully capture joint production at first glance, some of the assumptions systematically exclude important aspects of joint production.

An Arrow-Debreu economy comprises l commodities (labelled by an index h which runs from 1 to l), m consumers (labelled by an index i which runs from 1 to m), and n producers (labelled by an index j which runs from 1 to n). Let x_i be the consumption of consumer i and y_j be the output of producer j. Both x_i and y_j are vectors of the space $\mathbb{R}^l$ of all commodities. The vector of prices for all commodities $p \in \mathbb{R}^l$ may have components which are positive, zero or negative. Concerning production possibilities, it is assumed that for each production unit j there is a set Y_j of possible production plans. An element y_j of Y_j is a vector in $\mathbb{R}^l$, the h-th component of which, y_{jh}, designates the output of commodity h produced by firm j according to that plan. Inputs are treated as negative components. Apparently, this conceptualisation of production is so general as to also include the possibility of joint production, be it in fixed or in flexible proportions.

If Y denotes the set of all possible input-output schedules for the production sector as a whole (that is $y = \sum_{j=1}^{n} y_j$) and Ω denotes the non-negative orthant of $\mathbb{R}^l$, that is the set of all vectors of $\mathbb{R}^l$ with non-negative components $\Omega = \{y \in \mathbb{R}^l | y_h \geq 0 \ \forall_h\}$, then the following assumptions about the sets Y_j are made:

A1a: $0 \in Y_j$,
A1b: Y is closed and convex,
A2: $Y \cap (-Y) \subset \{0\}$,
A3: $Y \supset (-\Omega)$,

where $-Y = \{y | -y \in Y\}$. Assumption A1a says that an individual firm has the possibility of just doing nothing. Assumptions A1a together with A1b are crucial for the existence proof as they exclude increasing returns to scale. Yet, the assumption of convexity of Y is rather strong. Assumption A2 asserts that on the aggregate level production is irreversible.[46] Assumption A3 is the assumption of free disposal. It says that it is possible for all producers together to dispose of all commodities at no cost.[47] Under the assumptions specified above, and some additional assumptions concerning consumption, Debreu (1959: 84–88) showed the existence of a general competitive equilibrium. Furthermore, it has been shown already earlier that any competitive equilibrium is Pareto efficient in the absence of externalities (Arrow 1951a, Debreu 1951).

What is the relevance of these results in terms of joint production? One could argue that all the Assumptions A1–A3 are completely independent of joint production, and therefore conclude that the Arrow-Debreu formalisation is general enough to fully include the phenomenon of joint production. However, at least one aspect of joint production does indeed systematically interfere with two of the assumptions, convexity of the production set A1b and free disposal A3, namely the aspect that some of the joint outputs might be harmful bads. Actually, both assumptions are questionable when dealing with harmful joint outputs:

1. *Convexity of the production set:* A careful examination shows that with negative externalities stemming from harmful joint outputs and acting on other production processes, for example the waste water of a paper mill polluting a river and impairing the production possibilities of a downstream fishery, the total production possibility set Y may turn non-convex if the negative externalities are sufficiently strong (Baumol and Bradford 1972, Baumol and Oates 1988: 131–133, see also Baumgärtner 2000: Chapter 12). Put the other way, the convexity assumption A1b rules out harmful joint outputs that exert strong negative externalities on other production activities.

2. *Free disposal:* The assumption that an extra amount of some input or output can be disposed of at no cost is – although widely used in general equilibrium theory (Arrow and Hahn 1971: 20, Debreu 1959: 42, Mas-Colell et al. 1995: 131) – in general 'rather unrealistic' (Quirk and Saposnik 1968: 131, similarly Kurz and Salvadori 1995: 202, Pethig 1979: 12, Salvadori and Steedman 1988: 180).

   Furthermore, employing the free disposal assumption in a setting of joint production of desired goods and harmful by-products eliminates from the analysis all the problems originating from the harmful joint outputs: if a state of the economy is characterised by the fact that pollutants are emitted into the natural environment, then under the free disposal Assumption A3 another state of the economy is feasible in which consumption of economic goods is the same and there are no emissions into the environment. Hence, under the free disposal assumption environmental problems can always be solved 'in a trivial way' (Pethig 1979: 11). Formally, the effect of Assumption A3 is that in equilibrium all prices are non-negative.[48] That is, under the free disposal assumption all outputs have positive or zero value and there are no negatively valued outputs. So, the free disposal assumption, by offering a trivial, but artificial and unreal, solution to the problem of potential harm caused by joint outputs, renders the phenomenon of harmful joint products irrelevant in analytical terms.[49]

In order to overcome the serious limitation in scope which is imposed by the free disposal assumption, there have been attempts to prove the existence of a general competitive equilibrium without making use of this assumption – first in rather restricted models by McKenzie (1955, 1959, 1961)[50] and Debreu (1962); later in greater generality by Bergstrom (1976), Hart and Kuhn (1975), Nielsen (1990), Polemarchakis and Siconolfi (1993) and Shafer (1976). However, in these contributions the notion of 'equilibrium' has to be somehow modified for an equilibrium to exist. A general competitive equilibrium in the usual sense may fail to exist if free disposal is not assumed.

So, while the concepts and assumptions employed by Debreu (1959) are so general as to include important aspects of the phenomenon of joint production, in particular joint production of several desired goods, the treatment does not cover all aspects of joint production. In particular, it does not essentially cover joint production of desired goods and harmful bads.

6.6.2   Neo-Ricardian General Equilibrium Theory

While joint production is not explicitly studied in neoclassical general equilibrium theory, it is a major issue in the strand of literature that goes back to Sraffa (1960).[51] Piero Sraffa (1898–1983) had made a name for himself as a critic of Marshallian partial equilibrium analysis by showing that its logical foundations, the notions of a firm equilibrium and of a supply curve, are fragile and that the supply and demand curves are not independent of each other (Sraffa 1925, see Schefold 1989: 3). In the following, Sraffa focused on studying general equilibrium. The intense preoccupation with David Ricardo's theory, as the editor of Ricardo's works and correspondence, had a very stimulating impact on Sraffa (Kurz 1996: 173). His main interest became the consistent reformulation of the classical theory of value and distribution. The result of this research is *Production of Commodities by Means of Commodities* (1960) – Sraffa's main work. The book stimulated a renewed interest in the Ricardian theory of value and distribution and served as the starting point of what is today known as the neo-Ricardian school of general equilibrium theory.

In *Production of Commodities*, Sraffa takes a classical position. It is assumed that the income distribution problem is solved prior to and independently of the value problem (Pasinetti 1977: 84–85). In that perspective, the real wage rate and the rate of profit are not prices like any other commodity prices, as in a neoclassical perspective, but distribution parameters. Since the determination of distribution occurs prior to the analysis of the dynamic development of the economy, current output is taken as fixed in the analysis of distribution (Eatwell 1977: 62). As a consequence, the demand side is of no importance in Sraffa's system (Faber 1986a: 49). Therefore, demand is modelled in a very elementary way, namely it is assumed to be fixed and given by a vector of the 're-quirements for use' of all goods.[52] Then the prices of all commodities and the rate of profit can be determined from the size and composition of the output, the employed technique and the exogenously given real wage rate. The production side of the model is set up by assuming that there are a certain number of commodities and a certain number of production processes, such that a vector of inputs is transformed into a vector of outputs. A matrix of constants describes the input requirements in the production of all outputs. Labour is the only primary factor of production, all other inputs are producible commodities. It is further assumed that the system is in 'a self-replacing state' (Sraffa 1960: 4), that is in a steady state (or long-term) equilibrium.[53]

In Sraffa's *Production of Commodities*, joint production is extensively analysed. For Sraffa,

> [t]he interest of Joint Products does not lie so much in the familiar examples of wool and mutton, or wheat and straw, as in its being the genus of which Fixed Capital is the leading species. And it is mainly as an introduction to the subject of fixed capital that the [...] intricacies of joint products find their place. (Sraffa 1960: 63)

So, the analysis of joint production in *Production of Commodities* is 'in the main a preliminary to the discussion of Fixed Capital and Land' (Sraffa 1960: 43, footnote 1). Sraffa is well aware of the two most obvious problems that any classical theory of value faces in the presence of joint production. The first is that a pure labour theory of value cannot make any reasonable statements about the individual values of joint products:

> For in the case of joint-products there is no obvious criterion for apportioning the labour among individual products, and indeed it seems doubtful whether it makes any sense to speak of a *separate* quantity of labour as having gone to produce one of a number of *jointly* produced commodities. (Sraffa 1960: 56, Sraffa's emphasis)

The second problem is that the proportion in which some commodities are jointly produced together need not coincide with the proportion in which they are required for use. This problem has been noted from the very beginning. It has made Adam Smith introduce the 'rule of free goods' (cf. Section 6.2.1), but only with Frederik Zeuthen (1933: 15, cf. Section 2.2.1) has the underlying implicit assumption, that there are fewer processes of production than commodities produced, been given up.

Sraffa's conception of joint production from the beginning is that of not only one process of joint production but of a system of joint production processes. In particular, Sraffa always considers square systems of production, that is systems for which the number of production processes equals the number of commodities produced. The implicit justification is that with the number of production processes being smaller than the number of commodities, the commodities cannot be produced in the proportion in which they are required for use (Schefold 1983: 322). And if the number of processes exceeds the number of commodities, prices are overdetermined.

In the latter case a choice has to be made as to which processes to operate and which processes not to operate within a system of production. As a matter of fact, not all processes are necessary in order to produce the commodities in the proportions in which they are required for use. However, the choice of an efficient subset of production processes from an overdetermined system, while being trivial in a system of single production processes, is highly non-trivial in a system of joint production processes. Sraffa himself only devotes one and a half pages to this problem (Sraffa 1960: 86–87). Yet, the literature on the so-called choice-of-techniques problem stimulated by Sraffa's remarks is vast and still growing.[54] In essence, this literature shows that Sraffa's argument on this point cannot be sustained (Bidard 1984, Salvadori 1982, 1984, 1985).

There is another problem, which is related to the choice-of-techniques problem. With no substitution possibilities in consumption and a certain number of fixed coefficient techniques on the production side, the proportions in which commodities are required for use may not be matched by the proportions in which they are produced, even with the number of processes being equal to the number of commodities (Sraffa 1960: 47). As a consequence, there may be negative solutions for the prices. Sraffa (1960: 44) proposes that 'while the equations may be formally satisfied by negative solutions for the unknowns, only those methods of production are practicable which, in the conditions actually prevailing [...] do not involve other than positive prices' (Sraffa 1960: 44). Later work has specified this claim in the sense that prices in a square system of production are positive if and only if all processes are operated in the system (Lippi 1977, Filippini 1977, Filippini and Filippini 1982). Hence, negative prices in square systems are associated with inefficient processes, the operation of which is required in order to dispose of some products. This has led to employing the assumption of free disposal in existence proofs of cost-minimising square systems (Saucier 1984).[55] With free disposal, all prices will be non-negative. However, even under the assumption of free disposal a cost-minimising square system of production may not exist (Bidard 1984, Duménil and Lévy 1984, Lévy 1984, Salvadori 1982, 1984, 1985).[56] Therefore, non-square systems need to be studied as well.

As already mentioned, Sraffa's main interest in joint production is the preoccupation with fixed capital and land. Suppose that one single commodity is produced by the aid of a capital good. At the end of the production period the outputs of the production process are the amount produced of the commodity and the (deteriorated) capital good. In that sense, the existence of durable capital goods implies joint production over time.

With fixed capital the choice of techniques can be seen as a choice of how much and what kind of capital should be employed. One can show that in a system of production in which capital goods are employed in all industries, the prices of the new, not yet deteriorated, capital goods and of resources are positive for any rate of profit between zero and some maximal value (Baldone 1980, Schefold 1978a, 1980a, Varri 1980). In contrast, prices for older, already deteriorated capital goods may become negative. Negative prices of old capital goods can be avoided if the production processes, in which they are employed, are no longer operated beyond a certain point in time. This point in time has to be determined according to the choice-of-techniques criterion. This means that the economic life-span of a capital good differs from its physical life-span and, in particular, depends on the distribution in the economy. The choice of techniques from production processes with fixed capital, thus, is a choice of the optimal (economic) life-span of capital goods (Schefold 1983: 327). However, these neat properties of systems with fixed capital do not hold in general joint production systems.[57]

To sum up, while the neo-Ricardian school has produced a considerable amount of knowledge about joint production systems, their scope is restricted in several ways:

1. The demand side is modelled in such an elementary way as to include only goods which are required for use in exogenously given and fixed proportions. This focuses attention, in a very classical spirit, on wanted goods which serve basic needs but does, in particular, not allow for unwanted bads.

2. Since there is no subjective valuation of commodities other than the crude concept of 'requirements for use', negative prices in a

Sraffian system of production are not what they are usually taken to be, namely an indicator of negative subjective value. Instead, negative prices in Sraffian systems of production indicate the inefficient use of techniques.

3. The assumption of general free disposal is widely used by now in Sraffian analysis (for example by Brägelmann 1991, Schefold 1978b, 1988, 1989). While this assumption is sufficient to ensure that no price is negative in a cost-minimising system (Steedman 1976, Schefold 1978b, 1980b, Salvadori 1985), it is 'in general [...] not a realistic assumption' (Salvadori and Steedman 1988: 180).[58]

For these reasons, the scope of the Sraffian approach to joint production seems to be too restricted to address in an encompassing manner the issue of joint production of economic goods and environmental damages.[59]

6.6.3   Welfare Theory of Externalities

From the preceding sections it has become obvious that while modern general equilibrium theory has found a highly general way of dealing with the joint production of *desired goods*, joint production of *desired goods and harmful bads* is not explicitly an issue. This issue has been addressed in a different context during the same time period, namely from the perspective of welfare analysis. While general equilibrium theory as presented in this chapter so far is mainly positive theory, welfare analysis is motivated by a normative concern, namely the question of Pareto efficiency. The foundations of modern welfare analysis were laid by Arthur Cecil Pigou (1877–1959), Marshall's pupil and successor to the chair of political economy at Cambridge. He addressed the question how judicious government intervention can increase welfare in his monograph *Wealth and Welfare* (1912). In 1920, under the new title *The Economics of Welfare* and greatly elaborated, this became Pigou's major work and established welfare economics as a branch of economics (Niehans 1990: 320).

Pigou's basic condition for the efficient allocation of resources is the equality of their marginal net products in all different uses. Whenever this condition is violated, welfare can be raised by a suitable reallocation. The key to Pigou's contribution is the distinction between private and social marginal products. If the two coincide, the free interplay of self-interest tends, according to Pigou, to bring about an efficient allocation of resources if perfect competition prevails. However, Pigou notes that in reality private and social net products often diverge. The most important source of divergencies between the two are external costs and benefits, that is, costs or benefits that accrue to society but not to those who cause them.[60] An obvious and important example is the pollution of the natural environment by joint outputs of production, for example sulphur dioxide, heavy metals or CFCs. Pigou notes that activities with external costs ('negative externalities') would tend to be oversupplied in equilibrium as compared with the social optimum. His solution to the problem consists in a government intervention in order to close the gap between social and private marginal products, for example by suitable taxation.[61]

Pigou, being Marshall's pupil, studied *partial* equilibrium welfare analysis, by identifying specific sources of market failure in individual markets or industries. While this contribution is fundamental for applied welfare economics up to the present day, for instance in the field of environmental and resource economics (Baumol and Oates 1988, Dasgupta and Heal 1979, Hanley et al. 1997, Hartewick and Olewiler 1998, Kolstad 2000, Siebert 2004 and Tietenberg 2003), progress in the *general* equilibrium approach to welfare analysis beyond the pioneering contribution of Pareto (1896/97) only became accessible after general equilibrium theory had made substantial progress in the 1950s (cf. Section 6.6.1).

Since Pigou's analysis, it was known that with private goods efficiency requires that all individuals pay the same prices, and these prices must be equal both to the marginal amounts individuals are willing to pay and to the marginal costs of production. Paul Samuelson (1954), who addressed the field of welfare economics from a general equilibrium point of view, derived an analogous efficiency condition for the allocation of public goods in the framework of a highly aggregated general equilibrium model comprising private and public goods. The efficiency condition states that (i) the marginal amounts different individuals are willing to pay for an additional unit of the public good must be added over individuals, and (ii) the supply must be such that this sum is equal to the marginal cost of supplying an additional unit of the good.[62] These conditions imply that different individuals, who may be characterised by different willingness to pay for the public good, in general, have to pay different prices for the same public good. Whereas efficiently allocated private goods have the same price for individually different quantities consumed, public goods provide to all individuals the same quantity, but at different prices.

Samuelson's contribution initiated rapid further developments in welfare analysis (Niehans 1990: 437). One development started from the observation that instances of pure public goods are hard to find. In most cases a given supply cannot satisfy an unlimited number of consumers. Though the two polar cases of pure public and pure private goods may be analytically convenient, they turned out to make the application difficult. In a more general case, consumption by individual A was recognised as having some external effect on the utility of B. The theory of public goods thus became integrated into the more general theory of externalities with its numerous extensions and applications. Within the theory of externalities, joint outputs are typically modelled only in an implicit way, namely by representing their impact on some consumer or producer (cf. Section 2.2.1). With environmental quality as a public good, environmental damage caused by harmful joint outputs can then be considered as a public bad.

The two strands of literature on general equilibrium on the one hand and on externalities and public goods on the other were linked in the concept of Lindahl equilibrium (Roberts 1987: 198–200). The concept is due to Erik Lindahl (1891–1960), who had developed the idea in his doctoral dissertation *Die Gerechtigkeit der Besteuerung* (Lindahl 1919). In its modern formulation, Lindahl equilibrium has come to play a benchmark role in the study of economies with public goods, externalities and government expenditure which parallels the role played by Walrasian competitive equilibrium in the analysis of economies where these factors are absent (Roberts 1987: 198). The concept solves the problem of determining the amounts of public goods to be provided by adapting the price system of a market economy in such a way that the efficient allocation is the outcome of voluntary market activities under private property rights. The central idea is that in equilibrium each individual faces personalised prices for the consumption of the public goods. In equilibrium, these prices are such that everyone demands the same levels of the public goods. Since each individual buys and consumes the total production of the public goods, the prices to producers are the sum of the prices paid by consumers.

Foley (1970) later provided the basic general equilibrium treatment of Lindahl's idea in the framework of an Arrow-Debreu private ownership economy with both private and pure public goods where there are zero endowments of public goods, these goods are never used as inputs, and production is characterised by constant returns to scale.[63] In order to prove the existence of a Lindahl equilibrium he built upon Arrow's (1970) insight that externalities, and public goods in particular, can be viewed as a phenomenon of missing markets. To illustrate this approach, consider a public goods economy with I consumers, M private goods and N public goods. Then there is an associated, hypothetical economy with I consumers, $M + IN$ private goods and no public goods, in which each of the N public goods of the original economy is replaced by a collection of I private goods, each of which is of interest to, and consumable by, only one consumer and which together are joint products in production.

Walras equilibria of the associated hypothetical economy correspond to Lindahl equilibria of the original economy, with a parallel correspondence between the feasible allocations in the two economies and between the Pareto optima. It is then apparent that Lindahl equilibria are Pareto efficient and that any optimum can be supported as an equilibrium with a reallocation of resources.

Although Lindahl's original exposition of this equilibrium concept treats it as having both normative and positive value, the concept – as opposed to Walrasian general competitive equilibrium – is commonly not taken as having any predictive power in the description of actual economic action (Roberts 1987: 198). The usual complaint against the Lindahl solution of allocating public goods is that there would be no reason for an individual to take the Lindahl prices as given: there are incentives to hide one's true preferences for the public good and instead act as a free-rider.[64] Furthermore, the assumption of price-taking behaviour in equilibrium is questionable since there are only a finite number of participants in the market. And while for standard Walrasian equilibrium the case of 'large numbers' of individuals is very appealing, this intuition does not hold any more for public goods.[65] According to Roberts (1987: 200) all these problems give 'further reason for doubting the empirical relevance of Lindahl equilibrium'.

6.6.4 Theory of Multi-Product Firms and Industries

As described in the previous sections, joint production as an explicit issue has – with few exceptions, most notably in the neo-Ricardian strand of literature (cf. Section 6.6.2) – disappeared from the agenda of economic theory since the 1930s (although important aspects of the phenomenon are covered, to some extent, by more general theories as described in Sections 6.6.1 and 6.6.3). In the 1970s, the phenomenon is met with a renewed interest and explicitly studied in the field of industrial organisation. At the origin of this strand of literature are the following questions:

- What is the profit-maximising production programme of a multi-output firm, that is, amount produced and price set for each of their outputs, depending on their technology (in terms of economies of scale and scope) and different forms of interaction with competing firms in the same industry?

- What influence do multi-product firms exert on the market structure within an industry, and on the efficiency of market allocation?

- Based on these insights, what is the optimal policy to regulate multi-product firms and industries?

Generally, only marketable (that is positively valued) outputs are considered in this research strand, and the analysis is focused on partial equilibrium on the respective output markets.

Pioneering contributions in this field were the works of Baumol (1977), Panzar and Willig (1977a, 1977b, 1981) and Willig (1979). Further contributions have been made by Beckenstein (1975), Caves et al. (1980), Hasenkamp (1976) and Sharkey and Telser (1978).[66] The theoretical side has been most fully expounded by Baumol et al. (1988). By now the issue of multi-product firms and industries has found its way into many textbooks on industrial organisation (for example Tirole 1988).

6.7   SUMMARY AND CONCLUSION

Summing up the historical survey of Sections 6.2 through 6.6, what has been the role of joint production for the construction of modern economic theory? The analysis of joint production played an important role in the earlier stages of the development of economic theory, by serving as a catalyst for the abandonment of classical value theory and the establishment of neoclassical value theory (Kurz 1986). But thereafter, it was seen more as a troublesome obstacle, which was at odds with the newly developed mathematical tools. Today, the analysis of joint production as an explicit issue is – with few exceptions – not on the agenda of economics any more. While various economic theories capture particular dimensions of joint production, there exists no encompassing and general theory of joint production.

6.7.1   From 1776 until 1890: Joint Production as a Stimulus for the Development of Neoclassical Value Theory

The classical economists, while acknowledging that joint production is a ubiquitous and important phenomenon, recognised that an explanation of the value of joint products was not possible using the standard methods of classical value theory but required special patterns of explanation (Smith 1976[1776]: 234–235). Joint products were viewed – from an analytical point of view – as a 'peculiar case' (Mill 1965[1848]: 569). The analysis of joint production made obvious the shortcomings of the classical approach and, thus, 'played a significant role in the gradual abandonment of the classical approach to the theory of value' (Kurz 1986: 2).

The analysis of desired joint products, such as wool and mutton, as well as the analysis of undesired joint products, such as environmentally harmful wastes and emissions, also suggested what was needed to over-come the shortcomings of the classical approach: elements of utility and demand (Jevons 1911[1879], Marx 1959[1894], von Thünen 1921[1826]). The challenge therefore was to integrate the production side and the de-mand side in an encompassing explanation of value, leading to a so-called 'neoclassical' value theory.

With Alfred Marshall's *Principles of Economics* (1925[1890]) this task was completed, at least for partial equilibrium analysis. Marginalism ap-peared to be a general principle for the determination of equilibrium and value. Marshall (1925[1890]: 389) argued that this also held for joint pro-duction, and demonstrated how to determine the price of joint products in a partial equilibrium analysis. The conclusion was that joint pro-duction no longer needs to be considered a peculiar case which deserves special methods for the explanation of value. Instead, the explanation of value of joint products follows the same general explanatory principle that holds for all goods whatsoever (Marshall 1925[1890]: 395).

6.7.2   From 1890 until the 1950s: Joint Production as a Troublesome Obstacle for the Development of Neoclassical General Equilibrium Theory

As Marshall's analysis was in a partial equilibrium framework, the ques-tion of how to deal with joint production in a general equilibrium analy-sis remained open. The research programme after Marshall's *Principles*, hence, was guided by the question of how to extend neoclassical value theory from partial to general equilibrium analysis. The analysis of joint production did not play any significant role in this programme. Instead, the development of modern general equilibrium theory has been mainly stimulated by the development of new mathematical tools. Joint pro-duction was a troublesome obstacle for this development, because the multifaceted richness of the phenomenon was at odds with the newly developed formal concepts and methods.

Heinrich von Stackelberg (1932: 57, 60) demonstrated in a partial equi-librium framework that while the analysis of joint production in fixed proportions (interpreted as the production of 'packets') is formally equiv-alent to the analysis of single production, the general case of joint produc-tion in flexible proportions goes beyond any theory of single production in that it requires special formal methods even in a partial equilibrium analysis (for example the 'curve of the most favourable directions'). Von Stackelberg (1943: 26) recognised that, as a result, a general theory of joint production would be 'rather messy'. Also, he misinterpreted his results by concluding that joint production does not make a difference and, therefore, does not need to be explicitly studied. Although his results were obtained in a partial equilibrium analysis, he employed them as a fundamental assumption in his general equilibrium analysis (von Stackelberg 1934), where he restricted himself to single production.

John von Neumann (1937, 1945/46) pioneered modern general equilibrium theory. He also covered joint production, but explicitly sacrificed one important aspect of the phenomenon to the mathematical convenience of a particular method. His method rests on duality of prices and process intensities. Because the latter must not be negative, von Neumann simply assumed that the former are non-negative as well. That is, in order to apply a certain formal method, assumptions about the phenomena under study have been made to fit into the formalism. This discarded the fundamental and important aspect that joint outputs may be negatively valued. Again, joint production had turned out to be a troublesome obstacle which was in the way of applying some newly developed mathematical tools to economic theory.

Von Neumann's example of discarding the potentially negative character of joint outputs by assumption set the stage for modern general equilibrium theory. Following von Neumann's lead, Arrow and Debreu (1954) simply assumed prices to be non-negative in their analysis of general competitive equilibrium, which became foundational for neoclassical general equilibrium theory. Debreu (1959) was later a little bit more subtle in that he did not simply assume prices to be non-negative, but assumed free disposal, which implies non-negative prices. The assumption of free disposal is also widely used in the neo-Ricardian strand of general equilibrium theory.

6.7.3 Current State of Affairs: Many Theories, but No General Theory of Joint Production

With the completion of the 'marginalist revolution' and, again, after the establishment of general equilibrium theory, the case of joint production was mistakenly claimed to fall completely within the scope of some more general principle of explanation. Our discussion has revealed that this claim cannot be sustained.

Modern neoclassical general equilibrium theory purports that the assumptions and concepts employed are so general that they also encompass the phenomenon of joint production. Yet, as argued in Section 6.6.1, this claim may be questioned, in particular for the case of harmful joint outputs. But general equilibrium analysis does indeed provide a number of important insights that also hold under joint production, in particular, if all joint outputs are positively valued: (i) it specifies the conditions for existence and the properties of a general competitive equilibrium, and

(ii) it shows that a general competitive equilibrium is Pareto efficient if there are no (negative or positive) externalities.

The aspect that some of the joint outputs may be harmful bads was addressed in the framework of welfare analysis. Typically, the harmful joint outputs are not explicitly part of the models, but only implicitly insofar as their negative impact on other producers or households is modelled in the form of a negative externality or as a damage to a public good. In this case, the market equilibrium is no longer Pareto efficient. Welfare theory has suggested mechanisms to internalise such externalities, for example by Pigouvian taxes, thereby re-establishing the Pareto efficiency of the equilibrium. These insights form the working basis for current environmental and resource economics and lead to detailed suggestions for how to solve environmental problems. In the case of negative externalities exhibiting the character of public bads, however, this mechanism can only be established under very restrictive and unrealistic assumptions. In particular, every individual is assumed to reveal a personalised willingness to pay for the absence of the public bad, which is, in general, not incentive compatible. Each individual has an incentive to just free ride on the contributions of others to solving the public bad problem.

In summary, economic thinking has produced many interesting, relevant and applicable results concerning the existence, efficiency and other properties of economic equilibrium under different forms of joint production. But there are at least two major gaps in the current economics of joint production:

1. There are satisfying explanations for both (i) joint production of several desired goods (in the general competitive equilibrium theory à la Arrow-Debreu and in the partial equilibrium theory of industrial organisation) and (ii) joint production of desired goods and harmful bads (in the welfare theory of externalities). But both of these approaches presuppose an a priori knowledge of the character of outputs, that is whether they are positively or negatively valued, instead of determining it endogenously from the analysis. In the former approach, the positive character of the outputs is artificially imposed, for example by assuming free disposal in general equilibrium analysis or by limiting the analysis to solely the marketable outputs of a firm in industrial organisation; in the latter approach the negative character goes into the theory as a basic assumption. What is lacking is a general and encompassing theory of joint production that does not simply assume, or impose, the character of the outputs as positively or negatively valued, but endogenously derives this character.

2. In the case of harmful pollutants causing public negative externalities – a case that is characteristic for some of the most pressing
environmental problems of our time (for example the ozone hole,
climate change or biodiversity loss) and therefore is of utmost importance for environmental policy – economics essentially leaves
us without any operational result: while there are solutions (for
example Lindahl equilibrium) that work in theory, it is also clear
that they will not work in practice due to incentive incompatibility.

We will address both of these major gaps in this book. Concerning the
first gap, in Chapter 8 we will present a detailed analysis of how the character of joint outputs as being positively or negatively valued emerges in
a particular context, and how it may change over time. And concerning
the second gap, in Part III we will develop an alternative to the Pareto
efficiency criterion, based on the ethical concept of responsibility, to give
us normative guidance on how to act individually and collectively in the
face of complex environmental problems.

NOTES

1.   Needless to say, this presentation of 200 years of economic thinking on joint
production cannot be more than a rough sketch. Baumgärtner (2000: Chapters 5–7)
gives a more detailed account of this subject and contains many references to the
relevant literature. Kurz (1986) provides an excellent analysis of classical and early
neoclassical thinking on joint production. Ekelund and Thompson (2001) and West
(1994) discuss the issue with a focus on supply of, and demand for, joint products.
Blaug (1996) and Niehans (1990) provide encompassing treatments of the general
history of economic theory.
2.   Mill (1965[1848]: 436) claimed that '[h]appily, there is nothing in the laws of
value which remains for the present or any future writer to clear up; the theory of
the subject is complete'.
3.   Niehans (1990: 128) considers Mill's 'neat analysis of the prices of joint products'
as an illustration of how powerful the supply-and-demand-approach to value is as
opposed to the classical cost-of-production-approach. Mountifort Longfield (1802–
1894) had basically anticipated Mill's line of argument in his *Lectures on Political
Economy* (1971[1834]).
4.   Mill does not suggest any justification of this strong assumption, which is critical
for his argument.
5.   Von Thünen (1921[1826]: 58–60 and §§15–16) makes a considerable effort to provide empirical estimates of how productive dung is as a production factor in the
growing of different types of crops, such as wheat, rye, barley and oats.
6.   This idea is taken up today, under the heading of 'industrial ecology' (Ayres and
Ayres 2002, Hardy and Graedel 2002), as the recognition of environmental problems
caused by waste by-products has stressed the importance of establishing closed material cycles in the economy. On a local scale, firms do indeed already cooperate in
so-called 'eco-industrial parks' in such a way that the waste by-product of one firm
is used as a productive input by another firm (Strebel 1981, Dyckhoff 1996b).

7.   This assumption is untenable, as we know from the discussion throughout this book. As we have demonstrated in Chapter 3, the laws of thermodynamics imply that all industrial production is necessarily joint production (cf. Proposition 3.1). This is not to deny that there may be, in addition to the minimum amount of joint products required by the laws of thermodynamics, a considerable amount of joint products due to inefficiency, as also analysed in Chapter 3.

8.   Another way of reducing the amount of waste by-products and thus efficiently employing the given capital consists in the prevention of their occurrence (Marx 1959[1894]: 103).   According to Marx, this goal can be achieved by technological progress or by using raw materials of a higher quality as an input to production.

9.   An implicit assumption underlying Marx's reasoning is that the waste by-products are close substitutes of the raw or auxiliary materials that serve as inputs to production in the same or in different processes. In particular, Marx has in mind examples from the chemical industry and the textile industry where raw materials are not completely used up in the process of production and, thus, end up as waste by-products.

10.   In Chapter 8, we provide a detailed analysis of this interesting mode of dealing with originally undesired joint products. The case studies in Part IV provide illustrations from the paper, chlorine, cement and sulphur industries.

11.   This optimistic view was shared by many of Marx's contemporaries. For example, A.W. von Hofmann (1818–1892), one of the co-founders of the German Chemical Society and founder of the Royal College of Chemistry in London, argued that

> [i]n an ideal chemical factory [...] there is strictly speaking no waste but only products (main and secondary products). The better a real factory makes use of its waste, the closer [...] it gets to its ideal, the bigger is the profit. (von Hofmann 1866; quoted after Faber et al. 1996b: 272)

12.   The first edition of the *Theory of Political Economy* appeared in 1871 and was soon followed by an enlarged second edition in 1879. It is interesting that all the material of relevance for this survey, that is the sections on joint production, disutility and negative value, had been prepared by Jevons only for the second edition (Jevons 1911[1879]: xiii).

13.   Jevons realises that others had already reached the same conclusion. He refers explicitly to Mill and his treatment of joint production in Book III, Chapter xvi, 'Some Peculiar Cases of Value', which Jevons (1911[1879]: 197) considers to be 'one of the most interesting chapters of his *Principles of Political Economy*'.

14.   Gossen's (1854) Second Law is the first formulation of a marginal principle of allocation and had been published twenty years before the works of Jevons, Walras or Menger (1870–1874), who are today considered as the essential contributors to the 'marginalist revolution'. Jevons claims that he had developed this idea independently of Gossen. In the preface to the second edition of the *Theory*, which appeared in 1879 and contained for the first time the sections on joint production, he notes:

> The coincidence, however, between the essential ideas of Gossen's system and my own is so striking, that I desire to state distinctly [...] that I never saw nor so much as heard any hint of the existence of Gossen's book before August 1878. (Jevons 1911[1879]: xxxvi)

15.   Besides marginal utility of outputs, Jevons needs to assume technical relationships between inputs and outputs for a full explanation of equilibrium prices.

16.   Jevons' treatment of *discommodities* was not undisputed. For instance, Irving Fisher (1965[1906]: 120) criticised Jevons on the grounds that discommodities are never of great importance and need receive no special attention (Kurz 1986: 29; footnote 25).

17.   Jevons had already studied the connection between joint production and the environmental impact of production in his earlier work *The Coal Question* (1865).

18.   Many of Jevons' examples of joint outputs as environmentally harmful substances had already been described by Marx.

19.   See note XXI in the mathematical appendix to Marshall's *Principles of Economics* (1925[1890]).

20.   See note 6 on page 44 for Marshall's definition of *joint products*.

21.   Marshall's method is essentially identical to that suggested a little earlier by Hans von Mangoldt (1824–1868) in his *Grundriss der Volkswirtschaftslehre* (von Mangoldt 1863).

22.   In fact, its title established the term 'Economics' for the field that used to be called 'Political Economy' before Marshall's *Principles* (Niehans 1990: 239).

23.   The discussion of rail pricing in terms of joint production was to some extent obscured by the fact that prices in railroad systems are not only determined by technology (that is joint production) and demand, but that monopoly power and price discrimination are also relevant determinants of prices. See Ekelund and Thompson (2001: Section 2) for a detailed analysis of this discussion and its relationship to the current discussion of 'peak-load-pricing'.

24.   This argument should be compared to the argument of von Thünen (cf. Section 6.3.1) who also considers free disposal of unwanted outputs as impossible, but then concludes that the process should be located such that its otherwise unwanted by-product can be utilised as an input by a nearby process. This is a static view which ignores the possibility of technical change.

25.   Already Charles Babbage (1986[1832]: 217) had argued that large firms have an advantage over small firms because they can process and handle otherwise useless joint products through 'the union of two trades in one factory, which otherwise might have been separated'. For example, while small slaughter houses only process the meat and the hides of cattle and have to dispose of all the rest as waste, larger slaughter houses can also process in a profitable manner by-products such as the hoofs of the animals.

26.   Kurz (1986: 32–33) points out that 'by far [the ...] most important work in the [... nineteenth] century' about the treatment of unwanted joint outputs from manufacturing as well as the product and process innovations induced by them is P.L. Simmonds' *Waste Products and Undeveloped Substances* (1873). In some 500 pages it contains innumerable empirical examples of joint production and innovations which were induced by unwanted joint outputs.

27.   Fanno's contribution was recognised, though, in the strand of literature that goes back to Piero Sraffa (1960); see Section 6.6.2.

28.   The mathematician Karl Menger (1902–1985) was the son of Carl Menger (1840–1921).

29.   For instance, John von Neumann knew the Walrasian system only in its Cassel version (Weintraub 1983: 4–5).

30.   Already Marshall had argued, in his sparse comments on general equilibrium (1925[1890]: note XXI in the mathematical appendix), that a general equilibrium would exist if there were exactly as many unknowns as determining equations.

31.   For a carefully written and very readable historical overview of the evolution of general equilibrium theory from 1930 to 1954 see Weintraub (1983). Arrow and Hahn (1971: 1–15) give another useful historical account. A presentation which combines the historical perspective with an analysis of the formal structure of (classical and neoclassical) general equilibrium theories is that of Walsh and Gram (1980).

32.   For a detailed review and critical appraisal of von Stackelberg's contribution to cost theory under joint production see Baumgärtner (2001).

33.   Von Stackelberg presents a systematic and elaborated taxonomy of single and joint production in his textbooks (1943: 25–26, 1948: 31–32, 1952: 29). By 'joint production' (in German: 'verbundene Produktion') von Stackelberg (1932: 5) denotes

'the production of several kinds of products' within one firm, irrespective of whether they are necessarily jointly produced or not. This includes the case that a firm operates several completely independent production processes each of which yields one single output ('parallel production'). Another special case of joint production is that one of the outputs cannot be produced without jointly producing another one ('linked production', in German: 'Kuppelproduktion').

34.   These and all subsequent translations from von Stackelberg (1932) are ours.

35.   Isocost curves and isorevenue curves had originally been introduced, and also applied to the analysis of the decision problem of a multi-output firm, by Irving Fisher (1892).

36.   The assumption of strict concavity of the isocost curves amounts to saying that average output bundles are less costly to produce than extreme output bundles. In modern language, one would say that *economies of scope* prevail (Panzar and Willig 1981).

37.   One early example is the influential textbook on production theory by Erich Schneider (1934), one of the co-founders of the Econometric Society, who introduces his text with the statement that the theory of joint production poses no fundamental problem since von Stackelberg had shown how a theory of joint production could be reduced to the theory of single production in such a way that all propositions about single production can be as well applied to joint production. And Hans Möller, who was von Stackelberg's research assistant in Berlin, judges that

> [t]he decisive contribution of von Stackelberg to cost theory consists in showing that the theoretical statements about costs under single production can be applied as well under joint production. (Möller 1949: 402; our translation)

38.   Von Stackelberg had early on recognised the necessity of carrying out general equilibrium analyses (Möller 1949: 409). Immediately after completing the *Grundlagen einer reinen Kostentheorie*, von Stackelberg had studied the general equilibrium price theory of Gustav Cassel (von Stackelberg 1933). In his essay on problems of imperfect competition (von Stackelberg 1938) he criticises the Anglo-Saxon approach to price theory, which goes back to Alfred Marshall and prefers partial over total analysis. According to von Stackelberg (1938: 95–96) partial analysis has the drawback that it neglects important influences on price determination which are due to the interaction with other markets. He thus concludes that partial analysis has to be based on and controlled by a general equilibrium analysis.

39.   Leonard (1995) presents a detailed historical account of the emergence of game theory 1928–1944.

40.   For a detailed account of the genesis of von Neumann's (1937, 1945/46) paper see Weintraub (1983: 12–13 and 15), who considers this contribution 'the single most important article in mathematical economics' (Weintraub 1983: 13).

41.   Von Neumann (1937, 1945/46: 2) suggests that consumption of goods takes place only through the processes of production which include the necessities of life consumed by workers and employees. In other words, he assumes that labour is paid for at the minimum rate necessary for survival, wages are included in production inputs and all income in excess of the necessities of life will be reinvested. This resembles Sraffa's (1960) general equilibrium model (cf. Section 6.6.2), in which the demand side is also only contained in a very basic form, namely by assuming a vector of 'requirements for use' for all goods. This crude modelling of the demand side has led to the assessment that von Neumann proposes a classical theory of value (Kurz and Salvadori 1993). For a more differentiated appraisal as to whether von Neumann was more a classical or more a neoclassical economist see Leonard (1995: 735–736).

42.   See Baumgärtner (2000: 130–133 and Appendix 7A) for a more technical discussion of von Neumann's contribution.

43. This also becomes obvious from the equilibrium conditions: two of them are non-negativity conditions (for process intensities and prices), and two are complementary slackness conditions for the dual inequality systems.

44. McKenzie (1954) ruled out joint production by assumption, but he pointed out that this assumption may be relaxed and joint production allowed (McKenzie 1954: 158–159). In a later paper (McKenzie 1959), he worked out this more general proof, which also relaxes the free-disposal assumption (disposal is possible but not necessarily free) but is restricted in several other aspects (by assuming constant returns to scale and that the economy is 'irreducible').

45. Niehans (1990: 490) considers the Arrow-Debreu specification of an economy for a Walrasian general equilibrium system 'the neatest and most compact model of an economy since Cantillon's Tableau Economique in terms of land, and vastly richer and more general'. As a matter of history, Debreu's book *Theory of Value* (1959) became 'the bible of the new mathematical economics based on topology' (Niehans 1990: 491).

46. Actually, Assumption A2 captures *temporal* irreversibility but is too weak to capture *thermodynamic* irreversibility (Baumgärtner 2005).

47. This assumption is somewhat weaker than $Y_j \supset (-\Omega)$, that is it is *not* necessarily assumed that each individual producer can dispose of all commodities all by himself.

48. Within general equilibrium theory it is obvious and well known that negative prices may emerge as the combined effect of (i) fixed supply with some goods, as is the case with joint outputs, and (ii) absence of free disposal (Lager 2001). Negative prices have originally been dealt with in such a framework by Arrow (1951a) and Koopmans (1951: 91).

49. That free disposal results in non-negative prices is exactly the reason why the assumption is made. Non-negativity of prices, which was explicitly assumed by von Neumann, is necessary to use duality arguments and apply fixed-point theorems in the existence proof (see Section 6.5.2).

50. See also note 44.

51. For a survey of joint production analysis in a neo-Ricardian framework, see Kurz and Salvadori (1995: Chapter 8), Schefold (1983, 1989) or, in particular, Salvadori and Steedman (1988), who present a very careful survey in both conceptual clarity and formal rigour. Several contributions on joint production from a neo-Ricardian perspective are collected in Pasinetti (1980), Salvadori and Steedman (1990: Vol. II) and Steedman (1988).

52. Sraffa's term 'requirements for use' is not a standard term in economic analysis. Yet, Sraffa provides no definition or even explanation of this term. Salvadori and Steedman (1988: 168, footnote 2) suggest that Sraffa was seeking to de-emphasise the subjective elements in the determination of the pattern of output without denying them. As a matter of fact, the vector of the requirements for use does not need to be a constant. One could imagine that it is a function of the profit rate, the wage rate, the price vector, etc. However, nowhere in Sraffa's work or in the subsequent research is this vector treated other than as exogenously and fixed.

53. The similarity between Sraffa's model and that of John von Neumann (cf. Section 6.5.2) is striking. Both explicitly assume that commodities are produced from inputs which first need to be produced themselves. Hence, there is a 'vertical time structure of production' (Faber 1986a: 51). See Steedman (1976) and Schefold (1978b, 1980b) for a comparison as to the mathematical equivalence and conceptual difference between Sraffa's and von Neumann's analyses.

54. For an overview see Salvadori and Steedman (1988: 173–175).

55. On the use of the free-disposal assumption in Sraffian models see Brägelmann (1991: 40–42).

56. A *cost-minimising system* is a system of production at whose prices no known

process can pay extra profits. This means that only the cost-minimising system can prevail in the long run in a competitive economy. For a rigorous definition see Salvadori (1982: 285).

57.   In general joint production systems, the elimination of commodities which are characterised by negative prices for some rates of profit, and the elimination of the associated processes of production, only lead to a reduced square system capable of reproduction if one assumes equality of the growth rate and the rate of profit (Steedman 1976, Schefold 1978b, 1980b). In addition, further mathematical difficulties have to be addressed in this case.

58.   It has been suggested that free disposal should be introduced only for some commodities and that negative prices be allowed for those commodities which cannot be disposed of costlessly (cf. Franke 1986, Hinrichsen and Krause 1981). This has been done by assuming, for each commoditiy to be freely disposed of, the existence of a process into which that commodity is the sole input and from which there is no output. Salvadori and Steedman (1988: 180) comment on this procedure by stating that

> [w]hilst assuming the existence of free disposal only for some products is clearly superior to assuming free disposal for all products, however, it is still not acceptable. To assume free disposal for even one product is to deny the principle of the conservation of mass-energy, one of the most fundamental principles of Thermodynamics! Every process with some input must have some product.

59.   Nevertheless, the neo-Ricardian theory of joint production has been chosen as a framework for studying the joint economic and ecological impact of production, for example by O'Connor (1993, 1994, 1995) and Perrings (1986, 1994).

60.   The notion of external costs and benefits had originally been introduced by Marshall (1925[1890]) in his effort to reconcile rising supply curves for individual firms with falling supply curves for the industry (Niehans 1990: 321).

61.   Coase (1960) later pointed out that the inefficiency of equilibrium due to a divergence of social and private marginal costs does not necessarily require direct government intervention. In the absence of transaction costs and with property rights clearly defined, private contracts between the different parties are able to establish an efficient allocation.

62.   These conclusions were not new, and Samuelson had already mentioned earlier contributions from Richard Musgrave back to Knut Wicksell. In particular, Erik Lindahl (1919) had arrived at similar conditions. What was new, though, was the 'lucid and rigorous derivation of these results from a beautifully simplified model' (Niehans 1990: 437), which made Samuelson's (1954) three-page paper the departure point for the modern theory of public goods.

63.   See Milleron (1972) and Roberts (1974) for surveys.

64.   Roberts (1976) formally showed for an economy with public goods that if a mechanism always yields Pareto optima and if participation is voluntary, so that its outcomes must be unanimously preferred to the no-trade point, then it cannot be a dominant strategy always to report one's preferences correctly. In this sense, a Lindahl equilibrium cannot be the outcome of a mechanism which is incentive compatible in this dominant-strategy sense.

65.   Roberts (1976) has shown that increasing numbers can worsen the incentives for correct revelation of preferences for public goods and that as the numbers grow, the departure of the outcome from efficiency can also increase. Muench (1972) has shown that the core and the set of Lindahl equilibria do not coincide in large economies, and Champsaur et al. (1975) demonstrated that the core of a public goods economy may actually expand when the number of consumers increases.

66.   Bailey and Friedlaender (1982) give a survey of the literature.

7. Joint Production and the Philosophy of Economics

7.1 INTRODUCTION

The development in the analysis of joint production, which has been described in detail in the previous chapter, is characteristic of a general development in economic theory (identified by Niehans 1990: 313–315). The classical authors studied the phenomenon of joint production, and economic relationships in general, using concrete, empirically relevant examples. In the study of many different empirical examples some general relationships became obvious, for example the so-called 'rule of free goods' (Smith 1976[1776]: 178). Later, the formulation of abstract models became more fashionable. Jevons' (1911[1879]) breakthrough in the marginalist approach is entirely based on the study of a formal model. The same holds for Marshall's analytical treatment in his *Principles of Economics* (1925[1890]) and even more so for von Neumann's (1937, 1945/46) model of general equilibrium. Contributions to modern general equilibrium theory are even more abstract, so that it is hardly possible to directly link the assumptions employed to empirical facts about production. That is to say, the development in the analysis of joint production, just like the development in economic analysis in general, is characterised by an evolution from the study of empirical examples to the analysis of abstract models.

In order to understand this development, in this chapter we make recourse to the philosophy of economics. In Section 7.2, we distinguish between two different strategies for the enhancement of economic theory – the 'problem-oriented' strategy and the 'theorem-oriented' strategy. In Section 7.3, we argue that the current dominance of the theorem-oriented strategy over the problem-oriented strategy in economics is best understood as part of a broader intellectual movement, namely the general emergence of 'structuralism' across the natural and social sciences in the early twentieth century. Within the structuralist agenda, axiomatisation and formalisation play a central role, in particular in economics

---

*This chapter is based on Baumgärtner (2000: Chapter 8).

(Section 7.4). In Section 7.5, we place the development in the analysis of joint production in this context. This explains why, today, the analysis of joint production as an explicit issue is not on the agenda of economics any more.

7.2   Two Different Strategies for the Enhancement of Economic Theory

The philosophy of economics knows different strategies of enhancing economic theory. Among others, two distinct possibilities of building meaningful theories are the following, which may be termed 'problem-oriented' and 'theorem-oriented' theorising respectively (see, for instance, Albert 1996: 471).[1]

- The rationale behind *problem-oriented* theorising is to analyse models that, by the realism of the assumptions employed, represent realistic, empirically relevant problems, that is phenomena and contexts. The aim is to obtain results which might be hoped to yield reliable insights into, and predictions about, the real-world phenomena after which the model is built.[2] A theory is further enhanced, according to this strategy, by developing and studying a sequence of models which use ever more realistic assumptions with regard to the problem to be described. Obviously, the problem-oriented strategy presupposes some prior empirical knowledge about the phenomena and context to be described and studied.

- In contrast, *theorem-oriented* theorising is the systematic search for the strongest law-like hypothesis with regard to the particular problem to be studied, which can be obtained from a given theory. The strongest law-like hypothesis is usually considered to be known, once the model assumptions are known that are necessary and sufficient for the hypothesis to be fulfilled within the given theory. This strategy does not presuppose any prior knowledge about the empirical details of the problem to be studied.

Both strategies involve the use of models for the further development of economic theory. However, a difference can be seen as far as the *realism*[3] of the model assumptions employed is concerned. As a matter of fact, whereas realism of assumptions is crucial for the problem-oriented strategy, it is irrelevant for the theorem-oriented strategy. As a consequence, while the theorem-oriented strategy may result in insights about real-world problems, this need not be the case (Albert 1996: 472).

The development in the history of economic analysis of joint production as described in Chapter 6 may be interpreted in terms of the problem-oriented and the theorem-oriented strategy as follows. The classical and early neoclassical contributions are clearly characterised by a problem-oriented approach. At the centre of attention is a particular problem of empirical relevance. However, with the establishment of the neoclassical doctrine and method the theorem-oriented approach becomes more and more important. Heinrich von Stackelberg's scientific opus illustrates the transition from the problem-oriented to the theorem-oriented strategy. In his earlier works (von Stackelberg 1932), he studies a particular problem of empirical relevance, namely the consequences of joint production for the decisions of a firm. This corresponds to a problem-oriented strategy. However, by pursuing this strategy he encounters difficulties. For the results obtained turn out to be rather complicated and not very handy for further analysis. Consequently, in his later works (starting with von Stackelberg 1934) he prefers a theorem-oriented strategy and turns to studying the existence of general equilibrium under different forms of competition.

With John von Neumann (1937, 1945/46), whose contribution appears roughly at the same time, the theorem-oriented strategy dominates over the problem-oriented strategy in the mainstream of economic theory.[4] John von Neumann, whose model is actually capable of coping with joint production, is not concerned with studying a certain problem of empirical relevance, such as joint production; nor are Arrow and Debreu (1954) or Debreu (1959). Their aim is to make statements about the assumptions under which a certain result holds – the existence of a general competitive equilibrium. As a consequence, the result they are aiming for and the mathematical formalism of the proof determine what assumptions to make – be they realistic or not.

Similarly, the analysis of joint production of desired goods and harmful bads in the context of welfare analysis displays the very same transition from problem-oriented to theorem-oriented theorising. While Pigou (1912, 1920) is still concerned with finding solutions for certain concrete problems of empirical relevance, the development of the concept of Lindahl equilibrium was mainly motivated by an interest in the assumptions under which a certain result holds – namely the existence of a general equilibrium with private and public goods. The concept of Lindahl equilibrium, which was introduced for this particular theorem-oriented purpose, certainly cannot claim much empirical relevance.

Niehans (1990: 159) comments on the dominance of theorem-oriented theorising over problem-oriented theorising, and the resulting lack of realism in economic models, which has become apparent since the 1930s:

There is no question that this development was, overall, a decisive advance. There is also no question that [... it] is here to stay. Half a century later an observer might perhaps be forgiven for also feeling that this advance was increasingly bought at the expense of vision. To use Keynes' phrase, the 'art of choosing models which are relevant to the contemporary world' was not keeping pace with the 'science of thinking in terms of models'.

7.3   THE STRUCTURALIST RESEARCH PROGRAMME

The dominance of theorem-orientation over problem-orientation in the development of economic theory is best understood as part of a broader intellectual movement, namely the general emergence of what has been called 'structuralism' (Piaget 1971, Sturrock 1993), across the scientific spectrum in the early twentieth century. The underlying belief that logical analysis of formal structure, that is symbolic representation of a system, can yield insights about the subject matter of study was shared by a range of disciplines from philosophy to physics, from linguistics to economics. In this view, a scientific theory is not a set of statements about the world, which may be either true or false, and, consequently, may be corroborated or falsified on the basis of empirical data. But the fundamental claim of the structuralist programme is that scientific theories should be seen as purely formal structures rather than as statements (Hands 1985: 305).[5,6] One of the roots of this intellectual development can be found in the Vienna of the 1920s and 1930s – the Vienna of the 'Wiener Kreis' around Wittgenstein and of Menger's 'Mathematical Colloquium', the Vienna of Gödel, Neurath, Carnap, Menger, Morgenstern, von Neumann, Popper, Wald and Schlesinger, to mention just a few (Leonard 1995: 730, Weintraub 1983: 5).[7] The ultimate goal of the structuralist endeavour was to rigorously define and rule out metaphysics from scientific discourse (Velupillai 1996: 256).

In economics, the influence of structuralism shows in the increased effort with which more and more abstract models of a competitive economy were analysed starting in the 1930s in order to make statements about structural properties, such as the existence, uniqueness and stability of a general competitive equilibrium.[8] In this context, the emergence of game theory can be seen as an expression of structuralism in economics (Leonard 1995: 731, 756–757). This was recognised from the very beginning, not only by economists. For instance, Hermann Weyl, mathematician, physicist and representative of the Hilbert school at Göttingen, which had a great influence on von Neumann (see Leonard 1995: 732), noted:

> Perhaps the philosophically most relevant feature of modern science is the emergence of abstract symbolic structures as the hard core of objectivity behind [...] the colorful tale of the subjective storyteller mind. [...] J. von Neumann's and Oskar Morgenstern's recent attempt to found economics on a theory of games is characteristic of the same trend. (Weyl 1949: 237)

More generally, the works of Heinrich von Stackelberg, John von Neumann, Kenneth Arrow and Gérard Debreu on general equilibrium theory are prime examples of the influence of the structuralist research programme on economic theory.

7.4   FORMALISATION AND AXIOMATISATION

Since the structure of a scientific theory is most obvious when it is presented in its most elementary and concise form, formalisation and axiomatisation are key features of the structuralist approach to the construction of scientific theory. A theory is said to be *axiomatised* if some of its statements are singled out as unproved premises, and all the other statements are deduced from them (Vilks 1998: 28). Typically, premises and deductions are specified in a formal representation, since this enables a rigorous treatment.[9] When the theory is presented in this way the essential structure of the theory is manifest and is amenable to a logical analysis.[10]

Formalisation and axiomatisation of theories were on the agenda of all scientific disciplines in the first half of the twentieth century,[11] but particularly in economics. From the mid 1940s until the end of the 1950s many theories in economics were axiomatised: for example, expected utility theory (von Neumann and Morgenstern 1944), general equilibrium theory (Arrow and Debreu 1954, Debreu 1959), social choice theory (Arrow 1951b) and the theory of distributive justice (Harsanyi 1955). A case in point is Gérard Debreu's *Theory of Value* (Debreu 1959), which has the revealing subtitle *An Axiomatic Analysis of Economic Equilibrium* and may be taken as characteristic of modern general equilibrium theory with its emphasis on set-theoretic axiomatisation (Vilks 1998: 30). In the preface Debreu is quite clear about his commitment to axiomatisation and the structuralist agenda:

> The theory of value is treated here with the standards of
> rigor of the contemporary formalist school of mathematics.
> [...] Allegiance to rigor dictates the axiomatic form of the
> analysis where the theory, in the strict sense, is logically en-
> tirely disconnected from its interpretations. (Debreu 1959:
> viii)

It is the second sentence which explicitly demonstrates the structuralist
influence in Debreu's approach. Rather than being a set of statements
about the world, the theory is taken as a purely formal structure which
only yields meaningful statements about the world when the elements of
the structure are interpreted in a certain way. Debreu considers the fact
that the mathematical structure is 'free' of any specific economic interpretation as 'one of the sources of the power of the axiomatic method'
(Debreu 1983: 5).[12] Another hint is Debreu's reference to 'the contemporary formalist school of mathematics'. Given that N. Bourbaki is
Debreu's standard mathematical reference in both the *Theory of Value*
and much of his other work, Debreu is probably referring to the Bourbaki school (Hands 1985: 324).[13] The overriding goal of the Bourbaki
group was to unify the many different branches of mathematics based
on a fundamental (set-theoretic) axiomatic 'structure', a goal that also
motivated and influenced to some extent the structuralist reconstruc-
tion of other scientific theories, such as theoretical physics. One may
therefore conclude that 'Debreu's early (and influential) work on general
equilibrium theory was committed to exactly the same underlying Bour-
bakian philosophy of axiomatisation' (Hands 1985: 325) that influenced
the structuralist view of scientific theories in general.

The rise of formal models and their mathematical analysis in the first
half of the twentieth century, which was spurred by the structuralist
research programme and aimed at proving theorems, marked what was
called 'the formalist revolution' in economics (Ward 1972: 40). It was
much more than just a change in style or professional technique; it actually amounted to a fundamental change in the mindset of economists:

> [T]he contemporary theorist is not only well-grounded in
> mathematics, but finds it the natural medium for expressing
> his professional ideas: the proof has replaced the argument.
> (Ward 1972: 40–41)

With this development, the form of economic theory became more and
more important relative to its substantive content (Blaug 1997, 1998,
Hutchison 2000).[14] While this development was originally a consequence
of the increasing dominance of theorem-orientation and the structuralist influence on economics, it may conversely reinforce the dominance of

theorem-orientation over problem-orientation. In particular, formalisation systematically exerts, by itself, a strong force away from realism.[15] For,

> to fit formalization on to the [...] subject matter of economics [...] requires and encourages [...] intense simplification and abstraction – indeed, oversimplification and overabstraction [...] The formalist revolution did make [...] a very considerable substantive or empirical difference, by massaging assumptions to make them tractable, and by trimming or squeezing out substantive content at one point, and adding, at another, vital 'substantive' (even if often fantastic) content in the form of perfect knowledge. [...] At a more advanced stage of formalism the empirical element in economic theorizing and explanation not merely gets distorted or minimized but sometimes vanishes altogether. (Hutchison 2000: 18–19)

In particular, any given formalisation or formal analytical method has a tendency to impose the study of those problems which are particularly handy in that very formalisation (Velupillai 1996).[16] For instance, the methods available from topology actually asked to be applied to existence proofs rather than to other economic problems. John von Neumann's scientific career is a case in point (Leonard 1995). Coming from game theory and being familiar with the methods in that field, in particular with the advanced mathematical concepts of equilibrium and the related existence proofs, von Neumann sought other fields of application for these methods and, hence, came to economics where at that time the problem of the existence of a general competitive equilibrium was waiting to be solved. He successfully applied his method to solving the problem, but in order to do so he had to make the assumptions fit the formalism. In particular, prices must not be negative for duality concepts to apply. In order to fulfil this prerequisite, prices were simply assumed to be non-negative, which, however, discards the empirically relevant aspect of negatively valued joint outputs.

As this example illustrates, the structure of one particular formal method had shaped the substantive content of economic theory and the manner in which economists looked at reality from then on. One may only speculate that the use of alternative formal methods would have led to a substantially different development of economic theory and the subject matter of economics. Indeed, Velupillai's (1996: 268) conclusion 'that the formalisation of the [19]30s may have shunted us along paths that led to dead-ends, swamps and blind-alleys; because of inadequate care in the axiomatisation [... and] unnecessary appendage to one type of mathematics' also offers an answer to the question of why joint production is widely absent from modern economic theory as an explicit issue, and why today the study of joint production is scattered over a number of basically unrelated research strands where each one deals with only one particular aspect of joint production.

7.5   CONCLUSION

The analysis of joint production has played an ambivalent role in the history of economic thought. It acted as a stimulating force until the establishment of neoclassical theory by Alfred Marshall around 1890, but thereafter was more and more seen as a troublesome obstacle. At the origin of this change in perception was a change in the research strategy of mainstream economics, which became manifest around 1930, in particular in the works of Heinrich von Stackelberg and John von Neumann. At that time, under the influence of the structuralist paradigm, theorem-oriented theorising had taken over from problem-oriented theorising in guiding the further development of economic theory.

Under the theorem-oriented research strategy the result to be obtained and the mathematical formalism to be employed determine what assumptions are made. For instance, the duality concept introduced to the field of economics by von Neumann requires the assumption that all outputs are wanted goods (or free goods), or, more indirectly, some assumption which implies non-negativity of prices, such as free disposal. But that discards by assumption one fundamental and empirically important aspect of joint production, namely that joint products may be harmful and therefore negatively valued.

And so the problem of finding a scheme of explanation that is general enough to also include all aspects of joint production – a problem that had first been identified by Adam Smith and was later (mistakenly) claimed to have been solved by Alfred Marshall and Heinrich von Stackelberg – in the end was not solved in an encompassing manner, but has been abandoned. Today, there exist many different theories dealing with joint production – neoclassical and neo-Ricardian general equilibrium theories, the welfare theory of externalities, and the theory of industrial organisation – each addressing one particular aspect of the phenomenon. But there exists no general and encompassing theory of joint production. One important reason for this development and the current state of affairs is the significant influence in the twentieth century of the structuralist programme on the development of economic theory in general, and on the analysis of joint production in particular.

NOTES

1. What we have translated as 'problem-oriented' is actually called 'model-oriented' by Albert (1996: 471). However, the term 'problem-oriented' seems to be more appropriate.
2. For an example of this strategy see Lakatos (1970: 135ff), for an interpretation see Musgrave (1978: 186ff).
3. Before the 1950s, the 'realism' of economic theory used to be a concern shared by the majority of economists, especially among those writing on methodological issues (Mäki 1988: 90). *(Scientific) realism*, in this context, asserts 'the existence of the objects of research as independent of the enquiry of which they are the objects. [...] According to this doctrine, there is a material and social world that exists independently of any individual consciousness and which is knowable by consciousness' (Lawson 1989: 60–61). The realist holds that the aim of science consists in discovering new truths about the world (Hausman 1994: 5). As opposed to this view, some authors – most notably Friedman (1953) – have argued that the truth status of theories is irrelevant, but all that is required is usefulness of theories for predictive purposes. According to this *instrumentalist* view, scientific theories are not to be regarded as true or false but merely as better or worse instruments of prediction. The instrumentalist view became extremely influential in economics following Friedman's essay. However, in the philosophy of science and of economics there has recently been a renewed and growing interest in the realist approach (Bhaskar 1978, 1979, Keohane 1986, Lawson 1997, Leplin 1984 or Sayers 1985). On the question of whether (or how) realism and economics fit together, see Mäki (1989, 1998: 408–409, 2002).
4. Niehans (1990: 313–315) dates the transition, which marks the beginning of a new 'era', from 1920 to 1950. He judges that 'the principal purpose of these modern models was not to introduce concepts but to prove theorems' (Niehans 1990: 314). Others stress that the theorem-oriented strategy has always played an important role in economics, for example Blaug (1976: 357), who notes that '[a]nalytical elegance, economy of theoretical means, and generality obtained by ever more "heroic" assumptions have always meant more to economists than relevance and predictability'.
5. As far as the implications of the structuralist programme for scientific research are concerned, Weyl (1949: 630) remarks, expressing an opinion of David Hilbert: '[T]he question of truth [was] then shifted into the question of consistency'.
6. One prominent, yet very restrictive, interpretation of 'structuralism' is proposed by Sneed (1971), Stegmüller (1976, 1979) and their school. However, when using the term 'structuralism' in this chapter, we do not mean their restrictive interpretation but the more general 'semantic view' as advocated by philosophers of science such as van Fraassen (1980) or Suppe (1977, 1979). Note that the latter are in disagreement with some particular aspects of the Sneed/Stegmüller programme.
7. Janik and Toulmin (1973) give a detailed and charming intellectual and cultural history of Vienna at that time.
8. Lind (1992: 96) argues more universally that '[t]heoretical works in economics resemble more the picture of theoretical works presented by the so-called structuralist school'.
9. While formalisation and axiomatisation are, in principle, independent of each other, most often they come hand in hand.
10. Clower (1995) has argued that axiomatisation is useful in deductive or demonstrative disciplines, but that it has no positive value in disciplines based upon plausible reasoning. Since, according to Clower, economics is of the latter kind, axiomatisation may only be fruitful when and if it is used in a critical role, as contrasted with the constructive role which could only be played in the former disciplines. Otherwise, it is likely to be of 'as little use to an empirical scientist as a broken saw to a

carpenter' (Clower 1995: 310).

11.   As an example from physics, in 1909 Carathéodory published his axiomatic formulation of thermodynamics. And quantum theory was developed in the 1930s in different axiomatic forms by Paul Dirac, Werner Heisenberg and Erwin Schrödinger.

12.   Similarly, Arrow and Hahn (1971: vii) in the preface to their *General Competitive Analysis* defend general equilibrium theory as a purely formal representation, an 'idealized construction' of not much practical relevance.

13.   'Bourbaki' is actually a collective pseudonym used by a group of mathematicians beginning in the 1930s. Debreu is related to the Bourbaki group by the fact that he was a student of H. Cartan, one of the founders of that group (Vilks 1998: 29). For a detailed discussion of the Bourbaki school see Fang (1970).

14.   Blaug (1997, 1998) identifies the beginning of this development – which he calls an 'ugly current' and a 'disease' of modern economics – with the paper of Arrow and Debreu (1954). However, the development had already begun in the 1930s with the contributions of von Stackelberg (1932, 1934) and von Neumann (1937, 1945/46).

15.   Blaug (1997, 1998) argues that there is a direct trade-off between rigorous formalisation and substantive relevance. He sees current economics on the extreme side of rigorous formal analysis, with no longer any interest whatsoever in empirical or practical relevance: 'No Reality, Please. We're Economists' (Blaug 1998: 5).

16.   As a consequence, other problems may not get due attention:

> Formalism [...] brings clarity and rigour to arguments but such merits are almost always purchased at a price. To be dedicated to formal modelling at whatever cost is to close the door to the analysis of certain problems that so far have not lent themselves, and may never lend themselves, to rigorous treatment. (Blaug 1998: 27)

8. Ambivalence of Joint Outputs[*]

8.1 INTRODUCTION

It is usually assumed that the character of joint outputs – whether they are positively valued goods, free goods or negatively valued bads – is immediately obvious. For instance, in modelling the joint production of electricity and carbon dioxide in fossil-fuel-fired power plants, it seems to be apparent that electricity is a desired good while carbon dioxide is an undesired bad due to its harmful environmental impact. However, the character of an output, like its value, is not an inherent property of the substance itself but depends on the context in which the output comes into existence. For example, the waste heat generated in power plants may be a desired and positively valued commodity that could be used for space heating, given appropriate infrastructure and demand. But when released directly into ecosystems, such as rivers or lakes, it is a harmful and undesired bad.

In general, many factors will determine the value of an output and its character as a good, a free good or a bad (Debreu 1959: 33). Among them are the preferences of households for this output and other outputs, the technology by which it is produced, the scarcity of the resources from which it is produced, its environmental impact, etc. As a consequence, there are outputs of production which may be *ambivalent*. That is, they may potentially be both goods or bads, depending on the circumstances under which they are produced and perceived (Baumgärtner 2000: Chapter 10, 2004a). As all the factors that determine the value of an output and this output's character as a good, a free good or a bad may change over time, a particular joint output may change its character over time, from being a good to being a bad, or vice versa.

Typical examples of ambivalent joint outputs include material by-products or left-overs from production or consumption for which a recycling possibility or an alternative productive use exists. One could consider these materials as wastes, the dumping of which is costly be-

---

[*]Sections 8.1–8.3 and the Appendix are taken, with slight modifications, from Baumgärtner (2004a).

cause scarce dumping sites are required. Or one could consider them as secondary resources which substitute for scarce primary resources in some production process. Examples include the use of waste paper in the paper industry (see Chapter 15) and the input of used tyres into cement production (see Chapter 17). Which aspect prevails depends on the ecological-economic context. Empirical evidence of ambivalence comes, for example, from the spot market for waste paper in Germany (Baumgärtner and Winkler 2003; see Chapter 15 for details). The price on this market varies strongly, displaying positive values at some times and negative values at other times. This suggests that in a general equilibrium framework, not only the absolute value of prices but also their respective signs should be endogenously determined (Müller-Fürstenberger 1996: 2). At the same time, the ambivalence issue raises important policy issues. How should one deal with a material that is an undesired waste at some times and a scarce factor of production at other times?

This chapter addresses the question of what determines the character of a joint output as a good, a free good or a bad. It identifies conditions under which an output may be ambivalent. The analysis is based on a simple model of a vertically integrated two-sector economy with resources and waste. The model is inspired by the example of waste paper (Chapter 15), but aims at a more general analysis which goes beyond that particular example. Each sector produces a consumption good. The first sector jointly produces a by-product which is ambivalent in that it may potentially be both a harmful waste and a secondary resource for the other sector. The sign of the efficient shadow price[1] of this joint output indicates its character as a good (price > 0), a free good (price $= 0$) or a bad (price < 0). Thus, the character of the joint output is endogenously determined from a total analysis.

It is shown that the efficient shadow price of the joint output may be positive, zero or negative. As a consequence, with model parameters changing over time the joint output's character may change from being a positively valued good to being a negatively valued bad or vice versa. Rigid supply of the secondary resource as caused by joint production, limits to substitution between the primary and the secondary resource, and environmental damage due to waste disposal are identified as crucial for this result.

The outline of the chapter is as follows. In Section 8.2 we introduce a simple model of ambivalence which will then serve as a reference throughout the chapter. We characterise the efficient solution of the model in Section 8.3, and discuss how ambivalence may occur in principle. In Section 8.4, we expand this simple model by a number of dynamic amendments and discuss how ambivalence over time may come about. In Section 8.5, we identify implications of ambivalence for both ecological-economic theory and policy. Section 8.6 concludes.

8.2   A MODEL OF AMBIVALENCE

In order to gain a better understanding of how ambivalence emerges from the interplay of different economic forces and constraints, consider the following simple model, which is inspired by the waste paper example (cf. Chapter 15). It is not meant to be a fully detailed representation of the empirical situation, but it is intended to provide a simple analytical framework for the discussion of ambivalence. Therefore, it captures the key elements of the waste paper example in a stylised form. On the other hand, no attempt is made to strive for the highest possible generality. Instead, the model is specific and simple, as this allows one to analytically derive clear and illustrative results. All the results thus obtained, however, are robust to a fair amount of generalisation (see Baumgärtner 2004a).

Consider an economy in which there are two consumption goods, good 1 (high quality paper) and good 2 (low quality paper). They are produced from a primary resource (pulp) as depicted in Figure 8.1. There are two processes of production both of which use the primary

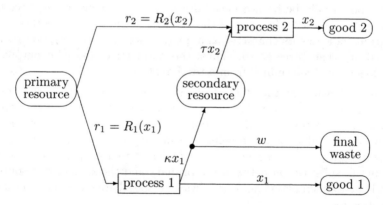

Figure 8.1   Material flow on the production side of the economy.

resource as an indispensable input. In process 1, good 1 is produced from the primary resource alone. Process 1 yields a by-product (waste paper)[2] which can either be a secondary resource and serve as input for process 2 or alternatively be disposed of as final waste. Good 2 is produced in process 2 from the primary resource and the secondary resource recovered from process 1's waste by-product. There may be other factors of production, for example labour, capital or other natural resources, but since they are not important with respect to ambivalence of the secondary resource they are not considered here.

Let $x_i \geq 0$ denote the amount of good i produced in process i and $r_i \geq 0$ the amount of primary resource input used in that process ($i = 1, 2$). Then the (convex) technology can be described by primary resource requirement functions R_i:

$$r_i = R_i(x_i) \qquad \text{with } R_i' > 0, R_i'' \geq 0 \text{ for } i = 1, 2. \qquad (8.1)$$

The function R_i is the inverse of a production function with non-increasing returns to scale and may be interpreted as a real cost function in terms of the primary resource. In process 1 the production of one unit of good 1 entails κ units of the by-product, where $\kappa > 0$ is a constant ('waste generation rate'). In process 2 the primary resource and the secondary resource are strictly complementary inputs. An amount τx_2 of the secondary resource is used together with r_2 units of the primary resource to produce x_2 units of good 2, where $\tau > 0$ is a constant ('secondary resource utilisation rate').

Strict complementarity of primary and secondary resource is, admittedly, a strong assumption. It reflects in extreme form the empirical fact that substitutability between recovered waste paper and primary pulp in producing low quality paper is limited for technical reasons (Kibat 1991: Section 2, Samakovlis 2003). As recovered waste paper is generally cheaper – even at times of a high price – than primary pulp, firms will use as much recovered waste paper as is technically possible. The constant parameter τ may then be thought of as given by this upper limit of substitutability between primary and secondary resource. Hence, it seems permissible to assume strict complementarity to start with.

Both κ and τ are assumed here to be exogenously given constant parameters (rather than price-dependent endogenous variables) as the waste paper example suggests that both the waste generation rate κ and the secondary resource utilisation rate τ are fixed in the short run.

With this technology the outputs of consumption goods, x_1 and x_2, are restricted by the following constraints. The amount of primary resource used as an input in the two production processes, $r_1 + r_2$, cannot exceed the total amount available in the economy, ρ. With (8.1):

$$R_1(x_1) + R_2(x_2) \leq \rho. \qquad (8.2)$$

With κx_1 of process 1's joint output produced, and τx_2 employed as a secondary resource input in process 2, the remainder is disposed of as final waste, w. The material balance condition for process 1's joint output thus reads:

$$w = \kappa x_1 - \tau x_2. \tag{8.3}$$

Furthermore, the amount of final waste cannot be negative:

$$w \geq 0. \tag{8.4}$$

Waste disposal is assumed to decrease the utility of households, for example due to emissions caused by waste incineration or leakage and odours from waste dumping sites. Let V be the additively separable utility function of a representative household. It depends on the amounts consumed of both consumption goods, x_1 and x_2, as well as the amount of waste, w:

$$V(x_1, x_2, w) = U(x_1, x_2) - D(w). \tag{8.5}$$

The consumption utility function U is assumed to exhibit positive marginal utility from the consumption of both goods, $U_i(x_1, x_2) > 0$ for all $x_1, x_2 \geq 0$, and infinite marginal utility for vanishing consumption of either good, $\lim_{x_i \to 0} U_i(x_1, x_2) = +\infty$, where $U_i \equiv \partial U / \partial x_i$ $(i = 1, 2)$. Furthermore, U is assumed to be strictly quasi-concave. The damage function D is assumed to exhibit non-negative and increasing marginal damage of waste, $D'(0) = 0$, $D'(w) > 0$ for $w > 0$ and $D''(w) > 0$ for $w \geq 0$, where $D' \equiv dD/dw$. Hence, the overall utility function V is strictly quasi-concave.

8.3   THE EFFICIENT ALLOCATION: POTENTIAL AMBIVALENCE

The efficient allocation is obtained by maximising the utility function (8.5) over $x_1, x_2, w \geq 0$ subject to the constraints (8.2), (8.3) and (8.4).[3] Taking constraint (8.4) into account explicitly may, at first sight, seem overly formalistic. It allows us, however, to analytically distinguish between the interior solution, $w > 0$, and the corner solution, $w = 0$. As will become apparent below, this distinction is crucial for the potential ambivalence of process 1's joint output. The Lagrangian for the constrained maximisation problem thus reads

$$\mathcal{L} = U(x_1, x_2) - D(w) + \lambda_R(\rho - R_1(x_1) - R_2(x_2))$$
$$+ \lambda_S(\kappa x_1 - \tau x_2 - w)$$
$$+ \lambda_W w$$

with λ_l $(l = R, S, W)$ as the Lagrange multipliers associated with the primary resource constraint, the secondary resource constraint, and the waste constraint. As the primary resource constraint (8.2) and the waste constraint (8.4) are inequalities, λ_R and λ_W are non-negative. In contrast, the secondary resource constraint (8.3) is a material balance condition which holds as an equality. As a consequence, λ_S is not restricted to non-negative values.

8.3.1 First Order Efficiency Conditions

According to the theorem of Kuhn and Tucker the first order conditions for a maximum are as follows:[4]

$$\frac{\partial \mathcal{L}}{\partial x_1} = U_1(x_1, x_2) - \lambda_R R_1'(x_1) + \lambda_S \kappa \quad = 0, \tag{8.6}$$

$$\frac{\partial \mathcal{L}}{\partial x_2} = U_2(x_1, x_2) - \lambda_R R_2'(x_2) - \lambda_S \tau \quad = 0, \tag{8.7}$$

$$\frac{\partial \mathcal{L}}{\partial w} = -D'(w) - \lambda_S + \lambda_W \quad = 0, \tag{8.8}$$

$$\frac{\partial \mathcal{L}}{\partial \lambda_R} = \rho - R_1(x_1) - R_2(x_2) \quad = 0, \tag{8.9}$$

$$\frac{\partial \mathcal{L}}{\partial \lambda_S} = \kappa x_1 - \tau x_2 - w \quad = 0, \tag{8.10}$$

$$\frac{\partial \mathcal{L}}{\partial \lambda_W} = w \quad \geq 0, \tag{8.11}$$

$$\lambda_W \frac{\partial \mathcal{L}}{\partial \lambda_W} = \lambda_W w \quad = 0. \tag{8.12}$$

Conditions (8.6) and (8.7) can be rearranged to yield

$$U_1(x_1, x_2) = \lambda_R R_1'(x_1) - \lambda_S \kappa \quad \text{and} \tag{8.13}$$
$$U_2(x_1, x_2) = \lambda_R R_2'(x_2) + \lambda_S \tau. \tag{8.14}$$

These conditions state that in the efficient allocation the marginal utility of both good 1 and good 2 should equal their marginal costs of production. With λ_R as the shadow price for the primary resource, both processes face marginal resource costs, $\lambda_R R_i'(x_i)$ $(i = 1, 2)$. With λ_S as the shadow price for the secondary resource, process 2 also faces marginal costs for this resource, $\lambda_S \tau$. Process 1 is a supplier of the secondary resource and, thus, obtains a marginal revenue for providing it, $\lambda_S \kappa$.

Concerning inequality (8.11), solving the system of first order conditions (8.6)–(8.12) makes it necessary to distinguish between two different cases: (i) an interior solution with $w > 0$, which implies $\lambda_W = 0$; and (ii) a corner solution with $w = 0$, in which case $\lambda_W \geq 0$. As a result of the optimisation both cases may occur.

8.3.2 Potential Ambivalence of the Joint Output

At this point, insights into the value of process 1's joint output can be gained from interpreting efficiency condition (8.8). It can be rearranged into

$$\lambda_S = \lambda_W - D'(w). \tag{8.15}$$

The value of the joint output as given by its efficient shadow price λ_S consists of two components. The first component, λ_W, is related to the scarcity of the secondary resource as an input into process 2. The Lagrange multiplier λ_W measures how binding the constraint $w \geq 0$ is, which limits the availability of process 1's joint output for use as a secondary resource in process 2. Thus, the first component adds a non-negative contribution to the overall shadow price λ_S, as $\lambda_W \geq 0$. Since process 1's joint output may also cause a welfare loss when disposed of as final waste the second component of λ_S is given by the marginal damage of waste. It makes a non-positive contribution to λ_S, as $-D'(w) \leq 0$. In general, the first component may outweigh the second, or vice versa, so that λ_S may be positive, zero, or negative. This is to say that the shadow price of process 1's joint output may be positive, zero, or negative, depending on whether or not the aspect of this substance being a scarce factor of production dominates over the aspect of this substance being a potentially harmful waste.

Two cases for the sign of λ_S (Equation 8.15) can be distinguished, depending on whether the efficient allocation is an interior solution ($w > 0$) or a corner solution ($w = 0$):

- *Interior solution.* With $w > 0$ it follows from condition (8.12) that $\lambda_W = 0$. Hence, condition (8.15) reduces to

$$\lambda_S = -D'(w) < 0. \tag{8.16}$$

  As long as there is a strictly positive amount of final waste the shadow price of process 1's joint output is given by the marginal damage of waste, which is strictly negative.

- *Corner solution.* In contrast, for $w = 0$ one has $D'(0) = 0$ by assumption. Condition (8.15) thus reduces to

$$\lambda_S = \lambda_W \geq 0, \tag{8.17}$$

  where $\lambda_S = 0$ holds for $\lambda_W = 0$ and $\lambda_S > 0$ otherwise. If there is no waste disposal and the entire amount of process 1's joint output is utilised as a factor of production in process 2, it is scarce and has a positive shadow price.

The ambivalence of the joint output thus coincides with the phase transition between the interior and the corner solution. The joint output has a non-negative value, $\lambda_S \geq 0$, in the corner solution ($w = 0$) and a negative value, $\lambda_S < 0$, in the interior solution ($w > 0$).

Although the model employed here is rather specific, the results are robust to a fair amount of generalisation. It derives from the combined effect of the following three features: (i) Process 1's by-product comes into existence as a joint output in fixed proportion to some desired good. (ii) The only alternative to recovering a secondary resource from that material consists in its environmentally harmful disposal. (iii) Substitutability between the secondary resource and the primary resource as factors of production in process 2 is limited. Any model displaying these three features in some form or other would reproduce the ambivalence result obtained here.

8.4 AMBIVALENCE OVER TIME

The simple model introduced in the previous section has shown that process 1's joint output may potentially be both a positively valued good and a negatively valued bad. Within that static model the output's character is uniquely determined. Once the model specification is known the character of the joint output as a good, free good or bad is also known. This amounts to what may be termed 'potential ambivalence'. From the potential ambivalence as laid out in Section 8.3, real ambivalence over time may now arise due to a number of different dynamic reasons. They can all be thought of as dynamic amendments to the basic model framework.[5] In this section, their effect, ceteris paribus, on the value of the joint output is discussed. For that sake, we consider the following model specification:

$$U(x_1, x_2) = x_1^{1-\beta} x_2^{\beta} \qquad \text{with } 0 < \beta < 1, \qquad (8.18)$$

$$D(w) = \frac{\delta}{2} w^2 \qquad \text{with } \delta > 0, \qquad (8.19)$$

$$R_1(x_1) = x_1, \qquad (8.20)$$

$$R_2(x_2) = x_2, \qquad (8.21)$$

$$\rho \equiv 1. \qquad (8.22)$$

The utility function is of the Cobb-Douglas type with β as the share of income spent on good 2, the damage function is quadratic with slope parameter δ such that the absolute and marginal damage vanishes as waste goes to zero, the two production processes are described by linear primary input requirement functions, and the amount of primary resource is normalised to one. This model is explicitly solved, and the properties of the solution are analysed in the Appendix.

8.4.1   Innovation of a New Production Process

Suppose that initially only process 1 exists. It yields a joint output for which no alternative use is known, but which causes welfare-decreasing environmental damage. Clearly, this joint output will be a negatively valued bad. If now a new process is innovated (corresponding to process 2 in the model), which opens up a productive use for the hitherto harmful joint output from process 1, the value of this joint output will increase. It might even increase to an extent that it turns into a positively valued good as the aspect of a scarce factor of production outweighs its character as a harmful waste. Examples include the recycling and recovery of secondary resources from material wastes, such as waste paper (cf. Chapter 15), the processing of hydrochloric acid into pure chlorine (cf. Chapter 16), and the processing of sulphurous wastes and emissions into sulphuric acid (cf. Chapter 18).

8.4.2   Gradual Technical Progress

With both process 1 and process 2 in existence, technical progress may lead to a change in their parameters. For example, the waste generation rate κ and the utilisation rate τ may change over time: $\kappa = \kappa(t)$, $\tau = \tau(t)$. As a consequence, the shadow price of process 1's joint output may change over time as well: $\lambda_S = \lambda_S(t)$. As some comparative statics with the efficient solution of the model reveals (see Appendix 8C), a decrease in κ will lead to an increase in the value of process 1's joint output, λ_S, as will an increase in τ. This is intuitively plausible since a decrease in κ will, ceteris paribus, reduce the supply of process 1's joint output, thus increasing its scarcity value. Likewise, an increase in τ will, ceteris paribus, increase the demand for process 1's joint output, also increasing its scarcity value. Depending on the value of the other model parameters, it is possible that this changes the sign of λ_S. This is illustrated in Figure 8.2.

If we now assume that technical progress leads to process 1 turning out less and less of the joint output with every unit of desired output (good 1) and process 2 is able to use more and more of the secondary resource input per unit of desired output (good 2) produced, that is κ decreases and τ increases over time, then the value of the intermediate product, λ_S, increases over time. Depending on the initial parameter values and the extent of parameter changes it may be that the joint output changes its character from being a negatively valued bad to being a positively valued good.

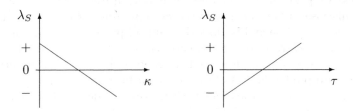

Figure 8.2   Ambivalence due to changes in the technical parameters κ (waste generation rate) and τ (utilisation rate).

8.4.3   Change in Preferences

Consumers' preferences are another factor in determining the value of process 1's joint output and its character as a good, free good or bad. In the model employed here they are represented by the utility function (8.18). The parameter β describes how much good 2 is appreciated relative to good 1. With β close to zero, consumers derive utility almost exclusively from good 1, while with β close to one they derive utility almost exclusively from good 2. As some comparative statics with the efficient solution reveals (see Appendix 8C), an increase in β will lead to an increase in the value of process 1's joint output, λ_S. This is intuitively plausible since an increase in β means a shift in preferences toward good 2 and, ceteris paribus, implies an increased demand for good 2 and a decreased demand for good 1. Since production of good 2 requires process 1's joint output as an input this increases the scarcity value of the joint output, λ_S. Depending on the value of the other model parameters it is possible that this increase changes the sign of λ_S from negative to positive. This is illustrated in Figure 8.3.

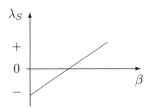

Figure 8.3   Ambivalence due to a change in preferences (β).

The parameter value β may change over time: $\beta = \beta(t)$. As consumer preferences shift from good 1, which by its joint output potentially causes the environmental problem, to good 2, the production of which helps to solve the problem, β increases over time and so does the value of process 1's joint output. Possibly, it may turn from a bad into a good. And likewise, if consumer preferences shift from good 2 to good 1, β decreases over time and so does the value of process 1's joint output.

This logic carries over to the case when goods 1 and 2 are not final consumption goods, but intermediate goods to be used by other firms as inputs into production. As firms' demand for these intermediate products changes, so does their value. Examples include the shift in demand for intermediate products of the chemical industry, in particular the shift away from soda and toward chlorinated plastics which resulted in chlorine turning from a harmful bad into a desired good (cf. Chapter 16).

8.4.4   Change in Perceived Environmental Damage

The welfare-decreasing environmental damage caused by process 1's joint output is another factor determining the value of this joint output. In the model the environmental damage was described by a damage function D (Equation 8.19). This damage function may be interpreted as describing the damage perceived by households rather than the actual damage. Based on such an interpretation it seems plausible that D may change over time. In particular, the damage parameter δ may change over time: $\delta = \delta(t)$.

As long as households do not perceive any environmental damage at all ($\delta = 0$) the value of process 1's joint output cannot be negative. It will be a positively valued factor of production for process 2, or a free good if it is produced in excess amounts. But as households pay more attention to damage to the natural environment and δ increases, it may be, depending on the other model parameters, that the joint output assumes a negative value and becomes a bad (see Appendix 8C). Its value λ_S decreases, that is, the absolute amount of λ_S increases, with δ (Figure 8.4).

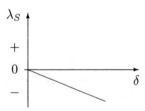

Figure 8.4   Ambivalence due to a change in perceived environmental damage (δ).

8.4.5   Waste Accumulation

In the model introduced in Section 8.2, the decrease in welfare due to environmental pollution was caused by the *flow* of waste, $w(t)$, disposed of at every point in time t. If one assumes, in contrast, that it is caused by the *stock*, $S(t)$, of waste accumulated over time, then the ambivalence of process 1's joint output may be an effect of the dynamics of the stock of waste (cf. Chapters 4 and 5).[6] If the stock of waste is zero to start with, $S(0) = 0$, it is likely that initially the joint output has a positive value since there is no noteworthy environmental damage yet. But as the waste piles up, especially when its natural degradation rate is very small, the damage increases and, consequently, the joint output's value may turn from positive to negative over time.

Accumulation of pollutants in the natural environment constitutes an important dynamic force which may have repercussions on economic decisions, for example on innovation and investment, and the formation of preferences. It thus creates a form of irreversibility and shapes the evolution of coupled ecological-economic systems (cf. Chapters 4 and 5). Accumulation of pollutants over time, and its role in determining optimal consumption and investment paths over time, will be the subject of a more detailed investigation in Chapters 9 and 10.

8.4.6 Uncertainty

Another important underlying cause of ambivalence may be uncertainty and its resolution over time. In Section 8.3, as well as in the discussion of ambivalence over time so far, we have always assumed perfect knowledge of all parameters and causal relationships, such as preferences, technology or environmental impact. This has allowed us to uniquely determine the efficient allocation of the economy and the efficient shadow price of process 1's joint output. Ambivalence over time was understood as an efficient phenomenon given perfect knowledge of all elements of the economy. But, of course, in reality all parameters and causal relationships are only known with considerable uncertainty. Over time people will learn more about them and some of the uncertainty may thus be resolved. As a consequence, the values of the various parameters describing the state of knowledge at some point in time change over time due to learning. And the value of the joint output will change over time accordingly. We will come back to the role of ignorance in assessing joint outputs, and the role of joint production in generating new knowledge, in more detail in Chapter 12.

8.4.7 Interaction of Different Causes

So far, we have discussed a number of causes of ambivalence over time under the ceteris paribus restriction. That is, we have looked at different dynamic developments in isolation. In reality, however, many of them act at the same time, and their effects overlap.

Consider, for example, a scenario where the waste generation rate $\kappa(t)$ increases rapidly from $t = 0$ to $t = 10$, and then at a slower rate from $t = 10$ to $t = 20$. In addition, the utilisation rate $\tau(t)$ also increases, but with a time lag starting at $t = 10$ (Figure 8.5). As a consequence of the first development, ceteris paribus, $\lambda_S(t)$ would decrease over time. And as a consequence of the second development, ceteris paribus, $\lambda_S(t)$ would increase over time. But as a combined consequence of both developments and depending on the other model parameters, $\lambda_S(t)$ may well develop as shown in Figure 8.5. The joint output's value first turns negative and

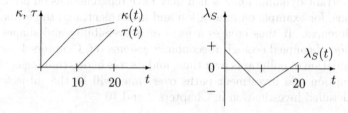

Figure 8.5   Ambivalence due to a combination of developments. $\kappa(t)$ increases rapidly from $t = 0$ to $t = 10$, and then at a slower rate from $t = 10$ to $t = 20$, while $\tau(t)$ increases only with a time lag starting at $t = 10$ (left). As a consequence, the joint output's value, $\lambda_S(t)$, first turns negative and later turns positive again (right).

later turns positive again. This example is not as far-fetched as it might appear at first. As a matter of fact, some of the repeated changes in the character of waste paper in Germany between 1985 and 2000 can be explained as the combined effect of uneven changes in the waste paper generation and utilisation rates (cf. Chapter 15).

8.5   IMPLICATIONS OF AMBIVALENCE FOR ECOLOGICAL-ECONOMIC THEORY AND POLICY

The phenomenon of ambivalence of joint outputs has a number of implications for ecological-economic theory (Sections 8.5.1 and 8.5.2) and policy (Sections 8.5.3 through 8.5.5).

8.5.1   Modelling Joint Production Processes

Since the character of outputs depends on the context of their production the description of the production side in ecological-economic models should, in general, not yet make any presumptions about the character of the jointly produced outputs. Models of joint production should be based on a material description of the production process, and they should not yet anticipate any value judgements concerning the outputs produced. Therefore a description of production activities in terms of a set of feasible production vectors or input-output matrices appears to be more appropriate than a description in terms of cost functions or production functions. For the latter, by focusing on the 'efficient' boundary of the set of feasible production vectors, presuppose a value judgement as to the outputs' character.

8.5.2 Total Analysis

The determination of an output's character as a good, a free good or a bad requires a total analysis. Other production processes, besides the one under study, households' preferences and environmental impact have to be considered as well when deriving the value of a particular output.

Furthermore, the analysis in Section 8.3 has revealed the crucial importance of the phase transition between the interior solution and the corner solution for establishing the ambivalence result. Therefore, economic analyses should not be restricted, as it is often done, to studying only the properties of interior solutions, but more attention should be paid to corner solutions and the phase transition between interior and corner solutions.

8.5.3 Hidden Externality

Joint outputs that are released into the natural environment may cause environmental damage and, thus, negatively affect the well-being of other people. That is, joint outputs may be a source of negative externalities. It is one of the tasks of environmental policy to efficiently internalise such externalities. Against this background, the corner solution derived in Section 8.3 poses a certain challenge for the regulation of environmental pollution. For as long as the real state of the economy is the corner solution there is actually no environmental problem. No single unit of pollution or waste is released into the environment, but the material is completely transferred to process 2 where it is used as a productive input. If some of the material were released into the natural environment there would be an environmental problem. But this potential problem is 'hidden'.

8.5.4 Link Between Different Production Processes

Ambivalence of a joint output and, in particular, the use of that output as a factor of production in some other production process link different production processes within the economy. They can then no longer be regarded and treated as independent. Joint production thus establishes a complex and integrated network of production within the economy (Baumgärtner and Jöst 2000). A case in point of utmost importance in both economic and environmental terms is the chemical industry. Due to the physical and chemical nature of the production processes, joint production is all-pervasive in this industry. Finding new uses for joint outputs that would otherwise be just waste characterises the historic evolution and current structure of the industry. Two examples, which will be discussed in more detail in separate chapters, include chlorine (cf. Chapter 16) and sulphuric acid (cf. Chapter 18).

Ambivalent joint production not only links different production processes *within* one sector of the economy, for example in the chemical industry. It may also establish rather rigid links *across* different sectors. This happens when a joint output emerges in one sector of the economy and is used in another sector. For example, the sulphurous emissions and wastes caused by metal production, crude oil refining and natural gas purification are mostly processed into sulphuric acid which is then used as an input in the production of textiles, dyes, and fertilisers (cf. Chapter 18). Thus, a link is established between two sectors of the economy which, otherwise, do not appear to be closely related.

8.5.5   Joint Externalities

While an upstream process's joint output may be used as an input by a downstream process, thus avoiding environmental pollution, the latter process may also yield a potentially harmful joint output. In such a case, the potential externality inherent in the by-product of the first process is replaced by another potential externality. Amending Figure 8.1, the situation can be depicted as in Figure 8.6. Thus, ambivalent joint production also links in a complex way the different negative externalities stemming from the different production processes.

Given that the externality of process 1 may be hidden due to ambivalence (see Section 8.5.3), when assessing process 2's externality one may not be aware of the circumstance that this process helps to mitigate externalities from process 1. As a matter of fact, when simultaneously internalising the two externalities, one faces a trade-off between reducing emissions from source 1 and from source 2. The policy issues related to such a situation of 'joint externalities', and the role of various uncertainties when devising regulatory policies for integrated production networks, are discussed in detail by Baumgärtner and Jöst (2000) with respect to the empirical example of the sulphuric acid industry (cf. Chapter 18).

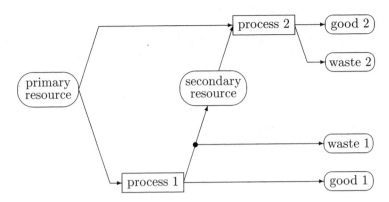

Figure 8.6   Joint externalities due to ambivalent joint production.

8.6 CONCLUSION

An output that is jointly produced with a desired good may be ambivalent. That is, it may potentially be a good, a free good, or a bad. In the framework employed here its character is determined in the interplay between two opposing forces. On the one hand the output is a potentially harmful pollutant when released into the natural environment. On the other hand it may also be used as a productive input in some other production process. Depending on which aspect dominates, the output will be regarded as a desired good or an undesired bad. With the economic context (preferences, technology, resource availability, environmental damage, or knowledge) changing over time, also the character of outputs may change over time. What used to be an unwanted bad may turn into a desired good, or vice versa.

The formal analysis has revealed that it is a combination of three properties of an economic system which generates potential ambivalence: (i) rigid supply of the secondary resource as caused by joint production, (ii) limits to substitution between the primary and the secondary resource, and (iii) environmental damage due to waste disposal. The detailed case study of waste paper in Chapter 15 will illustrate these conditions at work.

Ambivalence of joint outputs carries implications for the analysis of joint production, and for ecological-economic theory and policy in general. Since the character of joint outputs depends on the context of their production, general models of joint production should not presuppose any value judgements about the character of the outputs. Instead, they should be based on a material description of the production process. The outputs' character as goods, free goods or bads can then be endogenously determined within a total analysis. When devising environmental policies one needs to be aware of the possibility that due to ambivalent joint production certain externalities may be 'hidden' or 'joint'. Material flow analysis can help to detect such instances.

APPENDIX 8A   SOLUTION IN THE CASE $w = 0$ (CORNER SOLUTION)

With $w = 0$ conditions (8.11) and (8.12) are always fulfilled. Furthermore, $D'(0) = 0$. With the model specification (8.18)–(8.22) the system of first order conditions (8.6)–(8.10) thus becomes:

$$(1 - \beta)x_1{}^{-\beta}x_2{}^{\beta} - \lambda_R + \lambda_S\kappa \ = \ 0, \tag{8.23}$$
$$\beta x_1{}^{1-\beta}x_2{}^{\beta-1} - \lambda_R - \lambda_S\tau \ = \ 0, \tag{8.24}$$
$$-\lambda_S + \lambda_W \ = \ 0, \tag{8.25}$$
$$1 - x_1 - x_2 \ = \ 0, \tag{8.26}$$
$$\kappa x_1 - \tau x_2 \ = \ 0. \tag{8.27}$$

The system of five equations (8.23)–(8.27) determines the five unknowns x_1, x_2, λ_R, λ_S and λ_W. The non-negativity constraint $\lambda_W \geq 0$ determines the range of parameter values for which a corner solution holds.

x_1 and x_2 can be calculated from (8.26) and (8.27) as

$$x_1 = \frac{\tau}{\kappa + \tau} \quad \text{and} \quad x_2 = \frac{\kappa}{\kappa + \tau}. \tag{8.28}$$

(8.28) can be substituted into (8.23) and (8.24) which then becomes a system of two linear equations in λ_R and λ_S. It can be uniquely solved for all values of κ, τ and β to yield

$$\lambda_R \ = \ \frac{\kappa^{\beta}\tau^{1-\beta}}{\kappa + \tau} \quad \text{and} \tag{8.29}$$

$$\lambda_S \ = \ \frac{\kappa^{\beta-1}\tau^{-\beta}}{\kappa + \tau} \left[\tau\beta - \kappa(1 - \beta)\right]. \tag{8.30}$$

Taking the primary resource as numéraire good, the efficient relative shadow price of the secondary resource, λ_S/λ_R, can be obtained from (8.29) and (8.30):

$$\frac{\lambda_S}{\lambda_R} = \frac{1}{\kappa\tau} \left[\tau\beta - \kappa(1 - \beta)\right]. \tag{8.31}$$

Furthermore, with (8.30) it follows from (8.25) that

$$\lambda_W = \lambda_S = \frac{\kappa^{\beta-1}\tau^{-\beta}}{\kappa + \tau} \left[\tau\beta - \kappa(1-\beta)\right]. \qquad (8.32)$$

Consistency of this result with the restriction that $\lambda_W \geq 0$ requires that the case of a corner solution holds for parameter values characterised by

$$\tau\beta - \kappa(1-\beta) \geq 0 . \qquad (8.33)$$

Obviously, with this condition being fulfilled the value of λ_S/λ_R is non-negative, too. On the other hand, the first order conditions have an interior solution $(w > 0)$ for

$$\tau\beta - \kappa(1-\beta) < 0. \qquad (8.34)$$

APPENDIX 8B   SOLUTION IN THE CASE $w > 0$ (INTERIOR SOLUTION)

With $w > 0$ condition (8.12) implies that $\lambda_W = 0$. With the model specification (8.18)–(8.22) the system of first order conditions (8.6)–(8.12) thus becomes:

$$
\begin{align}
(1-\beta)x_1^{-\beta}x_2^{\beta} - \lambda_R + \lambda_S\kappa &= 0, \qquad (8.35) \\
\beta x_1^{1-\beta}x_2^{\beta-1} - \lambda_R - \lambda_S\tau &= 0, \qquad (8.36) \\
-\delta w - \lambda_S &= 0, \qquad (8.37) \\
1 - x_1 - x_2 &= 0, \qquad (8.38) \\
\kappa x_1 - \tau x_2 - w &= 0. \qquad (8.39)
\end{align}
$$

This system of five equations (8.35)–(8.39) determines the five unknowns x_1, x_2, w, λ_R and λ_S. From (8.38) one obtains $x_2 = 1 - x_1$. (8.37) can be solved for $\lambda_S = -\delta w$ and (8.36) can be solved for

$$\lambda_R = \beta x_1^{1-\beta}x_2^{\beta-1} - \lambda_S\tau. \qquad (8.40)$$

Substituting these expressions for x_2, λ_S and λ_R into (8.35) yields the following determining equation for x_1:

$$
\begin{align}
&- \delta(\kappa + \tau)^2 x_1^{1+\beta}(1 - x_1)^{1-\beta} - x_1 \\
&+ \delta(\kappa + \tau)\tau x_1^{\beta}(1 - x_1)^{1-\beta} + (1-\beta) = 0. \qquad (8.41)
\end{align}
$$

This equation uniquely determines the efficient value of x_1 in terms of the model parameters, β, δ, κ and τ. In order to obtain a closed-form expression for x_1 one can expand x_1 in δ around $\delta = 0$ up to linear order:

$$x_1 = x_1^0 + \bar{x}_1 \cdot \delta + \mathcal{O}(\delta^2), \qquad (8.42)$$

where x_1^0 and $\bar{x}_1$ are independent of δ and the symbol $\mathcal{O}(\delta^n)$ for $n \in \mathbb{N}$ denotes terms of order n and higher in δ which vanish at least as fast as δ^n when δ goes to zero. The approximation (8.42) holds for small δ. x_1^0 is the exact solution of equation (8.41) for $\delta = 0$. By setting $\delta = 0$ in (8.41) it is easy to verify that $x_1^0 = 1 - \beta$. $\bar{x}_1$ can be obtained by substituting (8.42) into (8.41) and expanding the following expressions in δ up to linear order:

$$x_1^\beta = x_1^0 + \beta \bar{x}_1 \cdot \delta + \mathcal{O}(\delta^2), \tag{8.43}$$

$$x_1^{1+\beta} = x_1^0 + (1+\beta)\bar{x}_1 \cdot \delta + \mathcal{O}(\delta^2), \tag{8.44}$$

$$(1 - x_1)^{1-\beta} = 1 - x_1^0 + (1-\beta)\bar{x}_1 \cdot \delta + \mathcal{O}(\delta^2). \tag{8.45}$$

Noting that $x_1^0 = 1 - \beta$ and keeping only contributions up to linear order in δ this yields

$$\delta\left[-\kappa(\kappa + \tau)\beta(1 - \beta) - \bar{x}_1\right] + \mathcal{O}(\delta^2) = 0 \tag{8.46}$$

from which it follows, since $\delta > 0$, that $\bar{x}_1 = -\kappa(\kappa + \tau)\beta(1 - \beta)$ and therefore

$$x_1 = x_1^0 + \bar{x}_1 \cdot \delta + \mathcal{O}(\delta^2) = (1 - \beta)\left[1 - \kappa(\kappa + \tau)\beta \cdot \delta\right] + \mathcal{O}(\delta^2). \tag{8.47}$$

From this it follows immediately that

$$x_2 = 1 - x_1$$
$$= \beta\left[1 + \kappa(\kappa + \tau)(1 - \beta) \cdot \delta\right] + \mathcal{O}(\delta^2) \quad \text{and} \tag{8.48}$$
$$w = \kappa x_1 - \tau x_2$$
$$= \kappa(1 - \beta) - \tau\beta - \kappa(\kappa + \tau)^2\beta(1 - \beta) \cdot \delta + \mathcal{O}(\delta^2). \tag{8.49}$$

Consistency with the assumption that $w > 0$ in the interior solution requires that

$$\delta < \frac{\kappa(1 - \beta) - \tau\beta}{\kappa(\kappa + \tau)^2\beta(1 - \beta)} \tag{8.50}$$

such that (8.49) is strictly positive. This condition indicates the range of validity of the employed approximation that δ be small. With (8.49) one then obtains from (8.37):

$$\lambda_S = -\delta w = \left[\tau\beta - \kappa(1 - \beta)\right] \cdot \delta + \mathcal{O}(\delta^2). \tag{8.51}$$

From (8.40) it follows with (8.47), (8.48) and (8.51) that

$$\lambda_R = \beta^\beta(1 - \beta)^{1-\beta} + \mathcal{O}(\delta). \tag{8.52}$$

Hence, with (8.51) and (8.52) one obtains

$$\frac{\lambda_S}{\lambda_R} = \frac{\tau\beta - \kappa(1 - \beta)}{\beta^\beta(1 - \beta)^{1-\beta}} \cdot \delta + \mathcal{O}(\delta^2). \tag{8.53}$$

APPENDIX 8C   COMPARATIVE STATICS OF THE SOLUTION

Some comparative statics with the results derived in Appendix 8A and Appendix 8B yields the following insights about how the efficient solution of the model depends on the exogenous model parameters (Table 8.1).

	interior solution				corner solution		
	x_1	x_2	w	λ_S/λ_R	x_1	x_2	λ_S/λ_R
β	−	+	−	?	0	0	+
δ	−	+	−	−	0	0	0
κ	−	+	?	−	−	+	−
τ	−	+	−	+	+	−	+

Table 8.1   Comparative statics of the efficient allocation and the joint output's relative shadow price. Left-hand columns refer to the interior solution ($w > 0$), right-hand columns refer to the corner solution ($w = 0$). '+' denotes that the respective endogenous variable (x_1, x_2, w, λ_S/λ_R) strictly increases with the respective exogenous parameter (β, δ, κ, τ), '−' denotes that it strictly decreases, '0' denotes independence, '?' indicates that the effect is ambiguous.

NOTES

1. A *shadow price* is an indicator of the scarcity of some good in an economy: it is obtained by maximising the social welfare in an economy and specifies by how much welfare would increase if one additional unit of the good were available. Hence, a positive shadow price indicates that an additional unit of that good would increase welfare, while a negative shadow price indicates that an additional unit of the good would decrease welfare.

2. In the case of waste paper (cf. Chapter 15), it is not only the *production* of paper which yields waste paper as a joint product, but also its *consumption*.

3. In this chapter we explain ambivalence as a property of the social optimum of an economy. Ambivalence can also be explained as an equilibrium of a competitive market economy with profit-maximising firms and utility-maximising households (see Baumgärtner 2004a). The results are qualitatively very similar to the ones obtained here.

4. With the utility function (8.5) it is obvious that efficient consumption of both goods will always be strictly positive. Therefore, conditions (8.6) and (8.7) are fulfilled with equality. Condition (8.8) holds as an equality because the non-negativity of w is explicitly controlled for by the Lagrange parameter λ_W. Furthermore, the primary resource is always scarce since an additional unit may be employed in such a way as to produce more of both good 1 and good 2 but not more waste, thus strictly increasing utility (8.5). As a consequence, the primary resource will be fully employed in the efficient allocation and condition (8.9) holds with equality.

5.   A proper dynamic analysis of ambivalence over time would actually require a dynamic optimisation, for example using the method of optimal control. However, in this chapter we take a short-cut: The comparative statics results of the model solution with respect to the parameters specifying preferences, technology, or environmental damage are interpreted as representing a change over time. All insights thus obtained in an easy way could also be obtained by employing a more rigorous, but also more tedious, approach.

6.   As discussed in Chapter 4, stock accumulation is commonly assumed to follow the equation of motion $\dot{S}(t) = w(t) - \delta S(t)$, where the parameter δ denotes the constant rate of natural degradation by which the pollutant stock decays.

9. The Investment Decision under Joint Production*

with John Proops

9.1 INTRODUCTION

As the discussion in Chapters 4 and 5 has made clear, and as illustrated by the case studies in Part IV of this book, when thinking about environmental issues we should think about the long run. Many, if not most, environmental problems have long historical roots and long-term consequences into the future. A branch of economics that deals with the long run is capital theory, which examines the motivations and technological conditions for the accumulation of capital, that is, the 'manufactured means of production', and its economic effects (Barro and Sala-i-Martin 1995, Bliss 1975, Bliss et al. 2005, Burmeister 1980, Faber 1979, 1986b, Faber et al. 1999, Hennings 1996, Hicks 1946[1939], 1973, Malinvaud 1953, Solow 1963, Sraffa 1960, Stephan 1995, von Hayek 1941, von Weizsäcker 1971).

From the perspective of capital theory, having a longer time horizon for decision makers is generally considered as acting in favour of investment, as this allows a more rapid rate of capital accumulation, with consequent long-run increases in consumption possibilities. However, a more rapid economic growth may lead to more rapid depletion of natural resources and more rapid production of polluting wastes. Furthermore, pollutants may accumulate in the natural environment, thus further aggravating the negative side-effects of economic growth over time. Therefore, it is a priori not clear whether employing a longer time horizon in economic decision making acts in favour or against investment in new technologies if environmental effects are taken into account.

Addressing this question, in this chapter and the next we seek to bring together long-run decisions about the economy and the environment within a unified dynamic modelling framework. In particular, we

---

*This chapter draws on Baumgärtner, Faber and Proops (2002).

shall consider the production of two sorts of long-lived stocks: a desired capital good and the stock of a harmful pollutant. This approach captures an important dynamic feature of economy-environment interactions: the dynamics of the coupled economy-environment system is essentially characterised by the existence of two different and independent internal time scales of the two subsystems (cf. Chapters 4 and 5). While the dynamics of the economic subsystem are determined by the (technical and economic) rate of deterioration of long-lived capital goods, the internal dynamics of the ecological subsystem are determined by the natural degradation rate of long-lived pollutants in the environment. Intertemporal ecological-economic decision making has to take both into account.

Within that framework we discuss the innovation of a new production technique which uses a produced capital good, and which jointly produces a consumption good and a polluting bad. To clarify language, a *production technique* is defined as the minimal combination of elementary production processes that enables the production of the consumption good from primary inputs (Faber et al. 1999: 44–45). A *technology*, in contrast, is defined as the set of all available production techniques. In particular, we study:

- how the decision to bring a new technique into use depends on the time horizon of the decision maker, and

- how the intertemporal nature of the polluting bad is crucial to the decision made.

We show that, in contrast to the conventional wisdom of capital theory, extending the time horizon when there is a pollution stock may make it *less* likely that the new technique of production is introduced. In general, it will turn out that fully taking into account dynamic aspects of environmental pollution considerably increases the complexity of economic valuation and the need for environmental precaution when making an investment decision.

The theoretical literature on the innovation of a new technique of production which employs a produced capital good and which entails long-lived pollutants is rather sparse. Keeler et al. (1971) analyse the choice of production technique with stock pollution in an optimal control framework. In contrast to our approach, 'to avoid irrelevant complications' (page 26) they consider labour as the only scarce factor of production and neglect production capital. Bidard (1990), Kurz and Salvadori (1995) and Salvadori (1982, 1985) use a neo-Ricardian framework to analyse the choice of techniques which are characterised by both the use of capital goods and general joint production. However, they do not consider harmful joint products such as environmental pollution (cf. Section 6.6.2). Downing and White (1986), Malueg (1989), Milliman and Prince (1989), Jung et al. (1996), Requate (1995, 1998) and Requate and Unold (2001, 2003) study different incentives for the adoption of advanced, less polluting techniques which are characterised by the use of capital goods as well as joint production of consumption goods and environmental pollutants. However, none of these studies considers long-lived pollutants accumulating to stocks.

Capital-theoretic work is usually presented in mathematical form, as this allows the complex intertemporal relationships to be rigorously explored. However, in this chapter we focus on economic and environmental intuition. This allows us to present our core argument mainly verbally, except for some simple algebraic representations, as the main capital-theoretic elements are reasonably straightforward. The following Chapter 10 will then address some more advanced questions in more detail, but also in a more technical manner.

The chapter is organised as follows. In Section 9.2, we develop a capital-theoretic framework with joint production of consumption goods and environmental pollutants. For that purpose, we first present a general notion of capital (Section 9.2.1) and sketch the standard capital model without considering the environment (Section 9.2.2). We then introduce joint production in Section 9.2.3 and in Section 9.2.4 consider a stock pollutant which comes into existence as the result of joint production. In Section 9.3, we analyse the implications for decision making of negative joint products in capital models. In particular, we study how the decision maker's time horizon and the pollutant's time characteristic affect the decision made. Section 9.4 concludes.

9.2 CAPITAL THEORY WITH JOINT PRODUCTION OF CONSUMPTION GOODS AND ENVIRONMENTAL POLLUTANTS

9.2.1 Capital and Pollutant Stocks

The theory of capital deals with the fact that capital goods, such as power plants, computer software, buildings, etc., supply services not just in one time period, but over many periods. The aggregated amount of services over time delivered by one unit of the capital good depends (technically) on its rate of deterioration over time, and (economically) on the decision maker's time horizon. The lower the deterioration rate, the longer the capital good can be used; and the longer the time horizon, the greater is the total amount over time of services supplied by the capital good and taken into economic consideration (Faber et al. 1999: 111–116). In a nutshell, this is the source of the conventional wisdom of capital theory: for a given rate of technical deterioration the longer the time horizon of decision making, the more advantageous it is to bring into use a new technique employing a new capital good.

However, use of the capital good may also have negative effects; it may give rise to environmental pollution. Very often, this pollution accumulates over time. The accumulated stock of pollution renders disservices, that is, welfare-decreasing environmental damage, in every time period. A full intertemporal analysis of the innovation of a new technique, therefore, requires one to take into account the dynamics of *both* the desired capital good and the undesired pollution stock. Both stocks, the capital good and the harmful pollution stock, share the economic characteristics that they are (i) produced and (ii) durable, and (iii) they render (dis)services in every period of their existence. Therefore, the pollutant stock can analytically be treated similarly to the capital good, namely as a 'capital bad'. In contrast to conventional capital theory with heterogeneous capital goods (for example two different kinds of machines), the production capital good and the associated pollution stock are not independent of each other. The latter is directly linked to the former as the beneficial service and the damaging environmental pollution are necessarily jointly produced (cf. Chapter 3).

9.2.2   The Case of One Capital Good and Single Production

In the economic realm, capital theory is usually employed to study how investment in a new technique allows the intertemporal substitution and expansion of consumption. The essential idea is that one unit of saved consumption today can be invested to build up the stock of a capital good, allowing the production of more than one extra unit of consumption tomorrow, by employing the capital-based technique.

Our basic model follows the usual approach in capital theory (Burmeister 1980: Chapters 2, 3; Faber et al. 1999: Chapters 2, 3). We consider an economy where one consumption good may be produced by two different production techniques. A *production technique*, again, is defined as the minimal combination of elementary production processes that enables the production of a consumption good from primary inputs (Faber et al. 1999: 44–45). The first technique comprises only one production process in which the consumption good is directly produced from the primary inputs (for example labour and natural resources). The second technique comprises two production processes; one in which the capital good is produced from primary inputs, and one in which a consumption good is produced by the use of the capital good plus some primary inputs. There is only one type of capital good, namely production capital, and every process of production yields only one desired output.[1] In particular, there are no polluting emissions.

We suppose that currently only the first technique is in use and the second technique is newly invented. We now ask: 'Under what conditions will this new technique be brought into use?' Standard theory (for example Nickel 1978) tells us that the following relationships hold:

1. The cost of producing the consumption good with the new technique has two parts. There is a fixed cost associated with the production and setting-up of the new capital good, and a variable cost associated with the use of the capital good (for example wages for labour, replacement of capital deterioration and cost of natural resources).

2. For there to be any chance of bringing this new technique into use, it will be necessary for the variable cost to be less than the selling price of the consumption good. The excess of price over cost makes a contribution in every time period to the fixed cost.

3. The firm considering the introduction of the new technique will generally have a finite time horizon. Therefore, we assume that outcomes up to that horizon are fully considered in decision making, while later events are ignored.

4. The longer the time horizon, the greater is the summed contribution to fixed costs recognised by the firm. Hence, the longer the time horizon, the more the technique will be able to cover its cost, and it may even produce a profit. Consequently, the longer the time horizon the more likely is the new technique to be profitable and to be brought into use.

Hence, for the case of one type of capital good, namely production capital, and single production techniques (that is, techniques which produce a consumption good without any harmful emissions), we have the result that the longer the time horizon, the more advantageous it is to bring the new technique into use. This 'rule of thumb' is appealing because it gives a simple and very general answer which does not depend on details of the technology under question, the decision maker's preferences, or the resource endowment of the economy.

9.2.3 Joint Production

The above description of the production process, as yielding only one single desired output, is standard in the literature. However, as widely discussed throughout this book, it is not a good representation of reality since it runs counter to the laws of thermodynamics (Baumgärtner 2000, Georgescu-Roegen 1971, Faber et al. 1998). In Chapter 3 we have seen that, due to the laws of thermodynamics, industrial production processes – for example the production of iron from iron ore – *necessarily and unavoidably* jointly produce high entropy by-products together with the desired good. That is, every process of industrial production is necessarily joint production. Since the by-products are characterised by high specific entropy, they will generally be considered as useless waste.

9.2.4   Accumulation of Pollutants

Pollutants and wastes that jointly emerge from production activities often accumulate in the natural environment and form pollutant stocks. Depending on their natural degradation rates, they differ in their lifetime (cf. Section 4.3.1). In the analysis of goods, one usually distinguishes between short-lived consumption goods (for example bread or electricity) and long-lived capital goods (for example buildings or machines). The distinction between the two is made on their lifetime: while consumption goods are 'eaten up' in the act of consumption (so they have a lifetime of only one time period), capital goods are *used* in the process of production but they are not *used up*. Instead, they have a lifetime of more than one time period and they can render their services over many time periods. In analogy, one may distinguish between short-lived flow pollution, for example waste heat or noise, and long-lived stock pollution, for example carbon dioxide or nuclear waste (see Section 4.3.1). Of course, any particular pollutant will have a particular degradation rate, so it will lie somewhere in the spectrum between a pure flow pollutant – with instantaneous degradation and zero lifetime – and an infinitely lived stock pollutant – with zero rate of degradation and infinite lifetime.

9.3   THE INNOVATION DECISION WITH CAPITAL, JOINT PRODUCTION AND POLLUTION

9.3.1   Setting the Scene

So far, we have introduced three components into our discussion. First, capital theory as means of describing production and of analysing how firms decide whether to bring a new technique into use. Second, joint production as a realistic approach to describing production, because of the constraints set by the First and Second Laws of Thermodynamics. Third, the time characteristic of the produced waste by-product, that is, the magnitude of its natural degradation rate.

We now turn to examining the implications of these three elements for long-run investment decision making. In particular, we study the question of whether a newly invented technique should be innovated, that is, brought into use. We shall see that the crucial variable in our analysis is the time horizon of the decision maker. Up to now, when speaking of the 'decision maker' and his or her time horizon we have left it open whether these terms refer to an individual firm which considers adopting a new production technique based on the goal of profit maximisation, or whether these terms refer to society at large, which aims at achieving some Pareto efficient or welfare maximising state. We should note that the time horizon for society at large (that is, the social time horizon) will often be considerably longer than the time horizons of businesses making investment decisions.[2] The discrepancy between the social and the private time horizon causes so-called 'market failure', that is, it causes the market equilibrium achieved by individual and independent decision making of profit-maximising firms and utility-maximising households to be suboptimal from the point of view of social welfare.

Problems of market failure however, while being central to a large part of the environmental economics literature, are not our main focus. Therefore, we simply adopt the perspective of a social planner who acts on behalf of society at large so as to maximise social welfare.[3] Consequently, whenever we use the term 'time horizon' it is meant to be the social time horizon. In any case, one should note that 'time horizon' attitudes, be they individual or social, are crucial determinants in this otherwise seemingly technological analysis. We base our analysis on a simple model characterised by the following assumptions:[4]

A1: Investment in the new technique is done at time $t = 0$. The fixed cost of investment is $f > 0$.

A2: The new technique produces a consumption good at constant output level $q > 0$ in every subsequent time period. The output is sold in every time period at price $p > 0$.

A3: The variable unit production cost in every time period is $c > 0$.

A4: The time horizon of the decision maker is $n \geq 2$ time periods.

A5: There is no deterioration of the production capital.

A6: The rate of discount is zero.

We shall show that the nature of the decision is crucially dependent on the time characteristic of the jointly produced waste, that is, the pollutant's natural degradation rate. We shall distinguish three cases:

- We start in Section 9.3.2 by briefly recasting in algebraic form the investment decision without any pollution (cf. Section 9.2.2).

- In Section 9.3.3, we analyse the case of pure flow pollution, that is, the jointly produced pollutant is short-lived.

- In Section 9.3.4, we analyse the case of a stock pollutant. In that section, we first look at the general case of a positive lifetime of the pollutant, and then at the extreme case of an infinite lifetime.

9.3.2 No Pollution

We first consider the case where there is no pollution at all. The (necessary and sufficient) condition for bringing the new technique into use is that the fixed cost of investment is at least covered by the total excess of price over variable cost, summed over the time horizon, that is,

$$q(p - c)\tau > f. \tag{9.1}$$

Thus, the longer the time horizon τ of the decision maker, the more advantageous it is, ceteris paribus, to bring the new technique into use. In passing, we note that the very same condition holds for society's decision to innovate a polluting technique when ignoring the effects of pollution. For, in this case, the existence of a polluting joint product does not influence the decision.

9.3.3 Flow Pollution

We now consider the case where the new technique is jointly producing a consumption good and a flow bad, that is, the polluting joint output is short-lived. For example, the technique may be producing electricity with windmills which also produce polluting noise. Concerning the effects of the pollution, we make the following assumptions:

A7: Production of the consumption good with the new technique entails an emission in each period of $e > 0$ per unit of consumption good.

A8: The social cost of damage from pollution in each period is $d > 0$ per unit of emission. The social costs include all direct and indirect costs that society at large or individual members of society incur due to the damages from pollution.

Thus, the social cost of damage associated with the production of one unit of the consumption good is de. Furthermore, we assume that the damage is taken into account by society when making the decision. The negative effects of the pollutant then count as social variable cost, and the decision whether to introduce the new technique would now have to take it into account. Including the social variable cost in the calculation gives the condition for innovation of the new technique as

$$q(p - c - de)\tau > f. \tag{9.2}$$

That is, the benefit of consumption is reduced in each time period as compared with the no pollution case by de per unit of consumption, but the time structure of decision making is effectively unaltered as compared with the case of no pollution (cf. Section 9.3.2 above).

Comparing the criterion for introducing the new technique without any pollution and with flow pollution (Inequalities 9.1 and 9.2) we make two observations:

- First, $(p - c) > (p - c - de)$, as both d and e are strictly positive because of Assumptions A7 and A8. This includes the possibility that $(p - c)$ is positive while $(p - c - de)$ is negative, that is, the new technology is profitable when there is no pollution (or, the pollution is not taken into consideration) while it is not beneficial when taking into account the costs of pollution. In the latter case, it will not be innovated, no matter what the time horizon is.

- Second, if pollution is properly taken into account and $(p - c - de) > 0$, it is a matter of the time horizon τ whether the new technique will be innovated. The longer the time horizon of the decision maker, the more likely it is that the new technique will be brought into use, although it produces a polluting by-product. The reason for this result is that the profitability of the technique increases with the time horizon (Faber et al. 1999: Chapter 5). This result is perfectly in line with the intuition from the case of no pollution.

9.3.4   Stock Pollution

Now we treat the case where the joint product causes a stock pollution. An example is the generation of electricity from fossil fuels producing carbon dioxide as a by-product which accumulates as a harmful stock in the atmosphere. In this case, the negative environmental impact of the pollutant increases over time as the pollutant accumulates. As a consequence, the variable social cost due to pollution also increases over time. Hence, as distinct from the above case, as the time horizon is extended, the new technique may be expected to become less and less likely to be introduced. However, the pollution stock dynamics is far from being obvious. It is, in general, the combined effect of three determinants:

- There might be an initial stock of pollution prior to any emission under consideration.

- The pollution stock is augmented by the yearly emission, which comes as a joint product when employing the new technique.

- As the pollution stock grows, so does the absolute amount of natural degradation in every time period, if we assume that in every time period natural degradation is a constant fraction of the existing stock (cf. Section 4.3.1).

In order to analyse this dynamic problem in detail, we shall first deal with the general case of stock accumulation and constant natural degradation rate. Then we shall look at the extreme case of no natural degradation. The latter case deserves explicit treatment, as it is not as unrealistic and irrelevant as it might appear at first glance. For, if the decision maker's time horizon τ is much shorter than the pollutant's lifetime, then as a good approximation one might neglect the natural degradation of the pollutant over the period of analysis. This is the case, for example, with nuclear waste. As mentioned in Section 4.3.1, it has a lifetime of up to 35 000 years, but it may be treated as living infinitely when analysing decisions under a time horizon of years or decades.

In order to represent the decision problem in algebraic form, we make three further assumptions concerning the time structure of pollution, in addition to Assumptions A1 to A6 above:

A9: Production of the consumption good with the new technique entails an emission in each period of $e > 0$ per unit of consumption good.

A10: Emissions accumulate to a stock of pollution. The negative social impact of pollution in each period is proportional to the size of the accumulated stock. The social cost of damages caused by one unit of pollution stock is $d > 0$ in every time period.

A11: There is no initial pollution, that is, the stock of pollution in $t = 0$ is zero.

Stock pollution with natural degradation

We first look at the general case of stock pollution with natural degradation. In addition to Assumptions A1 to A6 and A9 to A11 above, we make the following assumption concerning the natural degradation of pollution:

A12: In each time period a constant fraction of the accumulated stock of pollution naturally degrades. The natural degradation rate is δ with $0 < \delta < 1$.

Under these assumptions, the accumulated stock of pollutant in period $t + 1$ is given by the stock in period t plus the new emission minus the natural degradation, which is the fraction δ of the pollution stock in period t:

$$S_{t+1} = S_t + qe - \delta S_t. \tag{9.3}$$

With $S_0 = 0$ (from Assumption A11) this recursive formula for the dynamics of the pollution stock can be solved, giving the following explicit expression for the stock of pollution in period t (see Appendix 9A):

$$S_t = qe\frac{1 - (1 - \delta)^t}{\delta}. \tag{9.4}$$

Obviously, in the first period $(t = 1)$ the pollution stock is qe, that is, the stock consists of the first period's emission. In the following periods, constant yearly emissions of qe contribute to the accumulation of the stock, while the natural degradation grows in proportion to the growing stock. Eventually, as t goes to infinity the stock asymptotically approaches a stable level at qe/δ. This asymptotic level increases with increases in the yearly production level of the consumption good, q, increases in the emission fraction per unit of consumption, e, and decreases in the natural degradation rate, δ.

With this explicit expression for the pollution stock in period t, and with the social variable cost of damages from pollution, d, we can write the total social variable cost over the τ period time horizon, $D(\tau)$, as (see Appendix 9B):

$$D(\tau) = \sum_{t=1}^{\tau} dS_t = \frac{dqe}{\delta} \left\{ \tau - \frac{1 - \delta}{\delta} [1 - (1 - \delta)^{\tau}] \right\}. \tag{9.5}$$

If τ is large as compared with $1/\delta$, the first term in the braces dominates the second term. We thus see that for large τ, the total τ period social variable cost $D(\tau)$ is approximately given by

$$D(\tau) \approx \frac{dqe}{\delta}\tau. \tag{9.6}$$

We can, therefore, write the condition for the innovation of the new technique as:

$$q(p - c)\tau - D(\tau) = q\left(p - c - \frac{de}{\delta}\right)\tau > f. \tag{9.7}$$

Comparing this condition with the innovation condition in the flow pollution case, Inequality (9.2), we note the following:

- First, in the stock pollution case, there is an intertemporal 'leverage effect' on the social variable cost of pollution which is due to the fact that pollutants have a lifetime of more than one time period. Consequently, every unit of emission causes a negative effect not only in the period of emission but also – albeit in degraded form – in every subsequent period. The leverage factor on social cost de is given by $1/\delta$, which is the pollutant's lifetime (cf. Section 4.3.1). For instance, if the pollutant has a lifetime of ten years, then the social unit cost of pollution is weighted by a factor of ten in the innovation condition.

- Second, due to the leverage effect from the pollutant's lifetime, it is now less likely than in the flow pollution case that the new technique is beneficial within each period, that is, $(p-c-de/\delta) > 0$. Therefore, it is less likely that the new technique will be considered for innovation, irrespective of the length of the decision maker's time horizon.

Stock pollution with no natural degradation

We now look at the extreme case of stock pollution when there is no natural degradation at all. In addition to assumptions A1 to A6 and A9 to A11 above, we make the following assumption concerning the natural degradation of pollution:

A13: The natural degradation rate of the pollutant is zero, that is, the accumulated stock has an infinite lifetime.

By Assumptions A9, A10, A11 and A13, the accumulated stock of pollutant in period t is $S_t = qet$ and the social variable cost of damages from pollution is $D_t = dS_t = dqet$ in time period t. We can therefore write the total social variable cost over the τ period time horizon, $D(\tau)$, as (see Appendix 9C):

$$D(\tau) = \sum_{t=1}^{\tau} D_t = \frac{dqe}{2}\left(\tau^2 + \tau\right). \qquad (9.8)$$

We thus see that the total τ period social variable cost $D(\tau)$ increases with the square of the number of periods to the time horizon.

We write the condition for the innovation of the new technique, again, as:

$$q(p - c)\tau - D(\tau) > f. \qquad (9.9)$$

We see that as $D(\tau)$ increases with τ^2, increasing the time horizon will always eventually cause the social variable costs of pollution to increase to a level such that the technique would *not* be introduced. Thus, the longer the time horizon, the *less* likely is innovation of the new technique. This result is in stark contrast with the conventional wisdom of capital theory (cf. Section 9.2.2), according to which the longer the time horizon, the *more* likely is innovation of the new technique.

9.4 CONCLUSIONS

The consideration of environmental effects in investment decisions considerably extends the sphere of economic and social decision making, because the interactions between the purely economic domain and the environmental domain also have to be examined. While this is already true in the static case, it applies particularly to the case of a dynamic environment. The complexity of the latter increases if not only flows but also stocks are taken into account, and this considerably complicates the time structure of the analysis. This increasing complexity of dynamic cause-effect chains is a major reason why environmental policy measures are so difficult to design, to enact, and to carry through.

We have illustrated this increasing complexity with an analysis of how the innovation of a new technique depends on the time horizon of the decision maker and the intertemporal nature of the pollutant. Both determine, together with the time structure of production, the time structure of the environmental damages. While the conventional wisdom of capital theory states that the longer the time horizon of the decision maker the more likely is innovation, our analysis has shown that this result has to be qualified in several respects and may even be completely reversed:

1. In the case of flow pollution the innovation of a technique becomes less likely than in the case of no pollution. However, the dependence on the time horizon is as in the no-pollution case: the longer the time horizon the more likely is innovation.

2. If the pollutant accumulates to a stock, then there is an additional intertemporal leverage effect as to the damage and the associated social cost of pollution, which depends crucially on the lifetime of the pollutant.

3. If the natural degradation rate of the pollutant is zero, or if the pollutant's lifetime is long as compared to the time horizon of

the decision maker, which is, in practice, the case for all non-ferrous metals, chlorofluorocarbons (CFCs), nuclear waste, CO_2, etc., then the conventional wisdom of capital theory is completely reversed. In this case, the longer the time horizon the less likely is the innovation of a new technique.

The method and assumptions of our analysis limit the validity of the results. For this reason, we want to close this chapter by discussing those of our assumptions which seem to be particularly restrictive. Assumption A2 (constant output in every period) simplifies the analysis and can easily be relaxed. If q is replaced by $q(t)$ $(t = 1, ..., \tau)$ all formulae can be correspondingly altered and by direct economic argumentation one readily sees that our conclusions remain valid. A similar consideration holds if we employ non-linear cost functions instead of linear ones. In that case, the variable cost c has to be replaced by $c(q)$ but, apart from that, all of our conclusions remain valid.

If Assumption A5 (zero rate of capital deterioration) is given up and replaced by the assumption of a strictly positive, yet constant, rate of capital deterioration, then the variable cost c correspondingly increases by a constant amount representing the costs of replacing capital deterioration. Since this only changes the value of c but leaves unaltered the structure of all formulae derived, our qualitative results remain valid.

Assumption A6 (zero discount rate) does not restrict but merely simplifies our analysis as long as Assumptions A2 (constant consumption output over time) and A7/A9 (constant emissions over time) are maintained. As soon as one introduces variation of output of consumption and emissions according to different time profiles, however, the assumption of zero discount rate restricts the validity of our results. Under the assumption of non-constant output of consumption and emissions, varying differently over time, together with a strictly positive discount rate, the role of the time horizon is no longer uniquely determined. In that case, a longer time horizon might act in favour or against investment. As this raises interesting and relevant questions, they will be addressed in a more detailed, but also more technical and complex, analysis in the following Chapter 10.

On a different level, this chapter suggests another conclusion, which is rather general and will be further supported by the analysis in the following chapter: Taking into account the multiple stocks of ecological-economic systems, and their dynamics, considerably increases the complexity of economic valuation and the need for environmental precaution when making an investment decision. We will come back to this issue in Part III of the book from an alternative perspective.

APPENDIX 9A   PROOF OF EQUATION (9.4)

With $S_0 = 0$ we can recursively solve the dynamic difference equation (9.3). We have:

$$S_1 = qe,$$
$$S_2 = (1 - \delta)qe + qe,$$
$$S_3 = (1 - \delta)[(1 - \delta)qe + qe] + qe = (1 - \delta)^2 qe + (1 - \delta)qe + qe$$

and, in general,

$$S_t = qe\left[(1 - \delta)^{t-1} + (1 - \delta)^{t-2} + \ldots + 1\right] = qe\sum_{t'=1}^{t}(1 - \delta)^{t'-1}.$$

The sum involved in this expression is standard and known to yield

$$\sum_{t'=1}^{t} a^{t'-1} = \frac{1 - a^t}{1 - a} \qquad \text{for } 0 < a < 1.$$

Here, $a = 1 - \delta$ and therefore

$$\sum_{t'=0}^{t-1}(1 - \delta)^{t'} = \frac{1 - (1 - \delta)^t}{1 - (1 - \delta)} = \frac{1 - (1 - \delta)^t}{\delta},$$

which immediately yields Equation (9.4).

APPENDIX 9B   PROOF OF EQUATION (9.5)

With $S_t = qe[1 - (1 - \delta)^t]/\delta$ (from Equation 9.4) we have

$$D(\tau) = \sum_{t=1}^{\tau} dS_t = \frac{dqe}{\delta}\sum_{t=1}^{\tau}\left[1 - (1 - \delta)^t\right] = \frac{dqe}{\delta}\left[\tau - \sum_{t=1}^{\tau}(1 - \delta)^t\right].$$

The sum involved in this expression can be reduced to a standard sum, which is known to yield

$$\sum_{t=1}^{\tau} a^{t-1} = \frac{1 - a^\tau}{1 - a} \qquad \text{for } 0 < a < 1.$$

With $a = 1 - \delta$ we thus have

$$\sum_{t=1}^{\tau}(1-\delta)^t = (1-\delta)\sum_{t=1}^{\tau}(1-\delta)^{t-1} = (1-\delta)\frac{1 - (1 - \delta)^\tau}{1 - (1 - \delta)} = \frac{1 - \delta}{\delta}\left[1 - (1 - \delta)^\tau\right].$$

From this, Equation (9.5) follows immediately.

APPENDIX 9C   PROOF OF EQUATION (9.8)

With $D_t = dqet$ we have

$$D(\tau) = \sum_{t=1}^{\tau} D_t = \sum_{t=1}^{\tau} dqet = dqe \sum_{t=1}^{\tau} t.$$

The sum involved in this expression is a standard one,

$$\sum_{t=1}^{\tau} t = \frac{(\tau + 1)\tau}{2} = \frac{1}{2}\left(\tau^2 + \tau\right),$$

which immediately leads to the result expressed in Equation (9.8).

NOTES

1.   Processes in which capital is used will, in general, yield deteriorated capital as a by-product to the intended main product. Throughout this chapter, however, deteriorated capital will not be considered as a joint product. See Kurz and Salvadori (1995) for a treatment of fixed capital as joint product.

2.   This distinction between the social time horizon and the investment time horizon might be related to Sagoff's (1988) distinction between the consumer and the citizen. The former is concerned with individual, and generally short-term satisfaction; the latter has concern for wider society including future generations.

3.   Although our analysis focusses on the perspective of a social planner, our analytical framework can easily be expanded to deal with instances of market failure, too. For example, one could distinguish between the social time horizon and the time horizon of private businesses.

4.   In the concluding Section 9.4, we discuss how these assumptions restrict the generality of our results.

10. Structural Change under Joint Production[*]

with Ralph Winkler

10.1 INTRODUCTION

The basic idea of the analysis carried out in this chapter is similar to Chapter 9. As in Chapter 9, we will examine the trade-off between the production of a desired consumption good and an unwanted but jointly emerging environmental pollutant. We will also distinguish between flow pollutants which cause environmental damage solely in the period they occur, and stock pollutants which accumulate in nature and cause environmental degradation in every subsequent period. But in this chapter, we will use a more sophisticated model framework than in Chapter 9 and relax some of the assumptions made in that chapter. First, we formally introduce a time structure for the production process: the production of new capital goods does not occur instantaneously but takes time, and we suppose the existing capital stock to deteriorate at a given rate. Second, the valuation of the trade-off between consumption and the pollutant is carried out endogenously by assuming a representative consumer with intertemporal preferences. Third, we introduce two different methods of production, only one of which jointly produces the unwanted pollutant. This more sophisticated framework allows us to study the dynamics of structural change in the economy.

We speak of *structural change* if the different capital stocks within the economy change their relative composition. This takes place if a new production technique is *invented*, which is the emergence of a new production method, and *innovated*, that is bringing the new production method into use by investment in the specific capital goods.[1]

As we have seen in Chapter 3, all production is joint production from a thermodynamic point of view. As a consequence, production techniques do not only produce the goods they are innovated for, but necessarily

---

[*]This chapter is based on Winkler (2005).

also produce joint outputs. Although the character of a joint output may not be determined a priori as a good or a bad (cf. Chapter 8), in this chapter we will limit our attention to the case of an unwanted and at least potentially harmful joint output accruing in fixed proportion to the desired commodity. Given these assumptions, we will analyse the trade-off between increased production of consumption and natural degradation, both caused by the innovation of a new production technique, and derive necessary and sufficient conditions for structural change within the economy. In contrast to Chapter 9, we do not measure welfare benefits of consumption and welfare decreases due to environmental pollution in monetary terms. In fact, within the model framework presented here, both the consumption good and the pollutant retain their genuine characteristics as different commodities. Hence, the direct comparability between the two methods of production is lost as one technique produces solely the welfare-increasing consumption goods, and the other technique additionally produces a welfare-decreasing pollutant. In the following sections, we introduce three possible ways to deal with the joint output.

This chapter is organised as follows. As the model framework used in this chapter is an extension of the neo-Austrian three-sector model introduced by Faber and Proops (1991) and Faber et al. (1999: Chapters 3 and 4), Section 10.2 gives a brief introduction to this model. In Section 10.3, we extend this model framework by introducing joint production of an unwanted and at least potentially harmful pollutant. With the technical approach in Section 10.4, the ecological approach in Section 10.5 and the economic approach in Section 10.6, we introduce three idealised scenarios which are motivated by how politics may deal with unwanted joint outputs. Section 10.7 concludes.

10.2   The Neo-Austrian Three-Sector Model

Assume the intertemporal welfare function W of a representative consumer to be

$$W\{c(t)\} = \sum_{t=1}^{\tau}(1+\rho)^{-(t-1)}V(c(t)) , \qquad (10.1)$$

where V denotes a twice continuously differentiable, strictly increasing and concave instantaneous welfare function ($V_c > 0$, $V_{cc} < 0$), ρ the constant and positive discount rate and τ the time horizon.

Labour, the only non-producible input of production, is supposed to be fixed at the level $\bar{l}$ in each period and is allocated to three linear limitational production processes R_h, where $l_h(t)$ denotes the labour employed to process R_h at time t ($h = 1, 2, 3$). The consumption good can be produced by production processes R_1 and R_2. Process R_1 solely needs λ_1 units of labour, while Process R_2 combines λ_2 units of labour and κ units of the capital good k to produce one unit of the consumption good:

$$R_1 : \quad c_1(t) \quad = \quad \frac{l_1(t)}{\lambda_1} \; , \tag{10.2}$$

$$R_2 : \quad c_2(t) \quad = \quad \min \left[\frac{l_2(t)}{\lambda_2}, \frac{k(t)}{\kappa} \right] . \tag{10.3}$$

We suppose that the capital stock k is fully employed in every period.[2] Furthermore, we suppose an efficient labour allocation among the three processes. Then Equation (10.3) yields:

$$c_2(t) = \frac{l_2(t)}{\lambda_2} = \frac{k(t)}{\kappa} . \tag{10.4}$$

The consumption good is supposed to be homogeneous. Thus, total consumption is simply the sum of the production outputs produced by processes R_1 and R_2:

$$c(t) = c_1(t) + c_2(t) . \tag{10.5}$$

New capital goods are produced by the third production process R_3. Employing λ_3 units of labour yields one unit of new capital good:

$$R_3 : \quad i(t) = \frac{l_3(t)}{\lambda_3} . \tag{10.6}$$

The exogenously given technical coefficients λ_h ($h = 1, 2, 3$) and κ specify the production technology. As welfare is strictly increasing in consumption, in the optimum the labour supply $\bar{l}$ will be used up completely by the three production processes in every period t:

$$\bar{l} = l_1(t) + l_2(t) + l_3(t) . \tag{10.7}$$

The central assumption in this model is that the production of capital goods needs time. Thus, investment i in new capital goods in period t accumulates the existing capital stock k in period $t+1$. Furthermore, we assume that the deterioration of capital is proportional to the existing capital stock at a constant and exogenously given rate γ, which leads to the following equation of motion for the capital stock k:

$$k(t) = (1 - \gamma)k(t-1) + i(t-1) . \tag{10.8}$$

The model encompasses two techniques (Faber and Proops 1991: 147), where a *technique of production* is defined as the minimal combination of production processes which allows the production of the consumption good by the non-produced inputs (see also Chapter 9). The first technique T_1 consists solely of process R_1. The second technique T_2 comprises processes R_2 and R_3. Technique T_2 needs more time to produce consumption goods because of the time-consuming production of capital goods. Hence, technique T_2 is said to be more *roundabout* (Stephan 1995: 54).

Suppose that the first technique represents the status quo in the economy and technique T_2 has recently been discovered, that is the initial capital stock k_0 equals zero. The question we pose is, are there (i) necessary and (ii) sufficient conditions under which the new technique T_2 will be innovated and – at least partly – replace the existing technique T_1? Due to the structure of the model, both necessary and sufficient conditions can be derived without solving the intertemporal optimisation problem.

10.2.1   Superiority of a Production Technique

To derive a necessary condition for the innovation of the new technique, we first define superiority of a technique (Stephan 1995: 55). A production technique T_2 is *superior* to technique T_1 if for a given endowment of non-produced inputs the maximal producible sum of consumption goods within the time horizon τ is larger for technique T_2 than for technique T_1.

According to this definition, technique T_2 is superior to technique T_1 if the total amount of consumption produced by technique T_2 exceeds the consumption good production by technique T_1, which can be shown to be equivalent to (Faber et al. 1999: 112–116):

$$S(\tau) \equiv \frac{\lambda_1 - \lambda_2}{\lambda_3 \kappa} - \frac{\gamma}{1 - (1 - \gamma)^{\tau - 1}} + 1 > 1 . \qquad (10.9)$$

The left-hand side is called *degree of superiority* S (Faber and Proops 1991: 149). Thus, technique T_2 is superior to technique T_1 if $S > 1$. Note that S is bounded from above by $S(\infty)$, as $S(\infty)$ is finite and S is a positive and increasing function with respect to the time horizon τ. If the representative consumer is impatient to consume, that is $\rho > 0$, and the new technique is more roundabout than the existing technique, then the innovation of technique T_2 can only be optimal if technique T_2 is superior to technique T_1. Hence, superiority is a *necessary condition* for the innovation of technique T_2.

10.2.2 Sufficient Condition for the Innovation of a Production Technique

Nevertheless, being superior to the existing technique T_1 is not sufficient for the innovation of the new technique T_2. In addition, the new technique has to yield higher intertemporal utility than the existing technique to be preferred by the representative consumer. From the necessary and sufficient conditions for the optimal solution of the intertemporal maximisation problem one can show that the innovation of technique T_2 is optimal if (Winkler 2005):

$$\frac{\lambda_1 - \lambda_2}{\lambda_3 \kappa} > \frac{(1+\rho)^{\tau-1}(\gamma+\rho)}{(1+\rho)^{\tau-1} - (1-\gamma)^{\tau-1}} \ . \tag{10.10}$$

Defining the *criterion function* P (Faber and Proops 1991: 153) as

$$P(\tau) \equiv 1 + \frac{(1+\rho)^{\tau-1}(\gamma+\rho)}{(1+\rho)^{\tau-1} - (1-\gamma)^{\tau-1}} - \frac{\gamma}{1-(1-\gamma)^{\tau-1}} \ , \tag{10.11}$$

a sufficient condition for innovating the new technique T_2 is that $S > P$.

It can be shown that the innovation of technique T_2 is more likely as the time horizon τ expands (Faber and Proops 1991: 145). This is in line with the conventional wisdom of capital theory that, in general, innovation is more likely if the decision maker considers a longer time horizon (cf. Chapter 9). Note that the innovation of a new technique T_2 is independent of the exact functional form of the instantaneous welfare function V as long as it satisfies standard curvature properties. Note further that technique T_2 will fully replace technique T_1 if the innovation of technique T_2 is optimal and the time horizon τ is sufficiently long. In the remainder of this chapter, we analyse whether this result turns out to be robust if the new technique also produces an unwanted joint output.

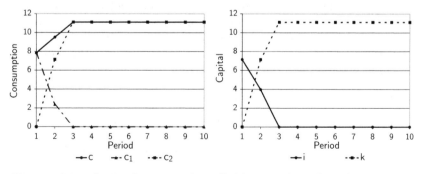

Figure 10.1   Optimal consumption (left), capital stock and investment (right) without joint production of an unwanted pollutant.

Figure 10.1 illustrates the structural change induced by the innovation of a new production technique by a numerically optimised example. The calculation details are given in Appendix 10A. For simplicity, we neglect capital deterioration. Hence, once the capital stock is established it can be used for the whole time horizon τ. We observe that in the early periods a part of the maximal producible consumption via technique T_1 is sacrificed to invest in the specific capital good needed by technique T_2. Once the capital stock is established, solely the production technique T_2 is used, yielding a higher consumption output than using the technique T_1.[3]

10.3   JOINT PRODUCTION

We now suppose that the newly invented production technique T_2 additionally yields an unwanted and at least potentially harmful joint output. Furthermore, we assume that the unwanted output occurs in fixed proportion to the desired output. Despite these limitations we have to examine a variety of different cases. First, the joint output can occur in the consumption-good-producing process R_2 or in the production of new capital goods in process R_3. Second, with regard to its time characteristic, the joint output and its potential harmfulness can be of two different types. In the case of a flow pollutant (cf. Sections 4.3.1 and 9.2.4) the emissions themselves can be regarded as the source of natural degradation, for example noise or SO_2 emissions.[4] In the alternative case that the emissions accumulate in the biosphere, it is a pollutant stock which causes environmental damage, for example greenhouse gases like CO_2 and CH_4. Third, there is the problem of comparability between the two techniques. In Section 10.2, both techniques produced a good of the same quality – the consumption good. Now technique T_2 also produces another good of a completely different quality – the unwanted pollutant. Hence, it is not adequate any more to simply compare the intertemporal quantity of consumption good output produced by both techniques. In the following three sections, we discuss three different idealised possibilities to solve this problem:

- a *technical approach*, based on an abatement process (Section 10.4),

- an *ecological approach*, based on a pollution limit (Section 10.5),

- an *economic approach*, based on valuation (Section 10.6).

These three approaches are motivated by the different ways in which environmental policy may address the problem of harmful pollutants.

10.4 JOINT PRODUCTION IN THE PRESENCE OF AN ABATEMENT PROCESS

For the technical approach we suppose that there is an additional process, the *abatement process* R_4. This process is capable of converting the unwanted and harmful pollutant in a completely harmless (and useless) output by the means of labour. If the amount of labour employed in the abatement process in period t is $l_4(t)$ and the process needs λ_4 units of labour to abate one unit of joint output, then the amount of abated joint output equals:

$$R_4 : \quad j^{ab}(t) = \frac{l_4(t)}{\lambda_4} . \tag{10.12}$$

Obviously, the labour restriction, given by Equation (10.7), has to be expanded to:

$$\bar{l} = l_1(t) + l_2(t) + l_3(t) + l_4(t) . \tag{10.13}$$

To ensure the comparability between the two production techniques the abatement process R_4 has to be employed to such an extent in every period that the total amount of joint output produced by technique T_2 is abated. We impute the additional labour needed for the abatement process to the production technique T_2. Hence, technique T_2 now encompasses a third process, the abatement process R_4. As a consequence, the net output of both techniques only consists of consumption goods. In particular, there are no more joint outputs.[5] Thus, the comparability between the two techniques is achieved again. As there is no net output of the unwanted and harmful joint product into the natural environment, we do not have to distinguish between flow and stock pollutants at this point.

10.4.1 Joint Output in the Consumption Good Production

First, assume that the unwanted and harmful joint output accrues in the production of the consumption good in process R_2. Furthermore, we assume that this process generates the joint output j in a fixed proportion α to the consumption good c_2:

$$j(t) = \alpha c_2(t) . \tag{10.14}$$

By assumption the net output of joint products equals zero, that is $j(t) = j^{ab}(t)$. Hence, per unit of consumption good c_2, $\lambda_4 \alpha$ units of labour are used to abate the emerging pollutant. Thus, processes R_2 and R_4 can be combined to form a clean production process with

$$c_2(t) = \min \left[\frac{\hat{l}_2(t)}{\hat{\lambda}_2}, \frac{k(t)}{\kappa} \right] , \tag{10.15}$$

where $\hat{l}_2(t) = l_2(t) + l_4(t)$ and $\hat{\lambda}_2 = \lambda_2 + \alpha\lambda_4$. The formal structure of the model is identical to the model framework in Section 10.2 if $l_2(t)$ and λ_2 are replaced by $\hat{l}_2(t)$ and $\hat{\lambda}_2$. As a consequence, the results simply have to be adjusted in the same manner. Note that λ_2 only appears in the degree of superiority S but not in the criterion function P. The adjusted degree of superiority $\hat{S}$ reads:

$$\hat{S}(\tau) = \frac{\lambda_1 - (\lambda_2 + \alpha\lambda_4)}{\lambda_3\kappa} - \frac{\gamma}{1 - (1-\gamma)^{\tau-1}} + 1 \ . \tag{10.16}$$

10.4.2   Joint Output in the Capital Good Production

Second, the unwanted and harmful pollutant is supposed to accrue in the production of new capital goods in process R_3. Assuming that the pollutant is produced in a fixed proportion β to the investment i, the amount of pollutant produced is:

$$j(t) = \beta i(t) \ . \tag{10.17}$$

Again, the abatement process R_4 and the capital-producing process R_3 can be combined to form a clean production process with

$$i(t) = \frac{\hat{l}_3(t)}{\hat{\lambda}_3} \ , \tag{10.18}$$

where $\hat{l}_3(t) = l_3(t) + l_4(t)$ and $\hat{\lambda}_3 = \lambda_3 + \beta\lambda_4$. Analogously, the adjusted degree of superiority can be written as:

$$\hat{S}(\tau) = \frac{\lambda_1 - \lambda_2}{(\lambda_3 + \beta\lambda_4)\kappa} - \frac{\gamma}{1 - (1-\gamma)^{\tau-1}} + 1 \ . \tag{10.19}$$

10.4.3   Innovation of the New Technique

The formal structure of the model with joint production and an abatement process is identical to the model presented in Section 10.2 if the degree of superiority S is replaced by the corresponding expression $\hat{S}$. Hence, all the results we have obtained in Section 10.2 are still valid. Note that, given identical parameter values, the degree of superiority is reduced when the joint production of a harmful pollutant is considered, that is $\hat{S} < S$. This is obvious as additional labour for the abatement process has to be employed, which reduces the amount of capital and consumption goods that can be produced by given labour supply $\bar{l}$ with technique T_2. Hence, as all production is joint production from a physical point of view (cf. Chapter 3), the superiority of a new production technique T_2 is, in general, overestimated if joint outputs are not considered explicitly. As a consequence, with harmful joint outputs taken into account, the innovation of the new technique is less likely to be optimal.

Figure 10.2 shows the optimal structural change for a numerically optimised example of joint production in processes R_2 and R_3. For better comparability, the parameters have been chosen as in Figure 10.1 (see Appendix 10A). If the joint output is produced in process R_2 a full replacement of technique T_1 is not optimal. If the joint output occurs in process R_3 we achieve full replacement of technique T_1, but it is delayed compared to the scenario without joint production (Figure 10.1). Hence, given identical parameters α and β, joint production is more restrictive if prevalent in process R_2 than in process R_3. This is obvious, as in process R_2 α units of pollutant are jointly produced with every unit of consumption good, while in process R_3 β units of pollutant jointly occur with every unit of new capital good which can be used to produce many units of consumption good for the rest of the time horizon τ.

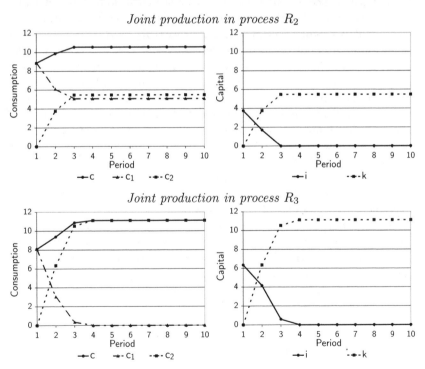

Figure 10.2   Optimal consumption (left), capital stock and investment (right) with joint production of a pollutant in the presence of an abatement process.

10.5   JOINT PRODUCTION IN THE PRESENCE OF A POLLUTION LIMIT

For the ecological approach we suppose that the natural environment has limited self-cleaning and assimilation capabilities which prevent harmful damage from pollutant emissions as long as the capacities of these mechanisms are not exceeded. Hence, we investigate the consequences of a pollution limit which accounts for these self-cleaning and assimilation capacities. Formally, an additional restriction, the pollution limit, is introduced to the model presented in Section 10.2. If the pollutant is a flow pollutant, then the restriction will limit the maximal amount of emissions in every period. Otherwise, if the pollutant is a stock pollutant then the stock will be restricted by a certain limit.

10.5.1   Innovation of the New Technique

In contrast to Section 10.4, we have to distinguish four different cases, depending on whether the joint output is a flow or a stock pollutant, and whether it is produced in production process R_2 or R_3. As long as the pollution limit is not reached, the necessary and sufficient conditions for the four cases are identical to Section 10.2. Hence, the degree of superiority S as well as the criterion function P, as defined in Equations (10.9) and (10.11), remain unaltered. As a consequence, it is always possible to replace (at least partly) technique T_1 by production technique T_2 if the pollution limit is strictly positive, irrespective of whether the joint output is a flow or stock pollutant, or whether the joint output accrues in process R_2 or R_3.[6]

But even if the general question about the innovation of the new technique seems to be untouched as long as the pollution limit is not exceeded, the dynamics of the system depends crucially upon the type of the joint output and in which process it is produced. If the joint output is produced by the production of the consumption good in process R_2, it may be optimal to not fully employ the capital stock in all periods. Furthermore, even for an infinite time horizon τ, a full replacement of technique T_1 by technique T_2 cannot be achieved in general due to the pollution limit. But we can derive necessary conditions for a full replacement.

10.5.2   Flow Pollutant as a Joint Output

If the joint output is a flow pollutant, then the exogenously given emission limit ϕ must not be exceeded in every period t, i.e. $\phi \geq j(t)$. First, let us assume that the joint output is produced by the production process R_2, the production of the consumption good. According to

Equation (10.14), the amount of joint output produced in every period is given by $j(t) = \alpha c_2(t)$. As the production of joint output is limited to a maximum of ϕ in every period, the production of the consumption good via production technique T_2 is also limited:

$$c_2(t) \leq c_2^{max_1} = \frac{\phi}{\alpha} . \tag{10.20}$$

The maximal amount of consumption good which could be produced without a pollution limit equals $c_2^{MAX} = \bar{l}/(\lambda_2 + \lambda_3 \kappa \gamma)$. It is the amount of consumption good produced if technique T_1 is completely replaced by technique T_2. As a consequence, if $c_2^{max_1} < c_2^{MAX}$ then the new technique T_2 cannot fully replace the established technique T_1, even if this would be optimal without an emission limit. Furthermore, the limit ϕ also limits the usable capital stock to $k^{max_1} = \kappa c_2^{max_1} = \kappa \phi / \alpha$ in every period.

Second, we suppose that the joint output accrues in the capital good production process R_3. According to Equation (10.17), the amount of joint output produced is $j(t) = \beta i(t)$. As the production of joint output is limited to a maximum of ϕ in every period, the production of new capital goods is also limited:

$$i(t) \leq i^{max_2} = \frac{\phi}{\beta} . \tag{10.21}$$

Two consequences arise from this limitation:

1. The replacement of technique T_1 by technique T_2 can take a longer time compared to the case without joint production, because the production of new capital i to accumulate the capital stock k is limited to i^{max_2} in every period.

2. Given a positive deterioration rate γ, the maximal sustainable capital stock k^{max_2} is reached when i^{max_2} is completely used to replace deteriorated capital, i.e. $k^{max_2} = i^{max_2}/\gamma$. According to Equation (10.3), a limited capital stock also implies a limited amount of consumption good $c_2^{max_2} = k^{max_2}/\kappa$. As a consequence, a complete replacement of technique T_1 is not possible if $c_2^{max_2} < c_2^{MAX}$.

Figure 10.3 shows a numerical example of the replacement of technique T_1 by technique T_2 with joint production of a flow pollutant in the consumption good process R_2 and in the capital good process R_3. The parameter values for the calculation have been chosen to be identical to Figures 10.1 and 10.2, and are listed in Appendix 10A. In the case of joint production in process R_2, the maximal producible amount of

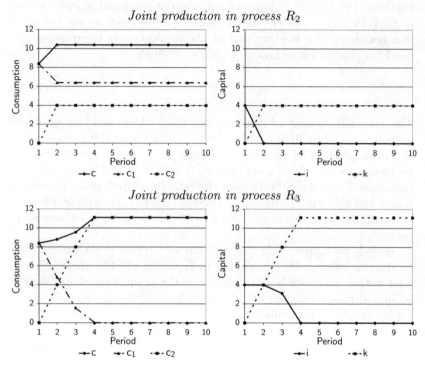

Figure 10.3   Optimal consumption (left), capital stock and investment (right) with joint production of a flow pollutant in the presence of an emission limit.

consumption good is limited to 4 because of the emission limit. Hence, a complete replacement is not possible. If the flow pollutant emerges jointly in process R_3 then we achieve full replacement, but it is delayed compared to the scenario without joint production (Figure 10.1), because in every period a maximum of 4 units of new capital can be produced due to the emission limit.

10.5.3   Stock Pollutant as a Joint Output

If the joint output is a stock pollutant, then the stock e of the pollutant is restricted to a certain amount ϕ in every period, that is $\phi \geq e(t)$. The stock e is assumed to be the stock of the last period plus the new emissions j less some natural decay. For simplicity, the natural decay is assumed to be proportional to the stock of the pollutant at a positive and constant rate δ (cf. Section 4.3.1). Thus, the equation of motion for

Structural Change under Joint Production

the stock of the pollutant reads:

$$e(t) = (1 - \delta)e(t-1) + j(t) .$$

(10.22)

The complexity of the model has significantly increased, since Equation (10.22) defines a second stock whose variations are described by a difference equation. Furthermore, if the joint output is produced in process R_2 then it might be optimal to produce a capital stock which is not fully employed in all periods: in early periods a huge capital stock is accumulated and fully employed while in later periods, as the stock of the pollutant reaches the upper boundary, the capital stock is employed under capacity to comply with the pollution limit.

In order to derive necessary conditions for a full replacement, the long-run *stationary state* is analysed, since optimal replacement is then completed. If the restriction ϕ is binding, then the long-run stock of pollutant equals $e(t) = \phi$. Hence, in every subsequent period the amount of pollutant emitted must not exceed the amount of pollutant degrading within this period, that is $j(t) \leq \delta\phi$. The problem is similar to the case of a flow pollutant where the emissions j are limited in every period. Depending on the production process which produces the joint output, the following restrictions hold:

$$\delta\phi = j(t) = \alpha c_2(t) ,$$

(10.23)

$$\delta\phi = j(t) = \beta i(t) .$$

(10.24)

In analogy to the case of a flow pollutant, full replacement of the technique T_1 by technique T_2 is not possible in the case where the joint output accrues in production process R_2 if $c_2^{MAX} > (\delta\phi)/\alpha$, and not possible in the case where the pollutant is produced by the production of new capital goods if $c_2^{MAX} > \delta\phi/(\beta\gamma\kappa)$. Furthermore, in the latter case the replacement of technique T_1 by technique T_2 can be delayed compared to the case of the unrestricted system because of the limitation of new capital production in every period.

Figure 10.4 shows a numerically optimised example for the case that the joint output is a stock pollutant and the stock of pollutant is restricted to a certain boundary. In addition to the previous figures, the stock of pollutant is also displayed (right). If the joint output accrues in the production of the consumption good, then full replacement cannot be achieved. Furthermore, from period 8 on the stock of pollutant reaches its boundary of 3 units. As a consequence, the capital stock is no longer fully employed to comply with the restriction, which is indicated by a drop of the consumption c_2 in period 9 and 10. If the pollutant is produced in process R_3 then the restriction of 3 units is already reached

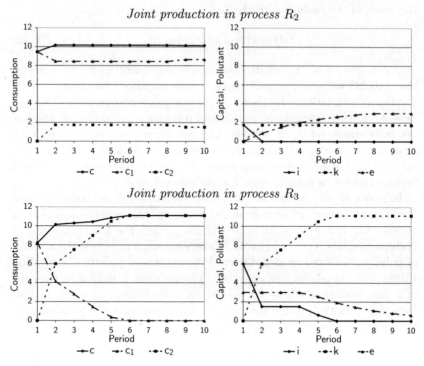

Figure 10.4   Optimal consumption (left), capital stock, stock of pollutant and investment (right) with joint production of a stock pollutant in the presence of a pollution limit.

in the first period. Hence, in all subsequent periods only such an amount of pollutant can be emitted which degrades within one period. As a consequence, the full replacement of technique T_2 is delayed compared to the case without joint production.

10.6   JOINT PRODUCTION AND ECONOMIC EVALUATION

Although it was assumed that the joint output interacts with, and degrades, the natural environment, the quality of the natural environment itself has not been an economic decision variable so far. In fact, in Sections 10.4 and 10.5, we simply assumed that either no pollutant at all was released into the environment, or the pollutant was emitted in amounts such that no natural degradation occurred. From an economic point of view, such an outcome will only be optimal if we presume that society has very strong preferences for environmental quality. As an alternative, in this section we shall perform an explicit *economic evaluation* of the trade-off between consumption good production via technique T_2 on the one hand, and the degradation of the natural environment by the emission of harmful pollutants on the other hand.

10.6.1 The Intertemporal Welfare Function

Suppose intertemporal welfare does not solely depend on the stream of consumption good c, but also on environmental degradation d which is assumed to be identical to the emissions $d(t) \equiv j(t)$ in the case of a flow pollutant, or to the stock of the pollutant $d(t) \equiv e(t)$ in the case of a stock pollutant. Again, we assume that intertemporal welfare is the discounted sum of instantaneous welfare in each period:

$$W\{c(t), d(t)\} = \sum_{t=1}^{\tau} (1 + \rho)^{-(t-1)} V(c(t), d(t)) . \qquad (10.25)$$

The instantaneous welfare function V is supposed to be twice continuously differentiable, concave and to exhibit the following standard properties:

$$\begin{array}{lll} V_c > 0 , & V_{cc} < 0 , & \\ V_d < 0 , & V_{dd} < 0 , & V_d(c(t), 0) = 0 . \end{array} \qquad (10.26)$$

10.6.2 Innovation of the New Technique

According to Equation (10.26), the marginal welfare loss caused by the joint output is zero if no joint output is produced. In this case the conditions for an optimal solution are identical to Section 10.2 in the following respect. As V_c is continuous by assumption, technique T_2 will be at least partially innovated in the optimum if this would have been optimal without joint output. Hence, the necessary and sufficient conditions for an innovation of technique T_2 remain as derived in Section 10.2.

Similar to the discussion of a pollution limit in Section 10.5, the system dynamics in the economic approach crucially depend on the type of joint output produced and the process in which it accrues. If the unwanted joint output is produced in the consumption good process, it might be optimal to accumulate a capital stock which is not fully employed in every period. In general, full replacement of technique T_1 by technique T_2 cannot be guaranteed. Furthermore, we cannot even derive the necessary conditions for full replacement without further knowledge of the instantaneous welfare function V.

10.6.3   Flow Pollutant as a Joint Output

If the joint output is a flow pollutant, then we assume that $d(t) \equiv j(t)$. Hence, the preferences of the representative consumer also depend on the emissions produced. Similar to the case of a pollution limit, there is an upper boundary of emissions which must not be exceeded in every period. This limit is not exogenously given and constant over time, but endogenously derived by economic valuation.

First, we suppose that the joint output is produced in the production of consumption goods in process R_2. As in the case of no joint output, investment in technique T_2 is only done if the welfare loss of an investment i in a marginal unit of the new capital good equals the sum of welfare gains in later periods. But the welfare gain of an investment in technique T_2 in period t is now reduced in *every subsequent period* by the welfare loss caused by the emissions, which are supposed to accrue in a fixed proportion to the production of consumption goods in process R_2. Depending on the evaluation of the emissions by the representative consumer, that is depending on V_d, full replacement is not possible. If $V_{cd} \neq 0$ then the emission tolerance of the representative consumer depends on the consumption level. Under these circumstances it is possible that the capital stock is not fully employed in every period. This was impossible in the case of an emission limit, as the upper boundary was constant in every period and in particular independent of the consumption level.

Second, if the pollutant accrues jointly with the production of new capital goods, the welfare gain of an investment in technique T_2 in period t is only reduced by the welfare loss caused by the emissions in the same period, as emissions only accrue in the production of capital goods which can be used in subsequent periods to produce consumption goods without emitting a harmful pollutant. As in the case of an emission limit, the replacement of technique T_1 by technique T_2 can be delayed as the welfare loss due to the emissions of the production of new capital goods restricts the maximal amount of new capital per period. Furthermore, a full replacement can be impossible as the amount of consumption good is restricted by the maintainable capital stock. Again, neither the limit itself nor a simple condition for full replacement can be derived.

Figure 10.5 shows a numerically optimised example for the economic valuation of a flow pollutant either produced in process R_2 or in process R_3. The results are similar to the ones obtained from the ecological approach (cf. Section 10.5) in the case of a flow pollutant with the difference that the emission target is determined endogenously. Again, we observe that full replacement of the technique T_1 is not optimal if the pollutant emerges jointly with the production of the consumption good.

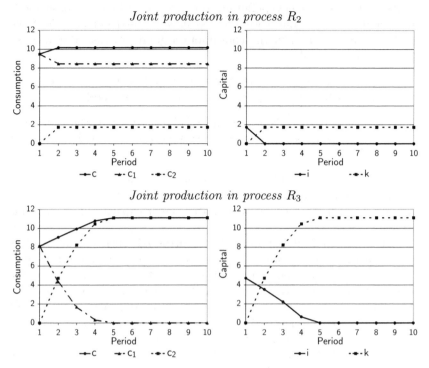

Figure 10.5 Optimal consumption (left), capital stock and investment (right) with joint production of a flow pollutant in the case of economic valuation.

Furthermore, full replacement is achieved if the joint output is produced in process R_3, but delayed compared to the case without joint production.

10.6.4 Stock Pollutant as a Joint Output

If the joint output is a stock pollutant, then we assume that $d(t) \equiv e(t)$. The equation of motion for the stock of the pollutant is given by Equation (10.22). If e_0 is the initial stock of the pollutant then Equation (10.22) can be rearranged to yield:

$$e(t) = (1 - \delta)^t e_0 + \sum_{m=1}^{t} (1 - \delta)^{t-m} j(m) . \qquad (10.27)$$

Hence, the preferences of the representative consumer also depend on the stock of the pollutant which itself, according to Equation (10.27), depends on the emissions in all former periods.

As in the case of a flow pollutant, the investment in new capital goods in period t suffers from a welfare loss in all subsequent periods if the pollutant is produced in the consumption good process. But now we face two different effects:

1. Every unit of new capital emits the pollutant in every subsequent period when used to produce the consumption good.

2. Every unit of emission accumulates the stock of the pollutant. Hence, the damage of a unit of emission spreads over all subsequent periods.

As a consequence, a full replacement of technique T_1 by technique T_2 cannot be guaranteed. Furthermore, these two effects can lead to an optimal capital stock which is employed under capacity in at least one period.

If the joint output is produced in process R_3, then the welfare loss for an investment in new capital in period t also spreads over all subsequent periods. Corresponding to the second effect mentioned above, the emissions accruing in the production of the new capital good i accumulate the stock of pollutant, which causes natural degradation in all later periods. As a consequence, the replacement of technique T_1 by technique T_2 can be delayed. Furthermore, a full replacement might be impossible as an (implicit) limitation on the investment i also implies a limitation on the sustainable capital stock k as long as the deterioration rate γ is positive.

Figure 10.6 shows the numerically optimised consumption, capital and investment path for the economic valuation of a stock pollutant which is produced in process R_2 and in process R_3 respectively. Again, we observe that full replacement of the production technique T_1 is not optimal in this example in the case of joint production in process R_2. If the pollutant is produced in the capital good process, we observe full but delayed replacement compared to the case without joint production. Note that, in contrast to the ecological approach, the size of the stock in the stationary state is determined endogenously by the valuation of the trade-off between consumption and the welfare loss due to natural degradation.

10.7   CONCLUSIONS

As in Chapter 9, the main conclusion is that the explicit consideration of unwanted joint outputs makes it less likely that a newly invented production technique is brought into use. The second conclusion from Chapter 9

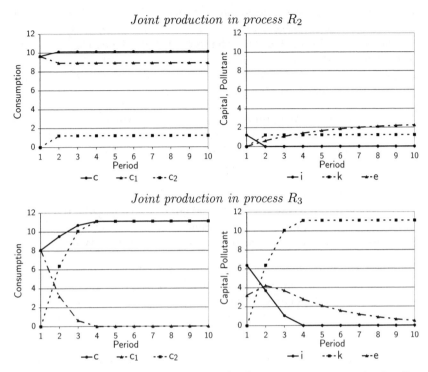

Figure 10.6   *Optimal consumption (left), capital stock, stock of pollutant and investment (right) with joint production of a stock pollutant in the case of economic valuation.*

remains valid, too: stock pollutants cause an additional intertemporal leverage effect, which makes them ceteris paribus more harmful than flow pollutants. The third conclusion from Chapter 9, that the innovation of a new technique which additionally produces a long-lived stock pollutant is the *less* likely the *longer* the time horizon, cannot generally be verified within the model framework presented here. The reason is that on the one hand we dropped the Assumptions A2 (constant output in every period), A6 (no discount rate) and A7/A9 (constant emissions over time), which leads to an ambiguous influence of the time horizon depending on the exogenously given parameters and the assumed welfare function. On the other hand, we have discussed three different approaches to the problem, of which only the economic approach is comparable to the exposition in Chapter 9. In any case, the emergence of the joint output, irrespective of whether it is a flow or a stock pollutant, is ceteris paribus more restrictive for the innovation of the new production technique if it is produced in the consumption good process R_2 than if it is produced in the capital good process R_3.

The results obtained in this chapter crucially depend on the three approaches to dealing with harmful joint outputs – the technical, the ecological, and the economic. In fact, the results for the innovation of the new technique T_2 are increasingly weaker:

1. In the technical approach (Section 10.4), which is based on an abatement process, the problem can be completely reduced to the original model framework. The degree of superiority decreases because of the additional labour needed to abate the pollutant.

2. For the ecological approach (Section 10.5), which is based on a pollution limit, the necessary and sufficient conditions remain unaltered, but full replacement cannot be guaranteed in general. Necessary conditions for full replacement have been derived.

3. For the most general case, the economic approach (Section 10.6), which is based on the valuation of consumption goods and environmental damage in welfare terms, the situation is similar to the ecological approach, but even necessary conditions for full replacement cannot be derived.

These approaches, to a different extent, go beyond the economic sphere and reach into the ecological sphere. The technical approach fully contains the joint output within the economic sphere as de facto no unit of the joint output is released into the natural environment. Hence, we do not have to distinguish between flow and stock pollutants – both being concepts to describe the impact of pollutants within the natural environment. In the ecological approach, there is an interaction between the economic and the ecological sphere, but it is limited to such a level that no change within the natural environment takes place – at least if the pollution limit is set correctly. In contrast, the economic approach leads in general to some natural degradation. Being a complex dynamic system, the natural environment will react with adjustment processes.

As a consequence, the level of information needed about the complex ecological system rises with increasing interaction with the ecological sphere. While there is no need for information about the complex ecological system if emissions of the joint output are completely banned, a substantial knowledge of the degradation processes of the joint output in the natural environment is necessary to set a limit for the emissions or the stock of the pollutant in the ecological approach. It is questionable if the natural sciences will ever be able to gain such an encompassing and detailed insight into the complex ecological system dynamics to satisfy these information requirements. This holds even more for the economic approach, as not only the limits to sustain a given status quo have to be derived, but the adjustment processes as reaction to the emissions of the pollutant have to be predicted. Thus, we face a twofold dilemma. Undoubtedly, the economic approach is the most powerful way to deal with joint production. But on the other hand, the result derived for this approach is the weakest, and the information requirements for an appropriate evaluation are the highest among the three approaches.

APPENDIX 10A   PARAMETERS FOR THE NUMERICAL OPTIMISATION

All numerically optimised examples (Figures 10.1–10.6) have been calculated with the advanced optimisation tool MUSCOD-II, which was developed by the Simulation and Optimisation Group of the Interdisciplinary Center for Scientific Computing, University of Heidelberg (Diehl et al. 2001). It exploits the method of multiple shooting state discretization (Leineweber et al. 2003).

λ_1	λ_2	λ_3	κ	γ	τ	ρ	$\bar{l}$
1	0.9	0.3	1	0	10	0.1	10

Table 10.1   Universal parameters for the numerical optimisation.

Table 10.1 shows the parameter values used for all numerical examples (Figures 10.1–10.6). As instantaneous welfare function V we have chosen $V(c(t)) \equiv \ln(c(t))$ in Figures 10.1–10.4, and $V(c(t), j(t)) \equiv \ln(c(t)) - \xi j(t)^2$ in Figures 10.5 and 10.6. In addition, we have used the parameter values given in Table 10.2.

	λ_4	α	β	ϕ	e_0	ξ
Figure 10.2	0.2	0.5	0.5	–	–	–
Figure 10.3	–	0.5	0.5	2	–	–
Figure 10.4	–	0.5	0.5	3	0	–
Figure 10.5	–	0.5	0.5	–	–	0.005
Figure 10.6	–	0.5	0.5	–	0	0.001

Table 10.2   Additional parameters for the numerical optimisation.

NOTES

1. This terminology was introduced by Schumpeter (1934[1911]).
2. If the economy starts with an initial capital stock of $k_0 = 0$ and given the intertemporal welfare W, as defined in Equation (10.1), full employment of the capital stock is *efficient* (Winkler 2005).
3. Solely using technique T_1 would yield a maximum of 10 units of the consumption good per period.
4. SO_2 emissions are washed out of the atmosphere by rainfall and are one of the main contributors to acid rain. See Chapter 18 for details.
5. The reason is that, since the output of the abatement process is – by assumption – completely harmless and useless, it is of no significance whatsoever and is left out of the model.
6. If the joint output is a stock pollutant and the time horizon τ is infinite, additionally the natural decay rate of the pollution stock has to be positive.

PART III

Ethics

INTRODUCTION

In the first two parts of this book, we have developed the conceptual foundations of joint production, and we have performed an economic analysis of the phenomenon. It has become obvious that the economic approach to joint production, while yielding a number of valuable and applicable insights, is nevertheless limited in its capacity to develop operational recommendations for environmental policy. Part III broadens the scope of our investigation to incorporate an ethical perspective: it links joint production to responsibility.* In this part, the argument will be based on philosophical reasoning. Accordingly, the presentation will be philosophical in style.

Responsibility and joint production are two terms which are central to a number of different disciplines: responsibility to philosophy – most significantly in the fields of ethics and political philosophy – and law; joint production to physics, engineering and economics. As we shall see in this part of the book, important relationships exist between responsibility and joint production. We, thus, intend to relate the terms to one another in consideration of the character of knowledge, and we draw conclusions for economic and political activity.

Responsibility is a ubiquitous phenomenon. In fact, one hardly needs to point out the ubiquity of responsibility. In practical life, someone or other is constantly assuming responsibility, or is having the assumption of responsibility demanded of them. A whole ethical doctrine of its own – the ethics of responsibility – has developed around this expression. With regard to modern environmental problems, the philosopher Hans Jonas (1979) has suggested an 'imperative of responsibility' as a reference point for the orientation of morality and politics.

The second term, joint production, also refers to a ubiquitous phenomenon (see Chapters 2 and 3). Whereas 'responsibility' is an expression belonging to the world of human thought and morality, 'joint production' refers to a reality of the physical world. At first glance, these two spheres appear to be independent of one another. For a description and evaluation of a situation in physical terms, it seems to be of no significance whether or not someone is responsible for it. Conversely, our ability to assume responsibility and to act in a morally commendable manner

---

*The four chapters of Part III are translated and revised from Petersen and Faber (2005).

does not appear to depend on circumstances outside of ourselves. Thus, Immanuel Kant (1996a[1785]) can declare that it is one's *good will* alone which makes an action morally 'good', that is morally responsible. For, in the evaluation of an action it does not matter what the action actually brings about.

> Even if [...] this will should wholly lack the capacity to carry out its purpose; if with its greatest efforts it should yet achieve nothing and only the good will were left [...] – then, like a jewel, it would still shine by itself, as something that has its full worth in itself. (Kant 1996a[1785]: 50)

However, the impression that physical and moral matters are completely separate from one another requires further consideration. For physical matters can undoubtedly have an effect on the moral quality of our actions. This becomes obvious if one considers the phenomenon of joint production.

Chapter 11 lays the philosophical foundations. It clarifies the concept of responsibility and elucidates its relationship to the concept of joint production. Chapter 12 discusses the relevance of knowledge and ignorance with regard to responsible behaviour, and explicates further the phenomenon of joint production. Chapter 13 introduces a distinction between different types of individual and collective responsibility. Chapter 14 investigates how the relationship between political and economic responsibility presents itself under the conditions of joint production. This chapter also contains a summary of Part III.

11. The Concept of Responsibility

with *Thomas Petersen*

11.1 INTRODUCTION

In the common usage of the word, the expression 'responsibility' is often ambiguous: Responsibility is a complex expression and the different connotations, along with the various layers of meaning, are often confused. For this reason, we start with a thorough analysis of the term. Section 11.2 analyses the term responsibility as in 'to assume responsibility for something' by distinguishing two meanings. We argue that responsibility is crucially related to human beings' freedom and power to act. Section 11.3 discusses limits of responsibility. In particular, due to the complexity which joint production introduces into the consequences of our actions, a problem of responsibility arises. In Section 11.4, we describe in what manner responsibility can be not only a foundation of ethics, but an ethical principle on its own, even a virtue. Section 11.5 summarises our findings.

11.2 TWO MEANINGS OF RESPONSIBILITY

In an elementary sense of the word, *responsibility* means primarily answerability – to give account to somebody for one's own actions. One bears responsibility if one is prepared to render account of one's deeds. And insofar as one is responsible for one's actions one can be held accountable for them (Jonas 1979: 174). Legal responsibility implies that we are liable for the consequences of our deeds, and from a moral perspective, we may be praised or rebuked. In this sense, to be responsible means that we are legally and morally compos mentis.

The concept of responsibility has always been explicitly or implicitly dealt with in political philosophy and philosophical ethics (for example Kant 1996b[1797]). But only in the twentieth century did responsibility become a 'key category' (Ritter et al. 2001: Column 569). It has received much attention in recent times and Hans Jonas, for example, has even viewed responsibility as an ethical principle in his monograph *Das Prinzip Verantwortung* ('The Imperative of Responsibility', Jonas 1979). The special attention which the concept of responsibility currently receives is, in our opinion, related to the consideration of two principal characteristics of human action: (i) the freedom of human action, and (ii) man's ability to unfold power to realise what they wish and intend (Arendt 1958 and – with respect to power – Plessner 2003). In particular, Jonas' (1979) book was written in light of the environmental crisis. It lends expression to the fact that economic activity, in combination with the dramatically increased power of modern technology, has a significant influence on the natural environment. Jonas' concept of responsibility directly implies the imperative that the natural environment, and therefore the foundation of human existence, be preserved. For, responsibility is the flip-side to freedom as well as to power.

There exists a close relationship between responsibility and freedom. A person is only the perpetrator of an action if this action can be described as the realisation of that person's intention. Only a free actor can have intentions and realise them. Responsibility therefore presupposes freedom. On the other hand, only he who can realise intentions through his own actions, and can assume responsibility for his actions, is truly free.[1] For, insofar as his actions bring about something he does not intend and is not responsible for, these actions do so *against his will*, that is, they are involuntary (Aristotle 2000: Book III). In this respect, he is not a free actor. Hence freedom demands the capability of being responsible.

Corresponding considerations hold for power and responsibility. A person is responsible only for what 'is in his power'. In all situations in which one is powerless, one not only does not need to bear responsibility, but is, in fact, unable to do so.

We can therefore conclude: The limits of one's freedom and one's power are the limits of one's responsibility. Only if one is free, is one able to bear responsibility, and only where one is able to bear responsibility, can one act freely. The responsibility of a person is one side of his freedom and power to do something. Corresponding to the two aspects of freedom and power, we differentiate between responsibility in two different meanings.

11.2.1 Primary Meaning of Responsibility: Ascription

To start with, responsibility means that one is the perpetrator of one's deeds. A person can determine his will *freely*; he is free to determine his aim of acting and to do something in order to realise this aim. These actions are ascribed to him, and in this sense he is responsible for these actions and their consequences. This is what we call the *primary meaning of responsibility*.

With this, the expression 'to assume responsibility' remains undefined. In the first instance, it only means that one ascribes an action to oneself and allows for it to be thus ascribed. So far, this does not address the consequences of responsibility, such as liability or any other obligations etc. We therefore conclude that responsibility in this primary meaning has, as such, no moral relevance. In Jonas' words, the primary meaning of responsibility 'is a precondition of morality, but not morality itself' (Jonas 1979: 179, our translation).

11.2.2   Secondary Meaning of Responsibility: Moral Obligation

Alongside the primary meaning of responsibility, there exists a secondary meaning of the word. It builds on the first and is of special significance in the fields of politics and, in particular, environmental politics. Whereas 'assuming responsibility' in the primary sense only means that an action and its consequences are ascribed to the perpetrator, in a stronger sense 'responsibility' means that legal and moral *obligations* arise for the perpetrator. For, the perpetrator is 'responsible' in the sense that his actions and their consequences meet certain legal and moral standards. We call this kind of responsibility the *secondary meaning of responsibility*. In its secondary meaning, responsibility imposes moral or legal obligations. Consequently, one has to give an account of their fulfilment or non-fulfilment.

Responsibility in the sense of ascription (primary meaning) is a precondition for assuming responsibility as a legal and moral obligation (secondary meaning). For a person can only accept legal and moral obligations for those actions and their consequences of which he is the perpetrator, that is, which are ascribed to him. However, moral meaning attains to the concept of responsibility only insofar as a person, as the perpetrator of his deeds, bears responsibility for his deeds in the stronger sense of the secondary meaning.

Based on the distinction between negative and positive obligations by Philippa Foot (1994), we distinguish between *negative* and *positive responsibility*:

1. *Negative responsibility* imposes the obligation that one's actions and their consequences do not damage another person or thing.

Assuming responsibility in this sense means that one has to give an account of the fulfilment or non-fulfilment of this requirement. Negative responsibility is limited in the sense that one is responsible only for one's deeds.

2. *Positive responsibility* means to assume responsibility for something in particular – for example for oneself, for another being, for a company, or for a specific field of action. As a consequence, one is positively responsible for the good state of being of this person, company, or field of action. A minister, for example, is responsible for a specific ministry or an area of affairs such as the finances of the state. Positively assuming responsibility for somebody or something implies that one is not only responsible for one's deeds but also for one's omissions. A minister, being positively responsible for the good state of being of his ministry, has to accept responsibility also for the failure of taking necessary action within the corresponding area of affairs.[2]

Assuming positive responsibility means that the well-being – or even existence – of what is placed in one's charge depends, at least in part, on one's actions. In this sense, Jonas (1979: 391) defines responsibility as '*care*, accepted as an obligation, for another being – care which, should the vulnerability of its charge be threatened, can become *concern*' (our translation). Hence, to be responsible for something in particular means that one is obliged in a legal or moral sense to care for its well-being. In order to fulfil this obligation one needs the capability to act; in particular one needs the *power* to do so. Thus, this meaning of responsibility accentuates the fact that those bearing responsibility must also be endowed with power to do what they wish and intend.

Generally, in the secondary meaning of the word one bears responsibility in a legal or moral sense for the compliance with certain rules or principles. One always bears this responsibility *to someone* or *some authority*. For example, an employee is responsible to his superior, a citizen is responsible before the law, the government is responsible to parliament etc.

Summarising, human beings are responsible for their actions and the consequences of those. In a moral sense, they bear responsibility for something in particular or somebody. Responsibility in the secondary meaning imposes legal or moral obligations on them, the fulfilment of which they have to give an account of. This is briefly summarised in Figure 11.1. Concerning environmental policy, a fundamental question arises from this: can one accept responsibility for the production of wanted goods despite the accompanying joint products?

Primary meaning:	Responsibility for the consequences of one's own action, in the sense of ascription.
	This is a precondition for morality, not morality itself.
Secondary meaning:	Responsibility for the consequences of one's own action or for something in particular, in the sense that moral and legal standards have to be met.
	This imposes moral or legal obligations.
Negative responsibility:	Actions must not damage another subject.
Positive responsibility:	Responsibility for the good state of being of something in particular, for example an object, an individual, a group or an institution.

Figure 11.1   Primary and secondary meanings of responsibility.

11.3   THE PROBLEM OF RESPONSIBILITY AND JOINT PRODUCTION

11.3.1   Limits of Responsibility

As has been mentioned, responsibility is the flip-side to a human being's freedom to act. Someone is only the author and master of his actions, insofar as he can assume responsibility for these actions and their consequences. That for which someone assumes responsibility can be ascribed to him. To this extent he is compos mentis. He who cannot assume responsibility for what he does is not compos mentis. Thus, only he who can assume responsibility is actually capable of taking concrete action. This raises the question of the extent of one's responsibility.

An action as the origin of effects or consequences is a complex matter. Every action has a variety of consequences which are not entirely discernible. Among those, human beings generally single out only one consequence as the objective of the action, thus elevating it above the others. Setting an objective is always a reduction of complexity – often the action is identified with its objective. Concerning the objective of an action, one speaks of the goal justifying the action. However, the means chosen have to be appropriate to the respective ends. What is appropriate is not an arbitrary affair, but always depends on a specific point of view – in general, that of the moral community as a whole. For example, if one cuts the main electrical cable of a house one cannot call this 'switching off the radio', even if this action does lead to the radio being switched off. One can say: as long as it is generally accepted that the means are appropriate to the end, the action makes sense. Conversely, it makes no sense to call cutting the main electrical cable 'switching off the radio'.

Along with the intended outcome, there exist further consequences. These unintended consequences we call side-consequences or *concomitants*. Many concomitants emerge as the material or energetic joint products of production activities. The general principle of joint production (see Section 4.4.3), however, points to the existence of a broader range of side-consequences. The perpetrator of an action does not intend such concomitants but, as far as he foresees them, he accepts or condones them. The range of concomitants which an individual 'foresees' in this manner is not entirely up to him. He must assume responsibility not only for the consequences he *actually* foresaw, but also for all those which he could, or should, have foreseen. Responsibility refers not only to the action itself, but to the prescience of consequences, at least insofar as such prescience is feasible at all.

These reflections indicate that an individual's responsibility has limits. For one can generally foresee only a part of the consequences of one's own actions. It is, for instance, impossible to foresee *chance consequences* of an action. These are consequences which an action does not lead to by necessity, but which arise from further circumstances that can be given or not. In other words, chance consequences are contingent consequences. An example of such chance consequences – entailing severely limited prescience – are the possible reactions of other human beings to one's own actions. An individual cannot be held liable for unforeseeable consequences. He need not assume responsibility for them. Furthermore, such consequences do not belong to the purpose of the action. In this manner, responsibility for the consequences of an action always has limits (Figure 11.2).

Limits of responsibility:

- Responsibility for foreseeable consequences.
- No responsibility for unforeseeable consequences, for example chance consequences.

Figure 11.2   The limits of responsibility.

11.3.2   Complexity and Responsibility

A severe problem for assuming responsibility arises in cases in which one can no longer overview the circumstances of one's action – that is, when the range of emerging concomitants displays high complexity. Due to such complexity, an individual is often unable to foresee certain crucial conditions for the achievement of his goals. This jeopardises the individual's possibility of taking responsibility for his action and, thus, his freedom (primary meaning). Thereby, it also impairs his capacity to assume negative or positive responsibility for something or somebody (secondary meaning). There are two aspects:

(a) In the political discourse, many people demand that the 'self-responsibility' or autonomy of the individual should be bolstered. Self-responsibility or autonomy means: 'I can take care of myself for my life, and I can support myself, particularly in my old age'. Such self-responsibility is becoming increasingly difficult in the modern world. For instance, hardly anyone can make sufficient provision for their old age nowadays without outside expertise.

(b) A second important aspect of complexity is the inherent possibility that one's actions are not dictated by one's own intentions, but by 'systematic regularities'. These arise from the intricacy of the concomitants of an action. The meaning of the action is thus defined by such regularities, not by the intentions of the enactor. In such cases, a concomitant of the action – that is to say, a concomitant from the point of view of the enactor – may become the defining aspect from an external perspective.

Such a perspective is common to social science. Examples may also be found in economics: according to Adam Smith, selfishness in market economies actually contributes to something which can by no means be called its original intention, namely, *general* wealth and well-being. Political economics provides further examples, such as the bureaucrat who has the public good in mind, yet only manages to contribute to the inefficient expansion of his administration (Downs 1967). In these cases the individual is no longer master of his actions; one could say he is unfree.

We can conclude that the complexity of our actions and their – intended and unintended – consequences places severe limits on our abilities and capabilities. In particular, it tends to jeopardise our potential to assume responsibility.

This problem has long been recognised in practical philosophy (Spaemann 1989: 186–202) but, thus far, has only been conceptualised and discussed with regard to social interaction. Concerning the relationship between humankind and nature, a quite different perspective seems to prevail. In modern times, nature has been viewed as being principally under man's stewardship and control: that man would 'rule nature in practice' was once the hope expressed by Francis Bacon (quoted after

Horkheimer and Adorno 1968: 14). Man bends nature to his service by shaping her according to his will, generating something out of her – in what is called 'production'. Now we recognise, however, that man's control of nature is limited. The ubiquitous phenomenon of joint production reminds us that we cannot produce something without simultaneously producing something else, which often was originally not intended.

One can map the structure of joint production and the problem of responsibility onto each other. In Section 2.4, we have defined joint production relative to a system representation and a time horizon which are both chosen by the observer. With respect to a thermodynamic system represention (Definition 2.4) – that is, in a complete 'image' of all nature – it was shown in Chapter 3 that all (industrial) production is joint production. Representations used in a typical analysis will, however, abstract from many outputs. Hence, in such representations it is an a priori open question whether or not the production of an output A necessarily brings forward joint products.

Although the category of intent is disregarded in this conceptualisation of joint production, one can still map the concept of joint production to the problem of responsibility. Consider a system with n outputs, such that in a thermodynamic representation output A is the main product and outputs $B_1,\ldots,B_{n-1}$ are joint products of A in the sense of Definition 2.6. However, in a different, 'incomplete' representation, the production of A may bring forward only the joint products $B_1,\ldots,B_m$ with $m < n - 1$. We can express this situation in terms of responsibility for the consequences of one's action. Let the action 'production' have an intention Z (production of output A) and the concomitants $Y_1,\ldots,Y_s$ (stemming from the joint products $B_1,\ldots,B_{n-1}$), whereby the enactor must assume responsibility for $Y_1,\ldots,Y_k$ (stemming from the joint products $B_1,\ldots,B_m$) with $k < s$. We can say: the enactor of the action is assigned responsibility on the basis of a certain representation of the system, whereby the choice of the representation is not up to him.[3]

The concept of joint production illustrates the fact that the economy in its 'material reactions between [man] and nature' (Marx 1902: 156) displays an equally unfathomable complexity as the sphere of social interaction. This holds for all cases in which one takes complex environmental issues into account. Let us consider the example of a newly produced vehicle. Before this vehicle one day becomes waste, it gives rise, at every use, to joint outputs and environmental effects in the form of waste from replaced parts and exhaust emissions which accumulate in the environment and themselves bring forth further joint effects. Whereas moral philosophy has discussed complexity in politics only with regard to social interactions, the concept of joint production makes it possible to extend such a discussion to the interaction of human action with nature. This will be subject to a detailed discussion in Chapter 12. Before that, we raise yet another important aspect of responsibility.

11.4 RESPONSIBILITY AS A PRINCIPLE OF ETHICS AND AS A VIRTUE

The complexity of the consequences of one's actions, for example the complexity emerging from joint production, which can hardly be completely overviewed, confronts us as human beings with a dilemma: how are we to act in a good manner under such circumstances? In light of such complexity, the philosopher Hans Jonas (1979) speaks of an 'imperative of responsibility' which – according to Jonas – must form the basis of all ethics. Such an imperative has been rejected, for example by Wieland (1999) who reasons that responsibility is not an autonomous ethical principle and thus cannot be a 'definitive norm'. Wieland's critique is directed at the particular 'ethics of responsibility' which seeks to justify actions by their consequences. Of course, such a justification is impossible where the consequences of an action cannot be entirely monitored. Hence, such an ethics of responsibility is not possible with respect to economic activity, if only for the reason that the consequences of, for example, an act of production can never be entirely monitored under conditions of joint production. Although responsibility cannot be *the sole* principle, we shall demonstrate that it is yet *one* principle of ethics and can even be conceived as an independent virtue.

At first glance, responsibility does not seem to be an ethical expression as such, but rather an indispensable precondition of all ethics (cf. Section 11.2.1). Only he who is capable of assuming responsibility for his own actions is praiseworthy or blameworthy in an ethical sense. He alone can act in a praiseworthy or blameworthy manner. In this context, responsibility was already conceptualised by Aristotle in his *Nicomachean Ethics* (2000). When Aristotle differentiates between voluntary and involuntary actions and declares that '[p]raise and blame are bestowed on that which is voluntary, whereas the involuntary requires pardon' (Aristotle 2000: Book III, Chapter 1), he is referring to the following circumstance: One is responsible only for that which one undertakes voluntarily. Insofar as responsibility is a precondition of all ethics, it is simultaneously a pre-ethical category and, thus, ethically neutral. Bearing responsibility for one's actions as such, is neither good nor bad in an ethical sense and therefore neither praiseworthy nor blameworthy.

As discussed in Section 11.2.2, responsibility only becomes a subject of ethical merit, or failure, in its secondary meaning – in the sense of

234 Joint Production and Responsibility in Ecological Economics

assuming negative responsibility for one's deeds, or positive responsibility for someone or something. Responsibility in the secondary meaning forms a *task* which one may, or may not, measure up to. In this sense, responsibility demands something of us, burdens us with an obligation. One is addressing such an obligation when stating that some person is acting 'irresponsibly'. This does not mean that this person *has* no responsibility for his actions (primary meaning); rather, it means that the person is not *assuming* responsibility (in the secondary meaning) for his actions. Someone is acting irresponsibly if, for example, he is in some way endangering himself or someone else in a manner he cannot justify.

Responsibility can therefore burden a human being with moral obligations. However, these moral obligations can come into conflict with other moral obligations. Situations may arise in which, in order to save the life of another person, one must resort to a lie or to breaking the law. The recognition of this conflict led Max Weber (1988[1919]) to contrast 'absolute ethics' with 'ethics of responsibility'. Such ethics of responsibility were not simply to justify lying or breaking the law, but to preserve one from being unqualifiedly damned from the point of view of absolute ethics. Weber's concept of ethics of responsibility remained extremely abstract, however. It implied only that one had to 'answer for the (foreseeable) consequences of one's actions' (Weber 1988[1919]: 522; our translation). Weber, however, has never specified in concrete terms what this means. Nor did he address the questions regarding how one is to choose in an ethical conflict, which consequences of one's actions one must assume responsibility for, or to whom or which authority one bears such responsibility.

So, what exactly do Weber's ethics of responsibility stipulate? A person who is taking his responsibility seriously confesses to his actions and their consequences. He is also willing to answer, or even be held liable, for them. Ethics of responsibility, therefore, lay down a simple imperative: you shall not deny yourself as a free individual. What the fulfilment of this imperative requires is simply 'good will' in the sense of Kant (1996a[1785]; see the discussion on page 224 in this book) which everyone can possess at any time. This demand is simple, but by no means trivial. The difficulty of assuming responsibility in this manner is demonstrated by the many in politics and economics who are not prepared to answer and accept responsibility for their decisions, but instead hide behind 'circumstances' and 'compulsions'. Willingness to answer for one's actions and to assume responsibility for them is, particularly in political ethics, an imperative directed at those involved in politics (see Chapter 13). Nevertheless, it is easy to assume responsibility in the sense of Weber. It requires nothing but the willingness to answer for all, possibly unpleasant, consequences of one's actions. For example, a minister in whose ministry a serious error has occurred resigns. Such a reaction does not require any specific capabilities other than good will.

On the other hand, European ethics knows another form of imperative which requires special talents that must be acquired and rehearsed – namely 'virtue', as Aristotle (2000) called it. In what follows, we argue that responsibility under the conditions of joint production is such a virtue. According to Aristotle, virtues (for example justice, temperance and courage) enable one to act in a good and correct manner in one's day-to-day living, and thus to live the 'good life' (Aristotle 2000: Book II, Chapter 1). Virtues require more than simply strength of will, however. Virtues always require practice and habituation (Aristotle 2000: Book II, Chapter 1), as well as an objective and ethically adequate evaluation of the specific situation and one's own possibilities. The ability to make such judgements must be carefully developed and cultivated. According to Aristotle, the most significant point is that every situation is unique in its particular complexity and that it is therefore impossible to formulate a general rule as to how to act or conduct oneself (Aristotle 2000: Book II, Chapter 2, 1104a 3–6): 'Matters concerned with conduct and questions of what is good for us have no fixity'. According to Aristotle, action always occurs under conditions of uncertainty, and virtue is to enable people to act correctly under such uncertainty.

This brings us to the very point at which responsibility under the conditions of joint production requires the capabilities Aristotle calls for. For the phenomenon of joint production confronts us with two separate types of uncertainty:

1. We know that our actions give rise to unintended joint products or – more general – side-consequences. But we do not know whether we are observing all of these or not.

2. Furthermore, we do not know what significance such identified or unidentified joint products or side-consequences have. The occurrence of joint production often gives rise to an inscrutable complexity, similar to that which Aristotle had in mind.

Under these uncertainties, if someone is to be responsible for someone or something in the secondary meaning, then this person must be able to answer questions such as the following:

- Which ethical and normative principles must my actions fulfil?

- What does the preservation and well-being of that which I am responsible for require?

- Which risks and dangers do my actions entail?

- Which risks may I accept?

- What degree of ignorance can I safely tolerate?

There exist no universally valid answers to these questions. In order to answer them, one requires a certain form of experience and ethical wisdom which Aristotle calls *phronesis* ($\varphi\rho o\nu\eta\sigma\iota\varsigma$) (Aristotle 2000: Book VI, Chapters 5, 8 and 9). Phronesis is the capability of judgement which can associate ethical edicts with the concrete necessities of any given situation. Phronesis deals with both normative and factual aspects and must relate them to one another in a meaningful manner. All this requires knowledge, not least of one's own inevitable ignorance.

For Aristotle, phronesis – or ethical wisdom – is the heart and soul of any virtue. He who is not wise in this manner cannot be virtuous (Aristotle 2000: Book VI, Chapter 5, see also Book II, Chapter 6, 1106b 36ff). As we have argued, one can only assume responsibility for someone or something insofar as one possesses such wisdom. Thus, responsibility, in the sense of assuming responsibility for someone or something (cf. Section 11.2) can be viewed as a virtue in Aristotle's sense of the word. We shall discuss in Chapters 13 and 14 what consequences these considerations have for politics, concerning the phenomenon of joint production.

11.5   SUMMARY

In this chapter, we have exposed the expression 'responsibility' in order to place this term in a shared context with the phenomenon of joint production. The complexity induced by joint production in nature gives rise to similar difficulties as they are observed in the complexity of social interactions. The problem of acting right, given that consequences are myriad and, hence, impossible to keep track of, leads to an understanding of responsibility as a virtue.

There seems to be a difference, however, between human interventions into nature and human behaviour in the social sphere. Joint products and their effects arise by necessity from the process of production, whereas such strict causality does not exist in the field of social behaviour. With respect to the latter, it was already observed by Aristotle (2000: 107; 1140b 1) that 'such thing might be otherwise' ($\alpha\lambda\lambda\omega\varsigma\ \varepsilon\chi\varepsilon\iota\nu$), in other words, that they are contingent. In acting there exists an element of unpredictability, namely novelty. For this reason, taking action was not an object of science ($\varepsilon\pi\iota\sigma\tau\eta\mu\eta$) for Aristotle, but an object of practical wisdom (phronesis). With regard to joint production, things 'can be otherwise' (Aristotle 2000: 107; 1140a 22/23) as well, namely whenever one views joint production, not as a natural, but as an economic phenomenon. This is discussed in detail in the following chapter.

NOTES

1.   The notion of freedom employed here is one in which one is only free insofar as one can realise one's intention in one's actions and, therefore, give reasons for one's actions (for example Hume 1978: 399–412 and Schelling 1997). This notion of freedom emphasises the inner self-determination of the actor, and goes beyond the weaker notion of, for example, Hobbes (1973) who defines freedom as the absence of external constraints in the following way: 'And therefore if a man should talk to me of [...] any *Free*, but free from being hindred by opposition, I should not say he were in an Errour; but that his words were without meaning: that is to say, Absurd' (Hobbes 1973: 20).

2.   Obviously, (positive) responsibility for something includes the (negative) responsibility not to damage this object. For example, if one has accepted the positive responsibility of taking care of a friend's house, this includes the obligation not to damage it by any action or its consequences.

3.   In the same way as there may be an asymmetric physical relationship between the production of A and B_i, with $i \in \{1, \ldots, m\}$ (see Definition 2.6 and the discussion on page 39), there may be an asymmetric relationship between the intention Z and a concomitant Y_j, with $j \in \{1, \ldots, k\}$. For the intention Z generally has concomitants which arise with necessity, whereas these concomitants, when being turned into the intention of an action, need not have the original intention Z as a concomitant. For example, if I purchase an expensive vehicle it follows by necessity that my payments for car insurance will increase. I can, however, also force up my insurance bill, without necessarily coming into possession of such an expensive vehicle.

12. Joint Production, Knowledge, and Responsibility

with *Thomas Petersen*

In the previous chapter, we discussed the close relationship between responsibility and joint production. Now we turn to the link between both concepts and knowledge. Joint products can be conceived of as intended or unintended concomitants of production processes which the producer must – under certain circumstances – take into account or assume responsibility for. However, as we have seen, responsibility requires the ability to foresee, to a certain extent, the consequences of one's action. Phrased differently, one must know what one's actions entail. Responsibility, therefore, raises a problem of knowledge. This problem was addressed in an instructive manner by Georg Wilhelm Friedrich Hegel (1970[1821]) who considers responsibility and knowledge in an ethical perspective.

12.1 HEGEL ON RESPONSIBILITY AND KNOWLEDGE[1]

The consequences are the part of one's actions that materialise in outer reality. In contrast, the purpose of those actions, that is, the essence of those actions, does not see the light of day but remains within. Therefore, the philosopher Georg Wilhelm Friedrich Hegel (1970[1821]: §118)[2] calls – in a somewhat poetic manner – the consequences of one's actions 'the shape which has the purpose of the action at its soul'. Hegel (1970[1821]: §118) goes on to differentiate between the necessary and the chance consequences of an action.

- *Necessary consequences* are those which an action 'in its general quality' (Hegel 1970[1821]: 225) always, or at least generally, entails.

- *Chance consequences* depend on further circumstances, separate from the action itself, which can be given or not.

One can expect a rational human being to have an awareness of the consequences of his actions. Contrary to general usage, Hegel calls this awareness the *intention* ('Absicht') of the executor of the action (Hegel 1970[1821]: §119). Thus, in the case of soda production (cf. Chapter 16), the *purpose* of the *Leblanc* process[3] is to create soda. Since this process inevitably also creates the joint product hydrogen chloride, something the producer has to be aware of, this fact is included in the intention. The production of hydrogen chloride is not actually intended, but it is willingly accepted by the producer. This implies that Hegel conceives the intention as a form of knowledge: the intention includes knowledge of the consequences which the action entails.

It is helpful to address Hegel here because he is clearly aware of the close connection between free and responsible acting and knowledge. Action is always the acting out of one's own free will. Hegel establishes that someone can act of his own free will if two complementary conditions are met:

1. The person must *know* what he is doing. He must therefore be capable of monitoring his actions and their necessary consequences. Should he be prevented by something or someone from monitoring these consequences, he does not know what he is doing and is not free in his actions. Hence, in Hegel's view, insofar as he is a free being, he has a claim, in an ethical sense of the word, to know about the consequences of his actions.

2. According to Hegel, there exists something similar to a claim which the consequences of our actions have on us. Namely, they place the claim on us that they are known to us and therefore they are actions which can be conceived as intended by us. Put differently, we have the duty to know these consequences and to assume responsibility for them.

Hegel calls these two different claims 'rights'. With respect to the first claim, he speaks of the 'rights of intention', and with respect to the second claim of a complementary 'right of the objectivity of the action to assert itself as known and intended by its subject as a consciously rational being' (Hegel 1970[1821]: §120). In the example of the *Leblanc* process, this means that the producer has the obligation to know that, apart from soda, hydrogen chloride with all its harmful effects jointly emerges.

Hegel's discussion of intention explicitly links the ethical problem of responsibility and the problem of knowledge. The right of responsible behaviour is the right to know. And he who has a responsibility also has the obligation to know – to know what his own actions are and what consequences they entail.

12.2 RESPONSIBILITY FOR KNOWLEDGE

Whoever wishes to act responsibly can only do so insofar as he has knowledge pertaining to his actions and their consequences. For only then can he know what he is doing. The question of responsibility therefore includes the questions: What can we know? What must we know? A further, closely related question is: What do we not know and to what extent can we reduce our ignorance (Faber et al. 1996c: Chapter 11)?

With regard to the knowledge which is required by responsibility, one can differentiate between factual and normative dimensions of knowledge:

1. We have already discussed the factual dimension of knowledge about the action and its consequences: one needs knowledge pertaining to the action itself, but also knowledge pertaining to the consequences and, thus, the end result.

2. The normative dimension of knowledge refers to the ethical quality of the action, that is whether the action can be classified as 'good', or at least, not morally dubious or even reprehensible. For only then can one take responsibility for the action. As a rule, this question is addressed against the background of moral principles.

Factual and normative knowledge are different dimensions which are investigated by separate scientific disciplines. Factual knowledge is the domain of the natural and social sciences while normative knowledge is assigned to disciplines such as practical philosophy, political philosophy, moral philosophy, and ethics, but is also addressed by normative economics.

Let us investigate the relationship between normative knowledge and factual knowledge: to what extent does normative knowledge depend on factual knowledge? One philosophical doctrine postulates the complete dependence of normative knowledge on factual knowledge. This is so-called 'consequentialism', which judges the moral quality of an action completely on the grounds of its consequences (Spaemann 1989: 157–171). If these are good on the whole, then the action is deemed good. Should they be negative overall, then the action is to be condemned.[4]

Other approaches of moral philosophy do not address the question of the moral quality of an action from the viewpoint of its consequences.

In Kant's moral philosophy, for example, there exist actions which are inherently good or bad. Thus, for Kant, a lie is always reprehensible, no matter what its consequences may be (Kant 1996b[1797]). Yet, even for Kant it is not possible to judge an action entirely without taking its consequences into account. As a case in point, no action can be labelled 'good' if only negative consequences are to be expected from it.

In order to judge actions on an ethical basis, therefore, knowledge pertaining to whether the consequences are good or bad is of crucial importance. An individual who wishes to act responsibly is obliged to obtain such factual and normative knowledge. Responsibility in general, hence, entails responsibility for one's knowledge – more precisely, a responsibility with regard to the prescience of consequences, as with the emergence of hydrogen chloride during the production of soda in the aforementioned example. According to Hegel, however, the obligation to obtain knowledge extends only to the necessary and not to the chance consequences of an action. Admittedly (as Hegel also recognises), it is often not possible to distinguish with absolute clarity between necessary and chance consequences (Hegel 1970[1821]: §118). However, such a clear distinction is generally not necessary.

In light of the modern environmental crisis, the problem of the distinction between necessary and chance consequences poses itself in a different manner. Jonas (1979) examines the demands which the modern environmental crisis burdens us with in his book *The Imperative of Responsibility* (see Section 11.2, all translations are ours). In light of the enormous ramifications of our technological activity, Jonas declares knowledge to be a 'most urgent obligation', and that this knowledge 'must be of equal dimensions to the causal scale of our activity' (Jonas 1979: 28). This means that our knowledge must be able to keep up with the consequences of our activity. Such 'dimensional equality' is, however, all but impossible to achieve because of

> the complexity of social and biospherical totalities which mock all mathematics; the unfathomable nature of mankind, forever lying in wait with surprises; and the unpredictability, that is to say, the non-pre-inventibility of future inventions. (Jonas 1979: 66)

The demand for prescience of the consequences of our actions cannot be met in the modern industrial civilisation. Thus, we must make do with knowledge regarding possible consequences (Jonas 1979: 67) if indeed, we can foresee only a part of the actual consequences. Our guide should be a 'heuristic of fear' rather than a 'principle of hope'.[5] For, we know far better what our worst evil is than we might recognise our greatest good (Jonas 1979: 63).

What Jonas is proposing is a form of 'ethics of knowledge' under the restriction of inevitable ignorance. But what can we know and where do the limits of our knowledge lie? Jonas remains relatively ambiguous with regard to these questions. The concept of joint production, however, allows us to define more precisely what degree of knowledge about the consequences can actually be achieved. At the same time, it can be used to demonstrate that the distinction between necessary and chance consequences discussed by Hegel no longer suffices for a determination of the limits of responsibility.

12.3   Joint Production and Ignorance

With respect to the joint products emerging from a production activity, let us make a threefold conceptual distinction. Joint products can be (i) classified into identified and unidentified joint outputs. With regard to the identified joint products, we can (ii) distinguish between identified and unidentified consequences or effects of these outputs. Additionally, as has been discussed extensively in Part II of this book, joint products (and their consequences) can be (iii) divided into desired and undesired joint products (and consequences). Whereas the distinctions (i) and (ii) are made on the basis of purely factual knowledge, the distinction (iii) is an economic one involving the valuation of outputs and consequences. Distinction (iii), hence, requires normative knowledge. The above classification is sketched in Figure 12.1. An example of a desired joint product would be mutton which is emerging as a joint product of wool. In contrast, an example of an undesired joint product would be dioxin arising from the burning of waste.

Knowledge and ignorance are relevant for these distinctions. With regard to the first two distinctions, the relevance is so explicit as to be almost trivial: identified joint products and consequences belong to the domain of knowledge, ignorance exists with regard to unidentified joint products and consequences. This is a matter of factual knowledge.

At first glance, the problem of ignorance does not seem to arise with regard to the question of the desirability of products. However, distinguishing between desired and undesired joint products also raises a problem of knowledge. This link is less obvious, but possibly more significant. Regarding oneself, one may assume that one knows for oneself whether one desires something or not. Hence, one would presumably also be expected to know whether one prefers the existence of a product to its non-existence or vice versa. Such knowledge does not exist, however, when one takes the dimension of time into account. Ambivalence of

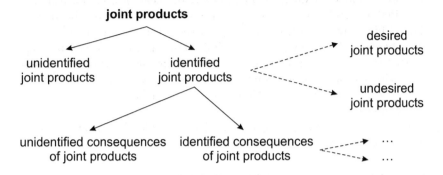

Figure 12.1   Factual and normative knowledge about joint production: joint products and their consequences can factually be identified or not, and they can be desired or undesired.

joint products (cf. Chapter 8 and, for a case study, Chapter 15) tells us that outputs which are desired today may later on become undesirable (or vice versa).

Recall that a transition of a product's desirability – from desired to undesired or vice versa – can arise for a number of reasons.

1. It can be due to the discovery of previously unidentified effects which may be perceived as positive or negative.

2. It can be the result of a shift in preferences.

3. It can result from technological change.[6]

Such a transition in the desirability of a joint product can generally not be foreseen. At any time, therefore, a certain ignorance with respect to the future character of joint outputs as being desired or undesired exists. A central question with respect to this ignorance is, however, whether or not it is possible to transform this ignorance into knowledge ex ante. With regard to joint production we find ourselves confronted with various forms of ignorance.

Factual knowledge about unidentified joint products and consequences

We first examine unidentified joint products and consequences – the latter being consequences of identified or unidentified joint products.

In Chapter 2, we have conceptualised a joint product as a *necessary* concomitant of a certain production process. With regard to joint production and its consequences, we are therefore dealing with scientifically identifiable correlations.[7] These correlations can, in principle, be known. That which hinders us from knowing *all* these things, and the interrelations between them, however, is the limit of our means of perception, our inattentiveness, as well as the difficulties of communicating the knowledge which a society has accumulated between separate research institutions and individuals. Viewed in this manner, the hole in the ozone layer and global warming through greenhouse gases should not have come as a surprise: each would have been completely predictable, given a certain research effort and scientific capabilities.

Factual knowledge about identified joint products and consequences

With regard to identified joint products and the effects of joint products, knowledge is available, but also limited. We can, however, keep moving the borders between knowledge and ignorance further and further into ignorance's domain. We are able to continuously transform ignorance into knowledge, even if we cannot hope ever to finalise this process.

Normative knowledge about the desirability of joint products

The situation is different with regard to the desirability or undesirability of joint products. Let us again examine the three aforementioned reasons for the transition of a product's desirability.

- Concerning the first reason, the desirability of products and joint products can be modified by the discovery of formerly unknown corollaries of these outputs. In this respect, the desirability of outputs seems to depend solely on scientifically observable facts. But this is misleading. Whether something is desirable or not is the outcome of a social valuation process which involves complex social interaction. Hence, the desirability of products does not exclusively depend on existing physical circumstances, but also on, for example whether and when these circumstances become known to the members of society. Such potential future recognition of presently unknown circumstances by society is not completely foreseeable in the same manner as the joint products themselves.

- The same is true for reasons 2 and 3 – a shift in preferences or the introduction of new technologies. In both cases hardly any ex ante predictability exists. New technologies derive from inventions and these are, by definition, not predictable. This holds equally for the shifting of preferences. Shifts in preferences, just as inventions, must be conceived as free results of human spontaneity. Shifts cannot be directly derived from the circumstances of their emergence. A shift in preferences, as well as an invention, has some characteristics of novelty and originality. The same applies to the progress of human knowledge with regard to nature's causality. Knowledge and its progress, as well as the shifting of preferences and inventions, are not phenomena of nature, but of the mind. They do not only restrict our prognostic knowledge in the manner in which the complexity of nature's causality does, but also bound it distinctly. Such intellectual phenomena are a source of causality on their own and cannot become the object of prognostic knowledge.[8]

Let us recapitulate. While we can investigate unidentified joint products and the unidentified consequences of joint products ever further, with regard to foresight we find ourselves faced with insurmountable obstacles.

These reflections on the possibilities of knowledge can be related to the problem of responsibility and the aforementioned differentiation between the necessary and the chance consequences of actions, as made by Hegel. Following Hegel's differentiation, it is solely the necessary consequences, not the chance consequences, which one must assume responsibility for. The phenomenon of joint production, however, casts a shadow over this for the following reason.

The *necessary* consequences of joint production are the joint products themselves, along with all the consequences they entail – be they identified or unidentified. However, as we have argued above, nature's complexity suffices to make it impossible to truly take all necessary consequences into account – that is, every single joint product and each and every one of their consequences. For our knowledge is inevitably limited. It is a *chance* consequence of joint production whether a particular joint product is desired or not, and whether it will be so in the future. For the desirability of a joint product is only partly determined by physical correlations. Following Hegel, it would therefore not be necessary to assume responsibility for the desirability of joint products. Yet, whether a joint product is desired or not is actually a *crucial aspect* of whether or not one can assume responsibility for a specific production process or not. At this point, we thus see the limitation of a conception such as that suggested by Hegel for the problem at hand.[9]

In light of the significance of knowledge and ignorance for the acceptance of responsibility in the following, we elucidate several categories of ignorance and the dynamics of the transformation of ignorance into knowledge.

12.4   CATEGORIES OF IGNORANCE AND THE TRANSFORMING OF IGNORANCE INTO KNOWLEDGE

In a first differentiation, ignorance can be divided into open and closed ignorance.[10]   A person is characterised by *closed* ignorance when he does not know that he is ignorant. In other words, that person has no knowledge as to his own ignorance. In the case of *open* ignorance, the person is conscious of his ignorance: he knows what it is that he does not know.

Open ignorance can be further differentiated according to whether it is reducible or not. *Reducible* ignorance may be individual and social ignorance. An individual can reduce his ignorance by learning; a society uses scientific research to transform its ignorance into knowledge. We want to subsume the knowledge which a society has accumulated under the expression *social knowledge*. The term 'social knowledge' does not imply that each individual member of society has access to this knowledge. Contrarily, individual knowledge is always smaller than social knowledge.

If ignorance cannot be reduced as described above, we speak of *irreducible* ignorance. For example, ignorance may be irreducible because of the overwhelming complexity of the object of research; irreducible ignorance also stems from the continuous possibility that true novelty emerges. The basic categories of ignorance are summarised in Figure 12.2.

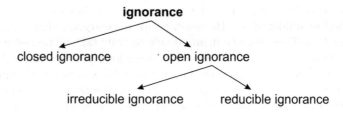

Figure 12.2   Basic categories of ignorance: one is conscious about open ignorance, but unconscious about closed ignorance. Open ignorance may or may not be reducible.

Let us investigate the relationship of these categories of ignorance to the concept of joint production and to our previous reflections. In principle, the concept of joint production lends itself to the process of transforming closed into open ignorance. According to thermodynamic considerations, all (industrial) production is ultimately joint production (cf. Chapter 3). Thus, the awareness of joint production demonstrates to the producer that every form of production necessarily entails joint production – that is, at least one joint product – and, moreover, also entails further effects. By that knowledge, the producer can actively attempt to reduce his ignorance through learning; society can reduce its corresponding social ignorance through scientific research.

As demonstrated above, however, joint production also entails an element of irreducible ignorance. In fact, we are dealing with irreducible ignorance induced by both of the aforementioned reasons:

- The complexity of scientifically researchable natural causality often makes it impossible to identify all joint products and every one of their effects.

- And whether a joint product is desirable or not in the long run depends on phenomena with the characteristic of novelty, namely changes in preferences and technological inventions. Thus, ignorance with respect to the desirability of joint products is not completely reducible (Baumgärtner et al. 2001: 369).

Knowing that irreducible ignorance exists can have an ambivalent effect. It can cause us to take greater care. On the other hand, it can also have the opposite effect in that it can lead us irrationally to allow ourselves to be guided by a 'principle of hope' (Bloch 1959) after all. That is to say that we, faced by evidently unsolvable problems with regard to undesired joint products or their dangerous consequences, choose to depend upon future discoveries to solve these problems and alleviate the dangers brought about by our actions today.

12.5   THE PRECAUTIONARY PRINCIPLE

Jonas' heuristic of fear (cf. Section 12.2) is closely related to the *precautionary principle*.[11] The principle demands that one takes precautionary measures to avoid harmful events, which are the object of fear. The precautionary principle is notoriously difficult to define. A frequently cited definition stems from the Wingspread Conference in 1988 (Raffensperger and Tickner 1999):

> Therefore it is necessary to implement the Precautionary Principle: Where an activity raises threats of harm to the environment or human health, precautionary measures should be taken even if some cause and effect relationships are not fully established scientifically.[12]

There is general agreement in the literature that the precautionary principle still lacks a sound conceptual foundation (Sandin 2004: 462, Turner and Hartzell 2004). In our view however, the proposal for a definition of the principle provided by Sandin (2004) can be used as a starting point. Sandin builds his argument on the premise that one can speak meaningfully of precaution only if one relates it 'to something' (Sandin 2004: 464). This implies that precaution is related not to general circumstances but always to a specific occurrence. It, hence, does not make sense to state that someone 'generally acts according to the precautionary principle'. Sandin (2004: 464–467) develops three criteria which an action must fulfil to meet the precautionary principle:

(i) The criterion of *intentionality*; it means that the action must be intentionally directed against the occurrence which is to be avoided.

(ii) The *uncertainty* criterion; it demands that the occurrence to be avoided is not 'certain or highly probable' (Sandin 2004: 466).

(iii) The *reasonableness* criterion; it demands that 'the agent has good reasons' that (ii) is fulfilled and, further, that the action 'will in effect at least contribute to the prevention of the harmful event' (Sandin 2004: 467).

Before proceeding, it is useful to define three types of ignorance – *risk*, *uncertainty*, and *ignorance*. Knight (1921) speaks of 'risk' if the outcomes and probabilities of an event are known, and of 'uncertainty' if only the outcomes are known, but not their probabilities. Faber et al. (1996c: 210) define 'ignorance proper' to be the 'inability to specify all future outcomes'.

Sandin's three criteria will now be discussed in light of the previous considerations in Part III of this book. In Sandin's conception, the precautionary principle relates only to the phenomena of risk and uncertainty. For, according to Sandin, the occurrence to be prevented by precautionary measures has to be known and must not be highly probable. Hence, ignorance proper, as defined above, is excluded from his considerations. Joint production on the other hand – in particular in its general principle (Section 4.4.3), giving rise to a high degree of complexity (Section 4.5) – implies that we cannot hope to know all possible outcomes of an event, either in the present or in the future. Moreover, it is important to emphasise that from the three types of ignorance defined above, ignorance proper is at the root of the most severe problems raised by joint production. For this reason, it is not adequate to restrict the precautionary principle to known events, that is to risk and uncertainty, as Sandin does.

From this, we derive the following two conclusions:

1. Precaution, as demanded by the precautionary principle, has to be precaution in general, not only towards specific events.

2. Humans exercising precaution are confronted with ignorance and, as we have shown in Section 12.4, they are confronted with irreducible ignorance.

Responsible action under conditions of ignorance (proper) requires the power of judgement (cf. Section 11.4). The power of judgement is implicitly addressed by Sandin (2004: 467) when he refers to 'good reasons' in criterion (iii). These good reasons are not 'objectively good' since they cannot be demonstrated by scientific methods, but they can only be 'somehow externally good', that is, they must be judged by others to be good reasons. To refer to the judgement of others is – as Kant (2000[1790]: 173f) has pointed out – a specific capability of the power of judgement, which he calls *sensus communis*.[13] Power of judgement is also employed by practical wisdom – phronesis in terms of Aristotle (see Section 11.4). Insofar as precaution is related to practical purposes, it requires phronesis, that is the practical power of judgement. In Section 11.4, we showed that responsible behaviour is a virtue if we are, at least partially, ignorant of the possible consequences of our actions. It is precisely this virtue which is demanded by the precautionary principle.

For a summary, the precautionary principle is a universal principle which concerns all possible consequences of one's actions. Although specific precautionary measures must be related to certain known outcomes, the principle itself cannot be restricted to known occurrences. The precautionary principle is encompassing, since it addresses the problem of ignorance, the capability of the power of judgement and it specifies responsibility in its secondary meaning (Section 11.2.2). Only if one is responsible for something or someone in particular must one act precautiously in that respect. Furthermore, since precaution demands the power of judgement and phronesis, it cannot be solely based on science. For this reason, the definition from the Wingspread Conference (Raffensperger and Tickner 1999, see above) states that 'precautionary measures should be taken even if some cause and effect relationships are not fully established scientifically'.

12.6 CONCLUSION: JOINT PRODUCTION AND THE OBLIGATION TO ACQUIRE KNOWLEDGE

Based on our reflections on joint production and ignorance in Sections 12.3 and 12.4, we can now come back to the argument introduced at the end of Section 12.2 and offer arguments in favour of the *heuristic of fear* put forward by Jonas (1979) – in contrast to the *principle of hope* as it was formulated by Bloch (1959). 'Heuristic of fear' means: when we are involved in something which has serious and far-reaching effects that we cannot entirely foresee at the present moment, we cannot be guided by hope with regard to some good outcome which might possibly occur as a result of our actions. Rather, the heuristic of fear demands of us that we ask before we act: 'What could be the worst case scenario?' In doing so, we must take into account that we will never be able to foresee each and every one of the relevant consequences of our actions in all detail. In keeping with the imperative of responsibility we may never trust entirely in our knowledge to date.

In Section 12.5, we have shown the close relationship between Jonas' 'heuristic of fear' and the precautionary principle. The latter is very encompassing; it contains the essential elements of our analysis in Part III so far, that is ignorance, the power of judgement, and responsibility in its secondary meaning. Thus, our analysis is suitable for substantiating the concept of the precautionary principle. Since ignorance proper – and not only risk and uncertainty – is the main problem for which the precautionary principle has been established, we cannot restrict ourselves to scientific methods but have to be aware of the possibility of closed ignorance (Figure 12.2).

Since we can never content ourselves with our knowledge to date, acquiring further knowledge becomes an obligation (Jonas 1979: 28). Our responsibility does not extend solely to the consequences of our past actions. Responsibility includes the obligation to do something specific in the future: we must, to the best of our ability, strive to know what the consequences of our actions are and will be. In doing so, however, we must never forget that we will never be able to foresee each and every one of them.[14]

Jonas' ethics of responsibility, with their obligation to acquire knowledge, can be substantiated by means of the concept of joint production. For instance, one assumes responsibility in the way Jonas addresses it, when one is aware of the fact that all production is joint production and takes this fact seriously.[15] In doing so, one brings to mind that every production process generates at least one unintended joint product, one which we might well not have identified yet. In this manner, the concept of joint production lends itself to transforming closed ignorance into open ignorance – namely as the means of developing knowledge about how ignorant we are. The concept challenges us to obtain knowledge of the unidentified joint products of our actions. At the same time, the concept of joint production reminds us that, due to the complexity of the consequences of our actions, we will never be able to obtain an overall view of each and every joint product and the corresponding consequences.

NOTES

1.   This section is for readers who are interested in the philosophical foundation of our approach. It can be skipped by those who are not particularly interested in this regard.

2.   All translations of Hegel are our own, but are based on the translation by T.M. Knox (1952).

3.   This specific production process for manufacturing soda, including a number of joint products, is discussed in detail in Chapter 16.

4.   This moral evaluation of actions is what Wieland calls 'consequence-based' (1999: 52, our translation). See also the discussion on page 233 on Wieland's critique of an ethics of responsibility.

5.   Cf. *Das Prinzip Hoffnung* ('The Principle of Hope') by Ernst Bloch (1959) to which Jonas (1979) constitutes a critical reply.

6.   For example, a previously undesired joint product can become a desired one because a new technology has been developed which allows it to be used as an input. A case in point is chlorine, which can be obtained from hydrogen chloride, an undesired joint product from producing soda (see Chapter 16): chlorine in the course of time actually became the (desired) main product of a certain branch of the (former) 'soda' industry because of a combination of a shift in preferences and technological change.

7.   Here, we use the expression 'scientifically identifiable correlations' in a deterministic sense and leave the problem of natural indeterminism aside.

8.   The differentiation of restrictions and bounds in respect to our ignorance goes back to Immanuel Kant's *Critique of the Power of Judgement* ('Kritik der Urteilskraft', § 80). Kant argues that, with regard to the perception of 'natural ends' (organisms), our mind is 'not only quite restricted, but also distinctly bounded', since the evaluation of organisms can only occur on the basis of a 'teleological principle' which is not a principle of reason, but of judgement (Kant 2000 [1790]: 286).

9.   For a discussion of Hegel's conception see Heidbrink (2003: 73ff).

10.   This classification is based on Faber et al. (1992).

11.   There is currently an extensive discussion on the precautionary principle, in particular in the environmental field (Bodansky 1991, Dorman 2005, Gollier and Treich 2003, Graham 2000, Harremoës 2002, Immordino 2003, Sandin 1999, 2004, and Turner and Hartzell 2004).

12.   The definition resembles the formulation of the United Nations' *Declaration on Environment and Development* (United Nations 1992: 3):

> In order to protect the environment, the precautionary approach shall be widely applied by states according to their capabilities. Where there are threats of serious or irreversible damage, lack of full scientific certainty shall not be used as a reason for postponing cost-effective measures to prevent environmental degradation.

Sometimes, a much stronger formulation is chosen, as for example by the City of San Francisco in a white paper on precaution (City of San Francisco 2003):

> Producers and proponents [of industrial activities] therefore must bear the burden of demonstrating and maintaining safety of products, projects, and technologies.

13.   Kant defines *sensus communis* as follows:

> By *sensus communis*, however, must be understood the idea of a com-
> munal sense, that is, a faculty of judging that in its reflection takes
> account (a priori) of every one else's way of representing in thought, in
> order as it were to hold this judgment up to human reason as a whole
> and thereby avoid the illusion which, from subjective private conditions
> that could easily be held to be objective, would have a detrimental
> influence on the judgment. (Kant 2000[1790]: 173f)

> To think in the position of every one else [...] is the maxim [...] of the
> broad-minded way. (Kant 2000[1790]: 174f)

14.   In this sense, the 'perspective' of joint production 'gives additional support to
applying the precautionary principle' (Baumgärtner et al. 2001: 370).
15.   'Inattention to joint production may therefore easily result in ethical negligence'
(Baumgärtner et al. 2001: 369).

13. Individual and Collective Responsibility

with Thomas Petersen

In the previous two chapters, we have investigated the term 'responsibility' and have placed it in one context with the phenomenon of joint production. Thereby, it became clear that responsibility is not only a precondition of ethics – at least insofar as one is free in actions of ethical relevance only if one is responsible for these actions – but that it is, furthermore, an ethical principle in its own right, and can even be regarded as a virtue in the sense of Aristotle.

Responsibility is a virtue, because the complexity of the consequences of any individual action makes it generally impossible to entirely foresee those consequences. Thus, an individual can become a hostage of his own actions insofar as he is not aware of what he is doing. Above all else, responsibility as a virtue comprehends the right handling of the ignorance which is inevitably inherent in all action. Such ignorance is a particularly serious problem wherever one encounters joint production. In Chapter 12 we have demonstrated how the problem of ignorance in the environmental field justifies what Hans Jonas calls a 'heuristic of fear'.

At this point, a number of questions remain to be addressed. We have already intimated that responsibility is by necessity limited in certain ways. According to Hegel, one only bears responsibility for the necessary consequences of one's actions. We have seen, however, that this limitation becomes inadequate under the conditions of joint production. If such a limitation is not possible in a general manner, then one must ask whether specific types of responsibility exist – types, some of which are more strictly limited, and others that are less so. At the same time, it remains to be clarified for each type of responsibility, who bears it and to whom.

In this chapter, we differentiate between four types of responsibility: legal, moral, political, and political-ethical responsibility. It will become clear that political-ethical responsibility is the most comprehensive. Each of these types of responsibility will be considered under the aspects,

- for what (or for whom),

- to whom (or toward which authority),

- and in regard to what (or according to which measure)

responsibility must be assumed. We shall begin with the sphere of law, as this is the area in which responsibility can be most clearly defined.

13.1   LEGAL RESPONSIBILITY

Legal responsibility means that the consequences of one's actions rebound on the perpetrator. In other words, they are certain forms of feedback, on the basis of which one is 'called to account for the consequences of one's deeds' (Wieland 1999: 26, our translation). Sanctions of the legal system 'guarantee that certain consequences of his deeds rebound onto the enactor' (Wieland 1999: 26). Such a feedback consists of either sanctions for violations of legal rulings, or liability for damage which one's actions cause to others. Such liability can refer to occurrences which are, at best, indirectly associated with one's own actions. Thus, parents are liable for the actions of their children, and the owners of an automobile for damage caused by that automobile, even if it is not directly their fault – for example, if it should catch fire and cause a major accident. An individual bears responsibility, in a legal sense, toward whichever authority passes laws and enforces them. The measure of his responsibility is the legal system. Under such a legal system, it is possible to precisely define and delineate responsibility so that, in general, an individual can be relatively certain of what to expect.

13.2   MORAL RESPONSIBILITY

The emphasis of *moral* responsibility does not primarily lie on the consequences of one's actions, but on the actions themselves. He who acts freely is responsible for his actions. Should these actions be good, then he acts responsibly – as long as his actions are compatible with serious ethical principles. Otherwise, his actions are bad and subject to reproach. Should his ethics be an ethics of virtue, then he must assume responsibility not only for his actions, but also for his attitudes and habits. He has to be prepared to justify them with respect to his

ethical principles. These principles constitute the measure according to
which he bears responsibility. In contrast, the authority toward which he
bears such responsibility can be defined in different ways: One can bear
responsibility toward oneself, toward 'one's own humanity', or toward
moral society as a whole.

Moral responsibility differs from legal responsibility in that the purpose of the action or the individual's intention plays a central role. An
action is not judged on the basis of its actual consequences; but the
judgement depends on the intention, and on the seriousness, with which
this action is executed. This holds even for utilitarianism, since, although
utilitarian ethics is based on the action's consequences, utilitarians must
judge the respective action according to the intended consequences (cf.
Tugendhat 1993: 109). However, the emphasis of moral responsibility on
the 'correct' intention does not mean that the consequences of an action
can be entirely neglected. For the correct intention includes taking the
consequences into account, and thus, no action can be labelled 'good'
from which only negative consequences can be expected with certainty,
or at least with high probability. There exist, as far as we can see, only
two exceptions to this rule:

1. The evil is justified by a higher ethical principle, for example in
   the manner in which punishment is justified by justice, or

2. the evil is balanced or compensated by a higher good so that one
   can justify accepting or condoning it.[1]

Moral responsibility shares with legal responsibility the characteristic
that, as a form of responsibility for the consequences of one's actions, it
is a *limited* form of responsibility. While law itself draws the limits for legal responsibility, in moral responsibility Hegel's differentiation between
necessary and chance consequences finds its place: as a rule, a person
must assume responsibility only for that which follows by necessity from
his actions and which he can overview. In this sense, Kant (1996b[1797]:
612) also declares: should someone act correctly, then he need bear no
responsibility for that which follows from his actions by chance. Chance
consequences, for example, can be actions and deeds stemming from the
will of another person. A person is not responsible for deeds of other
persons, even if such deeds only become possible due to the person's own
just acting in the first place.

Legal and moral responsibility, therefore, generally only refer to the
individual. They focus on the consequences of the individual's action (cf.
Section 11.2), and such responsibility is always limited as we have discussed above. In the legal case, responsibility is explicitly limited by law
itself, whereas in the case of moral responsibility, responsibility is limited

by the occurrence of chance consequences. However, an unambiguous differentiation between the necessary and the chance consequences of an action may be impossible to make. Also, a temporal limitation of responsibility can exist. In legal terms, this takes the form of the statute of limitations: one cannot be held liable – or, in other words, legally responsible – for consequences of actions which only appear or become enforced after a certain time period has elapsed.

13.3   POLITICAL RESPONSIBILITY

Political and political-ethical responsibility differs from the individual responsibility of the legal and moral kinds. Responsibility in the political and political-ethical sense does not primarily refer to responsibility for the consequences of an action, but rather to a form of responsibility for the state of being of something in particular – for example for the preservation and well-being of a political community. Being responsible for a state of being renders irrelevant the limits which apply to the responsibility for an action and its consequences. Responsibility in the political and political-ethical sense must be assumed for all foreseeable consequences which could be significant for the state of being of that which is placed under one's responsibility. Moreover, the subject which must assume responsibility is not necessarily a single individual. Instead, the subject is often a collective, a community or an individual who regards himself as a member of the community and is acting on its behalf.

Political responsibility is borne by all who take part in political activity. Political activity is the realisation of the interests of a political community, for example a state. We credit political activity with the capability of preserving such a community and, at the same time, shaping the world around us. Political activity is also the application and realisation of power. Insofar as power is ascribed to an individual in a political sense, he is burdened with responsibility for the consequences of all he does. Such political responsibility appears to be unlimited insofar as the one who bears it is furnished with power to guide the fate of the political community. Concerning this fate, the differentiation between necessary and chance consequences is irrelevant: the political subject has to assume responsibility with regard to necessary *and* chance consequences of his political acting. For example, a government is always held responsible for the state of the economy, even if this state is only partly – and that can mean by chance – a consequence of the government's own doing. Phases of prosperity are equally accredited to the government as recessions. A politician who wishes to live up to his calling must therefore have good fortune.

Furthermore, political responsibility appears to be temporally unlimited. Whether a politician has successfully reformed a political community or has effected its long-term collapse can only become discernible after several generations. How this case is evaluated, however, usually determines one's view of this politician.

13.4 POLITICAL-ETHICAL RESPONSIBILITY

Political responsibility is derived from the experience that those involved in the political process have, and exert, power. They are measured by the application of such power and by the realisation of the goals which are normally ascribed to them: in other words, by their success. Above all else, one assumes that the goal of such a political actor is the preservation, the ascendancy and the well-being of the political community. The conceptual content of political responsibility is, however, one-sided insofar as it is orientated solely toward success, but never asks about the means by which such success is achieved. One can, however, demand of political activity itself that it applies moral standards also to the means employed to achieve success.

If we wish to evaluate political responsibility along such lines, then we arrive at the notion of a 'totality of responsibility' as Jonas (1979: 189) developed it. Responsibilities have totality insofar as they 'encompass the total state of being of their objects, that is to say every aspect of it, from their naked existence to their highest interests' (Jonas 1979: 189). We label this form of responsibility *political-ethical* responsibility and relate it not only to the preservation and prosperity of the community – in other words to the *common good* – but also to the notion of *justice*. Justice, which belongs to the 'highest interests' of the community, includes at least the democratic principle, the rule of law, the guarantee of human rights, and the preservation of the possibility to act politically.

As political-ethical responsibility draws on the standards of the common good and justice, it is truly the most comprehensive of all categories of responsibility we have dealt with. The comprehensiveness of political-ethical responsibility raises the possibility that stipulations of the common good and of justice might come into conflict with one another – a conflict which may be irreconcilable and unsolvable. A war, for example, however legitimate and necessary it may be, always entails innocent victims. Such conflicts are of a tragic nature and, in the sense of Max Weber's ethics of responsibility, it becomes clear that the tragic nature of certain conflicts requires our special attention. The concept of ethics of responsibility emphasises the fact that in politics it is impossible to guarantee the moral integrity of actions by strictly limiting responsibility for the consequences of an action, as Kant and Hegel propose it for moral activity. In particular, someone involved in politics can never absolve himself of responsibility for the reaction of his counterpart to his own deeds.[2]

The comprehensive, total character of political-ethical responsibility emphasises another difficulty which the complexity of the consequences of an action entails. The power that someone involved in politics ascribes to himself allows him to disregard *none* of the concomitants of his actions. To a certain extent 'the difference between purpose, intent, action, main and side consequence is irrelevant' (Spaemann 1977: 180, our translation) to someone involved in politics. 'And wherever negative consequences arise from his actions, then their elimination is in turn also his task' (ibid.). In this manner, however, this person runs the risk of becoming entangled in the consequences of his actions so that in politics 'side effects of actions are processed rather than decisions made' (Meier 1983: 20, our translation). As a result he who lays claim to power is doomed to be powerless – he is no longer the master of his actions.

This danger appears to be particularly relevant under conditions of joint production. For the consequences which arise from joint production are irreversible in the majority of cases. The situation becomes additionally complicated by the fact that ignorance exists with regard to the possible joint products themselves, their consequences and their desirability in the future (cf. Section 12.3). Hence, there is a danger that a person who has to assume political-ethical responsibility becomes a prisoner of the joint products and side effects of his action: he may be completely absorbed by the elimination of undesired joint products and the neutralisation of undesired effects. He would then no longer be acting, but only reacting.

An example of this danger is the generation of electricity from nuclear energy. Radioactive materials are produced which must be stored or disposed of over generations, thus placing long-term obligations on politicians. The dangers of these radioactive joint products, and the extent of the measures which must be taken to deal with them, can hardly be ignored. The use of nuclear energy thus endangers the good of a political society, as well as its ability to act – in other words, its ability to assume responsibility for its own actions.

Nuclear reactors can also become the objective of terrorist attacks which would have terrible consequences. With the example of this possibility we may clarify the difference between moral and political-ethical responsibility. In Hegel's sense, a terrorist attack on a nuclear reactor is a chance consequence of a political decision in favour of nuclear energy. As the attack is a deed brought about by an evil will, the politician in question need not assume responsibility for such an attack and its consequences – in the moral sense of the term explicated above (cf. Section 13.2). However, in the political-ethical sense this, precisely, does not hold. It is not solely the terrorist himself who is responsible for the consequences of the attack, but equally those who assumed responsibility for the political decision in favour of the use of nuclear energy.[3]

13.5   CONCLUSION

Figure 13.1 summarises the four categories of individual and collective responsibility discussed in this chapter. At this point, we are left with a major problem of responsibility as imposing moral obligations (secondary meaning, cf. Section 11.2) with regard to joint production: how do, and how should, individual economic agents and the political community deal with unintended joint products which fall outside the social and legal order? We will address this question in the following chapter.

Individual responsibility
 • Legal responsibility; limited by law
 • Moral responsibility; limited by ethical principles

Collective responsibility
 • Political responsibility for the common good
 • Political-ethical responsibility: common good and justice

Figure 13.1   Individual and collective responsibility.

NOTES

1.   According to the ethical doctrine of utilitarianism, the second limitation is not the exception but the rule. From a purely utilitarian perspective, an action is *always* considered good if and only if it causes more good than bad. In other ethical doctrines, for example of the Kantian type, the second limitation holds under certain circumstances only.

2.   Thus, Max Weber's ethics of responsibility are not a consequential ethical concept which seeks to justify the means by the ends. However, since Weber is often ambiguous and misleading on this topic, ethics of responsibility are widely understood as 'a consequence-based concept of legitimisation, according to which decisions are not justified by intentions or individual consequences, but by the aggregate of all foreseeable consequences' (Wieland 1999: 56, our translation).

3.   The sociologist Ulrich Beck recognises a general tendency of modern societies to narrow down their range of possible actions due to the negligence of joint production which is actually taking place. Beck therefore calls the modern society a 'risk society' (Beck 1992). In a sociological sense, 'risk' denotes the danger of the emergence of undesired and hazardous events, where this danger is the result of one's own actions. Beck notes: 'In advanced modernity the social production of wealth is systematically accompanied by the social production of risks' (Beck 1992: 19). Insofar as one understands the production of risks as material environmental damage, the expression 'risk' can easily be translated into the terminology of joint production. Regarding the generation of 'wealth' as the quintessence of all intended and desired products, 'risk' can be understood as the quintessence of all possible undesired joint products and their consequences. The generation of 'risks' within the risk society also includes the problem of ignorance (Beck 1992: 24) with regard to 'growing hazardous side effects' (Beck 1992: 20) – as in the case of joint production with emerging undesired joint outputs. As in the case of joint production, the question of responsibility also arises with regard to the production of risks (Beck 1992: 33), namely the question of responsibility for the procurement of the best possible knowledge about risks. Beck recognises a general lack of responsibility ('One can do something and continue doing it without having to take personal responsibility for it.' Beck 1992: 33) as being predominant in a society which views risks as 'goods to be avoided, whose non-existence is implied until cancelled' (Beck 1992: 34).

14. Responsibility in Politics and in the Economy

with Thomas Petersen

In the previous chapter, we have differentiated four types of responsibility. We have pointed out that political-ethical responsibility is the most comprehensive one. This kind of responsibility is therefore potentially the most relevant for giving guidance when facing unintended joint products which fall outside the social and legal order. The question thus arises who bears this kind of responsibility, and what are the necessary attributes for someone to be able to do so. It is obvious that the standard conception of an individual as an economic agent (*homo economicus*) is not suitable to systematically characterise such a person. In this chapter, we shall argue that an individual who is to bear responsibility can, in particular, be conceptualised on the basis of the *homo politicus* hypothesis. To *homo politicus*, responsibility is to be ascribed as a virtue. On the basis of this argument, perspectives for environmental politics under the conditions of joint production can then be outlined. Thereby, special significance falls on the relationship between the responsibility of the economic agent and that of the politician.

14.1 Political-Ethical Responsibility and the *Homo Politicus*

Political-ethical responsibility, being the most comprehensive form of responsibility, places the highest demands on somebody to bear this kind of responsibility. Yet, how is such a political individual to be conceptualised, who is capable of living up to political-ethical responsibility? In earlier work, we have argued that the political individual is to be conceived of as a *homo politicus* (Faber et al. 1997, 2002, Petersen and Faber 2000). The *homo politicus* never acts only in his own interest. Rather, he views himself as a part of the community. He always acts for the community; what he undertakes on his own initiative is always orientated toward common activity and common decision-making. As a *homo politicus*, an individual involved in politics always orientates himself toward the demands of the common good and of justice. At the same time, he is characterised by the capabilities necessary to successfully pursue these goals. We have therefore described the *homo politicus* as someone possessing certain virtues. Thereby, we regard virtue as a capability, as a sort of virtuosity in the sense of Aristotle: justice, courage, temperance, as well as practical wisdom (phronesis) (Faber et al. 1997: 471). We can now ascribe a fifth virtue to the *homo politicus*, namely that of *responsibility* in the sense in which we developed it in Section 11.4.

Against the background of political-ethical responsibility, the virtue of responsibility can be thought of as the ability to decide which actions one can assume responsibility for. That is to say, the *homo politicus* must be able to live up to the stipulations of justice and the common good, while at the same time retaining the possibility of acting politically. He is therefore also responsible for conserving his ability to assume political responsibility.

Thus, the *homo politicus* must, on the one hand, strive to avoid the danger of becoming enmeshed in dealing with the concomitants of his actions, and, hence, ceasing to be the master of his actions. On the other hand, he must take care that his actions do not endanger the common good or violate justice. Political activity, of both a political community or the *homo politicus*, is always powerful activity which intervenes in the world, changing and shaping it. For the very reason that *homo politicus* as the bearer of political-ethical responsibility cannot limit his responsibility (cf. Section 13.4), he must limit his own actions, namely the exercising of political power. He must limit it under the provisions of his responsibility in the abstract sense, namely to those actions which he can assume responsibility for. Regarding environmental politics, this means: activity which changes the environment or nature must also be limited. And in this case, it is not only political activity itself which must be limited, but, in an appropriate manner, the activity of economic participants – who, after all, particularly intervene in the environment and nature.

So, how can the *homo politicus* live up to his responsibility? He is subject to the conditions of irreducible ignorance. Irreducible ignorance exists not only concerning social affairs, in other words, concerning the relationships between people, but also in the sphere of the relationship between man and nature. This became apparent from the discussion of joint production and ignorance in Section 12.3. Under the conditions of irreducible ignorance there are no concrete, universally valid rules on how to act. In order to decide what one can assume responsibility for, one requires practical wisdom (phronesis). For this reason, we have defined responsibility as a virtue.

In the field of environmental politics, however, this virtue must meet special requirements. Environmental politics cannot do without scientific expertise: the politician is dependent on science, without this lessening his own responsibility. Environmental politics 'must strive to achieve the highest possible level of information with regard to the consequences of its measures' (Spaemann 1977: 180, our translation). Yet, as exemplified by joint production, science cannot eliminate ignorance with regard to the environmental effects of political decisions, but only hope to reduce it to some extent. Thus, political activity in the field of environmental politics requires a specific form of practical wisdom with regard to scientific findings. From a person involved in politics we must, therefore, expect a certain level of scientific proficiency. He need not be a scientist himself. But he must be able to understand how scientific findings or recommendations come about. On the other hand, one must also demand of scientists that they assume political responsibility to a certain extent. Science shares responsibility for informing the society about the environmental effects of measures taken; and about the limits of its expertise – about that which it does know, that which it can know, and that which it cannot know.

14.2 THE RESPONSIBILITY OF THE ECONOMIC AGENT

The question of individual and collective responsibility under the conditions of joint production would not be adequately examined if we did not ultimately turn our attention to the specific responsibility of the *economic* agent. For it is actually far less the activity of politics than that of the economic agent, be he producer or consumer, that intervenes in nature and gives rise to joint products with all their consequences. The individual economic agent, however, is – in his role as economic agent – systematically not capable of monitoring all of the consequences of his actions – be they necessary or chance consequences. For in order to be able to take part in economic activity in the first place, the agent must be able to overview the relevant consequences of his economic actions, that is, those consequences for which he may have to account or be made liable. The responsibility for the consequences of his actions *must* be limited if he is to calculate them according to cost-benefit considerations, which is essential for economic activity.

Hence, the economic agent, if he is to be economically successful, cannot assume responsibility for all the relevant consequences of his actions. For he cannot entirely foresee them, and also would be completely overburdened by their neutralisation. He can therefore not be held accountable for some of the most significant consequences of his actions, in particular, in terms of environmental impact. If we take into account the intimate connection between responsibility and freedom explicated in Chapter 11, it follows that under the conditions of joint production, the economic agent is free in a limited sense only. The responsibility which he cannot assume himself must be assumed for him by politics. It is politics which must also decide on the limits of the individual agents' responsibility and the corresponding consequences.

The limited responsibility of the economic agent is therefore assigned politically. In defining this responsibility, we want to refer to the *representation* of a system as the object of a – scientific or other – investigation (see Section 2.3.2). Such a system representation takes only a certain portion of all joint products and consequences into account. Regarding the politically assigned responsibility of the economic agent, this means that the agent is assigned a specific system representation according to which he must consider and assume responsibility for joint products and their consequences in his production, consumption, or waste disposal activity.

How can politics assign a particular system representation to economic agents, so that they can act responsibly within this limited framework? This is typically done by creating a legal framework which specifies in detail who has to 'consider' which joint products in which manner. This includes the full range of environmental policy instruments, for instance:

- prohibitions and technical instructions ('command and control'), for example such that

    - the creation of a particular joint product must be avoided, by an appropriate modification of the production system or by shutting down the production of the corresponding main product, or

    - if it is created, it must be transformed into something non-harmful, such as sulphur-dioxide into plaster, or

    - it may only be created in certain amounts;

- market-based instruments and incentives, for example

    - a fee is to be paid for the production and emission of the joint product, or

- a tradable permit is required for the emission of the joint product, or

- a subsidy is paid for the development of a new technology that avoids the joint product;

• specific liability laws; that is, if damages should occur from any product or joint product within a certain time horizon, the producer can be held liable for those in specified ways.

In any case, whatever the economic agent cannot assume responsibility for falls back to politics. Ultimately, it is the political system which remains responsible for the political community as a whole and for the natural foundations of its existence.

14.3 SUMMARY OF PART III AND TWO CONCLUSIONS

In this part of the book, we have developed a new perspective on environmental politics which is relevant for politics as a whole. This perspective was derived from relating the concept of responsibility – an expression which has its place in the humanities and in practical philosophy – to the physical phenomenon of joint production. Thereby, it became clear that responsibility and joint production display significant terminological analogies.

Above and beyond this analogy, it became clear that the phenomenon of joint production poses new challenges for taking responsibility for human activity. This holds, in particular, for politics and those persons who are involved with it: they bear the most comprehensive form of responsibility – political-ethical responsibility. As we have demonstrated in Chapter 13, politics is always at risk of arriving at a tragic conflict or becoming entangled in the complexity of the consequences of its actions (cf. Section 11.3.2). This danger arises mainly from the fact that our activity is subject to conditions of irreducible ignorance (cf. Chapter 12).

The particular dangers of political activity are nothing new. Yet, for a long time, these dangers had only been taken into account in social affairs, that is, in the interactions among people. Something different appears to be the case with regard to our relationship to nature. This relationship was often seen in two different, but equally simplistic ways: either we are subject to natural phenomena and at nature's mercy, or we control these phenomena and thus reign over nature. Singular problems for responsible behaviour did not seem to arise in either case. The concept of joint production shows us, however, that both views of our relationship to nature are misleading. We are neither simply subject to nature, nor are we her sovereign lords. In the course of human production, we intervene in nature and subjugate her. By simultaneously giving rise to joint products with every product we produce, however, we instigate natural processes which are beyond our control. We act, as Arendt (1958) puts it, 'into nature' and nature responds as an autonomous counterpart. This leads to two conclusions.

Irreversibility in nature and in the social sphere

The same problems confront politics in the field of the natural environment as in the social field. Even if we regard solely the natural environment, that is, if we neglect the interests of the economic and political actors involved, politicians find themselves confronted by an unmanageable complexity of the consequences of their actions. This circumstance is even more momentous, since interventions in nature are often irreversible.

Irreversible consequences of actions exist also with respect to social affairs. However, in the social sphere there are ways to partly neutralise the irreversible consequences of individual actions. In the economic domain the traditional approach is that of monetary compensation. Arendt (1958: 236) points out another 'remedy against the irreversibility and unpredictability of the process started by acting' by which the consequences of actions may be reverted – namely the human 'power to forgive'.[1]

Evidently, neither of these ways hold for irreversible interventions in nature. Although we may have good reason to hope that nature will be able to physically neutralise the negative consequences of our actions to a sometimes surprisingly large, but limited extent, nature cannot be compensated in monetary terms, and it cannot forgive.

> Modern natural science and technology, which no longer observe or take material from or imitate processes of nature but seem actually to act into it, seem, by the same token, to have carried irreversibility and human unpredictability into the natural realm, where no remedy can be found to undo what has been done. (Arendt 1958: 238)

Responsibility of individuals and politics

Since the consequences of joint production are often not foreseeable and also irreversible, we can draw a second conclusion: The multifarious responsibility which is related to the phenomenon of joint production must be borne both by the economic agent and by politics. For in a modern economy it is above all the economic agent who produces, thus intervening in nature. Yet, this responsibility is always too great for the individual economic agent. There remains a problem in politics. Politics, science, and the public must fundamentally rethink the way of dividing up the enormous burden of responsibility which arises from economic activity through the phenomenon of joint production between politics and the individual economic agent.

NOTES

1.   Forgiving is independent of whether a damage resulting from an action has been compensated.

PART IV

Case Studies

INTRODUCTION

While the discussion in Parts I through III of this book has been mainly at the conceptual and theoretical level, in this part we present selected case studies. They serve to demonstrate the importance of the phenomenon of joint production in ecological-economic systems, to show the potential of the concept of joint production for analysing economy-environment interactions, and to illustrate the general results of the analysis obtained so far.

While many of the characteristics of joint production are eminent in most economy-environment interactions, the case studies in Part IV are selected such that each one highlights one particular aspect of joint production. Chapter 15 presents the case of waste paper, which is centred around the price ambivalence of this joint output. Chapter 16 discusses the history of the soda and chlorine industries, which illustrates the important role of joint production for innovation and industrial evolution. With the example of cement production, Chapter 17 shows how the development of an industry is being shaped by joint production and stock dynamics, with the result of increasing complexity. Finally, Chapter 18 uses the example of sulphuric acid to demonstrate how the ambivalence of joint products leads to the policy problem of joint externalities.

15. Waste Paper: Price Ambivalence*

with Ralph Winkler

15.1 INTRODUCTION

Many factors need to be considered in the design of environmental policies. Household behaviour, technology, environmental scarcities, market forces, political forces, delegation of responsibility and regulatory institutions interact in a complex way to determine the ultimate effect of policy measures on both the economy and the environment. In this chapter, we present a case study of how economic market forces, production technology and environmental legislation interact to generate price ambivalence of joint products – a phenomenon that we discussed in detail on a conceptual level in Chapter 8. The case we are drawing upon is the price ambivalence of waste paper on the German market between 1985 and 2000. The phenomenon of price ambivalence – that is the price of a commodity is positive at some times and negative at other times – is apparent in that particular market in a highly illustrative manner. Its causes are a number of technical and institutional characteristics of the German waste paper market. While some of these characteristics are common in all secondary resource markets, some characteristics are unique to the German waste paper market.

Natural resources are necessary inputs in many production processes and are usually paid according to their marginal productivity. Thus, primary resources like wood, pulp, crude oil etc. are only harvested or produced in amounts which enable a profitable sale on markets. The same goes, according to standard economic wisdom, for so-called secondary resources which are recovered from waste materials from consumption or production, for example waste paper, scrap glass and scrap iron. Profit-maximising firms in a free market would recover secondary resources from waste only in as much as it could be sold profitably in secondary resource markets. Hence, one would expect the price for secondary resources to be generally positive.

---

*This chapter is taken, with modifications, from Baumgärtner and Winkler (2003).

In contrast to this expectation, in the first half of the 1990s the price for low quality waste paper on the German market turned negative (Statistisches Bundesamt 2000). The recycling and disposal industry had to pay the paper industry, which uses waste paper as a productive input, for accepting waste paper. Since then the price for low quality waste paper has oscillated in such a manner that it is at times positive and at times negative (Statistisches Bundesamt 2000).

Recent publications on waste paper concentrate on the high volatility of waste paper prices (Ackerman and Gallagher 2002), examine inter-country differences in waste paper recovery and utilisation (Byström and Lönnstedt 1995, Berglund et al. 2002) or discuss whether waste paper should be recycled or incinerated (Hanley and Slark 1994, Leach et al. 1997, Byström and Lönnstedt 1997, Hekkert et al. 1999, UBA 2000, Samakovlis 2003). In the empirical technical literature, the observed price ambivalence on the German waste paper market has been documented since its occurrence at the beginning of the 1990s (Sudan 1992, Pothmann 1995). In particular, the relationship between waste management legislation and the excess supply of waste paper hass been pointed out (Holzey 1993, Kibat and Meißner 1994, Meißner 1995 and Hirche 1997). These contributions do not explain the reasons for price ambivalence but discuss potential consequences for the German paper industry as a result of changes in the legal framework, and criticise what is perceived as 'erroneous' trends (Kibat 1991, Grünewald 1992, Holzey and Pothmann 1993). In the theoretical economic literature, price ambivalence is a scarcely discussed subject. Only Wacker (1987) and Baumgärtner (2000, 2004a) analyse models of price ambivalent behaviour. Price ambivalence is, in general, only possible if, due to certain circumstances, supply of a secondary resource is independent of its price and demand. In Chapter 8, we have identified a combination of three particular model aspects causing price ambivalence: (i) The waste joint output emerges in fixed proportion to a wanted commodity. (ii) The only possibility of getting rid of the waste joint output, besides a productive use in a second production process, is a form of costly disposal. (iii) The use of the secondary material as a productive input and substitute for a primary resource is limited by technology. We will see in this chapter that the German waste paper market also exhibits these three characteristics.

In this chapter, we discuss in detail the case of price ambivalence in waste paper. We analyse how environmental policy, regulatory institutions, market forces and technology have interacted over time to generate this phenomenon, and we identify its underlying causes. Section 15.2 describes the German market for waste paper and the different actors in that market. The development of the market since 1950 and its relationship with the paper industry is outlined in Section 15.3. Section 15.4 deals with price ambivalence in detail, as observed since 1990, and explains the underlying economic, legislative and technological reasons. Section 15.5 concludes by summarising our results, assessing the waste paper industry in terms of responsibility, price ambivalence and welfare implications, and by giving an outlook on future developments.

15.2 THE GERMAN WASTE PAPER MARKET

Paper waste occurs as a joint output from production and consumption. The recycled part of paper waste is a secondary resource for paper production and is called *waste paper* to distinguish it from the *paper waste* which is disposed of in a costly manner, for example by dumping in landfills – which costs up to 230 euros per tonne – or incineration – which costs up to 255 euros per tonne (Behrens and Maydell 1997: 5–21, 5–22). In Germany, the utilisation of waste paper in the production of new paper has a tradition of 200 years (Pothmann 1996). Therefore it is not surprising that there exist market structures for trading waste paper. This market is called the *waste paper market*.

Waste paper is not a homogeneous good but is classified in over 50 different quality grades clustered in five groups (BIR and CEPI 1999). As a consequence, the waste paper market is split into various submarkets. Price ambivalence can be observed only in certain submarkets, namely for grades 1.02[1] and 1.04[2]. As the prices as well as demand and supply of different grades oscillate in a perfectly correlated manner, we sometimes refer to *the* waste paper market for brevity. In 1999, for example, the prices for waste paper oscillated between −5 euros and +46 euros per tonne for grade 1.02 and between +15 euros and +62 euros per tonne for grade 1.04. Over the same period, the prices oscillated between +46 euros and +92 euros per tonne for the medium grade 2.01[3], between +169 euros and +221 euros for the high grade 3.07[4], and between +359 euros and +544 euros per tonne for sulphite pulp.

Waste paper accrues in nearly every branch of production and consumption. These potential *suppliers of waste paper* can be clustered in three groups: the paper processing industry, commerce, and municipalities. The groups differ markedly from each other in terms of amount supplied and quality of waste paper (Table 15.1). The fraction of total domestic paper consumption entering the waste paper market is called the *waste paper recovery rate*. It is bounded from above at about 80 % (Göttsching 1998: V70) as a part of the paper produced is fixed in durable goods, such as books, or is disposed of as sanitary paper through sewage and cannot be recovered.

Waste paper supplier	Waste paper supply		Grades
	in million tonnes	in %	
Paper processing industry	1.2	12.7	medium and high quality
Commerce	4.7	48.2	mainly low quality
Municipalities	3.8	39.1	low quality
Total	7.7	100.0	

Table 15.1   Waste paper supply by different suppliers in Germany 1994. Source: BVSE (2000).

Only the *paper industry* is capable of using waste paper as a secondary resource on a large scale. The three main raw materials for paper production are mechanical pulp, chemical pulp and waste paper. In general, a limited substitution between the primary resources (chemical and mechanical) pulp and the secondary resource waste paper is possible (Samakovlis 2003). The ratio of recovered waste paper input to the total amount of paper produced is called the *recovered paper utilisation rate*.[5] The potential maximum extent of substitution between primary and secondary resources, and therefore the potential maximum recovered paper utilisation rate, is determined by the quality grade of paper or board to be produced. According to Kibat (1991: Section 2) the production of packaging paper and board allows the use of very high fractions of waste paper, while the production of graphic paper allows only limited use of waste paper (Table 15.2). The use of waste paper in the paper industry is mainly driven by economic considerations, as even in periods of high prices recycled fibres from waste paper are cheaper than chemical and mechanical pulp (Göttsching 1993: 152, 1998: V69). In 2000, 135 German paper mills used 11.0 million tonnes of waste paper for the production of 18.1 million tonnes of new paper and board. With 8.3 million tonnes (equalling 75.3 % of the utilised waste paper) the lower quality grades contributed the largest part (VDP 2002: 34, 47, 53).

The *recycling and disposal industry* coordinates the huge number of potential waste paper suppliers and the relatively few waste paper purchasers. The industry organises the logistics of waste paper collection from the various suppliers, cleans waste paper from impurities and sorts it into different quality grades. In 2000, the German recycling and disposal industry collected, sorted and sold 13.5 million tonnes of waste paper (BVSE 2001: 5). Due to the low price-to-weight ratio of waste paper, especially with low quality grades, transportation costs can cut

Paper grade	1988	1990	1992	1994	1996	1998	2000
Corrugated board	109	107	108	107	107	111	108
Packaging paper	55	55	60	60	60	72	54
Folding box board	72	78	81	80	88	79	82
Other packaging paper	83	86	76	79	69	68	71
Total	91	92	93	94	95	96	95
Newsprint paper	59	68	72	108	116	117	117
Other graphic paper	5	6	7	7	13	17	18
Total	15	18	20	28	36	37	37
Cellulose wadding	100	88	48	62	81	66	29
Tissue	29	49	54	63	63	67	76
Crepe paper	72	81	115	108	98	85	72
Total	37	55	62	69	68	69	74
Utilisation rate	46	49	52	56	60	61	60

Table 15.2   Recovered paper utilisation rates since 1988 for the production of different paper grades in %. Source: BVSE (2001: 4).

profits dramatically if waste paper is transported over long distances. Therefore the recycling and disposal industry commits 50–90 % of their waste paper by contract to nearby paper mills. The rest is sold on spot markets or is exported. The recycling and disposal firms face hardly any price risk since the risk is passed on to the waste paper suppliers or waste paper consumers by contracts with flexible prices. As a consequence, the recycling and disposal industry is a real intermediary just matching supply with demand.

15.3   DEVELOPMENT OF THE GERMAN WASTE PAPER MARKET 1950–2000

The German waste paper market has been subject to substantial changes over the last 50 years. As the biggest waste paper consumer the German paper industry and its development have influenced the German waste paper market to a great extent.

15.3.1   The German Paper Industry

Over the past 50 years, the German paper industry has experienced a period of extraordinary growth. Both paper production and consumption have increased tenfold over this period. Also paper imports and exports have soared significantly, while Germany is still a net paper importer. The excess paper demand reached its peak around 1990 because of the reunification of East and West Germany.[6] Due to large-scale investments in the paper industry in the 1980s and 1990s, this excess demand has been reduced significantly until today. As a result of the heterogeneity of paper, Germany still experiences high foreign trade activities (Table 15.3).

Year	Paper			
	Production	Consumption	Import	Export
	in million tonnes	in million tonnes	in million tonnes	in million tonnes
1950	1.6	1.6	0.1	0.1
1960	3.4	4.4	1.1	0.1
1970	5.5	7.6	2.7	0.6
1980	7.6	9.7	3.8	1.7
1985	9.3	10.8	4.3	2.9
1990	12.8	15.5	6.9	4.2
1990	14.8	15.8	7.2	6.2
2000	18.2	19.1	9.8	8.9

Table 15.3   Development of the German paper market 1950–2000. Source: VDP (2002: 43–45).

The mechanical and chemical pulp utilisation rates declined from 26.3 % and 38.3 % in 1950 to 8.6 % and 24.2 % in 2000. Over the same period, the recovered paper utilisation rate increased from 30.0 % to 60.4 % (own calculation from the data of VDP 2002: 47). According to Table 15.2, the main driver for the increased recovered paper utilisation rate since 1985 is the increased use of waste paper in the production of graphic paper and sanitary paper.

15.3.2   The Waste Paper Market

Both waste paper supply and domestic waste paper demand increased more than twentyfold from 1950 to 2000. Along with (absolute) domestic waste paper demand, the waste paper recovery rate increased drastically from 25.9 % in 1950 to over 70 % in 2000 (Figure 15.1). The development of the German waste paper market splits into two phases: In the first phase, until 1984, the waste paper supply followed the development of domestic waste paper demand. In the second phase, since 1985, waste paper supply and waste paper demand decoupled, and since then waste paper supply grew at a higher rate than the waste paper demand of the domestic paper industry (Table 15.4).

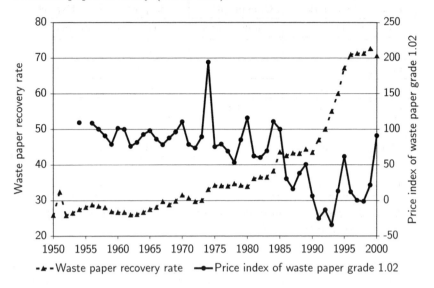

Figure 15.1   Price index of waste paper (grade 1.02, base year 1985) and waste paper recovery rate in Germany 1950–2000 in %. Source: Statistisches Bundesamt (2000) and BVSE (2001: 5).

Before 1985, foreign trade played a minor role in the German waste paper market but, due to the growing waste paper excess supply, waste paper exports have increased drastically since 1985. In 2000, the export of waste paper reached a level of about 4 million tonnes, which corresponds to an eightfold increase in only 15 years. Despite the domestic waste paper excess supply, waste paper imports have also increased because of the heterogeneity of waste paper. Germany exports mainly low quality grades and imports medium and high quality grades of waste paper. With a tripling of imports between 1985 and 2000, the import growth could not keep up with the development of waste paper exports (Table 15.4).

15.3.3   Price Ambivalence

Figure 15.1 shows the price index of grade 1.02 waste paper since 1950 (Statistisches Bundesamt 2000). The German Federal Statistical Office ('Statistisches Bundesamt') calculates this index based on a survey among 25 paper mills and recycling and disposing firms.[7] Before 1985, the waste paper price was always positive, although substantial variations in prices occurred (Figure 15.1) due to the fact that supply can only

Year	Waste paper			
	Production	Consumption	Import	Export
	in million tonnes	in million tonnes	in million tonnes	in million tonnes
1950	0.4	0.5	0.1	0
1960	1.2	1.3	0.2	0
1970	2.4	2.5	0.3	0.2
1980	3.3	3.2	0.4	0.5
1985	4.7	4.3	0.6	0.9
1990	6.8	6.2	0.8	1.4
1990	10.7	8.6	1.1	3.2
2000	13.7	11.0	1.4	4.0

Table 15.4   Development of the German waste paper market 1950–2000. Source: VDP (2002: 65–68).

react with a time lag to variations in demand, that is by an increase or decrease in collection activities. Strong price increases (for example in 1974, 1980 and 1984/85, Figure 15.1) motivated recycling and disposing firms to open up new sources of waste paper supply in commerce and private households by waste paper collections at fixed intervals.

While in the 1970s and 1980s increases in the waste paper recovery rate always followed periods of high waste paper prices, in the years 1991 to 1996 a drastic rise in the waste paper recovery rate can be observed, although waste paper prices during this period suffered a severe decline and even showed negative values in the years from 1990 to 1994. Figure 15.2 shows the development of the price index of waste paper grade 1.02 since 1985 on a monthly basis. Several periods of negative prices occurred during this phase. A number of reasons for this development can be identified. In the following, we discuss them in detail.

15.4   THE REASONS FOR PRICE AMBIVALENCE

15.4.1   Changes in the Waste Treatment Legislation and their Economic Consequences

After the federal government had obtained legislative power for waste treatment after a change in the Constitution, the lower house ('Bundestag') of the German parliament passed the *Waste Disposal Act* ('Gesetz über die Beseitigung von Abfällen') in 1972. The main objective

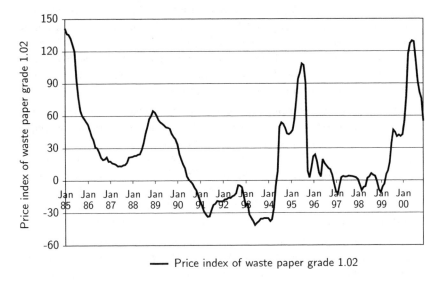

Figure 15.2   Price index of waste paper (grade 1.02) in Germany 1985–2000 on a monthly basis. Source: Statistisches Bundesamt (2000).

was to ascripe the proper disposal of waste to public corporations. This was the first step in a nationwide reorganisation of the disposal system.

With the passing of the fourth amendment of the *Waste Disposal Act* in 1986 it was renamed the *Waste Avoidance and Disposal Act* ('Gesetz über die Vermeidung und Entsorgung von Abfällen'). This law emphasised in particular the avoidance and recycling of waste, but did not yet legally establish a strict hierarchy of different waste treatment methods. Although this amendment did not enact mandatory regulations or collection quotas, it initiated the establishment of large-scale municipal waste paper collection systems.

This development was primarily motivated by economic reasons, as the cost of municipal solid waste disposal had risen dramatically between 1985 and 1995 due to stricter technical requirements for landfills and incineration facilities. The rate of cost increases varied regionally and ranged from 100 % to 1,000 % (Behrens and Maydell 1997: Section 6.3.2). As municipal solid waste contains up to 30 % (in weight) paper and board, many local authorities envisioned the possibility of cutting waste disposal costs by a separate collection of waste paper.[8] This led to an excess supply of waste paper in the years 1985 to 1987, resulting in a dramatic decline in waste paper prices (Figure 15.2).

After a failed attempt to amend the *Waste Disposal Act* again, the federal government enacted the *Regulation on Avoidance and Utilisation of Packaging Waste* ('Verordnung über die Vermeidung und Verwertung von Verpackungsabfällen') in 1991. This regulation contained a conditional retraction obligation for recycling for several kinds of packages in the form of mandatory collection and recycling quotas.[9] The *Regulation on Packaging Waste* was the turning point – in the legal sense – from a system of disposal to a system of recycling.

Thus, the excess supply of waste paper increased even more. The waste paper recovery rate as well as the total supply of waste paper rose dramatically. Despite a noticeable increase in the waste paper utilisation rate (Table 15.2), waste paper demand could not keep up with waste paper supply. As a consequence, the German waste paper market experienced a period of negative prices for waste paper grade 1.02 lasting about four years – from August 1990 until May 1994 (Figure 15.2), inducing a period of low prices for other waste paper grades.

The paper industry prevented a producer responsibility regulation for graphic paper, which was not included in the *Regulation on Avoidance and Utilisation of Packaging Waste*, through a voluntary self-commitment. In October 1994, the paper industry and the Federal Minister for the Environment signed an agreement on a *Voluntary Self Commitment for Retraction and Recycling of Used Graphic Paper* ('Selbstverpflichtung zur Rücknahme und Verwertung gebrauchter grafischer Papiere'). This agreement fixed a 60% recycling quota for the total consumption of graphic paper since January 2000.[10] In addition, the concept of producer liability and responsibility was included. As the recycling quota of 60% has already been over-fulfilled in 1996 by a quota of 82.6%, there is no need for further legal intervention at the moment (Krauthauf and Wiese 1998: 840).

In October 1994, the *Recycling Management and Waste Act* ('Kreislaufwirtschafts- und Abfallgesetz') passed the lower house of the German parliament, replacing the *Waste Avoidance and Disposal Act* from 1986. This law became effective after a two year transitional period in October 1996. New key aspects were a producer responsibility, which had already been indicated by the regulation on packaging in 1991 and the voluntary self-commitment in 1994, and an explicit waste treatment hierarchy: avoidance – recycling – disposal. It also put the combustion of secondary materials for energy recovery on a par with their productive recycling if certain technical conditions concerning efficient burning are met, which can easily be fulfilled for waste paper. Nevertheless, to date waste paper is not incinerated in Germany in significant amounts outside the paper industry. The reasons are that, first, in Germany the material recycling of waste paper is assessed to be more environmentally sound than its incineration, which is underpinned by several scientific studies (for example Hanley and Slark 1994, UBA 2000).[11] Second, due to the legal framework with its producer responsibility and its fixed recycling quotas, there are only small amounts of waste paper which could potentially be incinerated outside the paper industry. Third, in particular the paper industry has no incentive to advocate incineration on a large scale, as it has to fear an increase in competition for waste paper and higher prices. Nevertheless, small amounts of waste paper are incinerated by the cement industry (cf. Chapter 17). Furthermore, non-recoverable residuals from waste paper recycling are combusted by the paper industry in co-generation plants for heat and power.

With the *Recycling Management and Waste Act* still in effect today, a decline in the amount of collected waste paper is not very likely, even in the long run. The *Technical Instruction on Municipal Solid Waste* ('Technische Anleitung Siedlungsmüll') of 1993 has prohibited landfilling for municipal solid waste containing more than 5 % organic materials since 2005. As paper consists mainly of organic components, this means that all pulp and paper products and also the joint products of waste paper recycling are not allowed to be dumped in landfills without further treatment like recycling or incineration.

15.4.2   Influence of Foreign Trade

Since the disposal of waste paper as municipal solid waste is very costly and combustion is not an issue in Germany, only export remains to get rid of excess waste paper supply. Of course, waste paper is a useful secondary resource for paper fabrication in other countries, too. However, it suffers a disadvantage in these countries compared to home market waste paper due to higher transportation costs. Figure 15.3 shows the export shares for waste paper for different regions in the years from 1985 to 2000. Obviously, the dominant export region is still Western Europe, although its share decreased remarkably from 94.4 % in 1990 to 70.6 % in 2000 in favour of exports to Asia and Eastern Europe.

The expectation that foreign trade guarantees stable waste paper prices in Germany (Pothmann 1995: V68) has not turned out to be true. Despite stagnating waste paper recovery rates and waste paper utilisation rates, prices on German waste paper markets have continued to oscillate strongly. Because of the low price-to-weight ratio, in particular for low quality grades, transportation over long distances may be unprofitable. Thus, German disposal and recycling firms prefer exporting their waste paper to nearby West European countries. But as the national paper markets of the Western European countries tend to merge into a common paper market, the business cycles of the paper industries in the different countries are increasingly positively correlated. Thus, exports

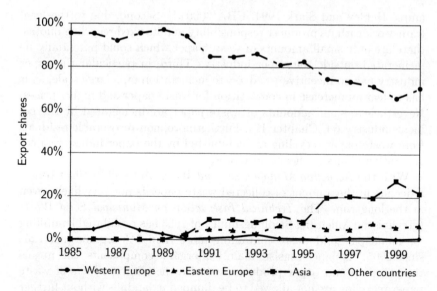

Figure 15.3   Shares of waste paper export from Germany to different regions 1985–2000 in %. Source: VDP (2000, 2002: 55).

into Western European countries are hardly capable of compensating for periods of weak domestic waste paper demand in Germany.

Waste paper exports to Asia are carried out by the cost-effective seaway, starting from German Northern and Baltic Sea harbours. Due to short distances to the coast, and corresponding low transportation costs to sea harbours, overseas exports are mainly attractive for disposal and recycling firms located in northern Germany (Friedrich 2000, Böcking 2000 and Braun 2000). Waste paper exports to Asia have been dominated by the US for quite a long time. Hence, German waste paper mainly competes with US waste paper exports on the Asian waste paper markets. The situation in the US is comparable to Germany: The US national paper industry is not able to use the whole domestic waste paper amount productively, leaving excess supply for export. Thus, the exported amount of US waste paper depends crucially on the business cycle of the US paper industry. As the business cycles of the US and the German paper industry are more and more correlated due to an increasing merging of national paper markets into a global paper market, the situation is similar to the situation in Western Europe. Yet, the cyclical match is not as perfect as between Germany and Western Europe. But overall, the problem remains that in periods of high excess supply of waste paper in Germany, German exports to Asia compete with high amounts of exported waste paper from the US.[12]

Exporting to Eastern Europe is mainly a cost-effective way of disposing of excess waste paper supply. Many Eastern European paper mills are happy to use waste paper as a secondary resource but are not able or willing to pay much for it. Thus, German disposal and recycling firms face transport costs of about 30 euros per tonne (transport ashore to the river Danube, then by ship; Friedrich 2000). Therefore the price of −30 euros per tonne is a lower limit for the German waste paper market. Effectively, until today no prices below this barrier could be observed. In fact, even during periods of negative prices the waste paper price was clearly above this lower limit.

15.4.3   Seasonal Fluctuations in Demand and Supply

Besides the fluctuations in waste paper demand due to the business cycle of the domestic and international paper industries, there are also seasonal fluctuations in demand and supply due to the consumption patterns of households. Paper demand is significantly higher at the end of the year because of the Christmas season. In fact, not only does the demand for packaging pulp and paper rise, but also print houses have increased demand for graphic paper in order to print advertorials and loose inserts for newspapers. To face this demand the paper industry increases its paper production in the second half of the year, which induces a rising waste paper demand. Collected packaging paper and advertorials increase the waste paper supply in the first months of the year. Yet, the paper industry does not demand this supply surplus.

In Figure 15.4, the monthly demand for waste paper grade 1.02 by the German paper industry and the waste paper price index of grade 1.02 is shown from July 1996 to January 2000. The seasonal fluctuations can be clearly observed: Low waste paper demand in the first months of the year gives way to an increasing demand in the second half of the year. Accordingly, waste paper prices show a decline in the first months of the year and a recovery during the rest of the year. As the seasonal fluctuations in this period do not overlap with longer-term trends, the waste paper price faces periods of negative prices at the beginning of the year due to a low waste paper price level.

15.5   CONCLUSIONS

Our analysis has shown that price ambivalence of waste paper is due to a complex interrelationship between environmental policy, regulatory institutions, market forces, and technology. Some of these characteristics

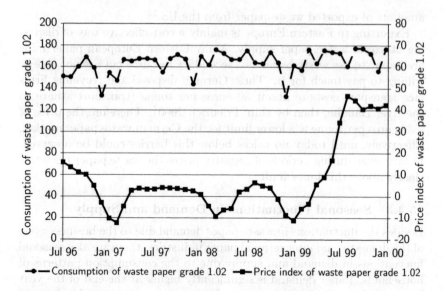

Figure 15.4   Monthly consumption in 1,000 tonnes and price index of waste paper (grade 1.02, base year 1985) in Germany 1996–2000. Source: VDP (2000) and Statistisches Bundesamt (2000).

are common to all secondary resource markets, while others are unique to the German waste paper market.

Summary of historic developments

Until 1985, developments in the German waste paper market followed the waste paper demand of the domestic paper industry. The market benefited from a rise in paper production which induced increasing waste paper demand. Since 1985 causality reversed. Within several years, as a consequence of rising disposal costs and changes in the legal framework, waste paper supply increased dramatically and independently of the development of waste paper demand. Since the use of waste paper in paper production is more cost-efficient than the use of primary fibres, paper mills reacted to this increase in supply with high investment in paper recycling technologies. This resulted in a dramatic increase in the waste paper utilisation rate, which today has reached the highest level worldwide given the product mix of the German paper industry (Berglund et al. 2002).

Since the input of recovered waste paper as a substitute for primary resources in paper production is technically limited, the paper industry is not able to use the entire amount of waste paper collected in Germany.

In 2000, there was an excess supply of approximately 2.5 million tonnes of waste paper, which had to be sold otherwise. As the incineration of waste paper in significant amounts is not an issue in Germany due to producer responsibility and fixed recycling quotas, there is no other productive use for waste paper, in noteworthy amounts, aside from paper production. Hence, the only possibility of getting rid of excess waste paper supply, beside the costly disposal of waste paper as municipal solid waste, is to sell it to the paper industry abroad. However, exports are suffering from a merging of national paper markets into a global market, which is generating a positive and increasing correlation between the business cycles of the paper industries of the individual countries. Thus, exports are not capable of compensating for periods of weak domestic waste paper demand during an economic downturn in the German paper industry, because the demand of the paper industry in the rest of the world is low, too. To avoid disposal of excess waste paper supply as municipal solid waste at very high costs, the German disposal and recycling industry has found a more cost-effective alternative way of disposal, namely by exporting this waste paper to the paper industry in Eastern European countries. Moreover, in this way the waste paper is used as a productive input and does not occupy scarce space at landfills.

Waste paper and responsibility

The development of the waste paper market can be reconsidered in terms of the concepts of individual, legal, moral and political responsibility developed in Part III. Paper waste occurs as a joint output from production and consumption and, therefore, has to be disposed of in a costly manner if it cannot be recycled. These costs have continuously risen during the 1980s and 1990s. Since waste paper is a secondary resource for paper production, it was demanded by the paper industry and supplied by the recycling and disposal industry. Obviously, representatives of both industries had an economic interest in establishing a waste paper market and acted accordingly, for instance by organising the logistics of waste paper collection, by cleaning waste paper from impurities and by sorting it into different quality grades. In so doing, they took individual responsibility in a manner that is typical of the economic agent (cf. Section 14.2).

But the issue of waste paper also had a social dimension, concerning the use of scarce resources such as primary resources and landfill areas. Hence, there is an issue of political responsibility, too. Accordingly, the waste paper market was regulated by a series of policy measures: The *Waste Disposal Act* in 1986 emphasised avoidance and recycling of paper waste. In particular, it initiated the establishment of large-scale municipal waste paper collection systems, which increased the supply of waste paper rapidly. In addition, the fees of municipal solid waste disposal were drastically increased, which led to a rapid rise in the amount of collected waste paper. In 1991, the federal government gave recycling top priority, as the *Regulation on Avoidance and Utilisation of Packaging Waste* calls for the recycling of paper waste.

These policy measures changed the legal framework within which individual economic agents could act. This also modified the individual responsibility of the agents. What used to be a matter of (implicit) moral responsibility now became a matter of legal responsibility and was thereby made explicit. In addition, the *Recycling, Management and Waste Act* of 1996 extended the scope of individual responsibility, by defining a producer responsibility for the whereabouts of all outputs produced.

The causes of price ambivalence

As a consequence of the multifarious developments in the paper and waste paper markets, the phenomenon of price ambivalence occurs. It is caused by three institutional and technical characteristics of the German waste paper market: (i) As a result of waste management legislation, the supply of waste paper is mostly independent of its price and its demand. Supply is bounded from below by collection and utilisation quotas fixed by federal regulation. (ii) The only alternative to costly disposal of waste paper as municipal solid waste is its use as a secondary resource in the production of new paper, as the paper industry is the only agent capable of using waste paper in a productive manner in significant amounts. (iii) Yet, its use as a substitute for primary inputs is technically limited. Exhibiting the three characteristics of price ambivalence identified in Chapter 8 in a theoretical model (see Section 8.6), the German waste paper market confirms the theory of the emergence of price ambivalence.

Obviously, the third characteristic is a common feature of all waste paper markets. Furthermore, at least in the European Union an increase in supply due to waste management legislation can be observed.[13] Another motivation for increased recycling rates may be an increase in environmental awareness (Ackerman 1997). The second market characteristic – the only productive use is in the paper industry, since incineration is not an issue – is unique to the German market. As a consequence of these three institutional and technical characteristics, the price of waste paper strongly oscillates and even turns negative at times. In this form the phenomenon of price ambivalence can be observed only in that particular market since 1985. Nevertheless, we consider the phenomenon of price ambivalence to be a general phenomenon which might, in principle, be observed in other secondary material markets exhibiting the three characteristics described above. We believe that price ambivalence is very likely to occur in other markets in the near future as we observe an increasing trend in the regulation of waste treatment. Recently, the German markets for waste oil and used tyres have displayed signs of price ambivalence.

Welfare implications of price ambivalence

The question of the overall welfare implications of the German waste management legislation is difficult to answer. Obviously, there has been a distribution effect. While the suppliers of waste paper are worse off today due to higher disposal costs and lower waste paper prices, the paper industry has benefited from both the higher availability of waste paper and the lower price, leading to higher utilisation quotas. As a pure intermediary, the recycling and disposal industry is largely unaffected. Furthermore, welfare increases due to decreasing amounts of municipal solid waste have to be considered, while the de facto prevention of the incineration of waste paper might have negative welfare effects. Therefore, the overall welfare effect is far from being obvious and has to be studied in further research.

Future perspectives for secondary resource markets

Concerning the future development of the German waste paper market, we expect neither in the short run nor in the long run drastic changes in the waste paper utilisation rate and the waste paper recovery rate. Therefore, the German waste paper market will continue to rely on foreign trade as the only possibility of getting rid of excess waste paper supply, since incineration is not an issue in Germany, and the disposal of waste paper as municipal solid waste has been prohibited since 2005 (Section 15.4.1). But one may expect that the share of today's main export region, Western Europe, will decline further due to waste treatment legislation and increasing supply abroad. Some European countries have already reached the German level: Austria, for example, has a waste paper recovery rate of over 70 % and Switzerland and the Netherlands have reached rates of about 65 % (VDP 2002). These countries face the same problem as Germany: excess waste paper supply has to be exported to other countries.

On the one hand, not only will the Western European export market cease to exist, but also waste paper from Germany will have to compete with increasing amounts of waste paper from other Western European countries for new export markets. On the other hand, a drastic increase in waste paper demand is expected in Asia (Pothmann 1995:

V68). Which one of these two effects will dominate in the future cannot be anticipated today, but Germany's exports in the Western European region are very likely to decline and exports to Asia will increase. Also, Eastern Europe could develop into an interesting waste paper consumer.

What will be the effects for waste paper prices? In the short run, the prices will continue to be influenced by cyclical (seasonal) fluctuations. Thus, further periods of negative prices cannot be ruled out. Because of the extremely high disposal costs and the fact that the disposal and recycling industry completely passes on the price risk to waste paper suppliers and waste paper consumers, there is no danger of a breakdown of the waste paper market during negative price periods. But in the long run, a Europe-wide increase in waste paper excess supply and a lack of alternative trade channels with other regions could lead to the necessity of seriously reconsidering alternative utilisations of waste paper, for example incineration.

NOTES

1. Mixed paper and board (sorted): A mixture of various qualities of paper and board, containing a maximum of 40 % of newspapers and magazines (BIR and CEPI 1999).
2. Supermarket corrugated paper and board: Used paper and board packaging, containing a minimum of 70 % of corrugated board, the rest being solid board and wrapping paper (BIR and CEPI 1999).
3. Newspapers, containing a maximum of 5 % newspapers or advertisements coloured in the mass (BIR and CEPI 1999).
4. White wood-free computer print-out, free from carbonless paper and glue (BIR and CEPI 1999).
5. Since both input and output are measured in mass units and usually the mass of all inputs exceeds the mass of the (desired) output, the utilisation rate may exceed 100 %, and a utilisation rate of 100 % does not necessarily mean that a particular paper product is produced exclusively from recovered waste paper.
6. All data used here refers to West Germany until 1990 and to unified West and East Germany since then.
7. Besides the German Federal Statistical Office ('Statistisches Bundesamt'), Wiesbaden, waste paper prices are also surveyed by the Society for Paper Recycling ('Gesellschaft für Papier-Recycling', GesPaRec), Bonn, and the European Economic Service ('Europäischer Wirtschaftsdienst', EUWID). Their data show an essentially identical development in German waste paper prices.
8. Recycling and disposal firms charge up to 100 euros per tonne for their service, depending on the waste paper price, which is considerably less than the disposal costs for municipal waste (Section 15.2).
9. The mandatory collection quota was raised from 30 % in 1991 to 80 % in 1995, the mandatory recycling quota of collected packages was raised from 60 % in 1991 to 80 % in 1995 in several steps.
10. The self-committed recycling quota was raised from 53 % in 1994 to 60 % in 2000 in several steps.

11.   There are also studies, however, which evaluate incineration of waste paper as more environmentally sound than recycling (for example Leach et al. 1997).

12.   Furthermore, the exchange rate between the euro and the US dollar influences the attractiveness of German waste paper, as waste paper is paid for in US dollars on the world market.

13.   The European Union passed a European regulation on packing waste in 1994 which had to be implemented in national law by 1996. Although the European regulation requires lower quotas than the German *Regulation on Avoidance and Utilisation of Packaging Waste*, in all Western European countries (with the only exception of Portugal) an increase in the waste paper recovery rate can be observed in recent years (Kibat 1998: 744).

16. Chlorine: Innovation and Industrial Evolution*

with Frank Jöst and
Georg Müller-Fürstenberger

16.1   INTRODUCTION: CHLORINE AS A KEY SUBSTANCE

In this chapter, we deal with the production of an important chemical substance of modern industrialised economies – chlorine in various forms and compounds. Chlorine in the colloquial sense is an ambivalent substance: On the one hand, the branch of the chemical industry dealing with chlorine is very significant in economic terms.[1] On the other hand, many of the produced (and consumed) chlorinated substances are extremely hazardous if released into the natural environment. So, chlorine is an interesting substance for investigating the connection between industry structure and environmental problems. It is an instructive example of how the phenomenon of joint production links environmental degradation – and its temporal development – and the temporal development of production systems.

In the following, we trace the history of the British soda and chlorine industry. We focus on the nineteenth century but also regard effects until the present. This historic development is a *paradigmatic case* for the interplay between the phenomenon of joint production and stock dynamics, which introduces time lags into the system's reaction (cf. Chapter 4). The case instructively shows the role which an environmentally harmful and economically ambivalent joint output of an industrial process – chlorine in various forms and compounds – can play in shaping the development of a whole branch of industry over a century. It thus shows how the emergence of environmentally harmful joint products can pro-

---

*This chapter is based on Faber, Jöst, Manstetten and Müller-Fürstenberger (1996a), Müller-Fürstenberger (1995) and Schiller (2002: Section 9.1).

vide the impetus for innovation and, beyond that, can shape industrial evolution.

The history of the soda and chlorine industry exhibits patterns of development which are similar to those that we have identified in Section 5.2 from a theoretical perspective in a stylised way: We see a rapidly developing industry emitting a hazardous joint output and creating a severe environmental problem. We observe the accumulation of significant socio-political pressure to avoid this problem, and the time-consuming change of the technology employed, resulting in conversion of the harmful by-product into a positively valued economic good. Consequently, we observe the development of a whole branch of chemical industry based on the use of chlorine. That industry in turn gives rise to various 'new' environmental problems today.

The chapter is organised as follows. In Section 16.2 the historic development of of the British soda and chlorine industry is sketched in five phases. Section 16.3 draws some more general insights from the analysis of the historic development.

16.2 THE HISTORY OF THE BRITISH SODA AND CHLORINE INDUSTRY IN THE NINETEENTH CENTURY

16.2.1 Phase 1: The *Leblanc* Industry without Environmental Restrictions

The story begins in the eighteenth century, when potash obtained from burning wood was used as an input into the British textile industry. Deforestation led to an increasing scarcity of the resource, finally resulting in its substitution by soda.[2] In France and Britain in those days, soda was produced from natural resources. It could either be obtained from the burning of seaweed or from Spanish 'barilla'. In the 1760s and 1770s, a British sea blockade of the French coasts cut off the French import of barilla from Spain. This shortage of supply of the natural resource input for the production of soda and a rising demand for soda led the French Academy of Science to announce a prize for the invention of a synthetic production process for soda in 1775 (Müller-Fürstenberger 1995: 181). This resulted in the invention of the first industrial process for producing soda from rock salt, sulphuric acid, lime, and coal in 1792 – the *Leblanc* process, named after its inventor Nicolas Leblanc (1742–1806). Figure 16.1 schematically shows the *Leblanc* process and its stoichiometric input and output flows.

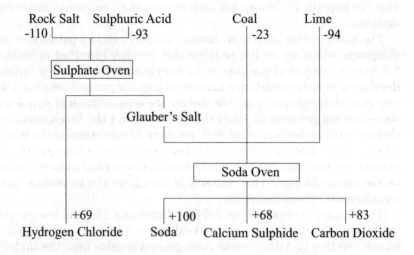

Figure 16.1   Scheme of the simple Leblanc process. The coefficients of the input and output flows indicate the lower bounds of the necessary resource inputs and joint outputs, as stoichiometrically derived, for the production of 100 kg of soda. (Figure adapted from Müller-Fürstenberger 1995: 182.)

However, *Leblanc* soda was of a slightly different specification compared to soda obtained from seaweed, which hampered its introduction in Britain. Only when British 'seaweed soda' users suffered serious disadvantages compared with their barilla-using competitors due to a cut in import duties for barilla was the *Leblanc* process introduced in Britain in 1822.[3] After its introduction, the *Leblanc* process rapidly penetrated the industry and led to a decrease in the soda price by 50 % between 1820 and 1830 (Haber 1958: 12).

In contrast to the former soda 'industry', the growth of the *Leblanc*-based soda industry that now followed was not restricted by any resource problems any more. However, new restrictions emerged due to the use of the natural environment as a sink for harmful joint products: The emissions of calcium sulphide (CaS, so-called 'tank waste') and highly poisonous gaseous hydrogen chloride (HCl) increasingly became a serious health problem for the neighbourhoods around the plants. Over time, these emissions also became increasingly problematic for the soda producers. Public pressure finally resulted in the passing of the Act for the more effectual Condensation of Muratic Acid Gas in Alkali Works in 1864 – the Alkali Act for short – according to which 95 % of the emerging hydrogen chloride had to be converted to hydrochloric acid. This hydrochloric acid was discharged into the neighbouring rivers.

The second joint output emerging in extensive quantities, calcium sulphide, was deposited in heaps and there accumulated to big stocks. Initially, this seemed to be an adequate treatment for this waste product. However, chemical reactions within the heaps resulted in the emergence of water-soluble sulphur compounds. These substances were washed out by precipitation and groundwater, and consequently entered the adjoining water bodies. The double pollution with hydrochloric acid and sulphur compounds caused significant damage not only to ecosystems, but also to economic assets. For instance, it fostered considerable corrosion of metal boats.[4] Again, in the course of time, there was a political reaction to the problem: An amendment to the Alkali Act also regulated the introduction of fluid wastes into water bodies.

16.2.2 Phase 2: The 'Cleaning' of the *Leblanc* Process

The socio-political pressure finally resulting in the passing of the Alkali Act had been noticeable already before its legal manifestation. It had been obvious for quite some time that alternative treatments of the joint products emerging from the *Leblanc* process had to be found. In 1869, the *Deacon* process was patented, making it possible to convert the unwanted hydrogen chloride into elementary chlorine by using sulphuric acid. Elementary chlorine could easily be converted into chloride of lime. This could be used as bleaching powder in the textile industry.[5] After the invention of the *Deacon* process, this method of treating the harmful hydrogen chloride output rapidly penetrated the *Leblanc* industry.[6]

The environmental problems associated with the second major joint output, 'tank waste', could be defused in the 1880s. Based on a patent from 1883 held by the chemist Claus, the entrepreneur Chance developed an industrial process by which 90 % of the sulphur contained in the tank waste could be recovered in elementary form. Elementary sulphur was a marketable good which, for example, could be used for producing sulphuric acid (see Chapter 18). Figure 16.2 illustrates the full-grown *Leblanc* process by the end of the nineteenth century: Both major joint products – the initially harmful hydrogen chloride and calcium sulphide – were now converted into desired outputs – chlorine, chloride of lime, and sulphur – which could be sold at positive prices.

16.2.3 Phase 3: The Co-Existence of two Processes

After a period of rapid growth until the mid-1870s,[7] the *Leblanc* industry entered a phase of stagnation for the following reasons: (i) Extensive investment was necessary to build up capital stocks related to the *Deacon*

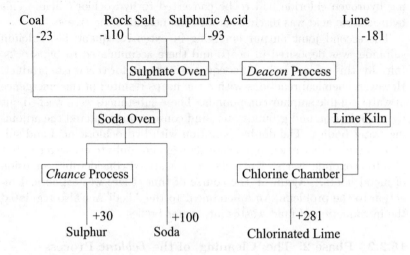

Figure 16.2   Scheme of the full-grown Leblanc process including Dea-con and Chance processes. The coefficients of the input and output flows indicate the lower bounds of the necessary resource inputs and joint out-puts, as stoichiometrically derived, for the production of 100 kg of soda. (Figure adapted from Müller-Fürstenberger 1995: 193.)

and *Chance* processes and (ii) a completely new competing technology for manufacturing soda was introduced in Britain, the so-called *Solvay* process. To understand the early phase of co-existence of both technolog-ical strands – the traditional *Leblanc* and the new *Solvay* technologies – it is important to note that British firms were quite conservative in their investment decisions. They were strongly inclined to invest in their own traditional technology instead of readily adopting new technologies.[8] Af-ter the implementation of the *Solvay* process two almost distinct soda in-dustries co-existed – the traditional *Leblanc* industry and the new *Solvay* industry.

The *Solvay* process (see Figure 16.3) had been developed since 1838. In 1864, Ernest Solvay (1838–1922) managed to produce the first quan-tities of soda using the new process. The *Solvay* process differs from the *Leblanc* process with respect to several aspects:

- The only joint output emerging in large quantities is calcium chlo-ride ($CaCl_2$), which could be handled much more easily than the gaseous hydrogen chloride. Moreover, calcium chloride is envi-ronmentally almost neutral.[9] Hence, it could be discharged into surface waters.

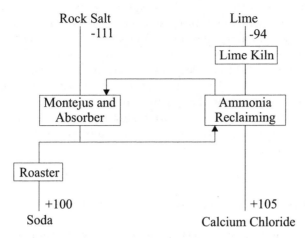

Figure 16.3   Scheme of the Solvay process. The coefficients of the input and output flows indicate the lower bounds of the necessary resource inputs and joint outputs, as stoichiometrically derived, for the production of 100 kg of soda. The emerging joint output calcium chloride ($CaCl_2$) is environmentally much less harmful than the joint products of the early Leblanc process. (Figure adapted from Müller-Fürstenberger 1995: 198.)

- The energy input per unit of output is lower for the *Solvay* process than for the *Leblanc* process. Instead of coal, other energy sources could be used, for example coal gas.

- Instead of sulphuric acid, the *Solvay* process uses ammonia (NH_3) as a processing chemical. In the nineteenth century, ammonia was initially quite expensive. However, there was an increasing supply of cheap ammonia as a joint product from gas works. In addition, Solvay managed to design the process in such a way that the flow of ammonia was a closed loop, which reduced the necessary input quantities of this chemical.

The industrial implementation of the *Solvay* process on a large scale, however, was delayed until 1874, mainly for the following reason. Due to cost savings and additional revenues from the sales of sulphur, chlorine and chloride of lime within the *Leblanc* industry, the soda price significantly dropped in the 1870s. For some time, this neutralised the general cost advantage of the *Solvay* process, leading to a slow penetration of the new technology.[10]

Ironically, it was the – initially unwanted – joint products from the *Leblanc* process which now protected the large *Leblanc* industry from a rapid decay: Sulphur, chlorine and chloride of lime more and more became the *main* products of this branch of the soda industry, when increasing efficiency of the *Solvay* process led to a further decrease of the soda price in the 1880s. Although many *Leblanc* works had to shut down in the 1880s, the remaining firms joined forces to form the *United Alkali Company* (UAC) and survived another 20 years. This was only possible due to increasing demand for chloride of lime and other substances based on elementary chlorine and sulphur.

16.2.4   Phase 4: The End of the *Leblanc* Process

It was the innovation of an electrolytic process for the production of elementary chlorine that finally made the *Leblanc* industry obsolete. The (joint) products of the chlorine-alkali electrolysis (cf. Figure 16.4) are chlorine and sodium hydroxide (NaOH). The joint output sodium hy-

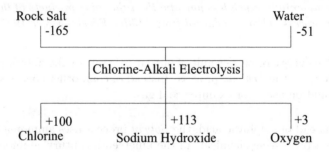

Figure 16.4   Scheme of the chlorine-alkali electrolysis. The coefficients of the input and output flows indicate the lower bounds of the necessary resource inputs and joint outputs, as stoichiometrically derived, for the production of 100 kg of chlorine. (Figure adapted from Müller-Fürstenberger 1995: 206.)

droxide is an important input in the paper and soap industries. The energy for the process is supplied by electric power. This was sufficiently and cheaply available by the end of the nineteenth century. After the introduction of the chlorine-alkali electrolysis, it was possible to produce almost the whole range of products of the *Leblanc* industry using more efficient production processes.

The innovation of the chlorine-alkali electrolysis was initially accomplished by German *Leblanc* producers in the 1890s, who like their British companions had to improve their competitive position against competitors employing the *Solvay* process. *Leblanc* producers in Britain – namely the UAC – however, missed the opportunity and were ruined.[11] Solvay himself bought the patents for the chlorine-alkali electrolysis and innovated the process in Britain at the end of the 1890s. The resulting rapid decline of the *Leblanc* industry is illustrated in Figure 16.5.

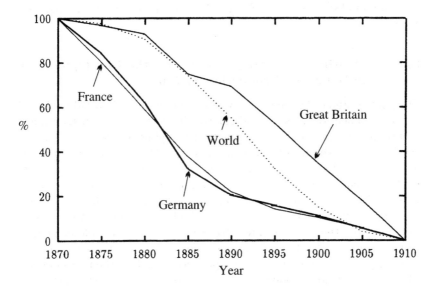

Figure 16.5   The decline of the Leblanc industry between 1870 and 1910: share of the Leblanc process in total soda production for Britain, Germany, France and the world. (Figure adapted from Müller-Fürstenberger 1995: 211.)

16.2.5   The Present

The main products of the chlorine-alkali industry, namely soda, chlorine and sodium hydroxide, are still important basic substances of the inorganic branch of the chemical industry.[12] Both the *Solvay* process and the chlorine-alkali electrolysis are in operation at present. The use of the *Solvay* process is, however, declining due to the comparatively high energy requirements of this process and due to problems concerning the disposal of the joint product calcium chloride. Both lead to the substitution of *Solvay* soda by natural sources of soda, in particular in the United States of America.

16.3   CONCLUSIONS: LESSONS FROM HISTORY

Investigating the historical development of the British soda and chlorine industry in the nineteenth and early twentieth centuries yields important insights into the structural long-term development of industrial production systems which are significantly characterised by joint production and are therefore closely linked to the emergence of environmental problems. Looking at industrial history, we empirically find a very similar pattern of temporal development to the scenario that we have investigated on an abstract level in Section 5.2. For a conclusion, we highlight five insights.

16.3.1   Chlorine as the 'Key Output' for the Development of an Industrial Production System

The joint product chlorine in its various compounds (i) notably shaped the development of the soda and chlorine industry in the nineteenth and twentieth centuries and (ii) entailed far-reaching repercussions for the development of the whole chemical industry. The jointly emerging output hydrogen chloride – initially in its gaseous form, later converted to fluid hydrochloric acid – hampered the growth of the *Leblanc* industry. The resulting environmental problems and the socio-political pressure that came with it led to strong research efforts to solve this problem. Consequently, the harmful unwanted joint product was able to be converted in a marketable wanted good. For a significant time span, this very output protected the *Leblanc* producers against their competitors who were using more modern production processes. Only when new technologies became available to deliberately produce the initially unwanted chlorine compounds, the *Leblanc* technology became obsolete and was abandoned. Based on the output chlorine, a huge branch of chemical industry developed, which still today is very significant in economic terms (see note 1). However, the outputs of this industry branch are still the subject of serious environmental concern.

16.3.2   Joint Production and Environmental Regulation as an Incentive for Innovation

Process requirements were imposed on the *Leblanc* industry by the different amendments of the Alkali Act. Compliance with these regulations forced the *Leblanc* industry into immense investment efforts and, hence, was very costly. *Leblanc* producers heavily controverted this legal regulation in advance (Müller-Fürstenberger 1995: 187), which can be understood considering the following argument.

Research and development into new technologies and their innovation is connected to a high degree of uncertainty – not only regarding direct technological and economic success but also with respect to the projected co-evolution of the broader economic, social and natural environment. The higher the degree of novelty involved in a new process compared to the existing technological standard, the higher is the level of associated uncertainty. Hence, the more economic actors tend to be reluctant to innovate such a new technology. This explains the observation of a certain tendency of technological systems to develop along 'old' and 'well-proven' paths.[13] The example of the British United Alkali Company (UAC) demonstrates this effect.

However, the occurrence of joint production together with adequate socio-political or legal pressure provides strong incentives to overcome this technological conservatism and to invest in technological development in order to adequately deal with the emerging joint products. These incentives may either be direct, for example in the form of a process regulation, or indirect in case the disposal of joint products is made costly by imposing, for example, emission taxes etc. Hence, the phenomenon of joint production can be regarded as a trigger to innovation.

Looking at the soda and chlorine case from an ex post perspective one could argue that due to its innovative consequences the legally required modifications of the *Leblanc* production technology with respect to the emerging joint products ensured the survival of the industry for several decades.[14]

16.3.3 Joint Production and Industrial Evolution

A production system like the soda and chlorine industry is integrated into a dynamic economic, social and natural environment. This environment exerts various influences on the system at hand, for example it may impose economic restrictions etc. Driven by exogenous factors, the environment evolves over time but is also influenced by the production system itself. Hence, there exists a co-evolution of the system and its environment.

Concerning the *economic* environment, the phenomenon of joint production can lead to the establishment of complementary structures due to the development of supply-demand relations.[15] The joint output is either available at no additional economic cost or it may even be undesirable and harmful so that its disposal is costly. In this case, there exist incentives to use the joint output as an input in further productive activities. As has been discussed in the preceding Section 16.3.2, this may lead to the invention and innovation of production structures that make use of the joint product. As a result, a new output-input relation is created, which interrelates the production system with its economic environment.

In the case of the soda and chlorine industry, the economic environment of the *Leblanc* industry adapted over time, so that the initially undesired by-product chlorine could be used as an input in subsequent production processes. The textile industry adapted in such a way that it could make use of the chloride of lime which was available after the innovation of the *Deacon* process. Similarly, the chemical industry developed a branch which is based on chlorine compounds. The availability of chlorine as a possible input facilitated the formation of huge stocks of capital goods, knowledge and know-how, and demand for chlorinated substances from subsequent industries and consumers. Once these stocks and the related demand structures had been established, there was a strong incentive for them to be satisfied – chlorine effectively became the main product of the *Leblanc* industry and ensured its survival for a long time.

We see that the ambiguity in economic evaluation of joint outputs – which we conceptualised as *ambivalence* in Chapter 8 and analysed empirically for the case of waste paper in Chapter 15 – in the case of chlorine originates from the adaptation of the economic environment to the emergence of the joint output. In contrast to short-term ambivalence as observed in the case of waste paper, ambivalence of this kind occurs over long time scales as it is intimately connected to the time-consuming change in economic structure, technology and capital stocks. The case of chlorine clearly shows how industrial evolution may be shaped by joint production.

16.3.4   Chlorine and the Dynamics of Environmental Problems

Recalling the general pattern of development of environmental problems that was postulated in Section 5.2, one finds a strong correspondence to the historical development of the soda and chlorine industry in the nineteenth century:

- With respect to the second joint output of the *Leblanc* process, calcium sulphide ('tank waste'), the scenario sketched in Figure 5.1 (on page 94) is directly applicable. As an adaptation of Figure 5.1, Figure 16.6 shows the stylised development of the *Leblanc* industry in a system representation including the output streams of soda and calcium sulphide. The 'tank waste' was first deposited in heaps until the environmental degradation caused by this pollutant stock became clearly noticeable. From then on, non-quantifiable stocks (cf. Section 4.2.4) were created, such as environmental legislation (the Alkali Act) and technological knowledge (the *Chance* process), and stocks of capital goods for operating the *Chance* process were accumulated. Employing those stocks, it was then possible to work off the pollutant stock, that is the heaps containing calcium sulphide.

- A modified but similar scenario can be traced for a system representation which includes soda, hydrogen chloride, elementary chlorine and various non-quantifiable stocks. In such a representation, the environmental problem due to the emission of hydrogen chloride is of central interest. This problem is effectively caused by a flow pollution – hydrogen chloride decays on a short time scale in the local atmosphere surrounding the *Leblanc* plants. Nevertheless, the emission of hydrogen chloride can only be avoided by the time-consuming modification of various non-quantifiable stocks (environmental legislation, technological know-how etc.) and quantifiable stocks (capital goods for the operation of the *Deacon* process etc.).

- Investigating a bigger production system comprising both the soda industry *and* the chlorine-based chemical industry, a cyclical pattern of the substitution of one environmental problem by another problem can be identified – as is illustrated on an abstract level in Figure 5.3 (on page 98): By converting hydrogen chloride into elementary chlorine (*Deacon* process) and re-using it in a multitude of chlorine compounds, one specific environmental problem of the nineteenth century had been solved. But concomitantly that created a whole range of new environmental problems connected with the chlorine-based chemical industry at later times. Examples are the adverse effects of chlorofluorocarbons (CFC) on the ozone layer or the extensive use of polyvinyl chloride (PVC), which can lead to the creation of dioxin in certain circumstances.

The patterns of industrial development observed in the soda and chlorine case show the importance of two structural elements. (i) Joint production can provide strong incentives for the invention and the innovation of new production technologies associated with the avoidance, the disposal or the re-use of the joint products. This leads to a co-evolution of economic sectors and to complex patterns of interaction between these. (ii) The time-consuming modification of stocks, which is necessary to modify ecological-economic systems, creates time lags that are responsible for the typical periodic or cyclical patterns of development.

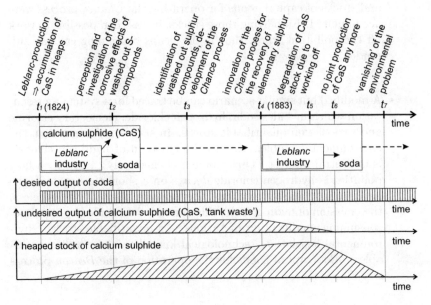

Figure 16.6   Stylised temporal pattern of the Leblanc process according to Figure 5.1 (page 94) in a system representation including soda and calcium sulphide (CaS): time series of the streams of the desired output soda, the undesired joint output CaS and of the heaped stock of CaS. After the innovation of the Chance process ($t = t_4$), the emergence of CaS declines. Later, the heaped stock of CaS is gradually worked off and at $t = t_7$ the environmental problem due to the washing out of sulphur compounds from heaps of calcium sulphide has ceased to exist.

16.3.5   Responsibility in the Soda and Chlorine Industry

Finally, let us briefly discuss the concepts of responsibility, and the limits of responsibility, in relation to the chlorine case. We differentiated between primary responsibility (in the sense of ascription of the consequences of one's action to oneself) and secondary responsibility (in the sense of moral obligation) in Part III, and we discussed various forms of individual and collective responsibility (Chapter 13). Now, we relate these concepts to the behaviour of the actors in the evolution of the soda and chlorine industry. In particular, we ask which actors were able and prepared to assume what kind of responsibility.

Our history of the soda and chlorine industry begins with a shortage of the natural resource input into soda production, and the rising demand for soda in the 1770s. This state of affairs hampered the increase of general welfare in France. As individuals, the members of the French

Academy of Science felt morally responsible (secondary meaning) in the positive sense (cf. Section 11.2.2) for the increase of general welfare. This was the reason why in 1775 they announced a prize for the invention of a synthetic production process for soda, which eventually led to the invention of the *Leblanc* process.

After the introduction of soda manufacturing using the *Leblanc* process the wider public noticed the harmful, but previously unidentified consequences of the joint product hydrogen chloride and attempted to stop its emission; the public assumed responsibility in the secondary meaning. The entrepreneurs operating the soda works, however, did not even feel responsible in the primary sense for the serious health problems and for the environmental damage in the neighbourhood of their factories. On the contrary, they actively tried to deny that the hydrogen chloride emitted by their plants had negative consequences at all.[16] That would allow them to avoid bearing responsibility for these consequences in the primary – and consequently also in the secondary – meaning due to the (pretended) non-existence of knowledge. Hence, the owners of the plants neither felt morally responsible, nor were they legally responsible. Thus, they did not change their behaviour.

It took several decades of public resistance against the emission of hydrogen chloride until politics considered being politically responsible and, hence, enacted the Alkali Act in 1864. From that time on, the entrepreneurs had to assume legal responsibility within certain limits. So, the awareness of individual responsibility finally led to a resumption of collective responsibility in politics.

As a result, the hydrogen chloride, which was now converted to hydrochloric acid, was released into rivers. The resulting damages led to public resistance, because individuals – again – felt morally responsible for public welfare. A decade later, politics assumed the corresponding political responsibility and amended the Alkali Act in such a way that the plant owners were made legally responsible for stopping the harmful disposal of hydrochloric acid into rivers. Thus, again individual responsibility induced political responsibility, which resulted in a change in legal regulations, that is legal responsibility.

NOTES

1. About 60 % of the chemical products produced in Germany (considering total quantity or total production value), about 300 basic chemicals and intermediate products, and about 30,000 refined chemical products involve the use of chlorine during their production (Meerkamp v. Embden 1992: 6, Nader 1996). In many cases, chlorine itself is not part of the final product but is used as a processing chemical (Jacob 1999: 1).

2. Soda (sodium carbonate, Na_2CO_3) is a basic substance still used today as an intermediate product in producing various sodium compounds. In addition, it is used as an input into the paper and soap industries and for water decarbonation.

3. An additional incentive to introduce the *Leblanc* process was a cut in the salt tax projected for 1824.

4. As an illustration, Haber (1958: 208) writes: 'The Sankey Canal fed by the Brook could not be used by iron boats and barges owing to the risk of corrosion. A sample of mud from the Brook contained 22.75 % of free sulphur.'

5. Another method of producing elementary chlorine and chloride of lime from hydrochloric acid had been available in the late eighteenth century already. This, however, gave rise to joint outputs which were extremely hazardous and could hardly be disposed of even at that time (Müller-Fürstenberger 1995: 189).

6. The *Deacon* process even survived the *Leblanc* technology and is still in use today.

7. Between 1852 and 1876 the number of *Leblanc*-based soda works in Britain almost doubled from 33 to over 60, the number of employees increased from 6,300 to 22,000, and the capital stock in monetary terms increased by a factor of 10 (Müller-Fürstenberger 1995: 194, Table 7.5).

8. For a discussion of this observation see Schiller (2002: 371–372). See also note 11.

9. Calcium chloride is used as road salt even today.

10. An additional reason for the delay was that due to its continuous process pattern, the *Solvay* process at that time was very challenging for the technical process management, because all flows of matter have to be carefully adjusted to match each other.

11. This observation of an apparently total lack of foresight, which is baffling from an ex post perspective, may be explained by the typical investment strategies of British firms. Murmann and Landau (1998: 36–44) extensively investigate the differences between the development of British and German chemical industries and their institutional background. They find that 'British chemical firms typically tried to maximize their profits by spending as little on R&D and new plants as possible' (1998: 43).

12. In 1991 the German chemical industry produced about 1.4 million tonnes of soda, amounting to 270 million euros, 3.2 million tonnes of sodium hydroxide, amounting to 800 million euros, and 3 million tonnes of chlorine, amounting to 460 million euros (Müller-Fürstenberger 1995: 212). Transporting just this production quantity of soda by rail would require approximately 700 heavy freight trains per year.

13. Schiller (2002: Chapter 6) discusses such effects. Patterns of technological change are conceptualised and empirically investigated in a branch of the literature on innovation, for example by David (1985), Kemp (1997), Landau (1998), Nelson and Winter (1977), and Rosenberg (1976).

14. Such positive effects of environmental legislation on the innovative power and long-term competitiveness of industries characterised by joint production are extensively discussed in the literature under the heading of the so-called 'Porter hypothesis' (Porter 1990, 1991, and Porter and van der Linde 1995).

15. This has already been observed by Alfred Marshall (1970[1911], see Section 6.4.2).

16. In the public hearings, one medical 'expert' went as far as to state that the inhalation of hydrogen chloride was advantageous for health (Müller-Fürstenberger 1995: 187).

17. Cement: Stock Dynamics and Complexity*

with Eva Kiesele

17.1 INTRODUCTION: CEMENT PRODUCTION – FROM A CHEAP SUBSTITUTE TO A KEY INDUSTRY

This case study focuses on the interplay of joint production and stock dynamics. In Section 4.4, we highlighted that by their very property of persistency over time, stocks are likely to create *future effects* on production and consumption possibilities, and economic choice. We then argued that stocks are a source of generalised joint production over time (cf. Section 4.4.2). Considering the example of cement manufacture in Germany from its beginnings in the early nineteenth century to the large-scale industrial production of today, we shall now demonstrate how the build-up of capital stocks and their interrelation can lead to an increase in the complexity of the economy. It is for several reasons that the cement industry is well suited for that purpose:

- *Ease of description.* The cement production is a primary industry. Its inputs and outputs are relatively few homogeneous and standardised mass products, and the production process is quite simple. The industry can thus be characterised completely by its input and output flows and a small number of technical properties.

- *Economic significance.* Although its annual turnover is rather small (in the 1990s about 0.15 % of German GDP, BDZ 1998), the cement industry is of major relevance to the gross domestic product: cement is a necessary input in the production of many investment goods, particularly in the whole construction industry, comprising about 13 % of GDP by the mid 1990s (BDZ 1998: 33). Hence, we may justifiably call it a key industry of the economy.

---

*This chapter is based on Schiller (2002: Section 9.2).

- *Environmental impact.* Some input and output flows are of high environmental significance. For instance, the main production step of cement production – the burning process – requires a very high energy input. As this energy input is predominantly supplied by fossil fuels, it necessarily implies enormous CO_2 emissions.

- *Transparency.* The industry's structure has developed slowly, that is the essential production principle has remained largely constant over the past 150 years. Therefore, the influence of other industries linked to it by joint production can be examined quite well in this example.

- *Joint production on the input and output side.* There is an extensive usage of other industries' joint products as input into the cement industry, and a variety of examples for generalised joint production on the input side, as we shall see later. Also, cement plants produce a number of joint outputs as well. This creates a considerable interconnectedness with other industries, which in combination with the above aspect of transparency makes the cement industry an instructive example for studying the resulting economic structures.

The chapter is organised as follows. In the following Section 17.2, we give a brief overview of the chemical composition of cement and its key properties, and roughly outline the production process. In Section 17.3, we then describe the historical development of cement production in Germany. Section 17.4 relates this development of the cement industry to knowledge the concept of responsibility as developed earlier in this book. Section 17.5 draws some conclusions.

17.2   Cement: What are we Talking about?[1]

Cement is a binding agent used to produce mortar and artificial stones. Its importance is defined by two key properties: First, it is a hydraulic-setting binder, that is, in contrast to lime mortar, for example, it does not require atmospheric CO_2 to set, so it may be used under anaerobic conditions such as underwater construction. Second, cement is of notably higher physical stability compared to other binding agents like lime mortar.

Its hydraulic-setting property comes into existence in the process of burning and originates from small amounts of clay that are either naturally comprised in the raw material, limestone, or artificially added

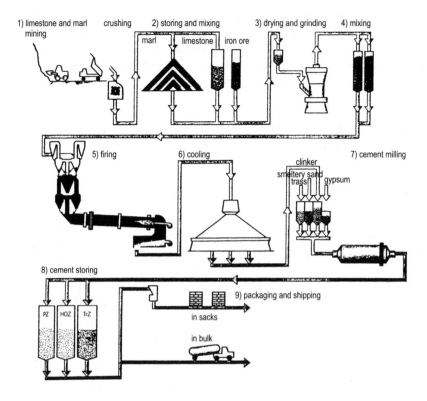

1) limestone and marl mining   crushing   2) storing and mixing   3) drying and grinding   4) mixing

marl   limestone   iron ore

5) firing   6) cooling   7) cement milling

clinker

smeltery sand   trass   gypsum

8) cement storing

PZ   HOZ   TrZ

9) packaging and shipping

in sacks

in bulk

Figure 17.1   Schematic representation of cement manufacture. (Figure adapted from Albrecht 1991: 94.)

before burning. In ancient times, hydraulic qualities were achieved by addition of *pozzolana*, a natural volcanic sand. Only when precision mechanic John Smeaton (1724–1792) found out about the clay admixtures in hydraulic materials by the end of the eighteenth century, was selective production of hydraulic-setting cement to start – so-called 'Roman Cement'. Today, cement presents itself as the most important binder of construction engineering. Although it usually makes just a small fraction of building material, enormous amounts are used: In 1995 annual sales in Germany amounted to 38.5 million tonnes, that is 471 kg per capita and year.

Let us now turn to a few details about the chemical composition of cement, and a rough description of the production process. Technically, cement consists of *cement clinker*, marl sintered at 1450°C, and a number of *aggregates* added after the process of burning. Cement clinker itself is a mixture of clay and limestone; the exact composition varies dependent on the geological circumstances of the respective quarry. The specific composition, however, defines the properties of the cement clinker, thus requiring thorough – and expensive – treatment of the raw material and, in many cases, the addition of further substances in order to achieve a constant quality.

Whereas lime mortar is recyclable in principle, the setting of cement is an *irreversible* process. Thus it is not possible to recycle cement; it can only be down-cycled. Moreover, destruction of concrete buildings is very energy-intensive. Large-scale usage of cement-based concrete therefore is to a great extent irreversible.

The process of cement production has not been fundamentally altered over time. A schematic representation of the basic steps of cement production, as given in Figure 17.1, illustrates both mid-nineteenth century cement manufacture as well as the functioning of a modern cement plant. The process naturally starts with the extraction of resources, limestone and marl, predominantly from the plant's own quarry. This is accompanied by major amounts of overburden as a joint product. In a second step, the extracted gravel is blended, homogenised and milled. This mixture is then heated to about 1450°C till the limestone sinters. The sintered material is called cement clinker. After the process of burning, aggregates are added in order to enhance the hydraulic-setting properties of the cement, and to generate other specific properties of the demanded output, such as a specific elasticity etc. The proportion of aggregates in the final output is in the range of 10–20%. Typical aggregates are natural substances and joint products from other industries such as hard coal flue ash or smeltery sand (blast furnace slag), both waste products from the iron and steel industry. Major joint products of cement manufacturing are overburden from resource extraction, waste heat, dust, and waste gases from the burning process such as CO_2, CO etc. (see Section 17.3.3).

17.3 STOCKS, KNOWLEDGE, CAPITAL, AND SOME USEFUL CONNECTIONS: THE HISTORY OF CEMENT PRODUCTION

17.3.1 Lime Kiln in the Early Nineteenth Century

Cement manufacture developed from the production of lime mortar or *quicklime*. It was intimately related to the production of brick-stones for three reasons: (i) There is a high complementarity between brick-stones and mortar. Hence, local markets for bricks provided sales markets for quicklime, simultaneously. (ii) The main production phase, namely burning, is so very similar for bricks and mortar that often they were actually burned in the same kiln – that is, the same capital stock was used for the production of bricks and mortar. (iii) In the extraction of clay for brick production, limestone may, depending on geological circumstances, accrue as a joint product (Albrecht 1991: 77). As transport and stocking of this overburden is costly, usage of the limestone components for quicklime production suggested itself quite naturally.

Ongoing industrialisation led to such a great increase in demand for mortar that a rising number of enterprises specialised in the production of quicklime: a new branch of industry developed from a joint product. The expansion of mortar-demanding and of quicklime-producing industries was connected to an accumulation of capital stocks, which was one defining factor of this development process in terms of time constants and time lags in the system's reaction.

Over this period, cement comes into play as a substitute for quicklime. Similar inputs are required for the production of cement and lime mortar and, again, both products are concerned with identical sales markets and identical producer-consumer relations. As the manufacturing principle of quicklime and cement was very similar, the specific capital and knowledge stock about lime kiln was used to build up cement production.

The rising demand for quicklime and cement necessitated a quest for suitable deposits of raw material. In those days, knowledge on how the chemical composition of the raw material related to properties of the final product was sparse. Production of the so-called 'Roman Cement' was largely reliant on naturally abundant limestone-clay compounds, and further development of product and production techniques rather resembled uncoordinated experimentation. More focused research was to start in the first decades of the nineteenth century, and the first scientific basics were discovered by Gustav Leube (1808–1881) by the end of the 1830s. As a result, small but still fairly primitive production plants emerged at various geologically suitable sites, all of them adopting the known technique of quicklime production. The heterogeneity of the raw materials and prevailing 'experimental' production techniques, which were still rather unsystematic, undermined the constancy of cement properties and quality.

At about the same time, by the first half of the nineteenth century, a major technological step was taken. From 2000 BCE onward, scove kilns had been in use – cylindrical cavities filled with limestone set on fire by fuel gases from a log fire below. This technique had several obvious shortcomings: first, such scove kilns could only be used discontinuously due to long periods of heating and cooling. Second, this led to a very

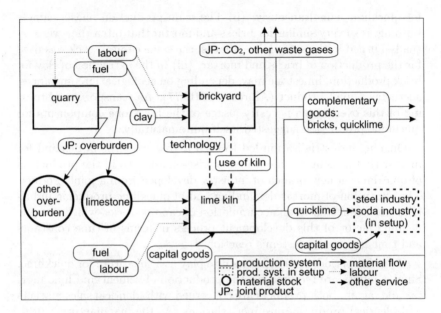

Figure 17.2   Schematic diagram of the interrelation between quicklime production and 'neighbouring' industries, such as the production of brick-stones in the first half of the nineteenth century. Material flows and accumulation of stocks are indicated by arrows.

high specific energy consumption. Third, this discontinuous operating method also resulted in notable fluctuations in quality. Finally, the capacity of scove kilns was limited, so that the fast increase in demand for mortar could not be met solely by relying on this technology. This problem was solved with the invention of the toploader kiln, a high cylindrical stack loaded with raw material and fuels (wood or coke) by turns. In a continuous 'first in first out' system, new material was added on top and burnt material – finished cement clinker and ash – was removed from the bottom. This innovation did not only increase quality and material throughput but also diminished specific energy consumption. The interrelation between quicklime/cement production and the production of brick-stones is summarised in Figure 17.2.

17.3.2   Cement Production and Transport: Transition to Industrial Production (1850–1914)

The second half of the nineteenth century saw the emergence of an independent cement industry. Small plants relying on technological knowledge from quicklime production developed into a multitude of large plants focused on cement manufacturing. This development was triggered by the following three factors:

1. *Increase in demand.* Progressive industrialisation generated a persistent further increase in demand. In particular, the build-up of transport infrastructure, that is railway construction and other state-run large-scale projects, created new profitable sales markets for cement and thus led to a continuous expansion of plants.

2. *Technological innovation.* New sorts of cement of a higher quality were innovated. Traditional 'Roman cement' produced from naturally abundant marl was substituted for 'synthetical' *portland cement* which, thanks to the addition of aggregates, had better and more constant properties. This technological innovation was accompanied by the accumulation of new stocks of knowledge and capital goods: The production steps for portland cement were more complex, and the raw material compounds had to be milled more thoroughly. A second innovation, sintered portland cement, required a higher burning temperature (about 1450°C). New fuels such as coke and a more modern kiln technology had to be used. Technological progress also made it possible to systematically search for marl deposits and exploit them even if the natural material composition did not match the exact input standards of traditional cement production. Both effects, the new possibility of extended resource exploitation as well as greater capital accumulation due to the changeover to portland cement, played a decisive role in the historical transformation of cement industry towards larger plants and industrial production.

3. *Changes on the input side.* Cement production increasingly required manufactured inputs such as a variety of energy sources, capital goods and transport services. Railway construction came into play as an important supplier of capital input: The new railway network enabled transport of the final product beyond regional boundaries and thus an expansion of sales markets. Likewise, railway transport was an indispensable prerequisite for the provision of the main energy sources, coal and coke, that had replaced wood and peat. Additionally, there was a new primary input: the iron and steel industry expanded rapidly, generating an increasing amount of blast furnace slag as a joint product. 'Smeltery sand' (furnace slag) has hydraulic-setting properties, and, thus, could be utilised as an aggregate for so-called metallurgical cement.

We will now have a closer look at the changes in production structure and technology. In the early stage, each step of production had taken place at a distinct location, as specific location factors had to be met such as the provision of water power. Typically, distinct enterprises carried out the individual steps of production. Over the course of the second half of the nineteenth century, a continuous process of integration and concentration took place for two main reasons: First, the building of great capital stocks was almost impossible for small companies. Second, increasing scarcity of resources in numerous quarries led to problems with input provision. In the remaining plants, production rates were growing fast.

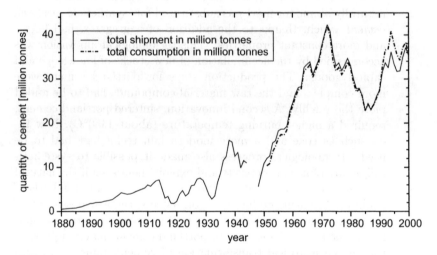

Figure 17.3   Total shipment of cement in Germany 1880–2000 (black line), and domestic cement consumption 1951–2000 (dash-dotted line); after 1990 including East Germany. Source: BDZ 1975, 1998, 2001.

Thanks to rapid progress in engine technology, all steps of production were mechanised more and more. By 1870, many bigger cement plants hosted steam engines to mill the raw material. Hence, the location factor of water power was no longer binding. Resource extraction and transport were carried out by dynamite blasting and cableways instead of manual labour, enhancing extraction rates enormously. Again, the accumulation of stocks of capital and knowledge in other sectors of the economy enabled further development of the cement industry. Along with mechanisation came a massive increase in production capacity, particularly with new techniques designed for greater output flows and realising increasing returns to scale (for an illustration of the increasing cement output, see Figure 17.3). Circular kilns substituted toploader kilns; these were favoured in spite of higher investment costs and higher energy consumption for their greater capacity – up to 20 times higher than for toploader kilns. This clearly indicates that enormous demand was the one dominant factor in the industry's evolution.

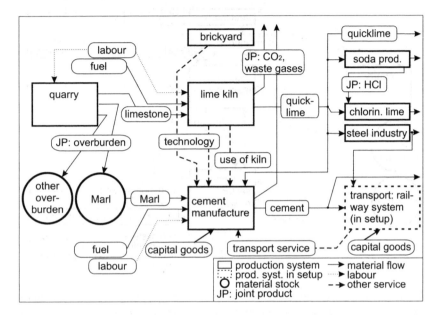

Figure 17.4 Schematic diagram of the interrelation between quicklime and cement production and 'neigbouring' industries, such as the steel industry and the emerging railway system in the second half of the nineteenth century. Material flows and accumulation of stocks are indicated by arrows.

The 'map' of industrial interconnections changed in various respects over this second phase – for a graphical view see Figures 17.4 and 17.5:

- In the beginning, essential elements of production were adopted from the quicklime industry, especially kiln technology. Undesired joint outputs of quicklime production, namely marl, were utilised as inputs (Roman cement).

- The soda and steel industries were fully developed and had great demand for quicklime. The developing railway system came to play a special role as both sales market and capital input. It provided transport services for final products and for extensive use of fuels of higher quality (hard coal, coke), thereby enabling transformation of the production in the form of better products.

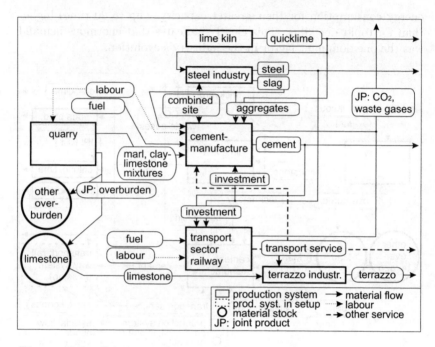

Figure 17.5   Schematic diagram of the interrelation between cement production and 'neighbouring' industries, such as the transport sector at the beginning of the twentieth century. Material flows and accumulation of stocks are indicated by arrows.

- By the early twentieth century, the mutual dependence between the railway system and cement production had reached its full extent. By means of existent capital stocks in the transport sector, the joint products of the cement industry could then be utilised, such as limestone from Blaubeuren, Germany, which contributed to the emergence of the terrazzo industry.

- Metallurgical cement makes up a new linkage between smelteries and cement plants. Slag, an undesired joint output from blast furnaces, was used as an aggregate for cement. As a result, many cement plants settled in close proximity to smelteries. Since metallurgical cements were much cheaper than portland cements, strong price competition arose, and there was a tremendous increase in the production of metallurgical cement by the beginning of the twentieth century.

17.3.3 Mechanisation and Environmental Concern: Modern Cement Industry in the Twentieth Century

General development

Over the course of the twentieth century, cement became an indispensable preliminary product for the construction industry. Hence, it came to play a key role in economic development. Along with general economic growth, the cement industry grew to eventually achieve an increase in annual production by a factor of ten by 1970 (as compared to annual production in 1900, see Figure 17.3). But its key role in the economy, on the other hand, implied greater sensibility to business fluctuations. Strong downturns during World War I and in the early 1930s as well as over the first postwar years were countered by cartel agreements; and besides these short-term collapses, the German cement industry was able to record constant growth until 1972, when the first energy crisis caused a general economic downturn.

The cement industry over this period of enduring growth is characterised by the ongoing substitution of the human workforce by mechanical drives, that is by capital stocks and energy input. Raw material extraction is automated completely; technical amendments within the cement plant are aimed at better product quality (for example more complete homogenisation of the raw material to guarantee constant quality), reduction of specific energy consumption, mitigation of harmful emissions (dust extraction, for instance), and minimisation of maintenance costs. Kiln technology is improved by using stocks of knowledge from the steel industry. Toploader kilns, which had already become obsolete in the nineteenth century, are automated with respect to material up and download, and then present a modern technology. Automated rotary kilns that can be fired with different fuels make up the standard of today. Likewise, the packaging and distribution of the finished product has become fully automated.

An abrupt end to incessant growth comes in 1972 in the form of the first energy crisis. Being an energy-intensive branch of industry, cement production is hit hard by rising energy prices. The industry puts great effort into saving primary energy input but, nevertheless, has to face a lasting decline of production over the next thirteen years. Only German reunification and the onset of 'Aufbau Ost' ('rebuilding the east') in 1990 bring back a stable positive trend in production figures (see Figure 17.3). A notable growth in production has been recorded since then, achieving a maximum output of 37 million tonnes in 1999, which, however, is much lower than the annual output in 1972 when cement production reached its climax. Short-term downturns and higher prices for energy inputs alone cannot explain this extended depression, considering that the cement industry managed to increase its energy efficiency significantly. Declining demand for cement seems a more plausible explanation here and may be caused by a rising awareness of the environmental impact of cement and its production, changing tastes in architecture turning away from concrete buildings, a more critical attitude towards large-scale construction projects etc.

Cement production and the natural environment

We shall now briefly investigate the environmental impact of cement production and examine how environmental concerns affected the development of cement industry. The general decline in cement production between 1972 and 1985 triggered a broad move towards innovation and modernisation. Many plants were closed down – predominantly those with higher specific energy consumption. Thus the decrease in demand led to both an increase in average energy efficiency and to an increasing market concentration.

Generally, the cement industry is characterised by high material throughput in proportion to the surplus value generated. Material flows are being exchanged with other industries and with the natural environment (Oss and Padovani 2002, 2003). Primary energy input (fossil fuels) and raw materials are examples of inputs from nature; a typical joint output of the cement industry released into the environment is CO_2, and of course cement itself represents a material flow to the environment. Here again, it is joint products of the industry under study that pose a threat to the natural environment. The negative environmental impact of the joint products of cement production has gained increasing public awareness since the 1970s, and socio-political pressure has prompted the industry to put some effort into reducing its emissions.

Two major strategies of the cement industry for emission reduction can be identified – investment in mitigation technologies and the use of alternative input compositions, such as the modification of the fuel mix. The attempts at emission reduction have succeeded to varying degrees. We shall illustrate this, considering three problematic joint products of the cement industry as an example: dust, sulphur dioxide (SO_2), and carbon dioxide (CO_2).

1. *Dust.* By downstream transformation processes, dust emissions can be abandoned. A stock of knowledge about this *end-of-pipe* technology was already in existence and cement fabricants chose to invest accordingly in stocks of specific physical capital, so that dust emissions were cut down to a large extent by the 1980s (cf. Figure 17.6).

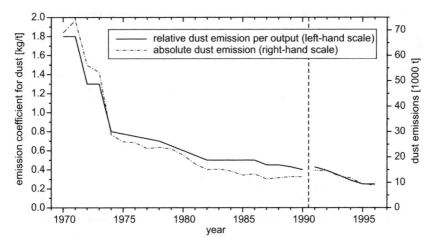

Figure 17.6   Dust emissions of the German cement industry 1970–1996: Relative dust emissions in kg dust emitted per tonne of output (solid line, left-hand scale), and absolute dust emissions (dash-dotted line, right-hand scale) for West Germany (until 1990) and Germany (from 1991 on). Source: Umweltbundesamt ('German Federal Environmental Agency', see Schiller 2002: 331).

2. *Sulphur dioxide* (SO_2). This joint product almost completely stems from sulphur contained in the energy sources being used. Although mitigation technologies are known (flue gas desulphurisation or upstream desulphurisation of fuels), these were not applied by the cement industry. The decreasing trend to be seen in Figure 17.7 was achieved by a change of fuel mix only. Over a period of three years (1979 to 1982, see Figure 17.9), coal was substituted for oil almost completely. Since coal has a lower specific SO_2 emission coefficient than oil, this led to an overall decrease in SO_2 emissions.[2]

3. *Carbon dioxide* (CO_2). For the past two decades, environmentalists have been focussing their attention on the cement industry as a major source of CO_2 emissions. While there is no true mitigation technology for CO_2, its generation per energy unit can be reduced either by means of using fuels with low carbon content in relation to the energy released in combustion or by increasing energy efficiency. About the first option, the alteration of fuel mix mentioned above (cf. Figure 17.9) led to an *increase* in CO_2 emissions per unit of output (see Figure 17.8b).[3] As to the second option, harsh limits are set upon energy saving by thermodynamical restrictions.

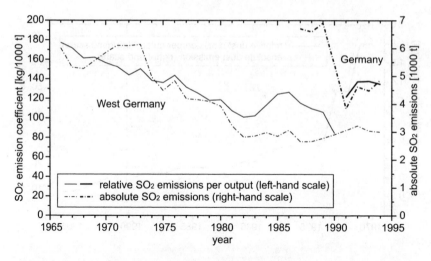

Figure 17.7   Sulphur dioxide (SO$_2$) emissions of the German cement industry 1966–1994: Relative SO$_2$ emissions in kg SO$_2$ emitted per tonne of output (solid lines, left-hand scale), and absolute SO$_2$ emissions (dash-dotted lines, right-hand scale) for West Germany (thin lines) and Germany (bold lines). Source: Umweltbundesamt ('German Federal Environmental Agency', see Schiller 2002: 335).

In any case, one should keep in mind that energy sources need not be fossil fuels. Indeed, climate concerns and related socio-political pressure incentivised the cement industry to search for alternative fuels. So-called *secondary fuels*, jointly emerging waste products of other industries characterised by a high energy content, such as oil residues, used tyres or waste plastics, substituted primary fuels by a significant share. The shift to secondary fuels led to a general decrease in carbon dioxide emissions per unit of output.[4] But this reduction was overcompensated for by the increase in production in the 1990s (Figure 17.3). Through this, CO$_2$ emissions from primary energy input rose to 10 million tonnes in 1994 – a benchmark that had not been hit since 1973 (cf. Figure 17.8).[5]

At the end of this section, we shall briefly list the intersectoral connections of the cement industry that emerged in the twentieth century. For an illustration, see Figure 17.10.

- Electrical energy makes a new input to cement production. Its proportion has been increasing continuously over the past three decades and currently holds at 15 %. This is a major contribution to emissions of the joint output CO$_2$.

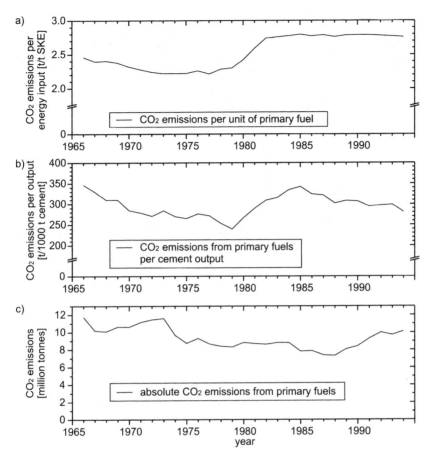

Figure 17.8   Carbon dioxide (CO₂) emissions of the German cement industry 1966–1994 (West Germany until 1990, then Germany): (a) CO₂ emissions per unit of primary energy put in, measured in tonnes CO₂ per tonne of standardised hard coal ('SKE'), (b) relative CO₂ emissions in kg CO₂ emitted per tonne of output, and (c) absolute CO₂ emissions. Source: Umweltbundesamt ('German Federal Environmental Agency', see Schiller 2002: 350).

- Cement production became a recycling industry for undesired joint outputs: Smeltery sand (blast furnace slag) and gypsum retained from fuel gas desulphurisation are used as aggregates.

- Primary energy input in the form of fossil fuels is partly substituted by secondary fuels such as waste plastics from the plastics manufacturing industry.

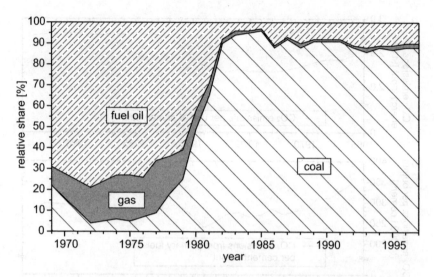

Figure 17.9   Fuel mix of the German cement industry 1969–1997: Relative shares of oil, gas, and coal as primary energy sources (West Germany until 1992, Germany afterwards).   Source: BDZ (1975, 1998, 2001, see Schiller 2002: 332).

- There is still a close bond with the transport sector. A new linkage emerged with combustion of old tyres – a joint product from the transport industry that serves as a secondary fuel in the cement industry.

- There is a new interrelation among cement plants: Overburden from one plant's quarry is being used as an aggregate by another plant, in order to meet the specific requirements of the chemical composition of the input material.

17.4   KNOWLEDGE AND RESPONSIBILITY FOR THE ENVIRONMENT

The case study of cement manufacture highlights the role of knowledge for responsibility. For a long time, cement manufacture was not seen to cause any major environmental problems; resource availability, apparently, was this industry's only relevant environmental constraint. Only in the 1960s and 1970s did the wider public notice the negative environmental impact of the joint products of the cement industry. It is this

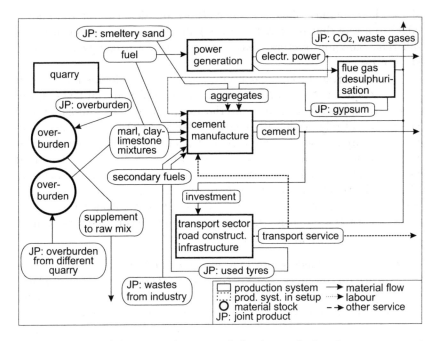

Figure 17.10   Schematic diagram of the interrelation between cement production and 'neighbouring' industries, such as the transport sector, at the end of the twentieth century. Material flows and accumulation of stocks are indicated by arrows.

public knowledge which has now raised an issue of collective responsibility for the natural environment.

Politics, prompted by public pressure, assumed political responsibility and enacted a number of regulations on air emissions. This change in the legal framework had implications for the individual legal responsibility of cement producers: Acting in a legally responsible manner from now on meant complying with emission standards. For example, they reduced harmful emissions by dust extraction (see Figure 17.6) and by changing the energy input mix – coal was substituted for oil, which lead to a reduction in sulphur dioxide emissions (see Figure 17.7).

17.5   CONCLUSIONS: STOCK DYNAMICS AND INTERACTION SHAPING A SECTOR OF INDUSTRY

Considering the historical development of cement production in Germany as an example, we have demonstrated how joint production may shape the dynamics of capital stocks (both physical capital and knowledge) in a way that is likely to create multiple interconnections between different economic sectors, that is to say, to form complex economic structures.

Up to the present, the cement industry and its development have been highly dependent on in- and outgoing energy and material flows. Local access to inputs, such as raw material from quarries, as well as a broad acceptance of related outputs – overburden and CO_2, for instance – are necessary prerequisites to run a cement plant. The technological evolution of cement production is characterised by largely constant technical principles. In particular, it turns out to be impossible to fundamentally alter production techniques in order to substitute the scarce input energy and thereby reduce or mitigate the undesired joint output CO_2.

Let us briefly summarise the main phases in the economic development of the German cement industry:

- The early phase before 1880 was governed by an extreme dependence on resources, since necessary stocks of knowledge were lacking as to how to access new deposits. The availability and usability of energy inputs was limited, hindering mechanisation of production. Growing stocks of knowledge and capital necessary for large-scale energy conversion then enabled mechanisation to a certain extent.

- The period from 1880 to 1970 presents itself as one of rapid expansion. The cement industry was subjected to hardly any input restrictions: access to resources, energy and transport services was almost unlimited. This was made possible by new technologies for energy conversion (engines etc.) and progress in railway transport. Scarce or locally unavailable resources then could be transported to production sites at low cost and on a large scale. Equally, the final product cement could be transported over much larger distances now. Technological change over this period mainly aimed at increasing returns of scale, that is expansion. The development of kiln technology (for example circular and rotary kilns) may serve as an example here. Decreases in production only occurred if caused by external shocks, such as World Wars I and II and the worldwide economic crisis in the late 1920s (cf. Figure 17.3).

- Since 1970, there has been a phase of new restrictions: oil crises and rising awareness of the environmental impact set limits to expansion and thus led to a saturation of the sector. The rising awareness of the environment led to socio-political pressure on cement plants to reduce emissions of undesired joint outputs. Those outputs for which mitigation technologies were known and applied, especially dust, were cut back to a great extent. Others were only partially improved on: Due to narrow limits to energy saving (see page 319), joint products resulting from the high energy consumption of cement production, namely CO_2, could only be dealt with by substituting secondary for primary fuels.

This development poses a contrast to the soda and chlorine industry (Chapter 16) in the following way. In the case of soda and chlorine, undesired joint products had accumulated into stocks in the natural environment and displayed harmful effects. This led to technological innovation either reducing joint products or opening up new fields of application. That is, the dominant macroeconomic factors of the industry's evolution were restrictions on certain output flows. As to cement production, there were no restrictions on output flows up to the early 1970s. Instead, restrictions on input availability acted as incentives for the selective accumulation of technological knowledge to overcome these restrictions.

The case of the cement industry demonstrates that the development of industrial systems is often shaped by the build-up and degradation of stocks, and by their interaction, which often stems from *unintended* effects of the stocks' existence. More specifically, the dominating factor in this case was the interaction of stocks of capital and knowledge that were initially not designed for cement production but, ex post, turned out to be essential for the cement industry's development: the invention of engines and electrical drives enabled the mechanisation of resource extraction, transport and kilns, and, thus, higher output rates. The effects of older stocks of capital goods or undesired substances on the cement industry were unforeseen and not intended by the time those stocks were built up. In its earliest phase, cement production used marl as a resource, which was an undesired joint output from quicklime production and costly overburden. At the same time, technological know-how regarding burning was adopted from the production of quicklime and brick-stones. This transfer of knowledge most likely had not been intended by former brick-stone fabricants. The usage of blast furnace slag is a similar example. For the iron-producing industry this was a joint product of negative value. The discovery of its hydraulic properties, however, turned it into a desirable input for the cement industry. Henceforth, it had a considerable impact on the industry's development, resulting in the construction of plants specialised in metallurgical cement.

A special case is the interconnectedness of cement production and the development of the railway system in the nineteenth century. Expansion of both sectors was mutually dependent on stocks of the other. Without the extremely loadable binder of cement and its large-scale availability many railway structures would not have been possible, whilst the development of the cement industry towards large-scale industrial production in big plants would not have been possible without the great expansion of the transport system. So ex post, the development of both economic sectors has to be considered a *co-evolution*, each step of development of one sector being a necessary base for the next step of the other. This interaction established a positive feedback mechanism on both sectors' growth. An increase in demand for cement here is coupled to an increase in factor inputs within the cement industry. Such complex interaction and development over time is usually unpredictable ex ante, but in many cases shapes economic evolution.

NOTES

1. This section is based on Keil (1971).
2. The modification of the fuel mix (Figure 17.9), however, also resulted in an *increase* in some emissions, notably carbon monoxide (CO), which accrues from incomplete combustion. Solid fuels generally lead to higher CO emissions than fluid or gaseous fuels.
3. Coal combustion leads to CO_2 emissions per unit of energy conversion which are higher than those associated with oil combustion by about one third.
4. There has been a heated debate on whether CO_2 emissions from burning secondary fuels should be ascribed to the cement industry or not. In Figure 17.8, they are not accounted for.
5. Moreover, there is another energy input to cement production, namely electrical energy. Ongoing mechanisation was accompanied by installation of many capital goods for material transport, preparation and milling, mostly powered and controlled by means of electrical energy. The proportion of electrical energy input amounts to 15 % of total energy consumption currently and is on the rise continuously. If we take the electrical component and combustion of secondary fuels into consideration, the total emission balance is increased by 35–45 % in addition.

18. Sulphuric Acid: Joint Externalities[*]

with Frank Jöst and
Georg Müller-Fürstenberger

18.1 INTRODUCTION

Sulphuric acid is a key compound in the chemical industry. A worldwide production of 155.6 million tonnes per year (in 1997) makes it, in terms of quantity, the chemical industry's single most important product (ESA-EFMA 1999: 6). Like the other case studies in this book, a study of sulphurous emissions and sulphuric acid offers important insights into how joint production links industrial structure and economic development on the one hand, and the dynamics of the natural environment on the other:

- Joint products – sulphur dioxide and other sulphurous wastes and emissions – which originate from the industrial production of desired goods, may cause environmental problems (cf. Chapter 5).

- The dynamics of economy-environment interactions are governed by various stocks. This leads to time lags between economic causes and environmental effects (cf. Chapters 4 and 5).

- As there is a (limited) potential for productive use of the sulphurous joint products by processing them into sulphuric acid, they are not just 'bads', but they are ambivalent. This means, they may be positively and negatively valued, depending on the context in which they come into existence (cf. Chapter 8).

- Joint production of different positively valued outputs may link different industrial sectors, which co-evolve as a result. This creates complexity in the structure of an economy (cf. Chapter 4).

---

[*]This chapter is based on Baumgärtner (2000: Section 2.3.3), Baumgärtner and Jöst (2000), Faber, Jöst, Manstetten and Müller-Fürstenberger (1996a), and Müller-Fürstenberger (1995: Section 7.2).

- Ambivalence of joint products results in a major policy challenge – so-called 'joint externalities'. This means that two environmental externalities are linked by the structure of the production system (cf. Sections 8.5.3–8.5.5).

This chapter is organised as follows. In Section 18.2, we describe how sulphurous emissions and waste from industrial production of desired goods may cause environmental problems. In Section 18.3, we discuss the ambivalence of sulphurous joint products and how this ambivalence gives rise to structural economic change. In Section 18.4, we analyse one important environmental policy implication of ambivalence, namely the problem of joint externalities. Section 18.5 concludes.

18.2   Sulphurous Emissions and Waste as the Origin of Environmental Problems

Environmental pollution by sulphurous emissions and waste is as old as the industrial way of production. During the nineteenth century, the burning of coal, the smelting and refining of metals, and chemical manufacturing resulted – given the lack of any serious attempt to control emissions – in ever increasing amounts of environmental pollution with sulphurous by-products (Ponting 1993: 361). One particular example is soda production, which was discussed in detail in Chapter 16. The industrial revolution created areas of concentrated pollution and environmental degradation, severely affecting the quality of life of the people living in these areas. While environmental regulation – in response to apparent threats to human life and health – set in as early as the 1860s, large-scale pollution with sulphurous by-products basically continued. Only in the second half of the twentieth century was it becoming clear that pollution by acid rain from sulphurous emissions was not just a national but an international problem.[1]

18.2.1   Emission of Sulphurous Pollutants

One of the most important sulphurous pollutants is sulphur dioxide (SO_2), which originates as a joint product in the combustion of fossil fuels (88 % of all SO_2 emissions, with 20 % from industrial combustion and the rest from automobile traffic), the refining of crude oil and the purification of natural gas (7 % of all SO_2 emissions), and various industrial production processes, mainly metal smelting and refining (5 % of all SO_2 emissions). Table 18.1 shows the annual emissions of SO_2 for Germany. Emissions reached a peak in 1980. The subsequent substantial reductions, by 60 % from 1980 until 1994, are due to the enactment of federal

year	1975	1980	1990	1994
sulphur dioxide (SO_2) emissions in 1,000 tonnes	7,483	7,514	5,326	2,995

Table 18.1   Annual emissions of SO_2 in Germany. Data for 1975 and 1980 are the aggregated data for the Federal Republic of Germany and the German Democratic Republic, data for 1990 and 1994 are those for unified Germany. Source: IW 1997: 107.

environmental regulation concerning sulphur dioxide and nitrogen oxide emissions from fossil-fuel-fired power plants.[2] In addition, around 1990 many inefficiently producing power plants and production facilities in former East Germany were shut down, which further decreased annual emissions.

18.2.2   Direct and Indirect Impact

Once emitted into the atmosphere, sulphurous pollutants are mainly carried by winds according to current weather patterns and either fall immediately onto plants, trees, soils, lakes and buildings ('dry deposition'), or are washed out by rain, snow, hail and dew ('wet deposition'). In the latter process, the pollutants chemically react with water (H_2O) in the air and are thus to some extent transformed into sulphuric acid (H_2SO_4). In this form they enter the soil and surface waters. 'Acid rain' denotes the entity of all acid-building air pollutants which are dissolved in the rain (Heintz and Reinhardt 1996: 73). Other emissions – besides sulphur dioxide – contributing to the formation of acid rain are nitrogen oxides (NO_x) and ammonia (NH_3), which are also joint outputs in the burning of fossil fuels.[3] About two thirds of sulphurous and nitrogen emissions into the atmosphere get back to the earth's surface as dry deposition, one third as wet deposition in the form of acid rain (Heintz and Reinhardt 1996: 149).

Sulphur dioxide has several negative effects on the natural environment as well as on the human economy. These comprise direct and indirect effects.[4]

Direct damages may be caused by dry or wet deposition. Deposited on needles and leaves of trees and crops, sulphur dioxide harms the plants' metabolism by impairing their ability to photosynthesise or transpire. Dry deposition also endangers human health. In particular, the respiratory tracts of elderly people and of children are affected.[5] Man-made structures such as buildings, fabrics, or materials, are negatively affected by the high corrosiveness of acid rain. Moreover, calcium is transformed into gypsum, which is then dissolved and washed out, so that buildings made from, for example, limestone or sandstone deteriorate much faster under the influence of acid rain.

All of this direct impact mainly depends on the concentration of the pollutants in the air (CDA 1988). In general, the severity of this impact declines rapidly with decreasing concentrations and increasing distances from the emitting sources (Persson 1982). Ecosystems are capable of assimilating a certain amount of sulphur dioxide during a certain time period ('critical load'). Any pollution exceeding this critical load will cause damage to the ecosystem.

Indirect negative effects of wet deposition consist in the acidification of soils and surface waters, thereby damaging both cultivated land (crops) and natural ecosystems (forests, lakes, streams, fish). Wet deposition of sulphur dioxide in the form of acids accumulates in the soil or surface waters to form a stock of immissions. Dry deposition may further increase this stock. The acidification effects depend on the absolute amount of dry and wet deposition and the natural sensitivity of soil and water bodies to acidification. These effects include the following (Hordijk et al. 1990):

- Accelerated acidification of lakes, which endangers fish species and may lead to their disappearance. For instance, Scandinavian countries, Canada and the Northeast of the USA experienced the death and disappearance of fish species from lakes and rivers (Newbery 1990), which has been attributed to the acidification of these waters.[6]

- Increased acidity of forest soils, which leads to nutrient deficiencies and high concentrations of aluminium and other toxic materials.

- Increased forest die-back ('Waldsterben') due to the combined impact of different gaseous pollutants, forest soil acidification, increased deposition of nitrogen, and other stress factors, such as extreme climatic episodes.[7] For instance, according to official estimates (BMELF 1991) 64% of German forests had been affected by acid rain and were suffering from the associated damages in 1991 (see Table 18.2).

Similarly as for direct impact, ecosystems are capable of assimilating a critical load of acids. Once the buffering capacity, that is the ecosystem's ability to chemically neutralise immited acids, is exceeded, any further immission of acids will cause damage to the ecosystem.

country	share of affected forest				
	1983	1985	1987	1989	1991
Poland					90.8%
Great Britain					94.0%
Switzerland					68.0%
Germany (East)					73.0%
(West)	34.4%	51.9%	52.3%	52.9%	60.0%
(Total)					64.0%
Belgium					56.6%
Norway					50.6%
Spain					35.7%
France					23.6%

Table 18.2   Share of forest suffering from damages caused by acid rain for various European countries in 1991, and for (West) Germany for the time span from 1983 to 1991. Source: BMELF 1991, 1992.

18.2.3   Temporal Structure of the Problem

The temporal structure of acid-rain pollution comprises both a *flow* pollution aspect and a *stock* pollution aspect (cf. Chapters 4, 9 and 10). The direct impact arises from the flow of pollutants at one point in time, whereas the indirect impact is caused by the accumulation of pollution over time into a stock of immissions (Klaassen 1996: 186).

The sulphur and nitrogen oxides emitted remain in the atmosphere for a relatively short time before they are either deposited directly onto the earth's surface or washed out by rain. How long exactly they persist depends on current weather; typically, this happens on a time scale of a few days to several weeks. Over such short time spans no large stocks of these pollutants can accumulate in the atmosphere. As a consequence, the amount of the pollutants that enter the ecosystems and cause damage – either as dry or as wet deposition – is approximately given by the flow of these pollutants emitted continuously from various sources. While the oxides cannot accumulate in the atmosphere, the resulting acids accumulate in soils and in surface waters into a stock of immissions. Hence, the damage to the ecosystem may have the character of flow pollution or of stock pollution.

The stock pollution aspect explains the seemingly paradoxical observation that while the flow of sulphur and nitrogen dioxide emissions actually decreased in many countries over the last two decades, the related environmental problems, such as damage to forests or acidification of lakes, nevertheless still increase. From Tables 18.1 and 18.2 it becomes obvious that in Germany, the indirect impact increased dramatically at a time, during the 1980s, when the underlying sulphur dioxide emissions were already sharply decreasing. This illustrates the conceptual discussion in Section 5.2.

18.2.4   Spatial Structure of the Problem

Since sulphur and nitrogen oxides remain in the atmosphere for a couple of days up to several weeks, the oxides may be transported hundreds, sometimes thousands, of kilometres from the original emission point. But they are certainly not diffused on a global scale, as opposed to long-lived substances such as carbon dioxide. As a consequence, the location of immission and, thus, damage is determined by both geographical location of the emission and weather, in particular wind direction and rain intensity.

Since the negative environmental impact of acid rain occurs downwind from the pollution sources, and western winds prevail in Europe, countries in Eastern Europe are comparatively more strongly affected than countries in Western Europe (cf. Table 18.2). In particular, damage in France or Belgium is almost exclusively due to emissions in Great Britain. This effect of the long-range transport of sulphur compounds in the atmosphere, hence, accounts for the fact that emissions and immissions have to be strictly distinguished. While Table 18.1 shows decreasing emissions of pollutants over time in Germany, actual immissions have indeed remained about the same. This is due to the large and growing amount of 'imported' immissions in Germany. For example, in 1994 only 56 % of the total sulphur deposition in Germany came from emissions in Germany (Statistisches Bundesamt 1996: 148). The rest was imported from other countries through wind drift.[8]

18.3   AMBIVALENCE OF SULPHUROUS JOINT PRODUCTS AS THE ORIGIN OF STRUCTURAL CHANGE

The ambivalent character of joint products, that is the fact that it is not a priori clear whether the by-products of some desired output are goods, free goods, or bads (cf. Chapter 8), has important dynamic consequences for the evolution of an economy.[9] This also holds for sulphurous by-products (Baumgärtner and Jöst 2000, Faber et al. 1996a, 1996b, Müller-Fürstenberger 1995).

During the nineteenth century many sites of sulphide metal ores were discovered and exploited. The production of pure metal from these ores, in particular the process of roasting,[10] yielded sulphur dioxide emissions as an unwanted joint output. The negative impact of sulphur dioxide had on the environment (see Section 18.2) entailed many claims for compensation. This urged producers, especially in Germany, to process unwanted sulphur dioxide into sulphuric acid (H_2SO_4). This in turn could serve as a useful input for the chemical industry, since many chemical production processes at that time required sulphuric acid as a processing chemical. In particular, the British textile sector needed large quantities of sulphuric acid. In the second half of the nineteenth century, demand for sulphuric acid further increased as the industrial production of fertilisers and coal tar dyes started.

Before the middle of the nineteenth century, the sulphuric acid demanded by the textile sector had been produced from elementary sulphur. This source, however, experienced a sharp price increase after Ferdinand II, King of Sicily, monopolised the export of sulphur in 1838. The production of sulphuric acid from sulphur dioxide, thus, solved two problems at once: the producers of metal from metal ores had found a way of disposing of their harmful and thus unwanted by-product and the chemical industry had found a substitute for elementary sulphur from Sicily. Figure 18.1 schematically shows the role of sulphuric acid as an intermediate product linking two sectors of the economy – the metallurgical industry and the chemical industry.

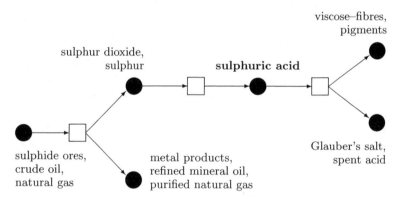

Figure 18.1   Schematic representation of an example of intersectoral joint production.   Square boxes represent production processes, filled circles represent the respective inputs and outputs. Sulphuric acid is an intermediate product between two sectors characterised by joint production – the metallurgical industry as well as the oil and gas industry on the one hand and the chemical industry on the other. (Figure modified from Faber et al. 1996a: 501.)

Today, sulphur and sulphuric acid are also produced in increasing quantities as joint outputs of natural gas purification as well as in the refining of crude oil (Müller 1994). Table 18.3 shows the origin of the sulphur which was used in the production of sulphuric acid in the chemical industry in Germany in 1991 (Strenge 1995; quoted after Faber et al. 1996a: 502, with own calculations). The first two lines of the table

source	amount [in tonnes of SO_3]	share
sulphides (except for pyrite)	745,185	
pyrite	348,810	58%
recovered sulphur	721,400	
elementary sulphur	388,450	
(except for recovered sulphur)		42%
other	951,300	
total	3,155,145	

Table 18.3   Sources of sulphur for the production of sulphuric acid in the chemical industry in Germany in 1991. Source: Strenge 1995; quoted after Faber et al. 1996a: 502, with own calculations.

give the amount of sulphur that enters the production of sulphuric acid as an input provided by the metal producing industry. Sulphides make the main part of non-ferrous metal ores and pyrite is the most important iron ore. In the process of roasting these ores, sulphur dioxide occurs as a joint output, which is then processed into sulphuric acid. Recovered sulphur (third line) is obtained in the process of refining crude oil or natural gas. Both oil and gas naturally contain sulphurous compounds that have to be removed before they can be processed further. Together, these three sources of sulphur make 58% of the total sulphurous input.

Table 18.3 shows that still today sulphuric acid is predominantly produced from joint outputs of other production processes. In particular, the metallurgical industry as well as the oil and gas industry are offered a way to dispose of their unwanted sulphurous by-products. With the chemical industry using sulphuric acid as an input, a link had been established between the metallurgical as well as the oil and gas industries on the one hand, and the chemical industry on the other. At the same time, this substance had changed its character from undesired to desired. As this input was cheap and easily accessible, technical developments within the chemical industry were stimulated that resulted in ever more products and production processes relying on sulphuric acid. The technological structure that has evolved in that way since the middle of the nineteenth century still persists. A considerable part of the products and the production technology of today's chemical industry is reminiscent of the fact that, in the beginning, there was an undesired by-product for which some way of disposal had to be found.

Today, sulphuric acid is a key compound in the chemical industry. A world-wide production of 155.6 million tonnes per year (in 1997) makes it, in terms of quantity, the chemical industry's single most important product (ESA-EFMA 1999: 6). It is mainly used as a processing chemical: about 70 % of the sulphuric acid used in the chemical industry is being reused within this industry.

18.4 JOINT EXTERNALITIES

As the previous section has revealed, originally undesired and harmful sulphurous emissions and waste from the metallurgical and the oil/gas industries have found new uses as inputs in the chemical and textile industries. That is, the ambivalence of joint outputs, and in particular the use of these outputs as inputs in other production processes, links different production processes within the economy, both within and across sectors (cf. Section 8.5.4). Joint production thus establishes a complex and integrated network of production within the economy.

The creation of this network was motivated by finding new uses for joint outputs that would otherwise have been waste. In this manner, some environmental problems could be solved, for example large-scale environmental damage from sulphurous emissions from the smelting and refining of metals or from the refining of crude oil and gas. But the activities that helped solve the primary environmental problems caused other problems. Often, the processes in the chemical industry that use sulphuric acid as a processing chemical yield sulphurous joint outputs themselves (see Figure 18.1). In the course of the chemical reactions, sulphuric acid undergoes physical and/or chemical changes and turns into unwanted by-products such as spent acid – a diluted 20 % acid enriched with heavy metals – or sulphurous salts such as sodium sulphate (Na_2SO_4, also known as 'Glauber's salt'). These undesired joint outputs leave the reaction vessels as part of the waste water.

Current environmental problems caused by sulphurous compounds, such as sulphates and spent acid, result primarily from the use of sulphuric acid in the chemical industry. Until 1989, some 750,000 tonnes of spent acid per year had been dumped into the ocean, where it caused a number of severe damages: it cauterised the gills and mucous membranes of fish, and due to the reaction heat when coming into contact with water, it contributed to the (local) warming of the ocean.

After the dumping into oceans had been banned, a recycling method for spent acid was developed. As for Glauber's salt, a decomposition into sodium and sulphuric acid is technically possible, but hardly lucrative as it requires high investment costs and high energy costs. As an alternative, the occurrence of Glauber's salt may be reduced or even completely avoided by reducing the input of sulphuric acid. This is technically possible for a number of production processes, for example in the production of ascorbic acid, boric acid, chlorine dioxide, hydroxylamine, formic acid, methionine or resorcinol.

But reducing the chemical industry's demand for sulphuric acid means that there is an excess of elementary sulphur and other sulphurous compounds from the metallurgical industry as well as from the oil and gas industry (Faber et al. 1996a: 500–501). This raises again the original disposal problem of sulphurous emissions and waste in these industries, which had been solved by the processing of these emissions and waste into sulphuric acid. Obviously, as a result of joint production and the ambivalence of a joint product, an industrial structure has emerged that is characterised by so-called 'joint externalities' (Section 8.5.5). This means that two sources of different forms of environmental damage are structurally linked by the production system: (i) emissions of sulphur dioxide from the metallurgical and the oil/gas industries causing acid rain, and (ii) the disposal of spent acid and Glauber's salt from the chemical industry into rivers and oceans causing damage to aquatic ecosystems.[11]

Joint externalities by sulphurous emissions and waste pose a major challenge to environmental policy (Baumgärtner and Jöst 2000): when simultaneously regulating the two types of environmental damage, one faces a trade-off between reducing emissions from one industry or from the other. And if the potential environmental problem due to emissions from the metallurgical and the oil/gas industry were to be largely reduced by processing the ambivalent joint output into sulphuric acid and trading it to the chemical industry, the original externality was not abandoned but just 'hidden' (see Section 8.5.3). As a result, when assessing the chemical industry's environmental performance, one may not be aware of the circumstance that this industry actually helps to mitigate problems from the former industries. This may lead to underestimating the chemical industry's environmental performance.[12]

18.5 CONCLUSIONS

The example of the sulphuric acid industry illustrates a number of typical features of present production systems in basic industries – for instance in the chemical industry, the metallurgical industry, the cement industry, or the oil and gas industry – and the impact of these production systems on the natural environment:

First, production processes in basic industries are characterised by the important role that chemical reactions and physical transformations play. It is typical of this kind of process that the quantitative amount of joint products is considerable and of economic relevance. It is also typical of these industries that their joint products, when released into the natural environment, cause damage.

Second, the existence of an unwanted joint output (here: sulphur dioxide from metal production or oil and gas refining) can act as the origin of innovation and structural evolution in the economy, and establish a complex interrelationship between different processes of production. Hitherto independent production processes are now linked within *integrated production systems* by the fact that one process uses the unwanted joint output of another process as an input. While such links are well known to exist *within* the various sectors of an economy, they may also exist *between* different sectors, for example between the metallurgical as well as the oil and gas industry and the chemical industry (Faber et al. 1996a).

Third, the character of these joint products may be *ambivalent*. On the one hand, the additional outputs are unwanted joint products which are often potentially harmful to the natural environment. On the other hand, they may also serve as inputs into other processes in which another desired good is produced. Often these other processes have originally been invented for the sole purpose of making good use of the otherwise unwanted joint product. However, while accomplishing this task, these other processes also yield joint outputs that may give rise to different negative externalities.

Fourth, this interrelationship links in a complex way different negative externalities stemming from different production processes, thus creating 'joint externalities' (Baumgärtner and Jöst 2000). As a result, there exists a trade-off between internalising different externalities. Internalising one externality may give rise to another externality which formerly did not exist. Environmental policy that solely aims at presently observable externalities and neglects other potential externalities may be associated with excessive costs. Materials flow analyses can help inform about the detailed structure of the production system and reveal 'hidden externalities' as well as 'joint externalities'.

NOTES

1. Ponting (1993: 365–368) gives a detailed account of the history of the acid rain problem. For a survey of the ecological and economic impact of acid rain, as well as a concise presentation of the chemical foundations underlying this phenomenon see Heintz and Reinhardt (1996: Chapter 6). Klaassen (1996: Chapter 8) gives a

brief overview of the acidification problem in Europe and deals at some length with institutions and regulations for dealing with the problem. See also Hordijk et al. (1990) and Persson (1982).

2.   The two most important regulations were the *Federal Immission Control Ordinance on Large Firing Installations* ('13. BImSchV – Verordnung über Großfeuerungsanlagen') as of June 22, 1983 and the *Technical Instructions on Air Quality* ('TA Luft') as of February 27, 1986.

3.   Nitrogen oxides (NO_x) and ammonia (NH_3) also chemically react with the water (H_2O) in the air and are thus transformed into nitric acid (HNO_3).

4.   Nitrogen oxides have essentially the same effects.

5.   Sulphur dioxide is known to be one of the most important causes of (winter) smog. Hitherto the most spectacular known smog disaster happened in December 1952 in London. During a smog period of several days an estimated 4,000 people were killed (Heintz and Reinhardt 1996: 74).

6.   Neutral acidity of a liquid, for example in water vapour, is indicated by a pH-value of 7; pH-values higher than 7 indicate an alkaline liquid; pH-values lower than 7 indicate an acid liquid. Normal precipitation is slightly acid, indicated by pH-values in the range from 7.5 to 6. Acid rain has pH-values of 5 and below. At pH-values of 5.5, fish reproduction is disturbed, and at pH-values below 5 fish die. When the phenomenon of acid rain was discovered, some lakes were found to have pH-values as low as 3. (For comparison: vinegar has a pH-value of 2.5.)

7.   It has by now become clear that the phenomenon of damage to forests cannot be attributed to one single cause, such as, for instance, sulphur dioxide. Rather, these damages are, like most other ecosystem stresses, multifactorial. This means that several causes synergetically interact in causing the effect. For instance, in the case of direct damages through dry deposition on leaves or needles of trees, small concentrations of sulphur dioxide can already cause relatively severe damage in the presence of nitrogen oxide or ozone (O_3) immissions (Lichtenthaler and Buschmann 1984).

8.   For example from Czechoslovakia (9 %), Great Britain (7 %), France (6 %), Belgium and Luxemburg (4 %), Poland (4 %) or the Netherlands (2 %) (Statistisches Bundesamt 1996: 148).

9.   Already Karl Marx (1959[1894]: 101–109), Johann Heinrich von Thünen (1921 [1826]: §29) and Alfred Marshall (1970[1911]: 238–240) were well aware of the fact that the occurrence of unwanted by-products may act as a dynamic force, shaping the structural evolution of an economy (see the detailed discussion in Chapter 6). For a conceptual analysis of this effect, see Section 5.2; for another case study, see Chapter 16.

10.   By 'roasting', one transforms iron sulphide (FeS_2) into iron oxide (Fe_2O_3) according to the chemical reaction:

$$4\,FeS_2 \;+\; 11\,O_2 \;\rightarrow\; 2\,Fe_2O_3 \;+\; 8\,SO_2\;.$$

The iron oxide (Fe_2O_3) can then be reduced, using coke (C), to elementary iron (Fe) according to the chemical reaction:

$$2\,Fe_2O_3 \;+\; 3\,C \;\rightarrow\; 4\,Fe \;+\; 3\,CO_2\;.$$

11.   The industrial structure which has emerged around sulphuric acid (cf. Figure 18.1) could be described in a more abstract manner by the model depicted in Figure 8.6, with 'process 1' representing the metallurgical or the oil and gas industry, 'waste 1' representing sulphur dioxide or recovered sulphur from these industries, 'secondary resource' representing sulphuric acid, 'process 2' representing the chemical industry, and 'waste 2' representing spent acid or Glauber's salt.

12.   The policy issues related to such a situation of joint externalities in the context of sulphuric acid, and the role of various uncertainties when devising regulatory policies for integrated production networks, are discussed by Baumgärtner and Jöst (2000).

19. Conclusions and Perspectives

In this book, we have addressed the questions of how environmental problems emerge from human economic activity, and what this implies for an all-encompassing and long-term environmental policy. At the centre was the concept of *joint production*. It captures the general principle that human action, which is directed towards a certain end, inevitably gives rise to additional side effects. The concept is constitutive for explaining how environmental problems emerge, and is also fruitful for pointing to their solutions. A thorough understanding of joint production and its consequences is, in our view, an indispensable prerequisite for taking responsible action that meets the challenge of sustainability (cf. Section 1.1). So, analysing joint production means rethinking the foundations of environmental policy.

19.1 Retrospect: Approach of this Book

We have analysed joint production and its consequences from different, complementary perspectives – that of the natural sciences, economics, and ethics. Our interdisciplinary approach was based on concepts, models, and case studies.

Taking the ubiquitous phenomenon of joint production as a starting point, Part I laid the conceptual foundations of joint production. We defined joint production in an encompassing way which captures the inevitability of joint outputs, and explicitly takes into account the time dimension of such inevitability. In a thermodynamic analysis, we demonstrated that all production is joint production. This ubiquity of joint production leads to a number of structural consequences for the development of ecological-economic systems. Economic action – due to joint production – interferes with a multiplicity of ecological, economic and social stocks. It thus induces many long-term consequences, and leads to high complexity in the consequences of economic activity. Both aspects matter when addressing sustainability.

In Part II, we analysed joint production from a welfare economic perspective. Essentially, this approach builds on the concept of (positive

339

or negative) value, which is assigned to joint products and used to determine their welfare-maximising allocation. In this perspective, joint production is linked to the concept of externalities, as joint products are often the cause of externalities. Environmental economics, in principle, tells us how to deal with these. Also, economics tells us how joint production influences the development of economies over time, for example by affecting the accumulation of capital or by causing the build-up of welfare-decreasing pollutant stocks in the natural environment. However, our analysis reveals that taking joint production and stock dynamics seriously, increases the complexity of economic valuation up to the point where an economic approach to environmental policy runs into severe difficulties.

As an alternative to the economic paradigm of *homo economicus*, in Part III, we considered a free human being who is able and obliged to assume responsibility for his actions or for something in particular. For an individual, assuming responsibility is only possible insofar as he has appropriate knowledge concerning the consequences of his actions. In a world dominated by joint production, however, these consequences are too complex to be completely foreseen by any individual. Hence, joint production systematically limits the ability of the individual to take responsibility for the consequences of his actions. This vindicates the need for collective responsibility in the form of political and political-ethical responsibility, which have to be assumed also for unforeseen consequences. Politics – and in particular the political actor (*homo politicus*) – has to assume unlimited responsibility for the consequences of human action. This has important and far-reaching implications for environmental policy, which we shall discuss in Section 19.3.

Part IV took a somewhat different approach to joint production. Considering four specific cases, we investigated in an empirical and historical perspective the role of joint production in the development of different industries. Consequences of joint production which were analysed in the preceding Parts I–III could be observed and investigated in the context of real-world ecological-economic systems.

19.2   KEY INSIGHTS

A number of key insights emerged from our analysis of joint production.

Phenomenon and concept of joint production

Many environmental problems due to human economic activity originate in the phenomenon of joint production: environmental pollution is jointly produced with desired economic goods. The concept of joint production is well suited analytically to a comprehensive investigation of this phenomenon as well as its environmental, economic and ethical implications. In particular, the concept of joint production emphasises the *multi-dimensionality* of the consequences of human action.

Thermodynamics of joint production

The concept of joint production can be analytically rooted in the natural sciences, in particular in thermodynamics, so that it captures the physical nature of energy and matter transformations in production processes. It is therefore suitable to describe relevant constraints of economic action in a realistic way. Performing a thermodynamic analysis, it turns out that all production is joint production. The phenomenon is necessarily ubiquitous. This insight is fundamental to the design of sustainable environmental policy.

Dynamics and complexity

The concept of joint production, along with the concept of stocks, enables a better understanding of the complex dynamics of economy-environment interactions. There are typical dynamic patterns characterising the long-term co-evolution of economy, society, and natural environment. This is important for an analysis of the long-term consequences of current economic activity as demanded by the imperative of sustainability. The complexity of ecological-economic systems poses a major challenge for scientific analysis as well as for sustainable policies and management strategies. The concept of joint production, together with the concept of stocks, allows us to address such complexity analytically.

Economics and the value of joint products

Over the course of time, economics has developed a vast body of knowledge about joint production. The economic approach in general, and as applied to joint production in particular, builds on the concept of (positive or negative) value in order to determine the optimal choice of the kinds and amounts of goods produced and consumed. This approach helps developing strategies to deal with joint products, for example in the context of a multi-product firm or in the context of environmentally harmful by-products, if there exists sufficient knowledge about the whole ecological-economic system so that the value of joint products is clear. But pursuing the value-based approach has led to an unfortunate division in the economic literature on joint production: one strand (business administration and industrial organisation) deals with the joint production of several *desired* outputs, while another, methodologically very different strand (externalities) deals with joint production of *desired and undesired* outputs. As a result, there is no encompassing theory of joint production dealing with both aspects in a unified way. On the contrary, there is a gap in economic theory concerning ambivalent joint production and its consequences.

Ambivalence of joint products

The character of joint products as 'desired' or 'undesired' depends on the whole economic, social and environmental context. Whether a particular joint product is desired or not may change over time. Such ambivalence gives rise to peculiar network effects in an economy, such as joint externalities or hidden externalities. As a result, solving one environmental problem may directly lead to another environmental problem, possibly in a different sector of the economy.

Against this background, ambivalence has implications for environmental impact assessment. System representations should be chosen in a comprehensive way in order to identify potential changes in the joint output's character from desired to undesired, or vice versa. For instance, the precautionary principle requires that an environmental impact assessment should not be limited to outputs and effects that are presently known to be harmful, but should be extended to outputs and effects with the potential to become harmful in the future.

Investment and capital accumulation

The consideration of environmental effects in investment decisions considerably extends the sphere of economic and social decision-making because ecological-economic interactions have to be taken into account. This may significantly alter standard economic results. While the conventional wisdom of capital theory states that the longer the time horizon the more likely is innovation, our analysis has shown that this result has to be qualified in several respects and may even be completely reversed when analysing investment in joint production technologies: Even for pollutants with a short lifetime the innovation of a technique becomes less likely than in the case of no pollution. And if the pollutant's lifetime is very long as compared to the time horizon of the decision maker, for example for some greenhouse gases or radioactive wastes, the standard result of capital theory is completely reversed. In this case, the longer the time horizon, the less likely is the innovation of a new technique characterised by joint production.

Joint production and responsibility

When human action is addressed from the perspective of ethics, it becomes apparent that human beings are responsible for their actions. The notion of responsibility has different aspects and implications. On the one hand, it imposes moral obligations on the actor. On the other hand, responsibility is always limited. The limits of responsibility are closely linked to the actual or potential knowledge (or ignorance) of the actor. Joint production systematically limits potential knowledge about the consequences of one's action and, therefore, limits the possibility of individually taking responsibility. But these limits are not simply given. For, responsibility for joint production also implies the obligation to acquire knowledge about the impact of the joint products.

Individual and collective responsibility

Four categories of responsibility can be distinguished: legal, moral, political and political-ethical. Whereas every individual is responsible in the legal or moral sense, and therefore only in a limited way, collective responsibility extends to political and political-ethical responsibility. It is therefore more encompassing than individual responsibility. For instance, collective responsibility includes the obligation to specify the scope and limits of individual responsibility, for example by establishing legal and moral standards.

Concerning joint production this has the following implications. Insofar as someone acts as *homo economicus* (for example as a consumer or business representative) his responsibility for joint products is limited. It is the collective responsibility of society at large – and of its members acting in the role of *homo politicus* – to define these limits, and to bear the responsibility for all those consequences of joint production which go beyond individual responsibility.

19.3 RESPONSIBILITY AND ENVIRONMENTAL POLICY

The joint production perspective that we have developed in this book has far-reaching implications for an encompassing and long-term environmental policy.

A common understanding of environmental policy making – often labelled 'rational' – is based on the following idea. It is the task of the natural sciences to produce an adequate understanding of 'how nature works'; likewise, it is the task of the social sciences to produce an adequate understanding of 'how human society works', and – on this basis

– to develop policy instruments that effectively direct the action of individual members of society, and thus society as a whole, towards a
desired development path of the ecological-economic system. The approach is based on a specific conception of the human being, namely the
behavioural hypothesis of *homo economicus*. According to this conception, humans are utility maximisers whose behaviour is determined by
preferences and is guided by external incentives. In principle, politics
can then achieve a desired path of development by appropriately setting
incentives for human behaviour. This approach is also advocated for
achieving sustainability.

But for such an encompassing policy goal as sustainability (Section
1.1), this approach faces unsurmountable problems. For instance, this
approach can only be effective if *detailed knowledge* about *every* actual
and potential external effect is available. In other words, one requires
complete and perfect knowledge of the world. Only then can incentives
be set appropriately. However, the analysis in this book has revealed
that joint production, along with a long time horizon, *systematically* induces irreducible ignorance. As a consequence, detailed and complete
knowledge concerning the long-term effects of economic activity is systematically not available. Hence, by relying solely on this approach to
policy making it is impossible to meet the challenge of sustainability.

The abstract conception of *homo economicus* highlights that a human
being acts according to external incentives; it neglects human creativity,
free will and freedom to act. While utility maximisation is the ethical category that guides *homo economicus* with given preferences under
external incentives, responsibility is the ethical category that provides
guidance with respect to these important dimensions of human existence. When developing strategies for sustainability, politics must take
these human dimensions into account. Also, the category of responsibility constitutes a means to guide human behaviour.

What does this imply for environmental policy? Responsibility, and
the moral obligations it imposes, guide both individual and collective
action. Individual members of society – for example in their role of economic actors – have to assume *individual responsibility* for the foreseen
and foreseeable consequences of their activity. This includes an obligation to acquire knowledge. Each individual, and the economic agent in
particular, actively has to acquire the information necessary to assess
the consequences of his action.

Individual responsibility is generally limited to the foreseen and foreseeable consequences of an action. But joint production severely limits
the ability of the economic actor to foresee the consequences of his activity and, hence, the responsibility that he can assume. If responsibility

were conceived only as individual responsibility, long-term ecological-economic consequences of economic activity would systematically remain outside the realm of responsibility. This is unsatisfactory, of course, if one is interested in the preservation of the natural environment and in the imperative of sustainability.

Individual responsibility, therefore, has to be complemented by *collective responsibility*. Politics – in particular members of society adopting the role of the political actor (*homo politicus*) – are responsible in the political and, eventually, political-ethical sense. That is, they have to assume unlimited responsibility, also for the unforeseen consequences of human activity.

It is part of the collective responsibility of politics to set the limits of individual responsibility. Where exactly these limits should be, however, is far from being obvious. On the one hand, politics should encourage individual members of society to bear individual responsibility in a broad manner. On the other hand, politics should not overburden individuals with obligations, since this would paralyse individuals and society at large.

As for individuals, there is an obligation to acquire knowledge also at the collective level. The task is to systematically grasp the major lines of economic, ecological, and societal development without getting stuck in irrelevant details. The analysis in this book suggests that the concept of *joint production* – along with the concept of *stocks* – is well suited as a fundamental perspective on how environmental problems emerge and how they may be solved in a sustainable manner. It enables a systematic exploration of the side effects of economic activity and the corresponding temporal structures due to stock dynamics, which are all too often simply ignored. Such a perspective can form a basis for 'good' decisions in light of the imperative of sustainability.

Against this background, the *precautionary principle* has to become a cornerstone of responsible policy making. The precautionary principle specifies the moral obligation of political and political-ethical responsibility. It demands of the political actor the capability of *power of judgement* as a virtue. Any political actor who lives up to his political and political-ethical responsibility with regard to long-term environmental degradation must take the precautionary principle seriously.

The imperative of sustainability poses a major challenge for politics. In order to meet this demand, it has to reorder itself completely. In particular, politics must truly accept responsibility for the unforeseen consequences of human action.

References

Ackerman, F. (1997), *Why do we Recycle? Markets, Values and Public Policy*, Washington, DC: Island Press.

Ackerman, F. and K. Gallagher (2002), 'Mixed signals: market incentives, recycling, and the price spike of 1995', *Resources, Conservation and Recycling*, **35**, 275–295.

Acosta, J.J. (2001), *Physische Input-Output-Rechnung: Ansätze, Möglichkeiten und Probleme einer aktivitätsbezogenen Stoffflussrechnung auf nationaler und regionaler Ebene*, Karlsruhe: Institut für Regionalwissenschaft, Universität Karlsruhe.

Albert, M. (1996), '"Unrealistische Annahmen" und empirische Prüfung', *Zeitschrift für Wirtschafts- und Sozialwissenschaften*, **116**, 451–486.

Albrecht, H. (1991), *Kalk und Zement in Württemberg. Industriegeschichte am Südrand der Schwäbischen Alb*, Ubstadt-Weiher: Regionalkultur.

Andresen, B., P. Salomon and R.S. Berry (1984), 'Thermodynamics in finite time', *Physics Today*, **37**(9), 62–70.

Arendt, H. (1958), *The Human Condition*, Chicago and London: University of Chicago Press.

Aristotle (2000), *Nicomachean Ethics*, ed. by R. Crisp (Cambridge Texts in the History of Philosophy), Cambridge: Cambridge University Press.

Arrow, K.J. (1951a), 'An extension of the basic theorems of classical welfare economics', in J. Neyman (ed.), *Proceedings of the Second Berkeley Symposium on Mathematical Statistics and Probability*, Berkeley: University of California Press, pp. 507–532.

Arrow, K.J. (1951b), *Social Choice and Individual Values*, New York: Wiley.

Arrow, K.J. (1970), 'The organization of economic activity: Issues pertinent to the choice of market versus non-market allocation', in R.H. Haveman and J. Margolis (eds), *Public Expenditures and Policy Analysis*, Chicago: Markham, pp. 23–39.

Arrow, K.J. and G. Debreu (1954), 'Existence of an equilibrium for a competitive economy', *Econometrica*, **22**, 265–290.

Arrow, K.J. and F.H. Hahn (1971), *General Competitive Analysis*, San Francisco: Holden-Day.

Ayres, R.U. (1978), *Resources, Environment, and Economics. Applications of the Materials/Energy Balance Principle*, New York: Wiley.

Ayres, R.U. (1998), 'Eco-thermodynamics: economics and the second law', *Ecological Economics*, **26**, 189–209.

Ayres, R.U. (1999), 'The second law, the fourth law, recycling and limits to growth', *Ecological Economics*, **29**, 473–483.

Ayres, R.U. and L.W. Ayres (eds) (2002), *Handbook of Industrial Ecology*, Cheltenham, UK and Northampton, MA, USA: Edward Elgar.

Ayres, R.U., L.W. Ayres and K. Martinás (1998), 'Exergy, waste accounting, and life-cycle analysis', *Energy*, **23**, 355–363.

Ayres, R.U. and A.V. Kneese (1969), 'Production, consumption, and externalities', *American Economic Review*, **59**, 282–297.

Ayres, R.U. and K. Martinás (1995), 'Waste potential entropy: the ultimate ecotoxic?', *Economie Appliquée*, **48**, 95–120.

Ayres, R.U. and U. Simonis (1994), *Industrial Metabolism: Restructuring for Sustainable Development*, Tokyo: United Nations University Press.

Babbage, C. (1986)[1832], *On the Economy of Machinery and Manufactures*, first published 1832, New York: Augustus M. Kelley.

Baldone, S. (1980), 'Fixed capital in Sraffa's theoretical scheme', in L. Pasinetti (ed.), *Essays on the Theory of Joint Production*, London: Macmillan, pp. 88–137.

Balian, R. (1991), *From Microphysics to Macrophysics*, vol. I, Berlin, Heidelberg and New York: Springer.

Bailey, E.E. and A.F. Friedlaender (1982), 'Market structure and multiproduct industries', *Journal of Economic Literature*, **20**, 1024–1048.

Barro, R.J. and X. Sala-i-Martin (1995), *Economic Growth*, New York: McGraw-Hill.

Baumgärtner, S. (2000), *Ambivalent Joint Production and the Natural Environment. An Economic and Thermodynamic Analysis*, Heidelberg and New York: Physica.

Baumgärtner, S. (2001), 'Heinrich von Stackelberg on joint production', *European Journal of the History of Economic Thought*, **8**(4), 509–525.

Baumgärtner, S. (2004a), 'Price ambivalence of secondary resources: Joint production, limits to substitution, and costly disposal', *Resources, Conservation and Recycling*, **43**(1), 95–117.

Baumgärtner, S. (2004b), 'Thermodynamic models: rationale, concepts, and caveats', in J. Proops and P. Safonov (eds), *Modelling in Ecological Economics*, Cheltenham, UK and Northampton, MA, USA: Edward Elgar, pp. 102–129.

Baumgärtner, S. (2005), 'Temporal and thermodynamic irreversibility in production theory', *Economic Theory*, **26**(3), 725–728.

Baumgärtner, S. and J. de Swaan Arons (2003), 'Necessity and inefficiency in the generation of waste. A thermodynamic analysis', *Journal of Industrial Ecology*, **7**(2), 113–123.

Baumgärtner, S., H. Dyckhoff, M. Faber, J.L.R. Proops and J. Schiller (2001), 'The concept of joint production and ecological economics', *Ecological Economics*, **36**(3), 365–372.

Baumgärtner, S., M. Faber and J.L.R. Proops (1996), 'The use of the entropy concept in ecological economics', in M. Faber, R. Manstetten and J.L.R. Proops, *Ecological Economics. Concepts and Methods*, Cheltenham, UK and Brookfield, USA: Edward Elgar, pp. 115–135.

Baumgärtner, S., M. Faber and J. Proops (2002), 'How environmental concern influences the investment decision. An application of capital theory', *Ecological Economics*, **40**(1), 1–12.

Baumgärtner, S. and F. Jöst (2000), 'Joint production, externalities, and the regulation of production networks', *Environmental and Resource Economics*, **16**(2), 229–251.

Baumgärtner, S. and J. Schiller (2001), 'Kuppelproduktion. Ein Konzept zur Beschreibung der Entstehung von Umweltproblemen', in F. Beckenbach, U. Hampicke, C. Leipert, G. Meran, J. Minsch, H.G. Nutzinger, R. Pfriem, J. Weimann, F. Wirl and U. Witt (eds), *Jahrbuch Ökologische Ökonomik, Band 2: Ökonomische Naturbewertung*, Marburg: Metropolis, pp. 353–393.

Baumgärtner, S. and R. Winkler (2003), 'Markets, technology and environmental regulation: price ambivalence of waste paper in Germany', *Ecological Economics*, **47**(2–3), 183–195.

Baumol, W.J. (1977), 'On the proper cost tests for natural monopoly in a multiproduct industry', *American Economic Review*, **67**, 809–822.

Baumol, W.J. and D.F. Bradford (1972), 'Detrimental externalities and non-convexity of the production set', *Economica*, **24**, 160–176.

Baumol, W.J. and W.E. Oates (1988), *The Theory of Environmental Policy*, 2nd edn., Cambridge: Cambridge University Press.

Baumol, W.J., J.C. Panzar and R.D. Willig (1988), *Contestable Markets and the Theory of Industry Structure*, rev. edn., San Diego: Harcourt Brace Jovanovich.

BDZ (1975), *Zement. Zahlen und Daten 74/75*, Köln: Bundesverband der Deutschen Zementindustrie e.V.

BDZ (1998), *Zahlen und Daten 97/96*, Köln: Bundesverband der Deutschen Zementindustrie e.V.

BDZ (2001), *Zahlen und Daten 2000/2001*, Köln: Bundesverband der Deutschen Zementindustrie e.V.

Beck, U. (1992), *Risk Society. Towards a New Modernity*, London: Sage.

Beckenstein, A.R. (1975), 'Scale economies in the multiplant firm: theory and empirical evidence', *Bell Journal of Economics*, **6**, 644–657.

Becker, G. and R. Michael (1973), 'On the new theory of consumer behavior', *Swedish Journal of Economics*, **75**, 378–395.

Behrens, F. and O. von Maydell (1997), *Analyse der Kostenstruktur der kommunalen Abfallentsorgung*, Berlin: Umweltbundesamt.

Bejan, A. (1996), *Entropy Generation Minimization*, Boca Raton: CRC.

Bejan, A. (1997), *Advanced Engineering Thermodynamics*, 2nd edn., New York: Wiley.

Bejan, A., G. Tsatsaronis and M. Moran (1996), *Thermal Design and Optimization*, New York: Wiley.

Berglund, C., P. Söderholm and M. Nilsson (2002), 'A note on inter-country differences in waste paper recovery and utilization', *Resources, Conservation and Recycling*, **34**, 175–191.

Bergstrom, T.C. (1976), 'How to discard free disposability – at no cost', *Journal of Mathematical Economics*, **3**, 131–134.

Bhaskar, R. (1978), *A Realist Theory of Science*, Brighton: Harvester.

Bhaskar, R. (1979), *The Possibility of Naturalism*, Brighton: Harvester.

Bidard, C. (1984), 'Choix de techniques en production jointe', in C. Bidard (ed.), *La Production Jointe: Nouveaux Débats*, Paris: Economica, pp. 186–207.

Bidard, C. (1990), 'Choice of techniques in joint production', in N. Salvadori and I. Steedman (eds), *Joint Production of Commodities*, Aldershot, UK and Brookfield, USA: Edward Elgar, pp. 198–214.

BIR and CEPI (eds) (1999), *European List of Standard Grades of Recovered Paper and Board*, Bureau of International Recycling and Confederation of European Paper Industries, Brussels.

Bisson, K. and J. Proops (eds) (2002), *Waste in Ecological Economics*, Cheltenham, UK and Northampton, MA, USA: Edward Elgar.

Blaug, M. (1976) 'Kuhn versus Lakatos *or* paradigms versus research programmes in the history of economics', in S. Latsis (ed.), *Method and Appraisal in Economics*, Cambridge: Cambridge University Press, pp. 149–180.

Blaug, M. (1996), *Economic Theory in Retrospect*, 5th edn., Cambridge: Cambridge University Press.

Blaug, M. (1997), 'Ugly currents in modern economics', *Policy Options*, **17**(7), 2–5.

Blaug, M. (1998), 'The disease of formalism in economics, or bad games that economists play', *Lectiones Jenenses*, **16**.

Bliss, C. (1975), *Capital Theory and the Distribution of Income*, Amsterdam: North-Holland.

Bliss, C., A.J. Cohen and G.C. Harcourt (eds) (2005), *Capital Theory*, Cheltenham, UK and Northampton, MA, USA: Edward Elgar.

Bloch, E. (1959), *Das Prinzip Hoffnung*, Frankfurt: Suhrkamp.

[BMELF] Bundesminister für Ernährung, Landwirtschaft und Forsten (ed.) (1991), *Waldzustandsbericht des Bundes. Ergebnisse der Waldschadenserhebung 1991*, Bonn.

[BMELF] Bundesminister für Ernährung, Landwirtschaft und Forsten (ed.) (1992), *Waldzustandsbericht des Bundes. Ergebnisse der Waldschadenserhebung 1992*, Bonn.

Böcking, B. (2000), Telephone interview with Mr Böcking, Executive Director, GesPaRec (Society for Paper Recycling), Bonn, March 2 and April 6, 2000.

Bodansky, D. (1991), 'Scientific uncertainty and the precautionary principle', *Environment*, **33**(7), 4–5 and 43–44.

Boulding, K.E. (1966), 'The economics of the coming spaceship Earth', in H. Jarrett (ed.), *Environmental Quality in a Growing Economy*, Baltimore and London: Johns Hopkins University Press, pp. 3–14.

Boulding, K.E. (1981), *Evolutionary Economics*, Beverly Hills: Sage.

Brägelmann, J. (1991), *Kuppelproduktion und Technikwechsel*, Marburg: Metropolis.

Braun, T. (2000), Telephone interview with Mr Braun, Vice Executive Director, BVSE (German Association for Secondary Raw Materials and Waste Disposal), Bonn, February 7 and March 23, 2000.

Brodyansky, V.M., M.V. Sorin, and P. Le Goff (eds) (1994), *The Efficiency of Industrial Processes: Exergy Analysis and Optimization*, Amsterdam: Elsevier.

Buchanan, J.M. (1966), 'Joint supply, externality and optimality', *Economica*, **33**, 405–415

Burmeister, E. (1980), *Capital Theory and Dynamics*, Cambridge, UK: Cambridge University Press.

BVSE (2000), Statistical data provided on telephone request by BVSE (German Association for Secondary Raw Materials and Waste Disposal), Bonn.

BVSE (ed.) (2001), *Zahlen, Daten, Fakten 2000/2001*, Bonn: BVSE (German Association for Secondary Raw Materials and Waste Disposal).

Byström, S. and L. Lönnstedt (1995), 'Waste paper usage and fiber flow in Western Europe', *Resources, Conservation and Recycling*, **15**, 111–121.

Byström, S. and L. Lönnstedt (1997), 'Paper recycling: environmental and economic impact', *Resources, Conservation and Recycling*, **21**, 109–127.

Callen, H.B. (1985), *Thermodynamics and an Introduction to Thermostatics*, 2nd edn., New York: Wiley.

Cassel, G. (1967)[1918], *Theoretische Sozialökonomie*, first published 1918, Leipzig: Winter.

Caves, D.W., L.R. Christensen and M.W. Tretheway (1980), 'Flexible cost functions for multiproduct firms', *Review of Economics and Statistics*, **62**, 477–481.

[CDA] Cambridge Decision Analysts/Environmental Resources Limited (CDA) (1988), *Acid Rain and Photochemical Oxidants Control Policies in the European Community*, Woodfolds Oaksey: Leopard.

Chambers, R.G. (1988), *Applied Production Analysis. A Dual Approach*, Cambridge: Cambridge University Press.

Champsaur, P., J. Roberts and R. Rosenthal (1975), 'Cores in economies with public goods', *International Economic Review*, **16**, 751–764.

City of San Francisco, Department of the Environment (2003), 'The precautionary principle and the City and County of San Francisco', *White Paper*, San Francisco.

Christensen, P.P. (1989), 'Historical roots for ecological economics. Biophysical versus allocative approaches', *Ecological Economics*, **1**, 17–36.

Cleveland, C.J. and M. Ruth (1997), 'When, where and by how much does thermodynamics constrain economic processes? A survey of Nicholas Georgescu-Roegen's contribution to ecological economics', *Ecological Economics*, **22**, 203–223.

Clower, R. (1995), 'Axiomatics in economics', *Southern Economic Journal*, **62**(2), 307–319.

Coase, R.H. (1960), 'The problem of social cost', *Journal of Law and Economics*, **3**, 1–44.

Connelly, L. and K.P. Koshland (2001), 'Exergy and industrial ecology', *Exergy – An International Journal*, **1**, 146–165 and 234–255.

Cornelissen, R.L. and G.G. Hirs (1999), 'Exergy analysis in the process industry', in A. Bejan and E. Mamut (eds), *Thermodynamic Optimization of Complex Energy Systems*, Dordrecht: Kluwer.

Cornelissen, R.L., P.A. Nimwegen and G.G. Hirs (2000), 'Exergetic Life-Cycle Analysis', in *Proceedings of ECOS 2000*, Enschede.

Cornes, R. and T. Sandler (1984), 'Easy riders, joint production, and public goods', *The Economic Journal*, **94**, 580–598.

Costanza, R. (ed.) (1991), *Ecological Economics. The Science and Management of Sustainability*, New York: Columbia University Press.

Creyts, J.C. (2000), *Use of Extended Exergy Analysis as a Tool to Optimize the Environmental Performance of Industrial Processes*, PhD Thesis, Berkeley: University of California, Department of Mechanical Engineering.

Daly, H.E. (1977), *Steady State Economics: The Economics of Biophysical Equilibrium and Moral Growth*, San Francisco: Freeman.

Dasgupta, P. and G. Heal (1979), *Economic Theory and Exhaustible Resources*, Cambridge: Cambridge University Press.

David, P.A. (1985), 'Clio and the Economics of QWERTY', *American Economic Review*, **75**, 332–337.

Debreu, G. (1951), 'The coefficient of resource utilization', *Econometrica*, **19**, 273–292.

Debreu, G. (1959), *Theory of Value. An Axiomatic Analysis of Economic Equilibrium*, New York: Wiley.

Debreu, G. (1962), 'New concepts and techniques for equilibrium analysis', *International Economic Review*, **3**, 257–273.

Debreu, G. (1983), *Mathematical Economics. Twenty Papers of Gérard Debreu*, Cambridge: Cambridge University Press.

de Swaan Arons, J. and H.J. van der Kooi (2001), 'Towards a metabolic society: a thermodynamic view', *Green Chemistry*, **3**(4), G53–G55.

de Swaan Arons, J., H.J. van der Kooi and K. Sankaranarayanan (2004), *Efficiency and Sustainability in the Energy and Chemical Industries*, New York: Dekker.

Dewulf, J., J.M. Mulder, M.M.D. van den Berg, H. Van Langenhove, H.J. van der Kooi and J. de Swaan Arons (2000), 'Illustrations towards quantifying the sustainability of technology', *Green Chemistry*, **2**(3), 108–114.

Diehl, M., D.B. Leineweber and A.A.S. Schäfer (2001), 'MUSCOD-II users' manual', *Preprint 2001-25*, Interdisciplinary Center for Scientific Computing, University of Heidelberg.

Dorfman, R., P. Samuelson and R. Solow (1957), *Linear Programming and Economic Analysis*, New York: McGraw-Hill.

Dorman, P. (2005), 'Evolving knowledge and the precautionary principle', *Ecological Economics*, **53**, 169–176.

Downing, P.B. and L.J. White (1986), 'Innovation in pollution control', *Journal of Environmental Economics and Management*, **13**, 18–29.

Downs, A. (1967), *Inside Bureaucracy*, Boston: Waveland.

Duménil, G. and D. Lévy (1984), 'The unifying formalism of domination: value, price, distribution and growth in joint production', *Zeitschrift für Nationalökonomie*, **44**, 349–371.

Dyckhoff, H. (1994), *Betriebliche Produktion. Theoretische Grundlagen einer umweltorientierten Produktionswirtschaft*, 2nd edn., Berlin, Heidelberg and New York: Springer.

Dyckhoff, H. (1996a), 'Kuppelproduktion und Umwelt: Zur Bedeutung eines in der Ökonomik vernachlässigten Phänomens für die Kreislaufwirtschaft', *Zeitschrift für angewandte Umweltforschung*, **9**, 173–187.

Dyckhoff, H. (1996b), 'Produktion und Reduktion', in W. Kern, H.H. Schröder and J. Weber (eds), *Handwörterbuch der Produktionswirtschaft*, 2nd edn., Stuttgart: Schäffer-Poeschl, pp. 1458–1468.

Dyckhoff, H., A. Oenning and C. Rüdiger (1997), 'Grundlagen des Stoffstrommanagement bei Kuppelproduktion', *Zeitschrift für Betriebswirtschaft*, **67**, 1139–1165.

Eatwell, J. (1977), 'The irrelevance of returns to scale in Sraffa's analysis', *Journal of Economic Literature*, **15**, 61–67.

Edgeworth, F.Y. (1925a)[1911], 'Contributions to the theory of railway rates', *The Economic Journal*, **XXI**, 346–370 and *The Economic Journal*, **XXI**, 551–571, reprinted as 'The laws of increasing and diminishing returns', in *Papers Relating to Political Economy*, vol. I (1925), London: Macmillan, pp. 61–99.

Edgeworth, F.Y. (1925b)[1915], 'Recent contributions to mathematical economics', *The Economic Journal*, **XXV**, 36–63 and *The Economic Journal*, **XXV**, 189–203, reprinted as 'On some theories due to Pareto, Zawadski, W.E. Johnson and others', in *Papers Relating to Political Economy*, vol. II (1925), London: Macmillan, pp. 450–491.

Ekelund Jr, R.B. and J. Thompson (2001), 'Joint supply and the development of economic theory: a historical perspective', *History of Political Economy*, **33**(3), 577–608.

Eucken, W. (1948), 'Heinrich von Stackelberg – Obituary', *The Economic Journal*, **58**, 132–135.

[ESA-EFMA] European Sulphuric Acid Association (ESA) and European Fertilizer Manufacturer Association (EFMA) (1999), *Best Available Techniques Reference Document on the Production of Sulphuric Acid*, Brussels.

Faber, M. (1979), *Introduction to Modern Austrian Capital Theory*, Berlin, Heidelberg and New York: Springer.

Faber, M. (1985), 'A biophysical approach to the economy: entropy, environment and resources', in W. van Gool and J.J.C. Bruggink (eds), *Energy and Time in the Economic and Physical Sciences*, Amsterdam: North-Holland, pp. 315–337.

Faber, M. (1986a), 'Relationships between modern Austrian and Sraffa's capital theory', in M. Faber (ed.), *Studies in Austrian Capital Theory, Investment and Time*, Berlin, Heidelberg and New York: Springer, pp. 44–59.

Faber, M. (ed.) (1986b), *Studies in Austrian Capital Theory, Investment and Time*, Berlin, Heidelberg and New York: Springer.

Faber, M., K. Frank, B. Klauer, R. Manstetten, J. Schiller and C. Wissel (2005), 'On the foundation of a general theory of stocks', *Ecological Economics*, **55**(2), 155–172.

Faber, M., F. Jöst, R. Manstetten and G. Müller-Fürstenberger (1996a), 'Kuppelproduktion und Umweltpolitik: Eine Fallstudie zur Chlorchemie und zur Schwefelsäureindustrie', *Journal für praktische Chemie (Chemikerzeitung)*, **338**, 497–505.

Faber, M., F. Jöst, R. Manstetten, G. Müller-Fürstenberger and J.L.R. Proops (1996b), 'Linking ecology and economy: joint production in the chemical industry', in M. Faber, R. Manstetten and J.L.R. Proops, *Ecological Economics. Concepts and Methods*, Cheltenham, UK and Brookfield, USA: Edward Elgar, pp. 263–278.

Faber, M., R. Manstetten and T. Petersen (1997): 'Homo politicus and homo oeconomicus. Political economy, constitutional interest and ecological interest', *Kyklos*, **50**, 457–483.

Faber, M., R. Manstetten and J.L.R. Proops (1992), 'Humankind and the environment: An anatomy of surprise and ignorance', *Environmental Values*, **1**(3), 217–242.

Faber, M., R. Manstetten and J.L.R. Proops (1996c), *Ecological Economics. Concepts and Methods*, Cheltenham, UK and Brookfield, USA: Edward Elgar.

Faber, M., H. Niemes and G. Stephan (1995)[1983], *Entropie, Umweltschutz und Rohstoffverbrauch: Eine naturwissenschaftlich ökonomische Untersuchung*, Berlin, Heidelberg and New York: Spinger, English translation as: *Entropy, Environment and Resources: An Essay in Physico-Economics*, 2nd edn. 1995, Berlin, Heidelberg and New York: Springer.

Faber, M., T. Petersen and J. Schiller (2002), 'Homo oeconomicus and homo politicus in ecological economics', *Ecological Economics*, **40**, 323–333.

Faber, M. and J.L.R. Proops (1991), 'The innovation of techniques and the time horizon: A neo-Austrian approach', *Structural Change and Economic Dynamics*, **2**, 143–158.

Faber, M. and J.L.R. Proops (1996), 'Economic action and the environment: problems of time and predictability', in T.S. Driver and G.P. Chapman (eds), *Time-Scales & Environmental Change*, London: Routledge, pp. 196–217.

Faber, M. and J. Proops (1998), *Evolution, Time, Production and the Environment*, 3rd edn., Berlin, Heidelberg and New York: Springer.

Faber, M., J.L.R. Proops and S. Baumgärtner (1998), 'All production is joint production. A thermodynamic analysis', in S. Faucheux, J. Gowdy and I. Nicolaï (eds), *Sustainability and Firms. Technological Change and the Changing Regulatory Environment*, Cheltenham, UK and Northampton, MA, USA: Edward Elgar, pp. 131–158.

Faber, M., J.L.R. Proops and S. Speck, with F. Jöst (1999), *Capital and Time in Ecological Economics. Neo-Austrian Modelling*, Cheltenham, UK and Northampton, MA, USA: Edward Elgar.

Fandel, G. (1994), *Produktion I: Produktions- und Kostentheorie*, 4th edn., Berlin, Heidelberg and New York: Springer.

Fang, J. (1970), *Bourbaki. Towards a Philosophy of Modern Mathematics*, Hauppauge, NY: Paideia Press.

Fanno, M. (1999)[1914], *A Contribution to the Theory of Supply at Joint Cost*, with forewords by L. Punzo and M. Morishima, London: Macmillan, 1999, first published as *Contributo alla Teoria dell' Offerta a Costi Congiunti*, supplement to *Giornale degli Economisti*.

Färe, R. (1988), *Fundamentals of Production Theory*, Berlin, Heidelberg and New York: Springer.

Färe, R., S. Grosskopf and C.A.K. Lovell (1994), *Production Frontiers*, Cambridge: Cambridge University Press.

Färe, R. and D. Primont (1995), *Multi-Output Production and Duality: Theory and Applications*, Dordrecht: Kluwer.

Filippini, C. (1977), 'Positività dei prezzi e produzione congiunta', *Giornale degli Economisti e Annali di Economia*, **36**, 91–99.

Filippini, C. and L. Filippini (1982), 'Two theorems on joint production', *Economic Journal*, **92**, 386–390.

Fisher, I. (1892), *Mathematical Investigations in the Theory of Value and Prices*, New Haven: Yale University Press.

Fisher, I. (1965)[1906], *The Nature of Capital and Income*, first published 1906, New York: Augustus M. Kelley.

Foley, D. (1970), 'Lindahl's solution and the core of an economy with public goods', *Econometrica*, **38**, 66–72.

Foot, P. (1994), 'The problem of abortion and the doctrine of the double effect', in B. Steinbock and A. Norcross (eds), *Killing and Letting Die*, 2nd edn., New York: Fordham University Press.

Frank, K. (2005), 'Metapopulation persistence in heterogeneous landscapes: lessons about the effect of stochasticity', *The American Naturalist*, **165**, 374–388.

Franke, R. (1986), 'Some problems concerning the notion of cost-minimizing systems in the framework of joint production', *The Manchester School*, **52**, 298–307.

Freeman, A.M. (2003), *The Measurement of Environmental and Resource Values. Theory and Measurement*, 2nd edn., Washington, DC: Resources for the Future.

Friedman, M. (1953), 'The methodology of positive economics', in M. Friedman, *Essays in Positive Economics*, Chicago: University of Chicago Press, pp. 3–43.

Friedrich, H. (2000), Telephone interview with Mr Friedrich, former Executive Director, Erich Böhm GmbH & Co. KG, Hochheim, February 16, 2000.

Frisch, R. (1965), *Theory of Production*, Dordrecht: Reidel.

Funk, M. (1990), *Industrielle Energieversorgung als betriebswirtschaftliches Planungsproblem*, Heidelberg and New York: Physica.

Georgescu-Roegen, N. (1971), *The Entropy Law and the Economic Process*, Cambridge: Harvard University Press.

Georgescu-Roegen, N. (1975), 'Energy and economic myths', *Southern Economic Journal*, **41**, 347–381.

Gollier, C. and N. Treich (2003), 'Decision-making under scientific uncertainty: the economics of the Precautionary Principle', *Journal of Risk and Uncertainty*, **27**, 77–103.

Gossen, H.H. (1854), *Entwicklung der Gesetze des menschlichen Verkehrs und der daraus fließenden Regeln für menschliches Handeln*, Braunschweig: Viehweg.

Göttsching, L. (1993), 'Steigerung des Altpapiereinsatzes unter dem Einfluss von gesetzlichen Maßnahmen in Deutschland', *Wochenblatt für Papierfabrikation*, **121**, 149–156.

356   *Joint Production and Responsibility in Ecological Economics*

Göttsching, L. (1998), 'Altpapier im Wettbewerb mit Primärfaserstoffen', *Das Papier*, **52**, V68–V71.

Graham, J.D. (2000), 'Perspectives on the precautionary principle', *Human and Ecological Risk Assessment*, **6**(3), 383–385.

Gray, L.C. (1913), 'The economic possibilities of conservation', *Quarterly Journal of Economics*, **27**, 497–519.

Gray, L.C. (1914), 'Rent under the assumption of exhaustibility', *Quarterly Journal of Economics*, **28**, 466–489.

Grimm, V. and C. Wissel (1997), 'Babel, or the ecological stability discussions: An inventory and analysis of terminology and a guide for avoiding confusion', *Oecologia*, **109**, 323–334.

Grimm, V. and C. Wissel (2004), 'The intrinsic mean time to extinction: a unifying approach to analyzing persistence and viability of populations', *Oikos*, **105**, 501–511.

Grünewald, H. (1992), 'Altpapierentsorgung aus der Sicht der GesPaRec: künftige Auswirkungen auf den Altpapiermarkt', *Allgemeine Papier-Rundschau*, **116**, 1320–1325.

Haber, L.F. (1958), *The Chemical Industry during the Nineteenth Century. A Study of the Economic Aspect of Applied Chemistry in Europe and North America*, Oxford: Clarendon.

Hands, D.W. (1985), 'The structuralist view of economic theories: the case of general equilibrium in particular', *Economics and Philosophy*, **1**, 303–335.

Hanley, N., J.F. Shogren and B. White (1997), *Environmental Economics in Theory and Practice*, London: Macmillan.

Hanley, N. and R. Slark (1994), 'Cost-benefit analysis of paper recycling: a case study and some general principles', *Journal of Environmental Planning and Management*, **37**, 189–197.

Hanley, N. and C.L. Spash (1993), *Cost-Benefit Analysis and the Environment*, Aldershot, UK and Brookfield, USA: Edward Elgar.

Hardy, C. and T.E. Graedel (2002), 'Industrial ecosystems as foodwebs', *Journal of Industrial Ecology*, **6**(1), 29–38.

Harremoës, P. (ed.) (2002), *The Precautionary Principle in the 20th Century: Late Lessons from Early Warnings*, London: Earthscan.

Harsanyi, J. (1955), 'Cardinal welfare, individualistic ethics, and interpersonal comparisons of utility', *Journal of Political Economy*, **63**, 309–321

Hart, O.D. and H.W. Kuhn (1975), 'A proof of the existence of equilibrium without the free disposal assumption', *Journal of Mathematical Economics*, **2**, 335–344.

Hartewick, J. and N. Olewiler (1998), *The Economics of Natural Resource Use*, Boston: Addison-Wesley.

Hasenkamp, G. (1976), 'A study of multiple-output production functions: Klein's railroad study revisited', *Journal of Econometrics*, **4**, 253–262.

Hausman, D.M. (1994), *The Philosophy of Economics. An Anthology*, 2nd edn., Cambridge: Cambridge University Press.

Hegel, G.W. (1970)[1821], *Grundlinien der Philosophie des Rechts oder Naturrecht und Staatswissenschaft im Grundrisse*, Frankfurt: Suhrkamp.

Heidbrink, L. (2003), *Kritik der Verantwortung. Zu den Grenzen verantwortlichen Handelns in komplexen Kontexten*, Weilerswist: Velbrück.

Heintz, A. and G.A. Reinhardt (1996), *Chemie und Umwelt*, 4th rev. edn., Braunschweig: Viehweg.

Hekkert, M., R. van den Broek and A. Faaij (1999), 'Energy crops versus waste paper: A system comparison of paper recycling and paper incineration on the basis of equal land-use', Paper presented at 4th Biomass Conference of the Americas, Oakland, CA, USA.

Hennings, K.H. (1996), *The Austrian Theory of Value and Capital. Studies in the Life and Work of Eugen von Böhm-Bawerk*, Cheltenham, UK and Brookfield, USA: Edward Elgar.

Hicks, J.R. (1935), 'Annual survey of economic theory: the theory of monopoly', *Econometrica*, **3**, 1–20.

Hicks, J.R. (1946)[1939], *Value and Capital. An Inquiry into Some Fundamental Principles of Economic Theory*, 1st edn. 1939, 2nd edn., Oxford: Clarendon.

Hicks, J.R. (1973), *Capital and Time: A Neo-Austrian Theory*, Oxford: Clarendon.

Hinderink, A.P., H.J. van der Kooi, and J. de Swaan Arons (1999), 'On the efficiency and sustainability of the process industry', *Green Chemistry*, **1**(6), G176–G180.

Hinrichsen, D. and U. Krause (1981), 'A substitution theorem for joint production models with disposal processes', *Operations Research Verfahren*, **41**, 287–291.

Hirche, W. (1997), 'Nachhaltige Entwicklung im Bereich der Kreislaufwirtschaft', *Das Papier*, **51**, 388–392.

Hobbes, T. (1973), *Leviathan*, London, Melbourne and Toronto: Everyman's Library.

Holzey, G. (1993), 'Das duale System und seine Auswirkungen', *Das Papier*, **47**, 337–344.

Holzey, G. and D. Pothmann (1993), 'Die Position der deutschen Papierindustrie zur Kreislauf- und Abfallwirtschaft', *Das Papier*, **47**, V102–V107.

Hordijk, L., R. Shaw and J. Alcamo (1990), 'Background to acidification in Europe', in J. Alcamo, L. Hordijk and R. Shaw (eds), *The RAINS Model of Acidification: Science and Strategies in Europe*, Dordrecht: Kluwer, pp. 31–60.

Horkheimer, M. and T.W. Adorno (1968), *Dialektik der Aufklärung*, Amsterdam: de Munter.

Hotelling, H. (1931), 'The economics of exhaustible resources', *Journal of Political Economy*, **39**, 137–175.

Hume, D. (1978), *A Treatise of Human Nature*, 2nd edn. with text rev. by P.H. Nidditch, Oxford: Clarendon.

Hutchison, T. (2000), *On the Methodology of Economics and the Formalist Revolution*, Cheltenham, UK and Northampton, MA, USA: Edward Elgar.

Immordino, G. (2003), 'Looking for a guide to protect the environment: the development of the precautionary principle', *Journal of Economic Surveys*, **17**, 629–643.

[IPCC] Intergovernmental Panel on Climate Change (1996), *Climate Change 1995. The Science of Climate Change – Contribution of Working Group I to the Second Assessment Report of the IPCC*, Cambridge: Cambridge University Press.

[IW] Institut der deutschen Wirtschaft Köln (ed.) (1997), *Zahlen zur wirtschaftlichen Entwicklung der Bundesrepublik Deutschland*, Köln: Deutscher Instituts-Verlag.

Jacob, K. (1999), 'Ökologische Modernisierung und Strukturwandel in der Chemischen Industrie: Der Fall Chlorchemie', *Forschungsstelle für Umweltpolitik (FFU)-Report*, 99–2, Berlin: Freie Universität

Janik, A. and S. Toulmin (1973), *Wittgenstein's Vienna*, New York: Simon & Schuster.

Jevons, W.S. (1865), *The Coal Question: An Inquiry Concerning the Progress of the Nation, and the Probable Exhaustion of our Coal-Mines*, London: Macmillan.

Jevons, W.S. (1911)[1879], *The Theory of Political Economy*, first published 1871, 2nd enlarged edn. 1879, 4th edn., London: Macmillan.

Jonas, H. (1979), *Das Prinzip Verantwortung. Versuch einer Ethik für die technologische Zivilisation*, Frankfurt: Suhrkamp. English translation: *The Imperative of Responsibility: In Search of an Ethics for the Technological Age*, Chicago: Chicago University Press, 1984.

Jung, C., K. Krutilla and R. Boyd (1996), 'Incentives for advanced pollution abatement technology at the industry level: an evaluation of policy alternatives', *Journal of Environmental Economics and Management*, **30**, 95–111.

Kant, I. (1996a)[1785], 'Groundwork of the metaphysics of morals', in *Practical Philosophy*, The Cambridge Edition of the Works of Immanuel Kant, Cambridge: Cambridge University Press, pp. 41–108.

Kant, I. (1996b)[1797], 'On a supposed right to lie from philanthropy', in *Practical Philosophy*, The Cambridge Edition of the Works of Immanuel Kant, Cambridge: Cambridge University Press, pp. 609–615.

Kant, I. (2000)[1790], *Critique of the Power of Judgement*, The Cambridge Edition of the Works of Immanuel Kant, Cambridge: Cambridge University Press.

Kakutani, S. (1941), 'A generalization of Brouwer's fixed-point theorem', *Duke Mathematical Journal*, **8**, 457–459.

Keeler, E., M. Spence and R. Zeckhauser (1971), 'The optimal control of pollution', *Journal of Economic Theory*, **4**, 19–34.

Keil, F. (1971), *Zement. Herstellung und Eigenschaften*, Berlin, Heidelberg and New York: Springer.

Kemp, R. (1997), *Environmental Policy and Technical Change. A Comparison of the Technological Impact of Policy Instruments*, Cheltenham, UK and Lyme, USA: Edward Elgar.

Keohane, R.O. (1986), *Neorealism and its Critics*, New York: Columbia University Press.

Kibat, K.-D. (1991), 'Altpapiereinsatz in der Papierindustrie. Ein Beitrag zur Lösung abfallwirtschaftlicher Probleme', *Wochenblatt für Papierfabrikation*, **119**, 941–945.

Kibat, K.-D. (1998), 'Altpapiereinsatz im Spektrum der europäischen Abfallpolitik', *Wochenblatt für Papierfabrikation*, **126**, 742–748.

Kibat, K.-D. and S. Meißner (1994), 'Aktuelle Gesetzgebung zur Kreislaufwirtschaft', *Das Papier*, **48**, V45–V51.

Klaassen, G. (1996), *Acid Rain and Environmental Degradation. The Economics of Emission Trading*, Cheltenham, UK and Brookfield, USA: Edward Elgar.

Knight, F. (1921), *Risk, Uncertainty and Profit*, Boston: Houghton Mifflin.

Knox, T.M. (1952), *Hegel's Philosophy of Right*, Oxford: Oxford University Press.

Kohn, R.E. (1975), *Air Pollution Control. A Welfare Economic Interpretation*, Lexington, MA: Heath.

Kolstad, C.D. (2000), *Environmental Economics*, New York: Oxford University Press.

Kondepudi, D. and I. Prigogine (1998), *Modern Thermodynamics. From Heat Engines to Dissipative Structures*, New York: Wiley.

Koopmans, T.C. (1951), 'Analysis of production as an efficient combination of activities', in T.C. Koopmans (ed.), *Activity Analysis of Production and Allocation*, New York: Wiley, pp. 33–97.

Koopmans, T.C. (1964), 'Economic Growth at a Maximal Rate', *Quarterly Journal of Economics*, **78**, 355–394.

Krauthauf, E. and H. Wiese (1998), 'Die Entwicklung der Rezyklierbarkeit von grafischem Altpapier', *Wochenblatt für Papierproduktion*, **126**, 839–845.

Krelle, W. (1969), *Preistheorie I: Produktionstheorie*, 2nd edn., Tübingen: Mohr.

Kuchling, H. (1988), *Taschenbuch der Physik*, Thun and Frankfurt/Main: Harri Deutsch.

Kümmel, R. (1989), 'Energy as a factor of production and entropy as a pollutian indicator in macroeconomic modelling', *Ecological Economics*, **1**, 161–180.

Kümmel, R. and U. Schüssler (1991), 'Heat equivalents of noxious substances: a pollution indicator for environmental accounting', *Ecological Economics*, **3**, 139–156.

Kurz, H.D. (1986), 'Classical and early neoclasical economists on joint production', *Metroeconomica*, **38**, 1–37.

Kurz, H.D. (1996), 'Piero Sraffa. Asket im Cambridge Circus', in N. Piper (ed.), *Die großen Ökonomen*, Stuttgart: Schäffer-Poeschel.

Kurz, H.D. and N. Salvadori (1993), 'Von Neumann's growth model and the "classical tradition"', *European Journal for the History of Economic Thought*, **1**, 129–160.

Kurz, H.D. and N. Salvadori (1995), *Theory of Production. A Long-Period Analysis*, Cambridge, UK: Cambridge University Press.

Lager, C. (2001), 'Joint production with restricted free disposal', *Metroeconomica*, **52**, 49–87.

Lakatos, I. (1970), 'Falsification and the methodology of scientific research programmes', in I. Lakatos and A. Musgrave (eds), *Criticism and the Growth of Knowledge*, Cambridge: Cambridge University Press.

Landau, R. (1998), 'The process of innovation in the chemical industry', in A. Arora, R. Landau and N. Rosenberg (eds), *Chemicals and Long-term Economic Growth. Insights from the Chemical Industry*, New York: Wiley.

Lawson, T. (1989), 'Abstraction, tendencies and stylised facts: a realist approach to economic analysis', *Cambridge Journal of Economics*, **13**, 59–78.

Lawson, T. (1997), *Economics and Reality*, London and New York: Routledge.

Leach, M.A., A. Bauen and N.J.D. Lucas (1997), 'A systems approach to material flows in sustainable cities: a case study of paper', *Journal of Environmental Planning and Management*, **40**, 705–723.

Leineweber, D.B., I. Bauer, H.G. Bock and J.P. Schlöder (2003), 'An efficient multiple shooting based reduced SQP strategy for large-scale dynamic process optimization. Part I: Theoretical aspects', *Computers & Chemical Engineering*, **27**, 157–166.

Leonard, R.J. (1995), 'From parlor games to social science: von Neumann, Morgenstern, and the creation of game theory', *Journal of Economic Literature*, **23**, 730–761.

Leplin, J. (ed.) (1984), *Scientific Realism*, Berkeley: University of California Press.

Lévy, D. (1984), 'Le formalisme unificateur du surclassement: valeur, prix, répartition et croissance en production jointe', in C. Bidard (ed.), *La Production Jointe: Nouveaux Débats*, Paris: Economica, pp. 37–51.

Lichtenthaler, H. and C. Buschmann (1984), *Das Waldsterben aus botanischer Sicht*, Karlsruhe: Braun.

Lieb, C.M. (2001), *Possible Causes of the Environmental Kuznets Curve. A Theoretical Analysis*, Dissertation, Department of Economics, University of Heidelberg.

Lind, H. (1992), 'A case study of normal research in theoretical economics', *Economics and Philosophy*, **8**, 83–102.

Lindahl, E. (1919), *Die Gerechtigkeit der Besteuerung*, Lund: Gleerup.

Lippi, M. (1977), *I prezzi di produzione. Un saggio sulla teoria di Sraffa*, Bologna: Il Mulino.

Longfield, M. (1971)[1834], *Lectures on Political Economy*, first published 1834, in R.D. Collison Black (ed.), *The Economic Writings of Mountifort Longfield*, New York: Augustus M. Kelley.

Mäki, U. (1988), 'How to combine rhetoric and realism in the methodology of economics', *Economics and Philosophy*, **4**, 89–109.

Mäki, U. (1989), 'On the problem of realism in economics', *Ricerche Economiche*, **43**, 176–198.

Mäki, U. (1998), 'Realism', in J.B. Davis, D.W. Hands and U. Mäki (eds), *The Handbook of Economic Methodology*, Cheltenham, UK and Northampton, MA, USA: Edward Elgar, pp. 404–409.

Mäki, U. (2002), 'Introduction: The dismal queen of the social sciences' in U. Mäki (ed.), *Fact and Fiction in Economics. Models, Realism and Social Construction*, Cambridge: Cambridge University Press, pp. 3–32.

Mäler, K.-G. (1974), *Environmental Economics: A Theoretical Inquiry*, Baltimore and London: Johns Hopkins University Press.

Malinvaud, E. (1953), 'Capital accumulation and efficient allocation', *Econometrica*, **21**, 233–268.

Malinvaud, E. (1985), *Lectures on Microeconomic Theory*, rev. edn., Amsterdam: North-Holland.

Malueg, D.A. (1989), 'Emission credit trading and the incentive to adopt new pollution abatement technology', *Journal of Environmental Economics and Management*, **18**, 52–57.

Marshall, A. (1925)[1890], *Principles of Economics*, first published 1890, reprint of the 8th edn. 1920, London and Baltimore: Macmillan.

Marshall, A. (1970)[1911], *Industry and Trade*, first published 1911, reprint of the 4th edn. 1923, New York: Augustus M. Kelley.

Marx, K. (1902), *Capital. A Critical Analysis of Capitalist Production*, London: Swan Sonnenschein.

Marx, K. (1954)[1867], *Capital*, vol. I, first published 1867 in German, Moscow: Progress Publishers

Marx, K. (1956)[1885], *Capital*, vol. II, first published 1885 in German, Moscow: Progress Publishers.

Marx, K. (1959)[1894], *Capital*, vol. III, first published 1894 in German, Moscow: Progress Publishers.

Marx, K. (1963/1968)[1905–1910], *Theories of Surplus Value*, vol. II, first published 1905–1910 in German, Moscow: Progress Publishers.

Marx, K. (1970)[1857–1858], *Grundrisse der Kritik der Politischen Ökonomie, Rohentwurf*, first published 1857–1858 in German, Frankfurt: Europäische Verlagsanstalt.

Marx, K. (1981), *Die technologisch-historischen Exzerpte*, ed. by H.-P. Müller, Frankfurt: Ullstein.

Marx, K. (1982), *Exzerpte über Arbeitsteilung, Maschinerie und Industrie*, ed. by R. Winkelmann, Frankfurt: Ullstein.

Mas-Colell, A., M.D. Whinston and J.R. Green (1995), *Microeconomic Theory*, New York: Oxford University Press.

McKenzie, L.W. (1954), 'On equilibrium in Graham's model of world trade and other competitive systems', *Econometrica*, **22**, 147–161.

McKenzie, L.W. (1955), 'Competitive equilibrium with dependent consumer preferences', in H. Antosiewicz (ed.), *Proceedings of the Second Symposium on Linear Programming*, National Bureau of Standards and Department of the Air Force.

McKenzie, L.W. (1959), 'On the existence of general equilibrium for a competitive market', *Econometrica*, **27**, 54–71.

McKenzie, L.W. (1961), 'On the existence of general equilibrium for a competitive market: some corrections', *Econometrica*, **29**, 247–248.

Meerkamp van Embden, I.C. (1992), 'Pauschalausstieg wenig hilfreich', *Chemische Industrie*, **3/1992**, 6.

Meier, C. (1983), *Die Entstehung des Politischen bei den Griechen*, Frankfurt: Suhrkamp.

Meißner, S. (1995), 'Rechtliche Rahmenbedingungen', *Das Papier*, **49**, V77–V84.

Menger, C. (1968)[1871], *Grundsätze der Volkswirtschaftslehre*, first published 1871, reprint of the 2nd edn. 1923, Wien: Scientia.

Mill, J.S. (1965)[1848], *Principles of Political Economy with some of their Applications to Social Philosophy*, first published 1848, ed. by W.J. Ashley, New York: Augustus M. Kelley.

Milleron, J. (1972), 'Theory of value with public goods: a survey article', *Journal of Economic Theory*, **5**, 419–477.

Milliman, S.R. and R. Prince (1989), 'Firms' incentives to promote technological change in pollution control', *Journal of Environmental Economics and Management*, **17**, 247–265.

Möller, H. (1949), 'Heinrich Freiherr von Stackelberg und sein Beitrag für die Wirtschaftswissenschaft', *Zeitschrift für die gesamte Staatswissenschaft*, **105**, 395–428.

Muench, T. (1972), 'The core and the Lindahl equilibrium of an economy with a public good: an example', *Journal of Economic Theory*, **4**, 241–255.

Müller, H. (1994), 'Sulfuric acid and sulfur trioxide', *Ullmann's Encyclopedia of Industrial Chemistry*, vol. 25, Weinheim: VCH, pp. 635–703.

Müller-Fürstenberger, G. (1995), *Kuppelproduktion. Eine theoretische und empirische Analyse am Beispiel der chemischen Industrie*, Heidelberg and New York: Physica.

Müller-Fürstenberger, G. (1996), 'Some implications of joint production on general equilibrium prices', *Discussion Paper* No. 96–1, Department of Economics, University of Berne.

Murmann, J.P. and R. Landau (1998), 'On the making of competitive advantage: The development of the chemical industries in Britain and Germany since 1850', in A. Arora, R. Landau and N. Rosenberg (eds), *Chemicals and Long-term Economic Growth. Insights from the Chemical Industry*, New York: Wiley.

Musgrave, A. (1978), 'Evidential support, falsification, heuristics, and anarchism', in G. Radnitzky and G. Andersson (eds), *Progress and Rationality in Science*, Dordrecht: Reidel, pp. 181–201.

Nader, F. (1996), 'Perspektiven der Chlorchemie', *Chemie Technik*, **25**(8), 66.

Nehring, K. and C. Puppe (2004), 'Modelling cost complementarities in terms of joint production', *Economic Theory*, **118**, 252–264.

Neisser, H. (1932), 'Lohnhöhe und Beschäftigungsgrad im Marktgleichgewicht', *Weltwirtschaftliches Archiv*, **36**, 415–455.

Nelson, R.R. and S.G. Winter (1977), 'In search of a useful theory of innovation', *Research Policy*, **6**, 36–76.

Newbery, D. (1990), 'Acid rain', *Economic Policy*, **5**, 297–346.

Nickel, S.J. (1978), *The Investment Decision of Firms*, Oxford: Cambridge University Press/Nisbert & Co.

Niehans, J. (1990), *A History of Economic Theory. Classic Contributions, 1720–1980*, Baltimore and London: Johns Hopkins University Press.

Niehans, J. (1992), 'Relinking German economics to the mainstream: Heinrich von Stackelberg', *Journal of the History of Economic Thought*, **14**, 189–208.

Nielsen, L.T. (1990), 'Existence of equilibrium in CAPM', *Journal of Economic Theory*, **52**, 223–231.

Norton, B.G. (1992), 'Ecological health and sustainable resource management', in R. Costanza (ed.), *Ecological Economics. The Science and Management of Sustainability*, New York: Columbia University Press, pp. 102–117.

O'Connor, M. (1993), 'Entropic irreversibility and uncontrolled technological change in economy and environment', *Journal of Evolutionary Economics*, **3**, 285–315.

O'Connor, M. (1994), 'Entropy, Liberty and Catastrophe: The Physics and Metaphysics of Waste Disposal', in P. Burley and J. Foster (eds), *Economics and Thermodynamics: New Perspectives on Economic Analysis*, Dordrecht: Kluwer, pp. 119–182.

O'Connor, M. (1995), 'Cherishing the future, cherishing the other: a "post-classical" theory of value', in S. Faucheux, D. Pearce and J. Proops (eds), *Models of Sustainable Development*, Aldershot, UK and Brookfield, USA: Edward Elgar.

Oenning, A. (1997), *Theorie betrieblicher Kuppelproduktion*, Heidelberg and New York: Physica.

Olson, M. (1965), *The Logic of Collective Action*, Cambridge, MA: Harvard University Press.

Oss, H.G. and A.C. Padovani (2002), 'Cement Manufacture and the Environment', *Journal of Industrial Ecology*, **6**, 89–106.

Oss, H.G. and A.C. Padovani (2003), 'Cement Manufacture and the Environment, Part II: Environmental Challenges and Opportunities', *Journal of Industrial Ecology*, **7**, 93–126.

Panayotou, T. (1995), 'Environmental degradation at different stages of economic development', in I. Ahmed and J.A. Doeleman (eds), *Beyond Rio: The Environmental Crisis and Sustainable Livelihoods in the Third World*, ILO Study Series, New York: St Martin's Press, pp. 13–36.

Panzar, J.C. and R.D. Willig (1977a), 'Economies of scale in multi-output production', *Quarterly Journal of Economics*, **91**, 431–493.

Panzar, J.C. and R.D. Willig (1977b), 'Free entry and the sustainability of natural monopoly', *Bell Journal of Economics*, **8**, 1–22.

Panzar, J.C. and R.D. Willig (1981), 'Economies of scope', *American Economic Review*, **71**, 268–272.

Pareto, V. (1896/97), *Cours d'Economie Politique*, Lausanne: Rouge.

Pasinetti, L. (1977), *Lectures on the Theory of Production*, New York: Columbia University Press.

Pasinetti, L. (ed.) (1980), *Essays on the Theory of Joint Production*, London: Macmillan.

Perrings, C. (1986), 'Conservation of mass and instability in a dynamic economy-environment system', *Journal of Environmental Economics and Management*, **13**, 199–211.

Perrings, C. (1987), *Economy and Environment: A Theoretical Essay on the Interdependence of Economic and Environmental Systems*, Cambridge: Cambridge University Press.

Perrings, C. (1994), 'Conservation of mass and the time-behaviour of ecological-economic systems', in P. Burley and J. Foster (eds), *Economics and Thermodynamics: New Perspectives on Economic Analysis*, Dordrecht: Kluwer, pp. 99–117.

364   *Joint Production and Responsibility in Ecological Economics*

Persson, G. (ed.) (1982), 'What is acidification?', in Swedish Ministry for Agriculture and Environment '82 Committee (ed.), *Acidification Today and Tomorrow*, Uddevall, Sweden: Risbergs Tryckeri AB, pp. 30–49.

Petersen, T. and M. Faber (2000), 'Bedingungen erfolgreicher Umweltpolitik im deutschen Föderalismus', *Zeitschrift für Politikwissenschaft*, 10(1), 5–41.

Petersen, T. and M. Faber (2005), 'Verantwortung und das Problem der Kuppelproduktion: Reflexionen über die Grundlagen der Umweltpolitik', *Zeitschrift für Politikwissenschaft*, 15(1), 35–59.

Pethig, R. (1979), *Umweltökonomische Allokation mit Emissionssteuern*, Tübingen: Mohr Siebeck.

Piaget, J. (1971), *Structuralism*, London: Routlege and Kegan Paul.

Pigou, A.C. (1912), *Wealth and Welfare*, London: Macmillan.

Pigou, A.C. (1913), 'Railway rates and joint cost', *Quarterly Journal of Economics*, 27, 535–536 and 687–692.

Pigou, A.C. (1920), *The Economics of Welfare*, London: Macmillan.

Plessner, H. (2003), *Macht und menschliche Natur* (Gesammelte Schriften, Bd. V), Darmstadt: Wissenschaftliche Buchgesellschaft.

Polemarchakis, H.M. and P. Siconolfi (1993), 'Competitive equilibria without free disposal or nonsatiation', *Journal of Mathematical Economics*, 22, 85–99.

Ponting, C. (1993), *A Green History of the World. The Environment and the Collapse of Great Civilizations*, London and New York: Penguin.

Porter, M.E. (1990), 'The competitive advantage of nations', *Harvard Business Review*, March/April, 73–93.

Porter, M.E. (1991), 'America's green strategy', *Scientific American*, 264(4), 96.

Porter, M.E. and C. van der Linde (1995), 'Toward a new conception of the environment-competitiveness relationship', *Journal of Economic Perspectives*, 9(4), 97–118.

Pothmann, D. (1995), 'Altpapier als Rohstoff', *Das Papier*, 49, V65–V71.

Pothmann, D. (1996), 'Altpapiereinsatz im 18. Jahrhundert: Wie war es damals? Was entwickelte sich daraus?', *Wochenblatt für Papierfabrikation*, 124, 80–86.

Proops, J.L.R. (1987), 'Entropy, information and confusion in the social sciences', *Journal of Interdisciplinary Economics*, 1, 224–242.

Proops, J.L.R. (2001), 'The (non-) economics of the nuclear fuel cycle: an historical and discourse analysis', *Ecological Economics*, 39, 13–19.

Quirk, J. and R. Saposnik (1968), *Introduction to General Equilibrium Theory and Welfare Economics*, New York: McGraw-Hill.

Raffensperger, C. and J.A. Tickner (eds) (1999), *Protecting Public Health and the Environment: Implementing the Precautionary Principle*, Washington, DC: Island Press.

Requate, T. (1995), 'Incentives to adopt new technologies under different pollution-control policies', *International Tax and Public Finance*, 2, 295–317.

Requate, T. (1998), 'Incentives to innovate under pollution taxes and tradable permits', *European Journal of Political Economy*, **14**, 139–165.

Requate, T. and W. Unold (2001), 'On the incentives by policy instruments to adopt advanced abatement technology if firms are asymmetric', *Journal of Institutional and Theoretic Economics*, **157**, 536–554.

Requate, T. and W. Unold (2003), 'Environmental policy incentives to adopt advanced abatement technology – Will the true ranking please stand up?', *European Economic Review*, **47**, 125–146.

Ricardo, D. (1951)[1817], *On the Principles of Political Economy and Taxation*, first published 1817, reprinted in P. Sraffa with the collaboration of M.H. Dobb (eds), *The Works and Correspondence of David Ricardo*, vol. I, Cambridge: Cambridge University Press.

Riebel, P. (1955), *Die Kuppelproduktion. Betriebs- und Marktprobleme*, Köln/Opladen: Westdeutscher Verlag.

Riebel, P. (1981), 'Produktion III: einfache und verbundene', in W. Albers, K.E. Born, E. Dürr, H. Hesse, A. Kraft, H. Lampert, K. Rose, H.H. Rupp, H. Scherf, K. Schmidt, W. Wittmann (eds), *Handwörterbuch der Wirtschaftswissenschaft*, vol. 6, Stuttgart: Fischer, pp. 295–310.

Riebel, P. (1996), 'Kuppelproduktion', in W. Kern, H.H. Schröder and J. Weber (eds), *Handwörterbuch der Produktionswirtschaft*, 2nd edn., Stuttgart: Schäffer-Poeschl, pp. 992–1003.

Ritter, J., K. Gründer and G. Gabriel (eds) (1971 ff.), *Historisches Wörterbuch der Philosophie*, Basel: Schwabe & Co.

Roberts, J. (1974), 'The Lindahl solution for economies with public goods', *Journal of Public Economics*, **3**, 23–42.

Roberts, J. (1976), 'The incentives for correct revelation of preferences and the number of consumers', *Journal of Public Economics*, **6**, 359–374.

Roberts, J. (1987), 'Lindahl equilibrium', in J. Eatwell, M. Milgate and R. Newman (eds), *The New Palgrave. A Dictionary of Economics*, vol. III, London: Macmillan, pp. 198–200.

Rosenberg, N. (1976), *Perspectives on Technology*, Cambridge: Cambridge University Press.

Ruth, M. (1993), *Integrating Economics, Ecology and Thermodynamics*, Dordrecht: Kluwer.

Ruth, M. (1995a), 'Technology change in the US iron and steel production', *Resources Policy*, **21**, 199–214.

Ruth, M. (1995b), 'Thermodynamic constraints on optimal depletion of copper and aluminum in the United States: A dynamic model of substitution and technical change', *Ecological Economics*, **15**, 197–213.

Ruth, M. (1995c), 'Thermodynamic implications for natural resource extraction and technical change in US copper mining', *Environmental and Resource Economics*, **6**, 187–206.

[RWE] Rheinisch-Westfälisches Elektrizitätswerk AG, Betriebsverwaltung Fortuna (ed.) (1986), *Braunkohle Kraftwerk Niederaußem*, Essen.

Sagoff, M. (1988), *The Economy of the Earth. Philosophy, Law and the Environment*, Cambridge: Cambridge University Press.

Salvadori, N. (1982), 'Existence of cost-minimizing systems within the Sraffa framework', *Zeitschrift für Nationalökonomie*, **42**, 281–298.

Salvadori, N. (1984), 'La choix de technique chez Sraffa: le cas de la production jointe', in C. Bidard (ed.), *La Production Jointe: Nouveaux Débats*, Paris: Economica, pp. 175–185.

Salvadori, N. (1985), 'Switching in methods of production and joint production', *The Manchester School of Economic and Social Studies*, **53**, 156–157.

Salvadori, N. and I. Steedman (eds) (1988), 'Joint production analysis in a Sraffian framework', *Bulletin of Economic Research*, **40**, 165–193.

Salvadori, N. and I. Steedman (eds) (1990), *Joint Production of Commodities*, Aldershot, UK and Brookfield, USA: Edward Elgar.

Samakovlis, E. (2003), 'The relationship between waste paper and other inputs in the Swedish paper industry', *Environmental and Resource Economics*, **25**, 191–212.

Samuelson, P.A. (1954), 'The pure theory of public expenditure', *Review of Economics and Statistics*, **36**, 387–389.

Sandelin, B. (1976), 'On the origin of the Cobb Douglas production function', *Economy and History*, **19**, 117–123.

Sandin, P. (1999), 'Dimensions of the precautionary principle', *Human and Ecological Risk Assessment*, **5**(5), 889–907.

Sandin, P. (2004), 'The precautionary principle and the concept of precaution', *Environmental Values*, **13**, 461–475.

Saucier, P. (1984), 'La production jointe en situation de concurrence', in C. Bidard (ed.), *La Production Jointe: Nouveaux Débats*, Paris: Economica, pp. 155–174.

Sayers, S. (1985), *Reality and Reason*, Oxford: Basil Blackwell.

Schefold, B. (1978a), 'Fixed capital as a joint product', *Jahrbücher für Nationalökonomie und Statistik*, **192**, 21–48.

Schefold, B. (1978b), 'On counting equations', *Zeitschrift für National-ökonomie*, **38**, 253–285.

Schefold, B. (1980a), 'Fixed capital as a joint product and the analysis of accumulation with different forms of technical progress', in L. Pasinetti (ed.), *Essays on the Theory of Joint Production*, London: Macmillan, pp. 138–217.

Schefold, B. (1980b), 'Von Neumann and Sraffa: mathematical equivalence and conceptual difference', *Economic Journal*, **90**, 140–156.

Schefold, B. (1983), 'Sraffas Theorie der Kuppelproduktion. Ein Überblick', *Zeitschrift für Wirtschafts- und Sozialwissenschaften*, **103**, 315–340.

Schefold, B. (1988), 'The dominant technique in joint production systems', *Cambridge Journal of Economics*, **12**, 97–123.

Schefold, B. (1989), *Mr. Sraffa on Joint Production and Other Essays*, London: Unwin Hyman.

Schelling, F.W.J. (1997), *Philosophische Untersuchungen über das Wesen der menschlichen Freiheit und die damit zusammenhängenden Gegenstände*, ed. by Thomas Buchheim, Hamburg: Meiner.

Schiller, J. (2002), *Umweltprobleme und Zeit. Bestände als konzeptionelle Grundlage ökologischer Ökonomik*, Marburg: Metropolis.

Schlesinger, K. (1933/34), 'Über die Produktionsgleichungen der ökonomischen Wertlehre', *Ergebnisse eines mathematischen Kolloquiums*, **6**, 10–11.

Schmidt, M., and A. Häuslein (1997), *Ökobilanzierung mit Computerunterstützung*, Berlin, Heidelberg and New York: Springer.

Schneider, E. (1933), 'Heinrich von Stackelberg – Grundlagen einer reinen Kostentheorie', *Schmollers Jahrbuch*, **57**, 627–629.

Schneider, E. (1934), *Theorie der Produktion*, Wien: Springer.

Schumpeter, J.A. (1934)[1911], *The Theory of Economic Development*, first published 1911 as *Theorie der wirtschaftlichen Entwicklung*, Cambridge, MA: Harvard University Press.

Schumpeter, J.A. (1954), *History of Economic Analysis*, New York: Oxford University Press.

Shafer, W.J. (1976), 'Equilibrium in economies without ordered preferences or free disposal', *Journal of Mathematical Economics*, **3**, 135–137.

Sharkey, W.W. and L.G. Telser (1978), 'Supportable cost functions for the multi-product firm', *Journal of Economic Theory*, **18**, 23–37.

Shephard, R.W. (1970), *Theory of Cost and Production Functions*, Princeton: Princeton University Press.

Siebert, H. (2004), *Economics of the Environment. Theory and Policy*, 6th edn., Berlin, Heidelberg and New York: Springer.

Simmonds, P.L. (1873), *Waste Products and Undeveloped Substances: A Synopsis of Progress Made in their Economic Utilisation during the Last Quarter of a Century at Home and Abroad*, London: Robert Hardwicke.

Smith, A. (1976)[1776], *An Inquiry into the Nature and the Causes of the Wealth of Nations*, first published 1776, ed. by R.H. Campbell, A.S. Skinner and W.B. Todd (The Glasgow edition of the works and correspondence of Adam Smith), Oxford: Clarendon.

Sneed, J.D. (1971), *The Logical Structure of Mathematical Physics*, Dordrecht: Reidel.

Solow, R.M. (1963), *Capital Theory and the Rate of Return*, Amsterdam: North-Holland.

Spaemann, R. (1977), 'Nebenwirkungen als moralisches Problem', in *Zur Kritik der politischen Utopie. Zehn Kapitel politischer Philosophie*, Stuttgart: Klett-Cotta, pp. 167–182.

Spaemann, R. (1989), *Glück und Wohlwollen. Versuch über Ethik*, Stuttgart: Klett-Cotta.

Spengler, T. (1999), *Industrielles Stoffstrommanagement*, Berlin: Schmidt.

Sraffa, P. (1925), 'Sulle relazioni fra costo e quantità prodotta', *Annali di Economia*, **2**, 277–328.

Sraffa, P. (1960), *Production of Commodities by Means of Commodities*, Cambridge: Cambridge University Press.

Statistisches Bundesamt (1996), *Fachserie 19 (Umwelt) Reihe 4: Umweltökonomische Gesamtrechnungen. Basisdaten und ausgewählte Ergebnisse 1996*, Stuttgart: Metzler-Poeschel.

Statistisches Bundesamt (1997), *Beiträge zu den Umweltökonomischen Gesamtrechnungen, Band 1: Physische Input-Output-Tabellen 1990*, Wiesbaden: Statistisches Bundesamt.

Statistisches Bundesamt (2000), Index of wholesale prices of mixed waste paper grade 1.02 of the German Federal Statistical Office in Wiesbaden, provided on telephone request.

Steedman, I. (1976), 'Positive profits with negative surplus value: a reply to Wolfstetter', *Economic Journal*, **86**, 873–876.

Steedman, I. (1988), *Sraffian Economics*, Aldershot, UK and Brookfield, USA: Edward Elgar.

Stegmüller, W. (1976), *The Structure and Dynamics of Theories*, Berlin, Heidelberg and New York: Springer.

Stegmüller, W. (1979), *The Structuralist View of Theories*, Berlin, Heidelberg and New York: Springer.

Stephan, G. (1995), *Introduction into Capital Theory. A Neo-Austrian Perspective*, Berlin, Heidelberg and New York: Springer.

Stigler, G.J. (1941), *Production and Distribution Theories*, New York: Macmillan.

Strebel, H. (1981), 'Umweltwirkungen der Produktion', *Zeitschrift für betriebswirtschaftliche Forschung*, **33**, 508–521.

Strebel, H. (1996), 'Ökologie und Produktion', in W. Kern, H.H. Schröder and J. Weber (eds), *Handwörterbuch der Produktionswirtschaft*, 2nd edn., Stuttgart: Schäffer-Poeschl, pp. 1303–1313.

Strenge, H.U. (1995), 'Vermeidung und Verwertung von Abfallsäuren aus der Chemischen Industrie', *UTA Umwelttechnologie Aktuell 1995*.

Sturrock, J. (1993), *Structuralism*, London: Fontana.

Sudan, J. (1992), 'Altpapiererfassung in der Bundesrepublik Deutschland', *Wochenblatt für Papierfabrikation*, **120**, 161–162.

Suppe, F. (ed.) (1977), *The Structure of Scientific Theories*, 2nd edn., Urbana: University of Illinois Press.

Suppe, F. (1979), 'Theory structure', in P.D. Asquith and H.E. Kyburg (eds), *Current Research in Philosophy of Science*, East Lansing: Philosophy of Science Association, pp. 317–338.

Szargut, J., D.R. Morris, and F.R. Steward (1988), *Exergy Analysis of Thermal, Chemical, and Metallurgical Processes*, New York: Hemisphere.

Taussig, F. (1891), 'A contribution to the theory of railway rates', *Quarterly Journal of Economics*, **5**, 438–465.

Taussig, F. (1913), 'Railway rates and joint cost once more', 'Railway rates and joint cost: rejoinder' and 'Railway rates and joint cost: comment', *Quarterly Journal of Economics*, **27**, 378–384, 536–538 and 692–694.

Taussig, F. (1933), 'The theory of railway rates once more', *Quarterly Journal of Economics*, **47**, 337-342.

Tietenberg, T. (2003), *Environmental and Natural Resource Economics*, 6th edn., Boston: Addison-Wesley.

Tinbergen, J. (1933), 'Heinrich von Stackelberg – Grundlagen einer reinen Kostentheorie', *Zeitschrift für Nationalökonomie*, **4**, 662–663.

Tirole, J. (1988), *The Theory of Industrial Organization*, Cambridge, MA: MIT Press.

Tugendhat, E. (1993), *Vorlesungen über Ethik*, Frankfurt: Suhrkamp.

Turner, D. and L. Hartzell (2004), 'The lack of clarity in the precautionary principle', *Environmental Values*, **13**, 449–60.

UBA (2000), 'Ökobilanzen für graphische Papiere', *Texte des Umweltbundesamtes*, 22/2000, Berlin: Umweltbundesamt.

United Nations (1992), *Rio Declaration on Environment and Development*, New York: United Nations.

van Fraassen, B. (1980), *The Scientific Image*, Oxford: Oxford University Press.

Varian, H. (1992), *Microeconomic Analysis*, 3rd edn., New York: Norton.

Varri, P. (1980), 'Prices, rate of profit and life of machines in Sraffa's fixed-capital model', in L. Pasinetti (ed.), *Essays on the Theory of Joint Production*, London: Macmillan, pp. 55–87.

VDP (2000), Statistical data provided on telephone request by the VDP (German Pulp and Paper Association), Bonn.

VDP (2002), *Papier '01 – Ein Leistungsbericht*, Bonn: VDP (German Pulp and Paper Association).

Velupillai, K. (1996), 'The computable alternative in the formalization of economics: a counterfactual essay', *Kyklos*, **49**, 251–272.

Vilks, A. (1998), 'Axiomatization', in J.B. Davis, D.W. Hands and U. Mäki (eds), *The Handbook of Economic Methodology*, Cheltenham, UK and Northampton, MA, USA: Edward Elgar, pp. 28–32.

von Hayek, F.A. (1941), *The Pure Theory of Capital*, London: Routledge and Kegan Paul.

von Hofmann, A.W. (1866), *Einleitung in die moderne Chemie. Nach einer Reihe von Vorträgen am Royal College of Chemistry in London*, Braunschweig: Viehweg.

von Mangoldt, H. (1863), *Grundriss der Volkswirtschaftslehre*, Stuttgart: Engelhorn.

von Neumann, J. (1928a), 'Sur la théorie des jeux', *Comptes Rendues de l'Académie des Sciences*, **186**, 1689–1691.

von Neumann, J. (1928b), 'Zur Theorie der Gesellschaftsspiele', *Mathematische Annalen*, **100**, 295–320.

von Neumann, J. (1937), 'Über ein ökonomisches Gleichungssystem und eine Verallgemeinerung des Brouwerschen Fixpunktsatzes', *Ergebnisse eines Mathematischen Kolloquiums*, **8**, 73–83, English translation as von Neumann (1945/46).

von Neumann, J. (1945/46), 'A Model of General Economic Equilibrium', *Review of Economic Studies*, **13**, 1–9, first published in German as von Neumann (1937).

von Neumann, J. and O. Morgenstern (1944), *Theory of Games and Economic Behavior*, Princeton: Princeton University Press.

von Stackelberg, H. (1932), *Grundlagen einer reinen Kostentheorie*, Berlin: Springer.

von Stackelberg, H. (1933), 'Zwei kritische Bemerkungen zur Preistheorie Gustav Cassels', *Zeitschrift für Nationalökonomie*, **4**, 456–472.

von Stackelberg, H. (1934), *Marktform und Gleichgewicht*, Berlin: Springer.

von Stackelberg, H. (1938), 'Probleme der unvollkommenen Konkurrenz', *Weltwirtschaftliches Archiv*, **48**, 95–141.

von Stackelberg, H. (1943), *Grundzüge der theoretischen Volkswirtschaftslehre*, Stuttgart: Kohlhammer.

von Stackelberg, H. (1948), *Grundlagen der Theoretischen Volkswirtschaftslehre*, English translation as von Stackelberg (1952), Bern: Francke.

von Stackelberg, H. (1952), *The Theory of the Market Economy*, English translation of von Stackelberg (1948), London: William Hodge.

von Thünen, J.H. (1921)[1826], *Der isolierte Staat in Beziehung auf Landwirtschaft und Nationalökonomie*, first published 1826, reprinted from the last edn. by the author 1842, 2nd edn., Jena: Fischer.

von Weizsäcker, C.C. (1971), *Steady State Theory of Capital*, Berlin, Heidelberg and New York: Springer

Wacker, H. (1987), *Rezyklierung als intertemporales Allokationsproblem in gesamt-wirtschaftlichen Planungsmodellen*, Frankfurt: Lang

Wald, A. (1933/34), 'Über die eindeutige positive Lösbarkeit der neuen Produktionsgleichungen', *Ergebnisse eines mathematischen Kolloquiums*, **6**, 12–20.

Wald, A. (1934/35), 'Über die Produktionsgleichungen der ökonomischen Wertlehre', *Ergebnisse eines mathematischen Kolloquiums*, **7**, 1–6.

Walras, L. (1954)[1874/77], *Elements of Pure Economics*, first published 1874 (Part I) and 1877 (Part II) as *Eléments d'Economie Politique Pure*, translation of the French Edition Définitive of 1926, London: George Allen & Unwin.

Walsh, V. and H. Gram (1980), *Classical and Neoclassical Theories of General Equilibrium. Historical Origins and Mathematical Structure*, Oxford: Oxford University Press.

Ward, B. (1972), *What's Wrong with Economics?* New York: Macmillan.

Weber, M. (1988)[1919], 'Politik als Beruf', in *Gesammelte Politische Schriften*, ed. by J. Winckelmann, Tübingen: Mohr, pp. 505–560.

Weintraub, R. (1983), 'On the Existence of a Competitive Equilibrium: 1930–1954', *Journal of Economic Literature*, **21**, 1–39.

West, E.G. (1994), 'Joint supply theory before Mill', *History of Political Economy*, **26**(2), 267–278.

Weyl, H. (1949), 'Ars combinatoria', in H. Weyl, *Philosophy of Mathematics and Natural Science*, Princeton: Princeton University Press, pp. 237–252.

Whitcomb, D.K. (1972), *Externalities and Welfare*, New York: Columbia University Press.

Wicksell, K. (1893), *Über Wert, Kapital und Rente nach den neueren nationalökonomischen Theorien*, Jena: Fischer.

Wicksteed, P.H. (1992)[1894], *The Coordination of the Laws of Distribution*, first published 1894, rev. edn., with an introduction by I. Steedman, Aldershot, UK and Brookfield, USA: Edward Elgar.

Wieland, W. (1999), *Verantwortung – Prinzip der Ethik?* Heidelberg: Winter.

Willig, R.D. (1979), 'Multiproduct technology and market structure', *American Economic Review*, **69**, 346–351.

Winkler, R. (2005), 'Structural change with joint production of consumption and environmental pollution: a neo-Austrian approach', *Structural Change and Economic Dynamics*, **16**(1), 111–135.

Zemansky, M.W. and R.H. Dittman (1997), *Heat and Thermodynamics: An Intermediate Textbook*, 7th edn., New York: McGraw-Hill.

Zeuthen, F. (1933), 'Das Prinzip der Knappheit, technische Kombination und ökonomische Qualität', *Zeitschrift für Nationalökonomie*, **4**, 1–24.

Index

The index contains references to subjects covered in the book. Comprehensive treatment of a subject is indicated by <u>underlined</u> page references; figures, tables, and notes are referenced in *italics*.